ਪਾਤਸ਼ਾਹੀ ਮਹਿਮਾ

PATSHAHI MEHIMA

Revisiting Sikh Sovereignty

RANVEER SINGH

Khalis House
Publishing

ਪਾਤਿਸ਼ਾਹੀ ਮਹਿਮਾ Patshahi Mehima:
Revisiting Sikh Sovereignty
Copyright © 2021 by Ranveer Singh
Bikramī 2078
Nanakshāhī 553

All rights reserved. No part of this book may be reproduced or transmitted in any form or by any means without written permission from the publisher.

ISBN 978-1-8381437-3-2
Printed in the United Kingdom
by KhalisHouse Publishing
www.KhalisHouse.com
info@KhalisHouse.com

Find us on:
Instagram/KhalisHouse
Twitter/KhalisHouse

੧ਓ ਸਤਿਗੁਰ ਪ੍ਰਸਾਦਿ
ਸ੍ਰੀ ਅਕਾਲ ਜੀ ਸਹਾਇ ॥

ਧੰਨ ਖਾਲਸੋ ਧੰਨ ਪੰਥ ਭੁਝੰਗੀ।
ਰਖਜੋ ਬੀਜ ਜਾਣ ਸਿੱਖੀ ਚੰਗੀ।
ਬਹੁਰ ਖਾਲਸਾ ਐਸ ਉਚਾਰਾ।
ਹਮੈ ਕੋਉ ਦਸੋ ਮੋਰਚਾ ਭਾਰਾ।

Great is the Khālsā, great are the youth of the Panth
who preserve the true spirit of Sikhi.
The Khālsā proclaimed to the Gurū,
"assign to us the most arduous of tasks"
-Rattan Singh, Panth Prakāsh (1841)

EARLY PRAISE

"Ranveer Singh skillfully weaves the evolving narratives of Sikh sovereignty since the days of Guru Nanak at Kartarpur to the twenty-first century by using the primary Sikh sources and secondary writings, offering a liberating alternative to the oppressive power structures of various regimes, giving voice to the unheard voices, and decolonizing the popular Sikh discourse in reverential language. The author deserves compliments for his brilliant achievement. This book belongs to every Sikh library and will have greatest appeal to the younger generation growing up in the Sikh diaspora."

Pashaura Singh, Distinguished Professor and Dr. J.S. Saini Chair in Sikh Studies, University of California, Riverside

"Ranveer Singh has put in his best intellectual effort to present a narrative on Sikh sovereignty and has thus, made a substantial contribution to Punjab and Sikh studies that deserves serious attention, engagement and reflection."

Pritam Singh, Emeritus Professor of Economy, Oxford Brookes

"As calls to 'decolonize' knowledge reverberate across the academy, Ranveer Singh engages in this very praxis. He asks us to consider the possibility of approaching Sikh sovereignty without the conceptual baggage that continues to weigh down mightily."

Rajbir Singh Judge, Assistant Professor of History,
California State University, Long Beach

"Ranveer Singh has done a great job in eloquently putting together the simmering issue of Sikh sovereignty which needs to be resolved with the mandate of Sikh people in the context of our historical sovereign past. This magnificent book should be in every university classroom in social sciences."

Hon. Justice Dr. Anup Singh Choudry, High Court Judge (retd)
B.sc. (Lond) LL.B (Cantab) LL.M .DipNotar (Cantab) Ph.D (KIU),
ACQI

FOREWORD

Ranveer Singh has put in his best intellectual effort to present a narrative on Sikh sovereignty and has thus, made a substantial contribution to Punjab and Sikh studies that deserves serious attention, engagement and reflection.

Given the current accelerating creation of an interconnected web of international flows of capital, commodities and labour which highlights the ongoing erosion of the sovereignty of nation states, it is becoming more clear each day that the era of absolute and complete sovereignty – if it ever truly existed – has come to an end. We are entering an era of varying degrees of negotiated sovereignties that recognise the imperatives of sustainability, pluralism and the co-existence of multiple identities. In his concluding chapter, Ranveer Singh makes an insightful remark about a vision of Sikh sovereignty that can 'fully realise the Guru's mandate and actualise Sikh ideals of *Sarbat da bhala*, the welfare of all beings, and *Sanjivalta*, the harmonious co-existence of humanity'. In a speech to the Indian Parliament, somewhat less clearly but following the same train of thought, the Sikh scholar and politician Kapur Singh discussed the aspirations and expectations of Sikhs as 'co-sharers in Indian sovereignty along with the majority community'.

With reference to 'the welfare of all beings', the wonderful Sikh ideal, I note the ecological imperative of going beyond a sole focus on human beings. Given the challenges to our planet stemming from the creation of an ecological catastrophe of biodiversity loss, due to capitalism, we need urgently to expand our imaginations to take into account the need for human spaces to be negotiated with non-human living beings. In Guru Granth Sahib's scriptural teachings on respect for nature, spirituality and social egalitarianism blend together in a marvelous manner; here, egalitarianism goes beyond humanity alone since Guru Granth Sahib's vision encompasses all living beings — human and non-human. Modern ecologists describe this as 'bio-egalitarianism'. To incorporate the human and the non-human into the web of inter-connected life, Guru Nanak represents the elements of nature as human beings, e.g., air as teacher, water as father, and earth as mother.[i]

The colonisation by human beings of non-human spaces, and the colonisation by one set of human beings of the spaces belonging to another set of human beings are inter-related. This calls for critique of all empires, including what is called the 'Sikh empire' of Ranjit Singh.

The Sikh community, which is increasingly becoming a global community through migration from its homeland, Punjab, faces a challenging task while it negotiates its universal ideals in multiple spaces. This challenge is even more acute at present in Punjab due to the ever-growing centralisation of economic, political and cultural power in India which has assumed menacing proportions with the rise to

---

[i] For further elaboration, see my article '*Shri Guru Granth Sahib: Understanding the Sacred Word*' (https://www.lse.ac.uk/south-asia-centre/assets/documents/18-0550-GGS-Report-New-Version-16ppV8-HR.pdf) that is also available as a podcast (https://richmedia.lse.ac.uk/dptevents/20180322_GGSJ_SAC_speaker3ProfPritamSingh.mp3).

power of the BJP, the party articulating majoritarian Hindu nationalism. The farmers' movement against this trend towards centralisation, despite its limitations, should be appreciated as the most powerful challenge to date to its dominance.[ii]

In this context, Ranveer Singh's analysis is welcome as a stimulus for further debate and critical reflection.

Pritam Singh
Oxford
October 2021.

[ii] Pritam Singh, 'BJP's Farming Policies: Deepening Agrobusiness Capitalism and Centralisation', *Economic and Political Weekly*, October 10, 2020, pp. 14-17.

ACKNOWLEDGMENTS

I bow in reverence to Akāl, the Gurū Sāhibān, the Gurū Granth and Panth, the known and unknown immortals whose weapons are forever loaded with the sovereign spirit of the Gurū's Darbār, which has, and shall always deliver on the Gurū's Bachan. I ask that the reader treat this book with respect as it contains various passages from Srī Gurū Granth Sāhib jī.

While this book came together over the past year, I thought about, and wrote various sections of the book, over the past seven years. That being said it would not be where it is today without the support and encouragement of many people.

I would like to thank my father Payara Singh and mother Amrit Kaur whose unconditional love, teaching and guidance allowed me to read, learn and write about the history of the glorious Sikh Panth. I would like to thank my wife and children for their love, comfort and support throughout the writing journey.

This book would not have been possible to write without the advice, direction and constant *Sangat* of my dear friends and colleagues Azadvir Singh, Baljit Singh, Charankamal Singh, and Shamsher Singh at the *National Sikh Youth Federation*. Our countless conversations over the past few years, whether in private or at various events held within Sikh spaces, have been a great source of knowledge, inspiration and encouragement in completing this book.

I would like to thank Harwinder Singh of *Naujawani* for reading the initial drafts of this book and for his thoughts and words of encouragement.

A very special thank you also to Prabjot Singh in Edmonton, for providing invaluable critique and feedback to numerous drafts of this book.

I must extend a heartfelt thank you also to Prof. Pritam Singh, Prof. Pashaura Singh, Prof. Rajbir Singh Judge and Hon. Justice Dr. Anup Singh Choudry for reading and reviewing this book. It is an honour to have such distinguished voices within the field of Sikh studies and History offer their valuable thoughts. I am grateful for their kind words of encouragement.

While I have authored this book, it has been the insight and wisdom imparted by all of those named above, as well as, countless members of the Gurū's Beloved Sangat who have empowered me to write.

Panth Sevak,
Ranveer Singh
19th November, 2021

CONTENTS

Introduction i

Part One: Sache Pātshāh 1

Srī Gurū Nānak Sāhib jī Maharaj 9

Srī Gurū Angad Sāhib jī Maharaj 26

Srī Gurū Amar Dās Sāhib jī Maharaj 37

Srī Gurū Rām Dās Sāhib jī Maharaj 49

Srī Gurū Arjan Dev Sāhib jī Maharaj 60

Srī Gurū Hargobind Sāhib jī Maharaj 79

Srī Gurū Har Rāi Sāhib jī Maharaj 97

Srī Gurū Har Krishan Sāhib jī Maharaj 110

Srī Gurū Tegh Bahādur Sāhib jī Maharaj 122

Srī Gurū Gobind Singh Sāhib ji Maharaj 138

Part 2: Rise of the Khālsā and Pursuit of Rāj 173

Bandā Singh Bahadur and the Khālsā Republic 181

Dal Khālsā and the Sikh Misl Confederacy 198

Ranjīt Singh and Darbār-e Khālsā 217

Part 3: Invasion and Occupation of Sikh Territory ... 232

Western Secularism and the Colonial Encounter 256

Sikh Opposition to Colonial Occupation 287

Part 4: Transfer of Colonial Power and the Rise of Indian Nationalism 312

Dharam Yudh and the Khalistān Sangarsh 338

Conclusion 368

Bibliography 374

Glossary of Terms 389

Introduction

The sacred land and waters of Panjāb, that region of the world upon which the Gurū Sāhibān graced us with their Divine presence, hold the glorious stories of the Sikh Panth. While Gurū Nānak Sāhib travelled far and wide, in search of the Gurmukhs[1], they ultimately returned to Panjāb and made Kartārpur Sāhib their temporal home.

Thus, with the founding of Kartārpur Sāhib in 1504[2], Gurū Nānak Sāhib initiated the movement that shaped Sikh consciousness, and with it, the tradition of founding independent Sikh territory became a defining aspect of Sikhi under the Gurū Sāhibān. For the purpose of avoiding ambiguity, in this book, I am adopting Gurbhagat Singh's definition of Sikh consciousness, which can be understood to be comprised of four key elements; "(i) faith in the One, both Sargun (with attributes) and Nirgun (without attributes); (ii) to work towards and be part of Gurū's Sangat and the Gurū Panth; (iii) become a non-egoic person, through the guidance of Gurū Sāhib; and (iv) develop the capability of hearing Anhad Shabad (the unstruck melody)".[3]

A new space was needed to cultivate the Sikh, or Gurmukh consciousness, amongst the Sangat and later the Panth, a process that required total autonomy. While the Sikh revolution under the Gurū Sāhibān expanded with the establishment of other towns, cities, reservoirs and wells, going beyond the region of Panjāb, the origins of *Sikh Sovereignty*[i] remained firmly rooted in the land of the five rivers. As we shall see, the cities of Amritsar and Anandpur Sāhib have

---

[i] Etymologically, the term sovereignty has Latin origins and, in the West, carries a specific meaning associated with superiority and dominance. In this book I use the term *Sikh Sovereignty* as a means of expressing the self-regulating and autonomous nature of the Sikh Panth, empowered by the Pātshāhī of Gurū Nānak Sahib.

served as strongholds of Sikh sovereignty at different times, as have other independent Sikh spaces carved out by the Gurū Sāhibān themselves.

The establishment of Kartārpur Sāhib, central to which was the institute of Gurū's Sangat and the Gurū's Darbār, is why in the Sikh world, Gurū Nānak Sāhib is revered as ਦੀਨ ਦੁਨੀ ਸੱਚੋ ਪਤਿਸ਼ਾਹਿ [4] (true Pātshāh in the mundane as well as the spiritual world), which provides a clear political resonance to the Gurū-ship, standing in opposition to other structures of temporal power and governance.

Over a period of approximately two hundred and nine years, Panjāb was culturally, politically, and socially redefined by the Gurū Sāhibān through the sovereign agency of the Gurū's Darbār. From Kartārpur Sāhib to Khadūr Sāhib, to Goindvāl Sāhib, Amritsar and Anandpur Sāhib, the Darbār evolved until it was the centre of both the learned and the armed. Where the Darbār evolved as a hub for propagating Gurmat and literature to increase people's understanding of both worlds, it was also a fortress adorned with weapons to protect Sikh sovereignty and fight oppression.[5]

Opposition to the Darbār of Gurū Nānak Sāhib

Ever since Gurū Nānak Sāhib established Kartārpur Sāhib, many forces have sought to establish their control over the Sikhs, and by extension, autonomous Sikh spaces. As we shall see, whether it was internal attacks from members of the Gurū's own family or attacks from external foes who tried to assert their logic and authority, the pursuit and preservation of Sikh sovereignty have been a perpetual command for Sikhs.

In this book, I shall explore the origins of that sovereignty which transformed life in Panjāb, and consider the various manifestations of Rāj, beginning with the centres of power under the Gurū Sāhibān, such as Kartārpur Sāhib, (1504), Amritsar (1577), and Anandpur Sāhib (1665); the Khālsā Republic under Bandā Singh Bahādur (1710-1716); the Confederacy of the Misls (1764-1799); and the Rāj consolidated by Ranjīt Singh (1799-1849). I shall offer analysis and commentary on the rise and temporary fall of Sikh political power following the colonial encounter, and also consider the pursuit of Sikh Rāj since 1849, thus bringing matters up to the present day as Sikhs continue to pursue the establishment of Khālistān, which was declared on 29th April 1986, following the Sarbat Khālsā of 26th January 1986.

Gurbānī and Gurmat

ਬਾਬਾਣੀਆ ਕਹਾਣੀਆ ਪੁਤ ਸਪੁਤ ਕਰੇਨਿ ॥
ਜਿ ਸਤਿਗੁਰ ਭਾਵੈ ਸੁ ਮੰਨਿ ਲੈਨਿ ਸੇਈ ਕਰਮ ਕਰਨਿ ॥[6]

Gurū Sāhib highlights the value of preserving and narrating the stories of one's ancestors. In revisiting those stories, there is a direct connection with the lived realities of the people; from those who first spoke the Divine words of Japjī Sāhib or experienced the depths of Sukhmanī Sāhib. These sacred words, when sung as ordained by the Gurū Sāhibān, "incarnate the whole cosmos",[7] and evoke Sikh consciousness; an awakening so strong it leads to the establishment of a force that tears down established orders of oppression and redefines land masses under the sovereign flags of the Gurū. Such is the blessing of Gurū Nānak Sāhib, who advocates that only those who follow Gurmat and subdue the five vices, are worthy of sitting on thrones,[8] that those war cries of truth continue to reverberate from those who find sanctuary and protection within the Gurū's Darbār today.

In exploring the origins of Sikh sovereignty, I aim to present the uniqueness of Gurmat and the Gurmukh, and in particular, Gurū Nānak Sāhib's worldview, that cultivates the notion of Halemi Rāj and the formation of the Khālsā, to actualise a model of governance in which Sarbat Da Bhala[ii] is permeated to all life forms. This

---

[ii] Sikh principle of welfare for all life forms, known and unknown.

governance model places Divine knowledge, or Brahmgiān, at the centre of human experience and interaction within the temporal world. Fundamental to this is the realization of Nām, a "holistic and loving meditative attunement to Vaheguru."[9] It is important to note that the need for sovereign Sikh territory arrived the moment Gurū Sāhib revealed Gurmat and introduced a radical new view of the world, which not only challenged the space and systems engineered by Mughal imperialism and Brahmanical hierarchy during the Gurū-period but also challenges today's dominant view rooted in Western secular philosophy and polity. The latter, in particular, is problematic for Sikh thought because it,

> "not only prioritizes empiricism and the material realm as the ultimate source of truth but actively prohibits the Divine (and non-Western perspectives) from all forms of public (social, political, and economic) life and knowledge-production."[10]

One of the underlying themes of this book is that Sikhi, as revealed and nurtured by the Gurū Sāhibān, is not the same as "Sikhism" the religion, engineered during the colonial encounter from the imagination of Christian missionaries and colonialists. We shall consider how "Sikhism" is in fact a suffocating label which seeks to compartmentalise Sikhī as one of the many "unilaterally conceived systems of classification"[11], which the West invented and utilised to exert their authority and control all over the world. I shall present how Gurmat challenges the very foundation upon which the colonial framework of "Sikhism" is built and imposed.

In revealing the treasure of Nām, Gurū Nānak Sāhib simultaneously unveiled the limits of the ego, which focuses on the material world, and on empirical thoughts that firstly sideline Divine wisdom, and then try to define and understand the latter from the limits of the former. Harinder Singh Mehboob, in his own unique style, provides comprehensive analysis and commentary on this when he frames the term '*Khalis Kudrat*', within which *Uchi Surat* (higher

Introduction

consciousness) contains greater awareness than the knowledge of mind which manifests 'psyche', 'absolute idea', 'spirit', and 'pure reason', of Western thinkers. This *Uchi Surat* enables one to experience the Divine and operate on a level beyond the limitations of the egoic mind, logic, and reason. We shall consider the effects of this, both on Sikh understanding of Gurmat and the connection to Sikh Sangarsh. The aim shall be to present how the idea of "Sikhism", as defined by colonial logic rooted in a particular ontology and epistemology, is poles apart from the Sikhī that Gurū Nānak Sāhib imparted.

Age of Kaljug

From the Gurū's own writings, and by looking at pre-colonial Sikh texts, we find, when Gurū Nānak Sāhib arrived on this earth, the stronghold of Kaljug[iii] was rampant. Human consciousness lay shattered in pieces; separated from the connection to Divine truth, it revolved around the circle of material tendencies.[12] In the pursuit of material wealth and fame, the condition of human life was one of great anxiety and doubt. Gurū Amar Dās Sāhib states the whole world had gone insane in egotism; in the love of duality, it wandered deluded by doubt.[13] This is a constant theme found within the Divine Words of the Gurū Sāhibān. Gurū Nānak Sāhib travelled far and wide, interacting with followers of Abrahamic and Brahmanical traditions, conversing with emperors and rulers. In doing so, the Gurū highlighted the pitfalls of ignoring the Divine, an act that exacerbates human consciousness due to the idolatry of the mind. Gurū Nānak Sāhib stated that *manmat*, mere intellect of the mind, is false.[14] The success of the Gurū Sāhibān did not lie in the mere rejection or criticism of other traditions or systems of governance, but upon the creation of the Tisar Panth, a radically new way, which became a

---

[iii] Kaljug is the Age of spiritual ignorance.

defining aspect of the Gurū's movement, actualised by the sovereign agency and authority of the Gurū's Darbār.

Not only did Gurū Sāhib outline the limits of the human mind but also introduced modes of social and political interaction based on Divine knowledge, in which Nām, Simran, and Shabad helped cultivate the Gurmukh and present a radical new shift on the socio-political landscape across South Asia. While this Gurū-inspired awakening was taking place in Panjāb, elsewhere in the world, individuals like Descartes were lauded for proposing, "I think, therefore I am", which followed the so-called Renaissance in Europe. When we analyze Western secular philosophy, a proposition in which Divine knowledge or experience was made but a literal afterthought, we find *haumai,* a defining aspect of Kaljug, at the epicentre of its glorification. With this ego-centric worldview, the benefactors of the colonial structure today constantly seek to impose not only their version of history but also their understanding of the seen and unseen world.

Haumai

There is an inextricable link between Gurū-inspired divinity and the establishment of Sikh Rāj. The origins of this relationship are found in the words and actions of the Gurū Sāhibān, all of whom contributed to and maintained the formation of a single, socio-economic, independent entity that garnered support from all members of society. Actualizing Sikh governance, based on ideals about the Creator, Creation, and all its manifested beauty, contained within Gurū Granth Sāhib, has been the perpetual Sikh command since Gurū Nānak Sāhib established Kartārpur Sāhib. The overriding purpose has been to heal a world drunk on the maladies of self-centred existence, *haumai* and *manmat*, perpetuated by power structures that profit from human control and collapse. In fact, the Gurū's explanation and examination of *haumai* is perhaps one of the most fascinating expositions throughout Gurbānī and completely lays bare

Introduction

the exploitative and dominating underpinnings of structures such as Brahmanism[15] and Western secular philosophy.

After revealing the sublime essence of Ik Oankaar, as recorded in the Mool Mantar, Gurū Nānak Sāhib goes on to declare that the eternal truth, which everyone so deeply craves, is realised when one accepts *hukam*. When *Hukam* is understood and accepted, as first described in the opening two *pauris* of Srī Japjī Sāhib, Gurū Nānak Sāhib assures us there is no room for *haumai*. But what is *haumai*, and what is *hukam*?

The condition of the human mind and its relationship with *haumai* is described using a variety of analogies and metaphors in Gurbānī, amongst which perhaps the most intriguing is the utterance in which Gurū Sāhib declares that *haumai* is a chronic ailment, but one which contains its own cure, if by *Kirpā* we earn Gurū's Shabad.[16] In the temporal sense, I have always understood the word to consist of two parts – 'hau' and 'mai'. Generally, it is taught that 'hau' means 'I' and 'mai' means 'me'. When joined together, the English interpretation of the word *haumai* is literally 'I-me'. The most common English word used to translate *haumai* is ego.

In Gurbānī, *haumai* has been referred to as ਦੁਖ (grief), ਪੀੜ (pain), ਰੋਗ (disease), ਸੰਤਾਪ (sorrow), ਪਰਦਾ (veil of illusion), and ਗੁਬਾਰੁ (spiritual darkness). Generally, the emphasis from Gurū Sāhib is that haumai is a state of existence in which one focuses on a worldview projected by one's own sense of individuality, devoid of Divine inspiration and knowledge. This state of being is what conceals the true reality of Creation and the Creative force and causes a separation from the Divine connection, which is the root cause of human suffering.

One of the perpetual directives ordained by Gurū Sāhib is to recognise the worth of this human life; to recognise with the Divine Creative power that resides within and connect with that Creative force[17] through the Gurū's Shabad. This is why reciting and singing Gurbānī and Nām Abiyas is a transformative process in which the veil of illusion is lifted, and the fire of egotism is extinguished.[18]

Speaking about the Gurū's way, Bhāī Gurdās ji elaborates further by describing how Gurū Nānak Sāhib showed us how to play the internal game, which made the biggest of egoists bow their heads. Before this revelation, all were engrossed in *haumai*, and the Gurmukhs were nowhere to be seen; the blind' were pushing the blind into wells.[19] Elsewhere Bhāī Gurdās ji notes the righteousness of the previous three Ages had vanished. In this Age of Kaljug, those with political power in the world turned unjust while their officers became butchers.[20]

Where Bhāī Gurdās ji is overtly critical of unjust political structures, he also rejects ideologies, philosophies, and religions that fail to acknowledge the truth of Akāl Purakh, as the power that Creates, Sustains, and Destroys. In the opening Vār from Bhāī Gurdās ji, we find commentary on the efforts of various Sages like Gautam, who deliberated on the Rig Veda, and Sage Jaimini, who studied Yajur Veda, but their doubts, suspicions, or illusions could not be dispelled without the help of a Satgurū.[21] Building on the writings of the Gurū Sāhibān, Bhāī Gurdās describes how Hindu gods such as Brahmā, Vishnū, Indrā, and Mahesh, or Shiv ji, remained engrossed in mundane pleasure because they acted out of ego. From a Gurmat perspective, their downfall lies in how they propagated their own supremacy.[22] In the critique of Buddhism[23], we find Bhāī Gurdās ji question those who revere knowledge and intelligence of the mind but remain ignorant of the Divine. Elsewhere Bhāī Gurdās ji critiques the development of Islamic culture, writing that saints, holy messengers, and learned people, became engrossed in arrogance and egoism, which led to seventy-two divisions, creating much enmity and animosity.[24]

Drawing upon the supplementary information we take from Bhāī Gurdās ji, it can be said therefore that *haumai*, the acceptance of one's sense of individuality, as a separate entity from Akāl Purakh, is the downfall of many in this Age of Kaljug. The construction of the word – "I Me" – is an assertion of one's individuality. In this state, the mind not only accepts the notion of individualism, perpetuated by external forces but thrives in this perception of life and the world around it, leaving little to no room for Divine agency or higher consciousness.

If we take this understanding and consider today's world, a world divided on arbitrary lines made primarily by European conquerors, who not only redefined land masses and peoples by exerting their own colonial logic but wiped out large amounts of indigenous peoples in order to assert their dominance, we can begin to unpack the damning role of *haumai*.

Western secularism and manmat

The creation of Nation States modelled on the secular framework, in which the Divine is but an afterthought, only serves to increase *haumai* by promoting man-made Nationalistic identities and economic systems based largely on the private ownership of the means of production and their operation for profit. These are all in the pursuit of temporal or materialistic gain.

In this state, the individual only suffers because *haumai* grows exponentially due to the demands of living in this type of society. As *haumai* grows, it strengthens the disconnect with the Divine. From Nationalistic agendas to centralised socio-economic structures built on Capitalism, the focus is always on the supremacy of individuality. If we acknowledge that the role of the Khālsā is to uproot all forms of oppression and establish an egalitarian society, this understanding of *haumai* is important not only to avoid the shortcomings of those who Bhāī Gurdās ji has critiqued and exposed but also other ideologies and philosophies, particularly those rooted in the manmat of Western secularism; "the foundation on which the entire gamut of social, political, administrative, educational and economic structures of the world are based."[25]

As mentioned, for Sikhs, the introduction to this secular worldview began in 1849 when Panjāb was annexed by the coloniser. We are still reeling from the effects of the colonial encounter in Panjāb because while colonial officers occupied Panjāb, fanatic Christian missionaries such as Ernest Trumpp made attempts to translate Gurbāṇī and redefine Sikhī. However, Trumpp and others such as Hew McLeod, failed to understand that Gurbāṇī is far more profound than a "religious scripture". The relevance of that today for a Sikh lies in the responsibility to oppose all structures of *manmat.* The secular model, for example, in which Divine agency is sidelined and categorised within the realm of Western religiosity, perpetuates an environment that allows *manmat* to grow exponentially. *Haumai* is idolised as the central component of this model in which the individual's attachment and pursuit of materialistic gain is considered of paramount importance.

The road to recovery from the chronic ailment that is *haumai* has also been revealed by Gurū Sāhib, if by Kirpā we earn the Gurū's Shabad.[26] This process is described by Gurū Amar Dās Sāhib in Anand Sāhib when the Guru speaks of Shabad being a jewel. The instruction is to focus on the Shabad, which radiates the light of divinity that Gurū Angad Sāhib tells us resides at the root of our being[27].

Timeless Victory of Satgurū

During the Gurū period, the Pundit, Qazi, and Mullah, who were responsible for the judicial and administrative facets of Mughal governance are condemned for the laws they wrote and passed.[28] We'll consider how the entire paraphernalia of government, including the rulers, the bureaucracy, the judiciary, and the administration, were overtly condemned by the founders of the Sikh movement.[29]

From Gurū Nānak Sāhib to Gurū Gobind Singh Sāhib, the Gurū Sāhibān were Kings of both the spiritual and temporal world, where having exposed the fallacy of those engrossed in *haumai*, they exercised their sovereign agency by founding towns and cities; holding courts; building forts; collecting *dasvandh*; disseminating emissaries who travelled far and wide to propagate Sikhī; and by waging war against other entities who stood against Gurmat. During the time of

Introduction

the Gurū Sāhibān, the main adversaries were the Mughals and the Hindu Hill Rajas, but empowered by the Pātshahi and Akāl Fateh[30] of Gurū Sāhib, the Sikhs have clashed with other forces such as the Afghans, British, and the Indian Government.

We shall see how the early success and survival of the Sikh movement was established because firstly, it was initiated by the Gurū Sāhibān, who spoke Truth, and secondly, because of the decision to remain independent from all external influences, threats, and attacks.

From the arrival of Gurū Nānak Sāhib to the passing of sovereignty to the Khālsā in 1699, the Sikh movement was both antiimperialist in nature and advocated against caste and class discrimination. It must be reiterated here that when I refer to the Gurū Sāhibān as rulers or kings, I am not doing so in the conventional sense. This wasn't a monarchy or merely sovereignty in the worldly sense, like the Mughal dynasty or the British Crown. The Gurūs certainly adopted regal attire, sat on thrones, held court, and adorned various symbols of royalty in their court, but they had no desire for materialistic gain or conquest for personal or familial goals like other empires and monarchies. Gurū Arjan Sāhib states:

ਰਾਜੁ ਨ ਚਾਹਉ ਮੁਕਤਿ ਨ ਚਾਹਉ ਮਨਿ ਪ੍ਰੀਤਿ ਚਰਨ ਕਮਲਾਰੇ ॥
I do not seek Rāj, I do not seek liberation.
May my mind remain imbued, at Your lotus feet.[31]

The movement initiated from the Gurū's Darbār was Divinely inspired, which stood for the welfare and dignity of all irrespective of how other power structures had defined, categorised, and controlled their existence for personal, temporal, and familial gains. This defiance and disregard of the temporal establishment and its categorisation of peoples were remarkable features of the Gurū period. It was possible due to how the Gurū Sāhibān simultaneously nurtured an environment to uplift, awaken, and empower society by firstly revealing the soul to be a light of the One Creator manifested in Creation, and then creating space for Sikhs to grow and flourish with a revived understanding of the world, its inhabitants, and its place in the universe. At the centre of this worldview is the notion that the world is sacred and any force that seeks to break this sacredness by way of its temporal governance ought to be challenged and removed.

Sikh sovereignty was and remains to be of utmost importance in establishing the environment that cultivates the Gurmukh, Sangat, and Nām realised souls. The Sikh worldview has its own map of reality, one derived from the knowledge and examples imparted by the Gurū Sāhibān, based on Gurmat and existence in both the physical and spiritual world.

[The Gurū Granth Sāhib is *Dhur kī Bānī*, Shabads that are Divinely inspired.] For over three centuries, the Sikhs have bowed in reverence to the Gurū Granth Sāhib, the nucleus of Sikh consciousness. Each time the Sikh has connected to and refocused their consciousness to the Gurū's Shabad, we've seen a new dawn of revolutionary Sikh action. The presupposed dichotomy between spiritual and temporal life has proven difficult for some to understand the significance of Gurū Nānak Sāhib fully. We live in a world where spirituality is continuously shown to be reserved for a select group of individuals or a select period of one's life, but the Gurū espoused that divinity resides in us all, accessible in one moment. The instruction is to unlock the Divine within, become Gurmukh and follow in the Gurū's steps to actualise the timeless within the here and now.

This is how Gurbānī is timeless and relatable to the common man with no façade of a "promised land" where there exists an abundance of indulgences that are otherwise sinful on Earth; nor is there the promise of a returning messiah; nor does the Gurū's message restrict the truth to a certain "class" or "caste" of people. The perpetual command in Sikhi is to experience the Divine here and now, to live according to the natural flow of events amidst the Creator's presence. The Gurū emphasises the need to live a householder's life and condemns renunciation as a sole means of salvation. The principle of

Chardi Kalā, which loosely translates to mean 'ever-rising spirit', is a prime example of this. A Sikh is directed to adopt a realist approach to life that does not allow pessimism or negativity. Chardi Kalā is a quality that empowers the Sikhs to rejoice in the face of extreme adversity, accept it as the Divine will of the Creator, and continue forth.

This work

In this book, I have considered the works of various writers from the 15th to the 21st Century, including but not limited to Persian sources, British accounts, European accounts, and eminent Sikh scholars who have produced invaluable early works that help contextualise the socio-political achievements of the Gurū Sāhibān. Individuals such as Sewā Dās (Parchīān, 1710); Sainapatī (Srī Gur Sobhā, 1711); Bhagat Singh (Gurbilās Pātshahi 6, 1718); Koer Singh (Gurbilās Pātshahi 10, 1751); Kesar Singh Chibbar (Bansāvalīnāmā Dasān Pātshāhīan Kā, 1769); Sarūp Dās Bhallā (Mehmā Prakāsh, 1776); Bhāī Swārūp Singh Kaushish (Gurū Kīān Sākhīān, 1790); Rattan Singh Bhangoo (Srī Gur Panth Prakāsh, 1841); Kavi Santokh Singh, (Sūraj Prakāsh, 1843); and Giānī Giān Singh (Tvārīkh Gurū Khālsā, 1891).

More importantly, I have also taken account of the Words of the Gurū Sāhibān, the Bhagats, the Bhatts, Bhāī Gurdās jī, and Bhāī Nand Lāl jī, both of whom were contemporaries of the Gurū Sāhibān. The English translations for the Gurbani references are taken from Dr. Sant Singh Khalsa (1972). As you may have already noted the pronouns I use for the Gurū Sāhibān are "they" and "them", as well as the possessive adjective "their". This is out of respect, since it is considered rude within both Sikh and Panjābi culture to refer to the Gurū as "him" or "he".

Where possible, I have purposefully refrained from providing an in-depth look at the anecdotes related to the childhood, upbringing, and family lineage of Gurū Nānak Sāhib; most commonly found in the four main Janam Sākhīs. That being said, since the Purātan Janam

Sākhī remains the most influential and accepted, I have taken this to be the main source of information from the texts of Janamsākhīs.[32]

I am presenting a work that focuses on how the Gurū Sāhibān proactively created new paradigms of existence that offered a liberating alternative to the clutches of totalitarian and oppressive power structures built and tied to *haumai*. The rise of Sikh consciousness became the source of a revolutionary transformation that empowered the disciple to realise the Divine power within. Integral to this was the doctrine of Sikh sovereignty that allowed the praxis of Gurmat to exist independently, empowering various manifestations of temporal Sikh Rāj. This was the overriding reason why the Gurū Sāhibān faced violent opposition from the ruling elite, and it is why the Sikhs continue to face persecution today.

Introduction

NOTES

[1] Guru Nanak Sahib, Raag Ramkali, Guru Granth Sahib, Ang 939 –
ਗੁਰਮੁਖਿ ਖੋਜਤ ਭਏ ਉਦਾਸੀ ॥ ਦਰਸਨ ਕੈ ਤਾਈ ਭੇਖ ਨਿਵਾਸੀ ॥
ਸਾਚ ਵਖਰ ਕੇ ਹਮ ਵਣਜਾਰੇ ॥ ਨਾਨਕ ਗੁਰਮੁਖਿ ਉਤਰਸਿ ਪਾਰੇ ॥੧੮॥

[2] ਸਰੂਪ ਦਾਸ ਭੱਲਾ, ੧੭੭੬, ਗੁਰੂ ਨਾਨਕ ਮਹਿਮਾ
Sārūp Das Bhalla, 1776, *Guru Nanak Mehima*, Edited by Dr. Uttam Singh Bhatia, 1971, Bhasha Vibhag, Panjab, p384

[3] Gurbhagat Singh, 1999, *Sikhism and Postmodern Thought*, Naad Pargaas, Sri Amritsar, p26

[4] ਰਤਨ ਸਿੰਘ ਭੰਗੂ, ਸ੍ਰੀ ਗੁਰ ਪੰਥ ਪ੍ਰਕਾਸ਼
Rattan Singh Bhangoo, 1841, *Sri Gur Panth Prakash*, (2:35) Translation by Gurtej Singh, 2015, Vol. 1, Singh Brothers, Amritsar, p14

[5] ਪ੍ਰੋ. ਪਿਆਰਾ ਸਿੰਘ ਪਦਮ, ਸ੍ਰੀ ਗੁਰੂ ਗੋਬਿੰਦ ਸਿੰਘ ਜੀ ਦੇ ਦਰਬਾਰੀ ਰਤਨ
Professor Piara Singh Padam, 1974, *Sri Guru Gobind Singh Ji De Darbari Ratan*, Singh Brothers, p33

[6] Gurū Amar Das, Gurū Granth Sāhib, Raag Ramkalee, Ang 951

[7] Gurbhagat Singh, 1999, *Sikhism and Postmodern Thought*, Naad Pargaas, Sri Amritsar, p31

[8] Guru Nanak Sāhib, Raag Maru, Guru Granth Sahib, Ang 1039 –
ਤਖਤਿ ਬਹੈ ਤਖਤੈ ਕੀ ਲਾਇਕ ॥ ਪੰਚ ਸਮਾਏ ਗੁਰਮਤਿ ਪਾਇਕ ॥

[9] Gurbhagat Singh, 1999, *Sikhism and Postmodern Thought*, Naad Pargaas, Sri Amritsar, p23

[10] Samvad, 7th June 2020, - https://sikhsiyasat.net/samvad-releases-important-draft-for-future-course-of-sikh-struggle/ p30

[11] Tomoko Masuzawa, 2005, *The Invention of World Religions*, University of Chicago Press, Chicago and London, p3

[12] ਹਰਿੰਦਰ ਸਿੰਘ ਮਹਿਬੂਬ, ਸਹਿਜੇ ਰਚਿਓ ਖ਼ਾਲਸਾ
Harinder Singh Mehboob, 1988, *Sahije Rachio Khalsa*, Third Edition, Singh Brothers, Amritsar, p930

[13] Guru Amardas Sahib, Raag Gauri, Guru Granth Sahib, Ang 159 –
ਹਉਮੈ ਵਿਚਿ ਸਭੁ ਜਗੁ ਬਉਰਾਨਾ ॥

ਦੂਜੈ ਭਾਇ ਭਰਮਿ ਭੁਲਾਨਾ ॥

[14] Guru Nanak Sahib, Raag Gauri, Guru Granth Sahib, Ang 222

[15] One of the most insightful definition of Brahmanism was put forward by Swami Dharma Theerta in 'The Menace of Hindu Imperialism" (1947). He wrote:

"It may be defined as a system of socio-religious domination and exploitation of the Hindus based on caste, priestcraft and false philosophy, - caste representing the scheme of domination, priestcraft the means of exploitation, and false philosophy a justification of both caste and priestcraft. Started by Brahman priests and developed by them through centuries of varying fortunes and compromises with numerous ramifications, it has under foreign rule become the general culture of the Hindu and is, at the present day, almost identical with organised Hinduism."

[16] Guru Angad Dev, Raag Aasaa, Guru Granth Sahib, Ang 466 –
ਹਉਮੈ ਦੀਰਘ ਰੋਗੁ ਹੈ ਦਾਰੂ ਭੀ ਇਸੁ ਮਾਹਿ ॥
ਕਿਰਪਾ ਕਰੇ ਜੇ ਆਪਣੀ ਤਾ ਗੁਰ ਕਾ ਸਬਦੁ ਕਮਾਹਿ ॥

[17] Guru Arjan Dev, Raag Aasaa, Guru Granth Sahib, Ang 378 –
ਭਈ ਪਰਾਪਤਿ ਮਾਨੁਖ ਦੇਹੁਰੀਆ ॥
ਗੋਬਿੰਦ ਮਿਲਣ ਕੀ ਇਹ ਤੇਰੀ ਬਰੀਆ ॥

[18] Guru Nanak Sāhib, Sri Raag, Guru Granth Sahib, Ang 20 –
ਸੁਣਿ ਮਨ ਮਿਤ੍ਰ ਪਿਆਰਿਆ ਮਿਲੁ ਵੇਲਾ ਹੈ ਏਹ ॥
ਜਬ ਲਗੁ ਜੋਬਨਿ ਸਾਸੁ ਹੈ ਤਬ ਲਗੁ ਇਹੁ ਤਨੁ ਦੇਹ ॥
ਬਿਨੁ ਗੁਣ ਕਾਮਿ ਨ ਆਵਈ ਢਹਿ ਢੇਰੀ ਤਨੁ ਖੇਹ ॥੧॥
ਮੇਰੇ ਮਨ ਲੈ ਲਾਹਾ ਘਰਿ ਜਾਹਿ ॥
ਗੁਰਮੁਖਿ ਨਾਮੁ ਸਲਾਹੀਐ ਹਉਮੈ ਨਿਵਰੀ ਭਾਹਿ ॥੧॥ ਰਹਾਉ ॥

[19] Bhāī Gurdās, *Vārān*, Vār 1, Paurī 26, translated by Shamsher Singh Puri, 2009, Singh Brothers, Amritsar, 1st Edition, p117

[20] Bhāī Gurdās, *Vārān*, Vār 1, Paurī 7, translated by Shamsher Singh Puri, 2009, Singh Brothers, Amritsar, 1st Edition, p79

[21] Bhāī Gurdās, *Vārān*, Vār 1, Paurī 9 and 10, translated by Shamsher Singh Puri, 2009, Singh Brothers, Amritsar, 1st Edition, p83-85

Introduction

[22] Bhāī Gurdās, *Vārān*, Vār 12, Paurī 7 to 10, translated by Shamsher Singh Puri, 2009, Singh Brothers, Amritsar, 1st Edition, p621-628

[23] Bhāī Gurdās, *Vārān*, Vār 1, Paurī 18, translated by Shamsher Singh Puri, 2009, Singh Brothers, Amritsar, 1st Edition, p101

[24] Bhāī Gurdās, *Vārān*, Vār 1, Paurī 20, translated by Shamsher Singh Puri, 2009, Singh Brothers, Amritsar, 1st Edition, p105

[25] Samvad, 7th June 2020, - https://sikhsiyasat.net/samvad-releases-important-draft-for-future-course-of-sikh-struggle/ p34-35

[26] Guru Angad Sahib, Raag Asa, Guru Granth Sahib, Ang 466

[27] Guru Amar Das, Raag Asa, Guru Granth Sahib, Ang 441 –
ਮਨ ਤੂੰ ਜੋਤਿ ਸਰੂਪੁ ਹੈ ਆਪਣਾ ਮੂਲੁ ਪਛਾਣੁ ॥

[28] Bhagat Kabir ji, Raag Bhaīrao, Gurū Granth Sāhib, Ang 1159

[29] Gurū Nānak, Raag Malaar, Gurū Granth Sāhib, Ang 1288

[30] ਹਰਿੰਦਰ ਸਿੰਘ ਮਹਿਬੂਬ, ਸਹਿਜੇ ਰਚਿਓ ਖ਼ਾਲਸਾ

Harinder Singh Mehboob, 1988, Sahije Rachio Khalsa, Third Edition, Singh Brothers, Amritsar, p930

[31] Guru Arjan, Raag Devgandhārī, Gurū Granth Sāhib, Ang 534

[32] According to Dr. Kirpal Singh, (2004) the source is known by a number of names; 'Walāyat vālī Janam Sākhī' because it is said in 1815, a copy was taken to England by Henry Thomas Colebrook, and 'Hafizābād vāli Janam Sākhī' because an almost identical copy was found by Bhāī Gurmukh Singh, leader of the Lahore Singh Sabhā in Hafizābād, Gujranwālā. Furthermore, eminent Sikh scholar, Bhāī Vīr Singh, refers to it as the Purātan Janam Sākhī because it dates back to 1588; however, the date is not corroborated by any reliable source. In Mahān Kosh, Kāhn Singh Nabhā attributes original authorship to one Bhāī Sewa Das. There is also some crossover with other sources, so I have invariably included reference to the version edited by Bhāī Vīr Singh (1926).

ਪਾਤਿਸ਼ਾਹੀ ਮਹਿਮਾ – Revisiting Sikh Sovereignty

Part One: Sache Pātshāh

SACHE PĀTSHĀH

ਮਾਰਿਆ ਸਿਕਾ ਜਗਤ ਵਿਚਿ
ਨਾਨਕ ਨਿਰਮਲ ਪੰਥ ਚਲਾਇਆ

Gurū Nānak Sāhib established the authority [of his doctrines] in the world, and started a Panth, devoid of any impurity.[1]

Before providing a brief overview of the Gurū period, it is important to acknowledge the relationship a Sikh has with their Gurū. Sikhs have always referred to the Gurū as Sache Pātshāh, which in English is perhaps best translated as the True Sovereign of both worlds. As such, the customs and traditions of conduct one adheres to whilst in the presence of the Gurū are reminiscent of the happenings in a royal court. However, the phrase Sache Pātshah invokes a greater reverence than that reserved for mere worldly rulers or monarchs. Utmost respect and honor are shown towards the Gurū, a practice the Sikhs continue till this day, for it is the Gurū who reveals the Shabad, Nām, and all the mysteries of the universe, both seen and unseen. If one were to walk into any Gurdwara across the globe, they would observe Gurū Granth Sāhib seated on a throne, usually at the front of the Darbār (Court), underneath a Chandoā (Royal Canopy) and an armed guard on duty waving a Chaur Sāhib (Wisk) over Gurū Granth Sāhib. These are the hallmarks of a sovereign Sikh space in which the King of kings resides.

According to Kapur Singh, in the Sikh world, there are, in essence, four distinct types of spiritual authority implied by "Gurū". They are, "(1) the eternal Gurū, referred to by Gurū Nānak Sāhib as Shabad; (2) the personal Gurū as personified by the line of ten Gurū Sāhibān; (3) Gurū Granth Sāhib, the repository of Divine power; and (4) Gurū Panth, the Khālsā bestowed with the temporal authority of

ਪਾਤਿਸ਼ਾਹੀ ਮਹਿਮਾ – Revisiting Sikh Sovereignty

the personal Gurū", which Kapur Singh refers to as "the condominium of Gurū Granth and Gurū Panth".[2]

Shabad

Understanding Shabad is important in appreciating the concept of Gurū; the two are inseparable. Whilst on the third Udassī, Gurū Nānak Sāhib meets the Sidhs and Nath Yogis of the North. Writing in Raag Raamkali, Gurū Sāhib records the conversation preserved in the Gurū Granth Sāhib and referred to as Sidh Gost (Discourse with the Sidhs). One of the enquiries the Sidhs make is centred on establishing who the Gurū's source of Divine knowledge was. Gurū Sāhib emphatically states, "the Shabad is my Gurū and my consciousness the disciple".[3] Throughout Gurbānī, Shabad is referred to as *anhad*, unheard primal sound and *alakh*, that which cannot be uttered. The emphasis throughout Gurbānī is that Shabad is eternal and realised when Haumai is replaced with Hukam.

As Kapur Singh states, the Gurū's mission was to awaken that inner Shabad, the "inner power of pure consciousness", which resides in each and every being. The concept of Gurū, of taking one from darkness to light, is a transformation like no other. Gurbānī places utmost importance on this transformation, emphasizing the need to recognise this as the true worth of human life. The Gurū is thus a portal to reach a higher consciousness. One who reaches this state is referred to as a Gurmukh (Gurū-facing), as opposed to a *manmukh* (ego-facing). The former experiences the oneness of Creation and works for the betterment of all of life, while the *manmukh* is trapped within the confines of his or her own haumai.

One of the key lessons for a Sikh to take from Sidh Gost is the understanding that liberation is found while living in this world, in living a householder's life but remaining detached from everything. It is not in the renunciation of the world per se; the Gurmukh knows both worldliness and renunciation. The Gurmukh saves oneself and others emancipated through the Shabad.[4]

Sangat

Empowered by the Shabad, the Gurmukh congregates with other Gurmukhs in the form of Sangat, and thus we see the rise of the Gurū Panth. In this way, all four interpretations of the word Gurū hold significance in Sikhī. Sangat in the presence of Satgurū keeps one in "a cosmic balance", and the Gurū's Sangat is not only a means of receiving Giān (knowledge) but is the act of transformation from *manmukh* to Gurmukh.

Referring to the lotus metaphor used throughout Gurbanī, Gurbhagat Singh describes how the closed lotus begins to open and grow in Gurū's Sangat. He describes how although the notion of Sangat and the metaphor of the lotus is linked to Buddhism, the "distinction of the Guru Granth is that it does not make the lotus symbolic of mere detachment and *karuna* (compassion). The relationship between the water which is the world or society of space and time and the lotus is of "preet" (love)".[5] According to Gurbhagat Singh, the Gurū Sāhibān insist that the closed lotus is not opened or awakened to its light without first associating with the Sangat.

> "...Individual effort is not enough. One needs to become part of the collective of saintly and truth-radiating persons, called "Sat-Sangat." It is they who enlighten multidimensionally, says Guru Amar Das in Rag Asa. If the seeker or subject desires to get his/her mind and body dyed with the colour of God, if he/she wills to live in God's eternity, only the Sangat can fulfil that aspiration... In the biogenetic or bio-structuralist idiom we can say that the Sangat works a neurogenic wonder, it opens up the entire nervous system with its multicentres, to its creative possibilities."[6]

ਪਾਤਿਸ਼ਾਹੀ ਮਹਿਮਾ – Revisiting Sikh Sovereignty

Gurbhagat Singh goes on to emphasise how "the original insight of Gurū Granth Sāhib is that a human being is a closed flower, a lotus bud awaiting to blossom up with the touch of Gurū's Sangat".[7] This is such a beautiful analogy, and as shall see, the rise of the Gurmukh and later the creation of the Khālsā was evidence of this transformation.

Bhāī Gurdās jī

Additionally, it may be of assistance to readers who are not familiar with the works of Bhāī Gurdās jī, a famous poet and scholar of the Gurū's Darbār, that I provide a brief introduction as I will invariably source his work. Bhāī Gurdās jī (1551-1636) was a leading Sikh scholar who was the first person to present an authentic commentary of Gurbānī in his famous voluminous works entitled Vaars & Kabitt Swayyas. Sikh tradition holds that Gurū Arjan Sāhib, the fifth light of Gurū Nānak Sāhib, blessed Bhāī Gurdās jī' work with the epithet of 'the Key to Gurbānī'. As such, Bhāī Gurdās jī' compositions are sung in Gurdwaras around the globe, and many have sought inspiration from his important texts. According to Kāhan Singh Nābhā, no Rehatnāmā, or code of conduct is more important than his compositions.[8] Having gained proficiency in contemporary languages such as Panjābī, Braj, Hindī, Sanskrit, and Fārsī, Bhāī Gurdās, under the stewardship of Gurū Arjan Sāhib undertook a comprehensive study and reflection of Gurmat. In addition to studying Hinduism and Islam, Bhāī Gurdās jī travelled to places such as Lahore, Agrā, Rajastān, Jammū, and Kāshī to spread the wisdom of Sikhī.[9]

Sikh tradition holds that Bhāī Gurdās jī was closely related to the Gurū Sāhibān in the following ways. Gurū Amar Dās Sāhib, the third light of Gurū Nānak Sāhib, was his Taya jī (uncle [father's older brother]), which made Bibī Bhānī jī (Gurū Amar Dās Sāhib' daughter) his first cousin. Sikh history holds that Bibī Bhānī jī married Gurū Ram Das, the fourth light of Gurū Nānak Sāhib, so Bhāī Gurdās jī became their brother-in-law. In the worldly sense, Bhāī Gurdās jī was also the Mama jī (uncle) of Gurū Arjan Sāhib and also knew Gurū Hargobind Sāhib, the sixth light of Gurū Nānak Sāhib. Therefore, Bhāī Gurdās jī knew four Gurū Sāhibān personally and may also have known of the sixth Gurū's son, who went onto become the ninth Gurū, Gurū Tegh Bahādur Sāhib.

As mentioned, Bhāī Gurdās jī was appointed as an emissary of the Gurū's Darbār and was the scribe of Adi Granth during the time of Gurū Arjan Sāhib. Gurū Hargobind Sāhib also chose him to lead construction works of the Akāl Takht alongside Baba Buddha jī, who incidentally knew all of the first six Gurū Sāhibān. The reason why I've detailed this is to demonstrate that Bhāī Gurdās jī' works are based on either a first-hand account from his own interactions with the Gurū Sāhibān or on the conversation he had with Baba Buddha about Gurū Nānak and Gurū Angad Sāhib, the second light of Gurū Nānak Sāhib. As such, Bhāī Gurdās jī is a leading authority on the lives and conduct of the Gurū Sāhibān.

Bhāī Nand Lal jī

Another primary source that requires special mention here is *Kalaam-e-Goya* Bhāī Nand Lal jī, a famous Sikh of Gurū Gobind Singh Sāhib, and one of Gurū Sāhib's most revered court poets. Bhāī Nand Lal jī was born in a town called Ghazni, situated in modern-day Afghanistan. He learnt Arabic and Persian from his father, a scholar of both languages and an employee of the court of Prince Dara Shikoh, the eldest son of Emperor Shah Jahan.

It is recorded that Bhāī Nand Lal jī left Ghazni following his father's death and headed to Multan, where he married into a Gursikh family. This is how he came to know of Sikhī and the Gurū Sāhibān. He went to Amritsar, and upon hearing about the greatness of Gurū Gobind Singh Sāhib, he went to Anandpur Sāhib.

Tradition holds that Bhāī Nand Lal jī felt much love and affection in the Gurū's presence and wrote a poem in Persian entitled 'Bandginama' (the Epistle of Worship). It is said Gurū Gobind Singh

Sāhib was very pleased upon reading the poem and said the poem should be called 'Zindiginama' (the Epistle of Life) instead because whosoever reads this poem, their birth in this world is made a success. Much like his father, Bhāī Nand Lal jī became a chief clerk within the Mughal Administration, serving Bahadur Shah, Aurangzeb's son.

It is said that Aurangzeb was struggling to understand a particular verse from the Quran, which his own Qazis could not explain. Bhāī Nand Lal jī explained the meaning of the verse, and Aurangzeb was very pleased with this and thought it would be beneficial to bring Bhāī Nand Lal into Islam. When Bhāī Nand Lal jī heard of this, he left for Anandpur Sāhib and sought refuge in service of the Gurū's Darbār. When the great separation took place during the siege of Anandpur Sāhib, Guru Gobind Singh Sāhib asked Bhāī Nand Lal jī to return to Multan and asked him to spread the Gurū's Wisdom as a Parcharak.

Bhāī Nand Lal jī's works remain a great source of inspiration and aspiration for Sikh artists, poets, and writers today, providing a unique insight into the perception Sikhs had of the Gurū and the Gurū's Royal Court. I will be referring to his compositions, and in particular, I'll be opening with couplets from his famous Ganjnāmā as I narrate the lives of the Gurū Sāhibān.

NOTES

[1] Bhāī Gurdās, *Vārān*, Vār 1, Paruī 45, translated by Shamsher Singh Puri, 2009, Singh Brothers, Amritsar, 1st Edition, p155

[2] Kapūr Singh, 1959, *Parasharprasna The Baisakhi of Guru Gobind Singh,* Lahore Book Shop, Ludhiana, p173

[3] Gurū Nānak Sāhib, Raag Raamkalee, Guru Granth Sahib, Ang 942

[4] Gurū Nānak Sāhib, Raag Raamkalee, Guru Granth Sahib, Ang 941

[5] Gurbhagat Singh, 1999, *Sikhism and Postmodern Thought*, Naad Pargaas, Sri Amritsar, p21

[6] Gurbhagat Singh, 1999, *Sikhism and Postmodern Thought*, Naad Pargaas, Sri Amritsar, p21

[7] Gurbhagat Singh, 1999, *Sikhism and Postmodern Thought*, Naad Pargaas, Sri Amritsar, p21

[8] Kahan Singh Nabha, 1930, *Gurshabad Ratnakar, Mahan Kosh,* Bāgh 1, Chattar Singh Jeevan Singh, 2004, Amritsar, p311

[9] Kahan Singh Nabha, 1930, *Gurshabad Ratnakar, Mahan Kosh,* Bāgh 1, Chattar Singh Jeevan Singh, 2004, Amritsar, p311

ਪਾਤਿਸ਼ਾਹੀ ਮਹਿਮਾ – Revisiting Sikh Sovereignty

Srī Gurū Nānak Sāhib Jī Maharaj
(1469-1539)

ਨਾਮਿ ਓੁ ਸ਼ਾਹਿ ਨਾਨਕ ਹੱਕ ਕੇਸ਼
ਕਿ ਨਆਇਦ ਚੁੰਨੁ ਦਿਗਰ ਦਰਵੇਸ਼ ॥੧੩॥

Known as Nānak the Emperor, imbued with righteousness.
There has been no other holy person, as distinctive as the Gurū. 13.[1]

Born in the modern-day province of Lahore, Pakistan, Gurū Nānak Sāhib was a revolutionary in every sense of the word. As Bhāī Gurdās comments, the Gurū quickly ascended in fame and established the authority of their doctrines, starting a new path devoid of any impurity.[2] Roaring like a lion, the Gurū recognised that humanity had been led astray, mainly by the corruption and falsehood of the ruling elite, but also in part due to the ritualistic idol worship within organised religions. Gurū Nānak Sāhib highlighted that, individuals who held seats of authority and power, whether in a political or religious establishment, had manipulated and exploited the people for personal and materialistic gains.

From an early age, Gurū Nānak Sāhib recognised the discriminatory social norms commonplace across South Asia. One such ritual was wearing a piece of thread tied around one's neck, common amongst followers of Brahmanism; the *janeu*. It was believed that without it, one would not be able to break out of the caste system and would forever remain in the lowest of castes. When young Gurū Nānak Sāhib was presented with the *janeu*, they spoke out against such superstitious beliefs and rebutted the claim by stating,

"make compassion the cotton, contentment the thread, modesty the knot and truth the twist. This is

the sacred thread of the soul, if you have it then go ahead and put it on me. It does not break, it cannot be soiled by filth, and it cannot be burnt, or lost. Blessed are those mortal beings, O Nanak, who wear such a thread around their necks." [3]

The Gurū continued to criticise the Hindu priest,

"You buy the thread for a few shells, and seated in your enclosure, you put it on. Whispering instructions into others' ears, the Brahmin becomes a Guru. But he dies, and the sacred thread falls, and the soul departs without it." [4]

Gurū Nānak Sāhib exposed the fallacy of such practices that had enraptured the masses, and as we shall see, shook the very foundations upon which fraudulent self-proclaimed leaders stood. Gurū Nānak Sāhib was critical of Muslim rituals, too, such as circumcision. He states,

"Let mercy be your mosque, faith your prayer-mat, and honest living your Quran. Make modesty your circumcision, and good conduct your fast. In this way, you shall be a true Muslim. Let good conduct be your Kaabaa, Truth your spiritual guide, and the karma of good deeds your prayer and chant. Let your rosary be that which is pleasing to the Will of Akal. O Nanak, God shall preserve your honour". [5]

The Mughals were the ruling elite and had adopted a monarchical political system in which the administrative jurisdiction of Panjāb was divided into three distinct *Subas*, comprised of Lahore, Doaba, and Sirhind. Each Suba was headed up with the approval and support of troops from the emperor. To stagnate society further, there were also perpetual divisions based largely on the *Varna Ashram Dharma*, which propped up the caste system. Gurū Nānak Sāhib saw the duplicity of both and declared no allegiance to either.

Udassi – In search of the Gurmukhs

Shortly after the famous incident in the river, Gurū Nānak Sāhib commenced the first of five journeys, by foot over an approximately 22-year period that saw them travel in all four directions. Gurū Nānak Sāhib writes how the purpose of the journey was to find the Gurmukhs.[6] The first journey was eastward towards Hindu centres, followed by a journey south towards modern-day Srī Lanka. The Gurū's third journey was north to visit the places of Yogis and Nathas before completing a fourth journey towards the West to the Abrahamic centres of influence.

Wherever Gurū Nānak Sāhib travelled, in addition to spreading knowledge of the Creator, Gurū Sāhib heavily criticised the political powers that ruled and questioned the superstitious rituals of self-proclaimed religious leaders, "tearing to shreds many cherished beliefs and establishing new social patterns".[7] The reason for Gurū Sāhib being so critical was due to the fallacies propagated by religious leaders and ruling officials who were both well-rehearsed in manipulating and exploiting the people for personal gains. From the offset, Gurū Nānak Sāhib was unapologetic in their overt condemnation of rulers; the Gurū used an analogy which likened the Kings to tigers and members of the Mughal Bureaucracy to dogs that went out to disturb and harass the people. Gurū Sāhib spoke of how public servants inflicted wounds with their nails, and the officials licked up the blood spilled. This was a reference to the mass exploitation taking place due to corrupt leadership and governance. At the same time, Gurū Sāhib forewarned that all beings would inevitably be judged, and those that had violated the people's trust would be disgraced in the True Court.[8]

In Gurū Granth Sāhib, the judicial and administrative set-up of the Mughal establishment is also criticised. The Pundit, Qazi, and Mullah, who were responsible for these two facets of Mughal governance, are heavily condemned for the laws they wrote and passed.[9] The entire paraphernalia of government, including the rulers, the bureaucracy, the judiciary, and the administration, are condemned too.[10]

Bhāī Gurdās jī reinforces this position by narrating the miserable plight of the rulers and their officers at the head of political, social, and religious institutions, stating that those who dispense justice have become corrupt and accept bribes to issue decisions favouring the offenders.[11] Gurū Nānak Sāhib also likened the Age to a knife in which the rulers are butchers, where righteousness has sprouted wings and flown away.[12] Highlighting the hypocrisy of what they preached and what they practiced, the Gurū constantly scrutinised their actions. There is no ambiguity in what Gurū Sāhib wrote;

> "the sacred marks on their foreheads, and the saffron loin-cloths around their waists; in their hands they hold knives – they are the butchers of the world".[13]

The Gurū adopted a no holds barred approach when exposing the duplicity of the men that abused their positions of power and authority. In this way, Gurū Nānak Sāhib remained resolute and continued to question the cowardice of individuals in positions of power irrespective of their lineage, house, or throne. This demonstrates Gurū Sāhib was not merely a *fakir*, a holy man, or some renunciate that preached of pacifism, but was prepared to engage in the world, prepared to challenge injustice and oppression, no matter how powerful the other regime was. This was a defining aspect of the Gurū period, from Gurū Nānak Sāhib right the way through to Gurū Gobind Singh Sāhib.

ਪਾਤਿਸ਼ਾਹੀ ਮਹਿਮਾ – Revisiting Sikh Sovereignty

Gurū Nānak Sāhib imprisoned

An incident occurred during the impending invasion by Mughal Emperor Babur, the grandson of Tamerlane (who himself was the great-grandson of Ghengis Khan), which highlights the Gurū's commitment to standing for the truth. It is recorded that during this time, the Yogis had refused to defend their people, relying instead on the recitation of mantras and assuring the people that their efforts to remain passive and chant mantras would blind the Mughal forces. When the Mughal forces attacked, Gurū Nānak Sāhib stated,

> "Millions of religious leaders failed to halt the invader, when they heard of the emperor's invasion. He burned the rest-houses and the ancient temples; he cut the princes limb from limb and cast them into the dust. None of the Mughals were blinded and no one performed any miracle".[14]

The Yogis chose not to oppose the brute of Babur's forces and instead abandoned their people. Perhaps the greatest teaching we can take from this is how the Gurū highlighted the importance of standing up against injustice and oppression, which when the time came, was an approach adopted by successive Gurū Sāhibān and later the Sikhs themselves.

The Purātan Janam Sākhī narrates that it was during this invasion that both Gurū Nānak Sāhib and Bhāī Mardana were arrested and imprisoned.[15] They were lodged in the Saidpur prison under the watchful guard of one Mir Khan and made to do forced prison labour. Gurū Nānak Sāhib ground corn and Bhāī Mardana attended to the horses. It is recorded that Gurū Sāhib remained overtly critical of the emperor's actions and recited a Shabad here, which condemned Babur for his actions, stating the priceless country had been laid to waste, defiled by dogs.[16]

Truthful living

Gurū Nānak Sāhib was an advocate of living a householder's life, and condemned empty rituals such as fasting and other forms of penance adopted to achieve enlightenment. The austerities of which the Yogis were so proud were of no value to the Guru, like the counterfeit coin, which may appear genuine but is ultimately rejected as it does not contain any properties of true worth. Whether travelling in the heat of Baghdad or the cold foothills of the Himalayas, the Gurū sang the glory of Akāl Purakh and declared the Divine as the source of his words and actions.

Professor Puran Singh sheds further light on Gurū Nānak Sāhib's revolutionary way when he writes how Gurū Sāhib "condemns false creeds, corrupt politics, and unjust social order." [17] The Gurū also condemns any ritual or tradition, whether religious or political, which breaks away from Akāl.

Gurū Nānak Sāhib not only promoted the idea that truth is the cornerstone upon which social ties are built, but as Satgurū also embodied it. An absence of truth leads to issues of mistrust and creates divisions between two or more communities. This is evident today and was evident to the Gurū in the 15th century. No government can effectively rule and administer a country or dominion if falsehood is strife amongst its ranks. The Gurū compares falsehood to the consumption of poison,

> "Thieves, adulterers, prostitutes and pimps, make friendships with the unrighteous and eat with the unrighteous. They do not know the value of the Lord's Praises, and evil is always with them. If a donkey is anointed with sandalwood paste, he still loves to roll in the dirt. O Nanak, by spinning falsehood, the web of falsehood is woven. False is the

cloth therefrom and its measurement; false are the raiment and pride thereof".[18]

Thus, Guru Nanak Sahib criticised not only the religious leaders for their duality but also became very critical of the people who followed them. The Guru remained steadfast in emphasizing the importance of spreading truth and eradicating falsehood, which went hand in hand with the message of upholding righteousness and uprooting oppression.

Building on the public rejection of the *janeu*, another way in which Gurū Nānak Sāhib eradicated falsehood was by denouncing the ritual of *sutak*, which was widespread amongst the followers of Hinduism. This was a superstitious belief that having given birth, a woman remained unclean for a specific number of days; the exact number itself depended on the caste to which the women belonged. Gurū Nānak Sāhib rejected the caste system and naturally condemned this practice. In Asa ki Var we find,

> "*The impurity of the mind is greed, and the impurity of the tongue is falsehood. The impurity of the eyes is to gaze upon the beauty of another man's wife, and his wealth. The impurity of the ears is to listen to the slander of others. O Nānak, the mortal's soul goes, bound and gagged, to the city of Death. All impurity comes from doubt and attachment to duality. Birth and death are subject to the Command of the Lord's Will; through the Will of Akal we come and go.*"[19]

Opposition to Brahmanism

Gurū Nānak Sāhib established that at its very core, the Brahmanical domination was traditionally very rigid, based solely on a hierarchical model where one's rights as an individual were limited to the caste in which one was born. An unyielding restriction was placed on one's ability to break out of the caste system, and as we have already seen, further disparities were placed on womenfolk. Gurū Nānak Sāhib exposed the errors prevalent within the Brahmanical system and remained outspoken and blunt with his view of the Mughal leaders and their discrimination against fellow humans. Gurū Nānak Sāhib's Divine mission was always centred on the idea of uplifting the world from the slums of spiritual blindness and worldly bigotry that had plundered humanity. For a much more comprehensive overview of how the caste system of Brahmanism has been the "quintessence of social exclusiveness and social inequality", I would urge the reader to study the exceptional work of Sardār Jagjit Singh[20]. His works consider the presence of caste-like discrimination in places like Iran, Assyria, Egypt, Japan and China, but show how over time they melted away into "fluid class distinctions".[21] On the contrary, explains Jagjit Singh, caste society across South Asia became ingrained as the four main groups were split up into more than 3000 hierarchical segments,[22] each one positioned to downgrade the other. This is how caste became systemic and was utilised as a constant mechanism for "downgrading and degrading groups and individuals".[23]

Sardār Jagjit Singh goes on to explain when there was conflict or clash between caste and economic interests, people "would rather forgo economic advantages than caste ones". The compartmentalization of the economy served to harden social segmentation, and the two forces reinforced each other. The position of each layer in the caste hierarchy was permanently fixed. Caste was hereditary, and the position was, by and large, unalterable. This caste-ridden society was driven by a specific caste ideology, namely Brahmanism, which had the full support of not only scriptures, but all systems, organs and institutions of the "orthodox" religion for millennia. After establishing what caste society and ideology are, Sardār Jagjit Singh then considers other movements that were essentially blocked out or consumed within Brahmanism, like the Radical Bhaktas, before providing a fascinating insight into how the

Gurū Sāhibān were the first to build a society outside the caste system. From Sangat to the Khālsā, the Sikh movement was and remains a wholly distinct and standalone proposition to, Brahmanism; which is rejected in its entirety by the Gurū Sāhibān, with the intent of building an inclusive and equal society, based on Gurmat.

Founding of Kartārpur Sāhib

Having discovered and exposed the hypocrisy and falsehood flowing throughout the world, and seemingly with no Gurmukh in sight, Gurū Nānak Sāhib set about starting a path based on Nām and Simran, the cornerstones of truthful living. After purchasing some land Gurū Sāhib established a base at Kartārpur Sāhib, on the banks of the River Rāvī, which was a completely autonomous space, outside the reaches of both the discriminatory caste system and the imperial government. Sarūp Dās Bhalla, the author of Mehma Prakash, makes reference to the founding of Kartārpur Sāhib and the initial meeting with Baba Buddha jī.[24] Dr. Uttam Singh Bhatia in his edits states the land for Kartārpur Sāhib was purchased in 1504, with the Gurū taking of residence in 1522 following the completion of the Udassīs. This demonstrates that the Gurū was not content with merely pointing out the problems leading society astray, nor was Gurū Nānak Sāhib a messenger or an *avtar* here on earth to merely convey a message; Bhāī Gurdās jī tells us Gurū Nānak Sāhib was Akāl Roop, the very form of the Timeless One.

In order to fully appreciate the greatness of the Sikh movement that Gurū Nānak Sāhib initiated from Kartārpur Sāhib, it is imperative to understand how Gurū Nānak Sāhib cultivated Nām consciousness, that gave birth to the Gurmukh and the Sangat, and how the former stood in opposition to both Mughal imperialism and the caste-ridden systems of Brahmanical hegemony. There was not a mere recognition or critique of the negative effects of the prevalent paradigms but, as Sache Pātshāh, the Gurū made a conscious move to create new paradigms of existence.[25] In Gurū Granth Sāhib we read from Bhatt Talh that Gurū Nānak Sāhib established Rāj, built on the foundations of Truth.[26] The choice of words, as later approved and endorsed by Gurū Arjan Sāhib, are very specific and worth noting. Bhatt Talh does not say Gurū Nānak Sāhib established a *mazhab* (religion), or even that they started a *dharam*, but that Gurū Nānak Sāhib established Rāj, political rule. Within this Rāj, a new home was thus created for the Gurmukh (Gurū-oriented, one who embodied the values imparted by Gurū Nānak Sāhib) to live, grow, prosper, and over time, tear down ego-driven structures of oppression and destruction.

Key Sikh teachings, such as dwelling amongst the society of saints, were actualised by the Gurū's Rāj upon the sacred soil of Kartārpur Sāhib[27]. With complete control and autonomy came the ability to control their own affairs and cultivate an environment in which the Gurmukh could be nurtured. The ideals of compassion, truthfulness, contentment, and love for the Creator and Creation were promoted, as Nām and Shabad formed the nucleus of the society Gurū Nānak Sāhib created at Kartārpur Sāhib. These are the ideals of Truth that Bhatt Talh referred to. Having heard of the Gurū's glory, people travelled from far and wide to attend the Gurū's Darbār. Not just from within Panjāb, but according to Kavī Santokh Singh, peoples from far off lands, including Turks and Brahmins, Muslims and Hindus alike, travelled to meet the Gurū and experience the joy and upliftment of attending the Darbār of Sache Pātshāh.[28]

It is plausible to suggest many of those who travelled from far off regions had either met the Gurū during the Udassīs or heard from others who had witnessed first hand what Gurū Sāhib had said and done. Furthermore, the pace of the mobilization that took place in Kartārpur Sāhib was a remarkable achievement. For such a diverse cross-section of society to travel, that too within decades of the Gurū's arrival on Earth, demonstrates the electrifying presence of Gurū Sāhib and how the people resonated with Gurmat.

Sangat and Pangat

The institute of Sangat was thriving within Kartārpur Sāhib, as people, irrespective of caste and class, gathered to contemplate and sing the praises of Akāl Purakh. As Gurbhagat Singh writes,

> *"the notion of Sadh Sangat in Sri Guru Granth Sahib is not merely an ethical concept but a physical place that nurtured an enlightened collectivity, which mediated the individual, deindividuating him/her with full awareness of the context."*[29]

Sangat went hand in hand with Pangat, both shining examples of how the Gurū demolished social barriers prevalent between different sets of communities. Pangat provided people with the opportunity to connect with one another and take part in Langar. It was a statement from the Gurū to bring about social change, which was a revolutionary act of its time when food was deemed dirty by followers of Brahmanism if the mere shadow of a person considered to be of low caste fell on the plate of a person considered to be of high caste. The underlying message of Langar was to break bread with a fellow human, irrespective of their social, political, or economic status in a totally autonomous and self-regulating environment.

The Gurū removed superstition and hypocrisy prevalent amongst the other "religions" of the world, which was tied to the socio-political movement initiated by the Gurū. In traditional South-Asian Brahmanical culture, any societal work involving manual labour was usually confined to those deemed of low caste. What Gurū Nānak Sāhib introduced with Pangat and Langar were practices, which, aside from spreading compassion, formed a bridge between the individual and society to better society and serve humanity.

Vismād

Having completed the Udassīs, Bhāi Gurdās jī comments how Gurū Nānak Sāhib conquered the nine regions of Earth, through the propagation of the authority of Satnam.[30] The early 16th century thus saw the rise of a new way of existing in the world. Gurbhagat Singh suggests this way may be called Sikh Consciousness[31]; put simply, it is the way of the Gurmukh. A spiritually complete and distinct form, in front of all other established so-called dharmic or religious creations. Spiritually complete because it counters the egoic tendencies of oppressive systems that have broken away from the Divine, and distinct because a Gurmukh acknowledges and experiences Vismād, the wonderous or joyous play in which Akāl Purakh resides within everything.

> *"In Vismād, knowing and existence cannot be separated. Knowing the Real is existentially being with the Beloved – the Real in His wondrous diversity become inspiring Love that transforms the knower into music. Vismādic knowledge therefore is a luminous and musical state of being. Once the Beloved begins to dwell in the body the ceaseless unstruck music is sensed and the Vismād experienced is unspeakable..."*[32]

Vismād, as spoken of in the Guru Granth Sahib, is explained by Gurbhagat Singh, as the "paradigm of heterogeneity and love, celebrating the Divine", and presented as an alternative to the two contemporary capital-based orders of Capitalism and Socialism.

According to Gurbhagat Singh, both orders alienate capital from the state of Vismād and the "sacred symphony of life",[33] which prevents any true revolutionary change for human life. He argues if the Sikh paradigm of Vismād is "adapted to redefine our understanding and relationship with capital and reorganise society by modifying the institutions that govern it",[34] it has the potential to bring radical change and create a state of "reflective and social equilibrium". In essence, Vismād offers a third option of governance over the two dominant ways of organizing the individual and society. While Socialism emerged when the masses of Europe revolted against the "single-centred" nature of Capitalism, the ideological position of all those revolutions (French, American and Russian), "was rooted in the philosophy of the so-called Enlightenment which prioritised Rationalism and its reason-centred narratives for the emancipation of all cultures."[35] This notion of Vismād helps to contextualise the distinct nature of the revolution that began from Kartārpur Sāhib. It opens up new possibilities of existence and governance in which the Divine permeates all spaces.

The radical approach

The early successes of Gurū Nānak Sāhib can be attributed to the fact that there were no forceful conversions or the waving of scripture to impose Sikhi on someone. It was the truth of the Gurū's Word that was revolutionary. The Gurū's Sikhia revolutionised some while alarming others. That has been the pattern throughout Sikh history and is why Sikhs have faced oppression and near extinction since inception. Sikhī was never a reformist movement. On the contrary, the Gurū was very critical of the followers of Brahmanism and Islam. The Gurū Granth Sāhib refers to Hindus as blind and Muslims as one-eyed in reference to their actions and practices[36]. This was of course in relation to the hypocrisy that prevailed across society. Despite this overt criticism, the Gurū Sāhibān did not attempt to steamroll the other traditions or attempt to subjugate or assimilate through any force. There was simply the creation of the Tisar Panth; the third way, which was grounded in Vismād, or pure wonder of the Creator, and the whole cosmos, revealed through Gurbānī.

The ego-driven rulers naturally labelled Gurū Nānak Sāhib an outlaw for such views, which they branded outlandish and directly opposed to their rule. Over time, due to the distinctiveness of Gurmat, it was viewed as a direct threat to power structures that sought to subjugate, control, and dominate through classification and stringent categorisation of peoples and land. It is important to note that this distinctiveness operates at an epistemological level, at the very foundation of a haumai-driven mode of knowledge-production, cultivation, and dissemination, which is prompted by a self-professed logical and rational mind to be the superior, over the Other. The resulting creation of temporal structures of power that crystalise this notion of individualism and perpetuate hierarchal control is, in essence, what Gurū Nānak Sāhib spoke out against.

Gurū Sāhib operated at a level beyond the confines of the mind, otherwise lauded for its logical, empirical, and intellectualizing abilities. Whether that ideology arrives from Brahmanism, Mughal Imperialism, or indeed Western Secular Philosophy, Gurmat opposes that imposition and the Tisar Panth, founded on Gurmukh consciousness, comprised of Nām, Shabad, and Vismād, exists to resist and overcome the egoic forces, whether in an individual or an entire power structure.

Passing of the Gurūship

When Gurū Nānak Sāhib chose their successor, instead of passing the reign to their son(s), they adopted a meritocracy model and chose a committed Sikh in Bhāī Lehna. Gurū Granth Sāhib records, via Bhatts Satta and Balvand that,

> *"Gurū Nānak established Rāj; building the true fortress on the strongest of foundations. Gurū Sāhib installed the royal canopy over Lehna's head; who in praise, drank in the immortal nectar. The Guru implanted the almighty sword to illuminate the soul.*

> *The Guru bowed down to the disciple, while alive. The king, while still alive, applied the ceremonial mark to [Bhāī Lehna's] forehead".*[37]

Bhāī Gurdās jī builds on this by poetically declaring,

> *"Guru Nanak created Guru Angad from their limbs as the waves are produced by River Ganges out of itself...The love between Guru and the Guru's disciple was such that the disciple became Guru and the Guru disciple".*[38]

Mahakāvī Santokh Singh, in his masterpiece Srī Gur Nānak Prakāsh states,

> *"In Kartārpur, the King of the world, Srī Gurū Nānak, gave the glorious gift [of the Guru's Throne] to Srī Gurū Angad Dev jī".*[39]

Kavī Santokh Singh goes on to describe how Gurū Nānak Sāhib infused their light in Gurū Angad Sāhib. The transition was seamless,

> *"Just like a King, taking off one of his royal robes and wearing a second robe, [Gurū Angad] now sits in the Gurū's Darbār".*[40]

All three sources depict this moment with strong emphasis on the oneness of Gurū Nānak Sāhib and Gurū Angad Sāhib, as well as with strong reference to the sovereignty of the Gurū's Darbār. In this way, the Sikh revolution continued forth, and in 1539 Bhāī Lehnā, the Gurū's most loyal disciple was placed upon the Throne of Gurū Nānak Sāhib. Thus, began the reign of Sache Pātshāh Srī Gurū Angad Sāhib jī Maharaj.

Srī Gurū Nānak Sāhib ji Mahārāj

NOTES

[1] Bhāī Nand Lal (1633-1713), *Ganjnama*, Kalaam-e-Goya, translated by Sardar Pritpal Singh Bindra, 2003, Institute of Sikh Studies, Chandigarh

[2] Bhāī Gurdās, *Vārān*, Vār 1, Paurī 45, translated by Shamsher Singh Puri, 2009, Singh Brothers, Amritsar, 1st Edition, p155

[3] Gurū Nānak Sāhib, Raag Aasaa, Gurū Granth Sāhib, Ang 471

[4] Gurū Nānak Sāhib, Raag Aasaa, Gurū Granth Sāhib, Ang 471

[5] Gurū Nānak Sāhib, Raag Maajh, Gurū Granth Sāhib, Ang 140

[6] Gurū Nānak Sāhib, Raag Rāmkalī, Gurū Granth Sāhib, Ang 939

[7] Rajinder Singh, 1988, *Five Hundred Years of Sikhism*, Amritsar Chief Khalsa Diwan, Department of History, Panjab University, Patiala, p6

[8] Gurū Nānak Sāhib, Raag Malaar, Gurū Granth Sāhib, Ang 1288

[9] Bhagat Kabir ji, Raag Bhāīrao, Gurū Granth Sāhib, Ang 1159

[10] Gurū Nānak Sāhib, Raag Malaar, Gurū Granth Sāhib, Ang 1288

[11] Bhāī Gurdās, *Vārān*, Vār 1, Paurī 30, translated by Shamsher Singh Puri, 2009, Singh Brothers, Amritsar, 1st Edition, p125

[12] Gurū Nānak Sāhib, Raag Maajh, Gurū Granth Sāhib, Ang 145

[13] Gurū Nānak Sāhib, Raaj Aasaa Gurū Granth Sāhib, Ang 472

[14] Gurū Nānak Sāhib, Raaj Aasaa Gurū Granth Sāhib, Ang 418

[15] *Purātan Janam Sakhi* (1588), edited by Bhāī Vir Singh, 1926, Sākhī 35

[16] Gurū Nānak Sāhib, Raag Aasaa, Gurū Granth Sāhib, Ang 360

[17] Professor Puran Singh, 1930, *Spirit of the Sikh*, Part 1, Publication Bureau Punjabi University, Patiala

[18] Gurū Nānak Sāhib, Raag Soohee, Gurū Granth Sāhib, Ang 790

[19] Gurū Nānak Sāhib, Raag Aasaa, Gurū Granth Sāhib, Ang 472

[20] Jagjit Singh, 1981, *Percussions of History, The Sikh Revolution & in the Caravan of Revolutions*, The Nanakshahi Trust, Panjab

[21] Jagjit Singh, 1981, *Percussions of History, The Sikh Revolution & in the Caravan of Revolutions*, The Nanakshahi Trust, Panjab, p12

[22] Jagjit Singh, 1981, *Percussions of History, The Sikh Revolution & in the Caravan of Revolutions*, The Nanakshahi Trust, Panjab, p17

[23] Jagjit Singh, 1981, *Percussions of History, The Sikh Revolution & in the Caravan of Revolutions*, The Nanakshahi Trust, Panjab, p17

[24] ਸਰੂਪ ਦਾਸ ਭੱਲਾ, ੧੭੭੬, ਗੁਰੂ ਨਾਨਕ ਮਹਿਮਾ
Sārūp Das Bhalla, 1776, *Guru Nanak Mehima*, Edited by Dr. Uttam Singh Bhatia, 1971, Bhasha Vibhag, Panjab, p383

[25] Gurbhagat Singh, 1999, *Sikhism and Postmodern Thought*, Naad Pargaas, Sri Amritsar, p60

[26] Bhatt Talh, Raag Raamkalee, Gurū Granth Sāhib, Ang 966

[27] Guru Arjan Sāhib, Raag Bilaaval, Gurū Granth Sāhib, Ang 816

[28] Kavī Chūrāmanī Bhāī Santokh Singh, 1843, *Srī Gur Pratap Sūraj Granth*, Steek 2, Utarāradh, Adhiāi 53, Line 20-24, edited by Dr. Ajeet Singh Aulakh, 2014, 3rd Edition, p629

[29] Gurbhagat Singh, 1999, *Sikhism and Postmodern Thought*, Naad Pargaas, Sri Amritsar, p60-61

[30] Bhāī Gurdās, *Vārān*, Vār 1, Paurī 37, translated by Shamsher Singh Puri, 2009, Singh Brothers, Amritsar, 1st Edition, p139

[31] Gurbhagat Singh, 1999, *Sikhism and Postmodern Thought*, Naad Pargaas, Sri Amritsar, p26

[32] Gurbhagat Singh, 2013, *Vismād The Sikh Alternative*, Naad Pargaas, Sri Amritsar, p8

[33] Gurbhagat Singh, 2013, *Vismād The Sikh Alternative*, Naad Pargaas, Sri Amritsar, p1

[34] Gurbhagat Singh, 2013, *Vismād The Sikh Alternative*, Naad Pargaas, Sri Amritsar, p1

[35] Gurbhagat Singh, 2013, *Vismād The Sikh Alternative*, Naad Pargaas, Sri Amritsar, p1-2

[36] Bhagat Nām Dev, Raag Gond, Gurū Granth Sāhib, Ang 874

[37] Bhatt Satta & Balwant, Raag Raamkalee, Gurū Granth Sāhib, Ang 966

[38] Bhāī Gurdās, *Vārān*, Vār 24, Paurī 6, translated by Shamsher Singh Puri, 2009, Singh Brothers, Amritsar, 1st Edition

[39] Kavī Chūrāmanī Bhāī Santokh Singh, 1843, Srī Gur Nānak Prakāsh, translated by Resham Singh & Jīvanpal Singh, 2019

[40] Kavī Chūrāmanī Bhāī Santokh Singh, 1843, Srī Gur Nānak Prakāsh, translated by Resham Singh & Jīvanpal Singh, 2019

ਪਾਤਿਸ਼ਾਹੀ ਮਹਿਮਾ – Revisiting Sikh Sovereignty

Srī Gurū Angad Sāhib Jī Maharaj

ਦੋ ਆਲਮ ਚਿਹ ਬਾਸ਼ਦ ਹਜ਼ਾਰਾਂ ਜਹਾਂ
ਤੁਫ਼ੈਲਿ ਕਰਮਹਾਇ ਓ ਕਾਮਰਾਂ ॥ ੫੬ ॥

> Let alone the two worlds, through [Guru Angad Sāhib's] kindness, thousands of other domains are flourishing. 56.[1]

Gurū Angad Sāhib collected the Shabads of Gurū Nānak Sāhib and composed Divine melodies of their own. In addition to preserving the writings of Gurū Nānak Sāhib, they added a further 63 Saloks[2]. Bhāī Gurdās jī has commented that Gurū Nānak Sāhib had merely transformed themself, by merging the light of Gurū with Bhāī Lehnā.[3] The appointment of a successor while alive shows the Gurū's intent to grow the community and the founded institutions. However, others were vying for the opportunity to sit on Gurū Nānak Sāhib's Throne. Gurū Angad Sāhib moved to Khadūr Sāhib and established a new centre because, as J.S. Grewal notes, "the law of the state could be invoked by the legal heirs of Guru Nanak to claim Kartarpur as a matter of right".[4]

Other Sikh historians too have noted how Gurū Angad Sāhib strategically avoided confrontation with the sons of Gurū Nānak Sāhib, who felt it was their birthright to sit on the throne of their father.[5] Despite the hostilities from Srī Chand and Lakhmi Das, which are first narrated by Bhāī Gurdās jī and recorded in Gurū Granth Sāhib by Satta and Balvand, Gurū Angad Sāhib managed the aspirations of a growing Panth by relocating to Khadūr Sāhib and initiated a regular system of collecting offerings made by Sikhs to finance the development of the Sikh movement. This demonstrates the importance Gurū Sāhib placed on maintaining autonomy, following in the footsteps of Gurū Nānak Sāhib, and on the need to establish independence to nurture the Gurmukhs in a space that was free of the imposition of external influences and ideologies. Sovereign Sikh spaces was fundamental to the Sikh movement.

Building the Sikh movement

In this way, Gurū Angad Sāhib continued the revolution and was responsible for the ratification of the Gurmukhī script. The Guru's overt rejection of the Devnagari script, a script considered sacred by Hindus, in favor of the new Gurmukhī script, further cemented the notion of giving rise to a new shared identity among the Sikhs. It served the Sikhs with a constant reminder,

> "...that they were something distinct from the common mass of Hindus. It also dealt a powerful blow to the domination of the priestly class, whose importance rested on their knowledge of Sanskrit which had so far been the language of religion".[6]

This was a clear rejection of not only the superiority of Devnagari and Persian scripts, but also the hegemonic authority these scripts had amassed in religious and scholarly groups of the time.[7]

> "The disciples of [Gurū] Nanak...do not recite the mantras of Hindus and do not pay respect at idol temples. They do not count the avtārs for anything. They do not have any attachment to Sanskrit, which the Hindus call the language of the angels"[8]

The decision to formally adopt Gurmukhī supported the distinct and unique nature of Gurmat. This was not met favourably by the upper-class Hindus, Brahmins, Kshatriyas, and Vaishahs, who were conditioned in Vedic ideas expressed in the Sanskrit language.

Srī Gurū Angad Dev Sāhib jī Mahārāj

Professor Puran Singh narrates how they questioned Gurū Sāhib about the exclusion of the Sanskrit language, which they deemed the only language in which great truths could be told. The answer from Gurū Sāhib, according to Puran Singh was,

> *"Sanskrit, now that is no longer the people's tongue, is like well water – sufficient for the irrigation of a small tract of land; whereas Panjābi, being the living language of the people, even if it be nothing but a dialect, is as the rain, which falls in showers all over the country".* [9]

This is a beautiful analogy of how the Gurū sought to break the stranglehold of upper-class rulers, who had restricted the passing of knowledge to an exclusive group defined by their own terms. Gurū Angad Sāhib also continued the practise of Langar, which Gurū Nānak Sāhib had established before him. The supervision of Langar was entrusted with Mātā Khivī jī who ensured necessary provisions were made for those who travelled from all directions to the Gurū Dārbār at Khadūr Sāhib. Professor Puran Singh again comments,

> *"The whole people came to the new Master: some to be healed and blessed, others to be initiated as disciples. But, once they had come, they all continued, in one way or another, to however round the magic personality of the Master, Angad, as moths hover a lamp in darkness".* [10]

Gurū Sāhib led by example by fully embracing the tradition of Pangat and Sangat. Those who did not adhere to this tradition were not allowed to meet with the Gurū.[11] Further centres were opened, and the Gurū established a regular stream of revenue through the offerings brought by those who arrived in Khadūr Sāhib

Gurū Angad Sāhib was very fond of physical exercise and sports.[12] They took a keen interest in wrestling and encouraged those in

Khadūr Sāhib to remain fit and healthy, ready at a whim for any service the Gurū may need of them. It is evident this move was a precursor to Miri Piri, which Gurū Hargobind Sāhib formally established. The decision to champion physical training alongside spiritual growth became a defining attribute of Sikh existence during this period and thus demonstrated the ideological connectedness of the Gurū Sāhibān. The Gurū was also instrumental in setting up institutes of education.

The Gurū's Darbar at Khadūr Sāhib

Upon reading Gurbānī, and building on the Rāj established by Gurū Nānak Sāhib, it becomes evident that the Gurū Angad Sāhib was introducing a kind of Court etiquette in which the attendees had to adhere to certain protocols before receiving an audience with the Gurū. Mahakavi Santokh Singh describes how Gurū Angad Sāhib, sat on a throne from Khadūr Sāhib, which is located in the Amritsar district of Panjāb, and much like the founding of Kartārpur Sāhib by Gurū Nānak Sāhib, Khadūr Sāhib was also strategically founded along a river, this time the River Beas.

ਤਖਤ ਬੈਠਿ ਅੰਗਦ ਗੁਰੂ ਕੀਨ ਖਡੂਰ ਨਿਵਾਸ ॥
ਨਰਨ ਉਧਾਰਨ ਕਾਰਨੇ ਕਰਤਿ ਸੁ ਭਗਤਿ ਪ੍ਰਕਾਸ ॥ ੯ ॥ [13]

Gurū Angad sitting on the throne, came to live at Khadūr Sāhib, for the sake of saving the people, he manifested the path of loving devotional worship.

The socio-political success of Gurū Angad Sāhib in Khadūr is confirmed by the diverse array of Sangat that arrived and filled the Gurū's Darbār. Bhāī Gurdās ji provides an extensive list of names and describes their traits and professions. From community leaders such as Bhagirath of Malsihan and ironsmiths such as Gujjar to soldiers such as Malu Shahi and famous intellectuals such as Lalu, Durga, and Jiwandh[14], it is clear the Gurū was attracting a wealth of gifted people under their entourage to help build a society that could provide the best opportunities for society to develop and flourish. The Gurū's decision to use metaphors from trade in Gurbānī is not merely coincidental. [They were purposeful and intended to create a mindset in which the Sikhs understood the importance of creating a prosperous Panth.]

Indeed, Bhāī Gurdās ji has dedicated large sections of Vār 11 to naming the Sikhs of the Gurūs. It is likely the names of Sikhs that Bhāī Gurdās ji refers to stayed in close proximity to the Gurū's Darbār. These Sikhs were likely the most trustworthy and dedicated members of the Gurū's Sangat, who worked to further the Gurū's Darbār. In the *paurīs* immediately preceding the names, Bhāī Gurdās ji does mention the qualities of a Gursikh, a Gurmukh and the way of the Gurū's Sikh, stating a Gurmukh accepts and follows the instructions of the Gurū and loves doing necessary tasks for the welfare of all.[15] This vivid depiction of Bhāī Gurdās is built on the first Paurī of Vār 11[16]:

ਸਤਿਗੁਰੁ ਸਚਾ ਪਾਤਿਸਾਹ ਪਾਤਿਸਾਹਾਂ ਪਾਤਿਸਾਹ ਜੁਹਾਰੀ।
ਸਾਧ ਸੰਗਤਿ ਸਚਿਖੰਡਿ ਹੈ ਆਇ ਝਰੋਖੈ ਖੋਲੈ ਬਾਰੀ।
ਅਮਿਉ ਕਿਰਣਿ ਨਿਝਰ ਝਰੈ ਅਨਹਦ ਨਾਦ ਵਾਇਨ ਦਰਬਾਰੀ।
ਪਾਤਿਸਾਹਾਂ ਦੀ ਮਜਲਸੈ ਪਿਰਮ ਪਿਆਲਾ ਪੀਵਣ ਭਾਰੀ।
ਸਾਕੀ ਹੋਇ ਪੀਲਾਵਣਾ ਉਲਸ ਪਿਆਲੇ ਖਰੀ ਖੁਮਾਰੀ।
ਭਾਇ ਭਗਤਿ ਭੈ ਚਲਣਾ ਮਸਤ ਅਲਮਸਤ ਸਦਾ ਹੁਸਿਆਰੀ।
ਭਗਤ ਵਛਲ ਹੋਇ ਭਗਤ ਭੰਡਾਰੀ ॥੧॥

Salutation to the True Gurū, the True Emperor who is Emperor of the emperors. The True Gurū comes to the realm of truth and dispenses words of wisdom to all present. The Divine nectar flows perpetually in their discourse and those present in the Darbār experience the melody of unstruck music. Drinking the cup of spirituality in the court of worldly emperors is difficult. (It would not be elixir-like as that of the True Gurū).

ਪਾਤਿਸ਼ਾਹੀ ਮਹਿਮਾ – Revisiting Sikh Sovereignty

Whosoever is blessed with the Divine nectar by the True Gurū, is ever found in the intoxication of Lord's Name. Such a devotee lives in the loving devotion of the Lord. Renounced from the world and yet remaining attentive and wise. Lord fulfils all the desires of such a devotee.

This is perhaps one of the clearest examples of how a contemporary of the Guru describes the institute of Gurū's Darbār as a standalone and distinct sovereign centre of power. The eulogy is similar to the compositions of Bhāī Nand Lāl jī, who describes Gurū Gobind Singh as the Emperor of emperors, which confirms the wholeness and continuity of the Gurū's Darbār. The glorification of Gurū Sāhib by Bhāī Gurdās ji is in many ways reflective of the distinguishable writings of Gurū Angad Sāhib whose devotional Shabads, which speak to the liberating power and authority of Akāl, and Gurū Nānak Sāhib.[17] Acknowledging the socio-political accomplishments of the Gurū, against the context of their Words as recorded in Gurbānī, helps one to understand the necessity of sovereignty of the Gurū's Darbār.

Condemning false rulers

The policy of scrutinizing the ruling elite continued with Gurū Angad Sāhib, which is evident not only from the written accounts about the Gurū's life but also in the Gurū's own writings contained within the Gurū Granth Sāhib,

> "The beggar is known as an emperor, and the fool is known as a religious scholar. The blind man is known as a seer; this is how people talk. The trouble-maker is called a leader, and the liar is seated with honour. O Nānak, the Gurmukhs know that this is justice in Kaljug".[18]

We've already seen how Gurū Nānak Sāhib likened the Age of Kaljug to a knife in which the rulers are butchers, and elsewhere Gurū Sāhib has also stated that in this Age those individuals who act like tyrants are accepted and approved, such is the state of the world[19]. This truth is as relevant today as it was during the time of the Gurū Sāhibān. Gurbānī informs us of the various forms taken by Akāl throughout the Ages, maintaining that in the Age of Kaljug, Akāl arrived in the form of Gurū Nānak Sāhib, Gurū Angad Sāhib, and Gurū Amar Dās Sāhib:

ਕਲਿਜੁਗਿ ਪ੍ਰਮਾਣੁ ਨਾਨਕ ਗੁਰੁ ਅੰਗਦੁ ਅਮਰੁ ਕਹਾਇਓ ॥
ਸ੍ਰੀ ਗੁਰੂ ਰਾਜੁ ਅਬਿਚਲੁ ਅਟਲੁ ਆਦਿ ਪੁਰਖਿ ਫੁਰਮਾਇਓ ॥੨॥

In the Age of Kaljug, they are known and accepted as Gurū Nānak, Gurū Angad and Gurū Amar Das. The sovereign rule of the Great Guru is unchanging and permanent, according to the Command of the Primal Being, Akāl. [20]

Opposition from other established orders

As Gurū Sāhib's fame spread, Kavi Santokh Singh narrates an episode in which a number of yogis, including the renowned Gorakh, Bhartar, Charpat, and Gopichand, came to see Gurū Angad Sāhib in Khadūr Sāhib.[21] In a similar manner to how the Siddhs posed questions to Gurū Nānak Sāhib, they question the Gurū on various matters concerning his decision to remain involved in worldly affairs, an approach they felt was improper. As ascetics, they felt the Gurū too should become a recluse and leave the mundane affairs of society. They declared without undertaking yoga, none could achieve salvation. Gurū Angad Sāhib listened to their questions and then addressed them in a forthright and direct manner quoting Gurū Nānak Sāhib's own writings. Gurū Angad Sāhib listed all the different ways of the yogis, from wearing a patched coat and earrings to shaving one's head and sitting in trances or bathing at sacred shrines, and told them that ultimately such measures alone were not the real union. They had to look upon everyone and view them all as equals; that's when they would begin their journey towards a true union. Remaining unattached whilst living in the real world, that was the true way to achieve union.[22] The courage and conviction of the Gurū's Words left a lasting impression upon the yogis who soon left the Gurū's Darbār.

Gurū Angad Sāhib's reign correlated with the reign of the second Mughal king Nasir-ud-Din Muhammad, also known as Emperor Humayun, and with Sher Shah, who was the founder of the Sur Afghan dynasty. Sikh tradition holds that Emperor Humayun once came to see the Gurū[23] after being defeated by Sher Shah Suri in the Battle of Kanauj (May 1550). This was a common practice amongst the Muslim world as they believed a *fakir* had the power to forewarn of impending misfortune.

When the emperor arrived, however, Gurū Angad Sāhib was engaged in other affairs and refused to meet the emperor. This enraged him, and he became hostile. In a fit of anger, he reached for the hilt of his sword, to which the Gurū uttered,

> *"Beaten by Sher Shah, you can do no better than strike a faqir with your sword. Better go back to your motherland before you seek to regain your throne".*[24]

Keeping with the tradition of speaking against falsehood, Gurū Angad Sāhib displayed the same spirit with which Gurū Nānak Sāhib had challenged the power regime. Interestingly, Puran Singh suggests the Guru told the emperor to go back to his motherland because it would imply, certainly in the mind of Puran Singh writing in 1920, there was a clear distinction between the political jurisdiction or dominion of the Emperor of Delhi, and the Gurū's Darbār in Khadūr Sāhib, Panjāb. As we shall see, other prominent Sikh writers and scholars, including pre-colonial writers such as Kavī Santokh

Singh, are conscious of this separation between the government in Delhi, and the parallel structure of power of the Gurū's Darbār.

Passing of the Gurūship

Much like Gurū Nānak Sāhib, Gurū Angad Sāhib felt their sons were not worthy of the Gurū's Throne and thus when the time arose, based the decision to pass on the Gurgaddī to the next successor, on merit and merit alone. This was a bold and radical decision since the Gurū would have known the impact it would cause from the encounter with Srī Chand, who had laid claim to the seat of Gurū Nānak Sāhib, and refused to recognise Gurū Angad Sāhib as the successor. This had caused many to be taken in by Srī Chand's claims who joined him in Kartārpur. Despite this Gurū Angad Sāhib remained steadfast, and as we shall see in the coming chapters, this became a constant struggle that the Gurūs embraced and overcame each time. The person chosen by Gurū Angad Sāhib was Bhāī Amar Dās, who in 1552 become Gurū Amar Dās Sāhib, the 3rd light of Gurū Nānak Sāhib.

NOTES

[1] Bhāī Nand Lal (1633-1713), *Ganjnama, Kalaam-e-Goya*, translated by Sardar Pritpal Singh Bindra, 2003, Institute of Sikh Studies, Chandigarh

[2] Dr Sarbjinder Singh, 2008, *Divine Revelation*, Sikh Foundation, Delhi, p26

[3] Bhāī Gurdās, *Vārān*, Vār 1, Paurī 45, translated by Shamsher Singh Puri, 2009, Singh Brothers, Amritsar, 1st Edition, p155

[4] J.S. Grewal, 1994, *The Sikhs of The Punjab*, Cambridge University Press, p47

[5] Kushwant Singh, 1963, *A History of the Sikhs*, Vol. 1, Second Edition, Oxford University Press, and Dr Sangat Singh, 2014, *The Sikhs in History*, Singh brothers, Amritsar

[6] Teja Singh and Ganda Singh, 1950, *A Short History of the Sikhs (1469-1765)*, Volume One, Publication Bureau, Punjabi University, Patiala, p19

[7] Pashaura Singh, 2000, *The Guru Granth Sahib*, Oxford University Press, p16

[8] Mobad, 1645-46, *Dabistān-i Mazāhib, Sikhism and the Sikhs*, translated by J. S. Grewal & Irfan Habib, 2001, *Sikh History from Persian Sources*, Tulika Books, Delhi, p66

[9] Professor Puran Singh, 1920, *The Book of The Ten Masters*, Singh Brothers, Amritsar, p62

[10] Professor Puran Singh, 1920, *The Book of The Ten Masters*, Singh Brothers, Amritsar, p52

[11] Kavī Chūrāmanī Bhāī Santokh Singh, 1843, *Srī Gur Pratap Sūraj Granth*, Steek 3, Rās 1, Adhiāi 10, Line 12, edited by Dr. Ajeet Singh Aulakh, 2014, 3rd Edition, p74,

[12] Kavī Chūrāmanī Bhāī Santokh Singh, 1843, *Srī Gur Pratap Sūraj Granth*, Steek 3, Rās 1, Adhiāi 10, Line 15, Edited by Dr. Ajeet Singh Aulakh, 2014, 3rd Edition, p75

[13] Kavī Chūrāmanī Bhāī Santokh Singh, 1843, *Srī Gur Nānak Prakāsh*, translated by Resham Singh & Jīvanpal Singh, 2019, Bhai Gurdas Educational Trust, page 126

[14] Bhāī Gurdās, *Vārān*, Vār 11, Paurī 14-15, translated by Shamsher Singh Puri, 2009, Singh Brothers, Amritsar, 1st Edition, p573-575

[15] Bhāī Gurdās, *Vārān*, Vār 11, Paurī 4, translated by Shamsher Singh Puri, 2009, Singh Brothers, Amritsar, 1st Edition, p553

[16] Bhāī Gurdās, *Vārān*, Vār 11, Paurī 1, translated by Shamsher Singh Puri, 2009, Singh Brothers, Amritsar, 1st Edition, p547

[17] Gurū Angad, Gurū Granth Sāhib, Raag Majh, Ang 145-146

[18] Gurū Angad Sāhib, Raag Malaar, Gurū Granth Sāhib, Ang 1288

[19] Gurū Nānak Sāhib, Raag Raamkalee, Gurū Granth Sāhib, Ang 902

[20] Bhatt Kalh, Svaiyay, Gurū Granth Sāhib, Ang 1390

[21] Kavī Chūrāmanī Bhāī Santokh Singh, 1843, *Srī Gur Pratap Sūraj Granth*, Steek 3, Rās 1, Adhiāi 10, Line 22, Edited by Dr. Ajeet Singh Aulakh, 2014, 3rd Edition, p76

[22] Gurū Nanaak Sāhib, Raag Soohee, Gurū Granth Sāhib, Ang 730

[23] Kavī Chūrāmanī Bhāī Santokh Singh, 1843, *Srī Gur Pratap Sūraj Granth*, Steek 3, Rās, Adhiāi 10, Line 51, Edited by Dr. Ajeet Singh Aulakh, 2014, 3rd Edition, p81

[24] Professor Puran Singh, 1920, *The Book of The Ten Masters*, Singh Brothers, Amritsar

ਪਾਤਿਸ਼ਾਹੀ ਮਹਿਮਾ – Revisiting Sikh Sovereignty

Srī Gurū Amar Dās Sāhib Jī Maharaj

ਜਹਾਂ ਰੌਸ਼ਨ ਅਜ਼ ਨੂਰਿ ਅਰਸ਼ਾਦਿ ਉ
ਜ਼ਮੀਨੋ ਜ਼ਮਾਂ ਗੁਲਸ਼ਨ ਅਜ਼ ਦਾਦਿ ਉ ॥੬੬॥

Through [Gurū Amar Dās'] expositions this world is radiating, and through [Gurū Amar Dās'] justice the Earth is a celestial garden. 66.[1]

As an active member of Gurū Angad Sāhib's Darbār in Khadūr Sāhib, Gurū Amar Dās Sāhib had contributed to all aspects of life there. From serving the Gurū to working in the Langar, Gurū Amar Dās was accustomed to the daily happenings in the Gurū's Darbār. In addition to writing a total of 869 Shabads in 17 Raags that are included in the Gurū Granth Sāhib[2], Gurū Sāhib also initiated the work of collecting not only the writings of the previous Gurū Sāhibān but also commenced the process of collecting the writings of other Bhagats. This demonstrated that the Gurū was preparing to collate and bundle the writings for future preservation to serve as the nucleus of the Panth, or as Professor Pashaura Singh has noted, this was a moment of "consolidation and crystallisation".[3]

Gurū's Darbar at Goindvāl Sāhib

Gurū Sāhib moved to Goindvāl Sāhib, which was situated on the highroad to Lahore, not far away from Khadūr Sāhib. Bhatt Nalh, whose compositions are preserved in Gurū Granth Sāhib, notes that Goindvāl Sāhib was built on the banks of the River Beas[4] and we learn from Kavi Santokh Singh that Goindvāl Sāhib was a sovereign Sikh space established following the request of Gurū Angad Sāhib.[5] This was a strategic move, to avoid confrontation with the sons of Gurū Angad Sāhib, who like the sons of Gurū Nānak Sahib, felt they had a claim to the throne. The decision was an indication of the Gurū's intent to remain autonomous and free from external influences.

Bhāī Gurdās jī too mentions that it was through the timeless blessings of Gurū Nānak Sāhib's Throne, that Gurū Amar Dās Sāhib came to raise the town of Goindvāl Sāhib, where the Gurū's actions were beyond comprehension.[6] The Gurū purposefully chose this location, as it was an ideal spot to build new houses and capture travelers heading to and from both Lahore and Delhi.[7] The Gurū did not just build the town but also helped populate it by encouraging folks from the Gurū's own village to relocate to Goindvāl Sāhib, including family members.[8]

We know from the writings of Bhāī Gurdās jī, the names of at least two individuals who were singers and scribes of Gurbānī within the Gurū's Darbār; Bhāī Pāndhā and Bullā.[9] In this particular Paurī, we learn about twenty-four other Sikhs of Gurū Amar Dās Sāhib, who were in close service to the Gurū. These Sikhs likely formed the Counsel or inner circle of confidants who pledged allegiance to the Gurū's Darbār. In fact, from Paurī 13 to 31 of Vār 11, Bhāī Gurdās jī mentions by name (alongside occupation, skills, or attributes), all the Sikhs considered to have formed the immediate circle of confidants of each of the first six Gurū Sāhibān.

Panth begins to assemble

It was during the reign of Gurū Amar Dās Sāhib that Sikhs first started to assemble during the month of Vaisakhi. At the suggestion of Bhāī Pārro, writes Kavī Santokh Singh, Gurū Sāhib issued Hukamnāme to Sikhs living close by and far away in foreign lands to join him in Goindvāl Sāhib during the month of Vaisakh.[10] There was great excitement amongst the Sikhs, many of whom had rejected the social order of Brahmanism and its discriminatory caste system that was allowed to prosper under the Mughal rule. They were excited at the prospect of joining the Gurū and meeting other Sikhs for the first time at one big gathering. Ordinarily, up until that point, they would have travelled to the Gurū's Darbār in small groups, at their own leisure and around their own lives, but now for the first time, there was a date in the calendar, following the Gurū's Hukam, for them to gather as a collective.

It was during this first gathering in Goindvāl Sāhib that Gurū Amar Dās Sāhib is said to have asked about Rām Dās, who had not yet come to meet the Gurū. Bhāī Bullā[11] is said to have informed Gurū Sāhib that Rām Dās was seeing to the Sangat, helping feed and accommodate their needs during the inaugural gathering. This pleased Gurū Amar Dās Sāhib, who is said to have sung Rām Dās' praises for serving the Sikh Sangat with such love and devotion.[12]

The Manjī System

Keeping to the tradition of Gurū's Darbār, Gurū Amar Dās Sāhib placed great emphasis on physical training to ensure the Sikhs were ever ready in service of the Panth and honoured the gift of life that had bestowed upon them. Historian Hari Ram Gupta writes,

> *"He declared that human beings were created in the image of God. The human body was the temple of God. It was the duty of his Sikhs to keep the body quite fit to the last. It was a valuable gift of God, and must not be spoilt by bad habits. He sanctified human life by condemning torturing the body by yogis and sadhus. He denounced the use of intoxicants."*[13]

In order to further the objective of creating a new Panth, as well as upholding the institutions of Sangat, Pangat, and Kīrtan that Gurū Nānak Sāhib had established from Kartārpur Sāhib, we know from the writings of Rattan Singh Bhangoo, that Gurū Amar Dās Sāhib established 22 Manjīs. The number is significant because it reflected the number of provinces under Mughal rule.

Srī Gurū Amar Dās Sāhib jī Mahārāj

ਅੰਗਦ ਤੇ ਗੁਰ ਭਯੋ ਅਮਰਦਾਸ ਕੀਯੋ ਪਾਤਸ਼ਾਹੀ ਦਾਵਾ ਜਾਸ।
ਬਾਈ ਸੂਬੇ ਜਿਨੈ ਨਿਵਾਏ। ਪਤਿਸ਼ਾਹੀ ਦਾਵੈ ਜਿਤਨ ਜਤਾਵੈ ॥੩॥

'Next to Angad, Amardas was the Guru who laid claim to a sovereign status. Organising twenty-two provinces the Gurū claimed kingship over them". [14]

The Manjīs were seats of delegated authority that worked to grow the Sikh movement. In so far as direction and guidance on Sikh affairs was concerned, the Manjhīs were held by nominated individuals authorised to act on behalf of the sovereignty of the Gurū's Darbār. In this way the Gurū was able to build upon the foundation laid by the previous Gurū Sāhibān and meet the demands of the exponential rise of Sikhī. Regular grassroots engagement had already become the norm, as the Gurū held discussions with the community on a whole host of social and spiritual topics. Shabad and Kirtan were central to this development, and the Gurū's decision to install both men and women within these districts empowered role models from both genders who taught the Sikhs about connecting with the Divine and imparting worldly knowledge.

Sikh historians do differ slightly on the locality of the Manjhīs. For example, when one compares the list of Manjhīs presented by Bhāī Kahn Singh Nabha with the list compiled in Mehmā Prakāsh, and the list at Gurdwara Haveli Sāhib, Goindvāl Sāhib, we find there to be thirteen commonalities; however, it appears more research is needed in this area to clarify why there appears to be a difference in the location of nine of the Manjhīs.

Nevertheless, the establishment of Manjīs signified a unique and revolutionary approach because we know during those days there was generally heavy gender bias against women, let alone women in positions of power. In addition to these 22 Manjhīs, the Gurū opened 52 sub-centres (Piris) [15], which mirrored the 52 bodyguards of the

ਪਾਤਿਸ਼ਾਹੀ ਮਹਿਮਾ – Revisiting Sikh Sovereignty

emperor. This was another way in which the Gurū laid down the gauntlet of rebellion. Gokul Chand Narang writes,

> "The Sikhs had now asserted their own individuality...some slight foundation of organization had been laid by the establishment of the twenty-two...and the public institutions founded by that Guru and his successor, together with the prestige derived from the friendship of the emperor, had considerably strengthened the foundation..."[16]

Gurū Amar Dās Sāhib had also completed the construction of Baolī Sāhib at Goindvāl, a project delegated to them by Gurū Angad Sāhib. This was an open well with steps leading down to the water, made accessible to all, regardless of caste, colour, or creed. Much like in his previous forms, the Gurū was breaking down the artificial barriers of sect and caste, so rife amongst the people. In this way, the Gurū was not only changing the psyche of the people; he was changing the geographical landscape of Panjāb. In addition to setting up independent Manjhīs from where he could grow the Panth, he was also responsible for abolishing Jazia, a tax levied upon non-Muslims by the emperor.

Gurū Sāhib summoned to Lahore

Sarūp Dās Bhalla, author of Mehmā Prakāsh (1776), offers a fascinating insight into the socio-political foresight of Gurū Amar Dās Sāhib. His portrayal of the first gathering in Goindvāl Sāhib came approximately seventy-five years before the portrayal we considered earlier by Kavī Santokh Singh. He narrates Gurū Sāhib held discussions with Bhāī Pārro Julka, who Sarūp Dās Bhalla states was a Manjīdār (who incidentally appears on all three lists mentioned above), on the necessity of introducing annual gatherings between the appointed Sikh leaders. Sarūp Dās Bhalla states how Gurū Amar Dās Sāhib instructed the Manjīdārs to assemble in Goindvāl Sāhib on the day of Vaisākhī. As mentioned, letters were sent to all Sikhs, and henceforth this became an annual event marking a key milestone in the evolution of the Sikh Panth.

The annual assembly provided an opportunity for the Manjhīdars and other Sikhs to discuss matters of utmost importance to the development of the Sikh Panth, whether that be parchār related or otherwise. The annual assembly promoted solidarity and a real sense of nationhood amongst the Sikh faithful.

This inaugural meeting in Goindvāl Sāhib alarmed both the Brahmins and the Khatri traders and merchants, who convened a meeting of their own and decided to petition the emperor.[17] They felt the propagation of Gurmat, and the positive manner in which the active mobilization of Pangat and Sangat had been greeted by the people, would lead to the demise of their own control and authority. The Gurū's Word was already alleviating people from mental and spiritual entanglement, and with the establishment of Gurū's Darbār at Goindvāl, they had a place to gather and attain physical liberation. The Brahmins and Khatrīs went to see Emperor Akbar and, according to Kavī Santokh Singh proclaimed:

ਤੁਮ ਮਿਰਜਾਦਾ ਰਾਖਨ ਹਾਰੇ। ਬਿਗਰਤਿ ਕੋ ਜਗ ਦੇਤਿ ਸੁਧਾਰੇ।
ਗੋਇੰਦਵਾਲ ਅਮਰ ਗੁਰੁ ਹੋਵਾ। ਭੇਦ ਬਰਨ ਚਾਰਹੁੰ ਕਾ ਖੋਵਾ ॥੩੫॥
ਰਾਮ ਗਾਇਤ੍ਰੀ ਮੰਤ੍ਰ ਨ ਜਪੈ ॥ ਵਾਹਿਗੁਰੂ ਕੀ ਥਾਪਨ ਥਪੈ।
ਜੁਗ ਚਾਰਹੁੰ ਮਹਿੰ ਕਹੀਂ ਨ ਹੋਈ। ਜਿਮਿ ਮਿਰਜਾਦ ਬਿਗਾਰੀ ਸੋਈ ॥੩੬॥
ਸ੍ਰੁਤਿ ਸਿੰਮ੍ਰਿਤਿ ਕੇ ਰਾਹੁ ਨ ਚਾਲੇ। ਮਨ ਕੋ ਮਤਿ ਕਰਿ ਭਏ ਨਿਰਾਲੇ।
ਹਮਰੀ ਕਰਹੁ ਅਦਾਲਤ ਏਹੀ। ਦ੍ਰਿੜ ਹੁਇ ਧਰਮ ਸੁ ਰਾਜੁ ਬ੍ਰਿਧੇਹੀ ॥੩੭॥
ਪਸਰ ਜਾਇ ਸਭਿ ਜਗਤ ਬਿਸਾਲਾ। ਪੁਨ ਮੁਸ਼ਕਲ ਇਹੁ ਟਲਹਿ ਨ ਟਾਲਾ।
ਸੁਨਿ ਅਕਬਰ ਨੇ ਦੀਨ ਦਿਲਾਸਾ। 'ਕਰਹੁੰ ਨਯਾਉਂ ਰਾਖਹੁ ਭਰਵਾਸਾ ॥੩੮॥ [18]

You preserve the social conventions, and resolve that which has been ruined. In Goindvāl resides Guru Amar Das, who has ended the order of the four castes. 35.

ਪਾਤਿਸ਼ਾਹੀ ਮਹਿਮਾ – Revisiting Sikh Sovereignty

> They do not recite the Ram mantra, they sing "Vaheguru".
> Throughout the four ages this has never occurred before; in the way in which he has changed the social conventions. 36.
> They do not walk on the path of the Simritees, they have become distinct by following their own ways. Please now deliver justice for us, strengthening our Dharam, your rule will prosper. 37.
> If their new social conventions spread into the whole world, it will be difficult to undo their backward ways. Listening to this Akbar reassured them, "have some faith, I will deliver you justice". 38.

The success and speed at which the Gurū was progressing had alarmed some individuals, namely those to whom the Gurū was a direct threat. Puran Singh states,

> *"A movement against him developed, and he was charged with wishing to make all castes one. By his teaching he had polluted, they said, the religion of his and their ancestors. Guru Amar Das was accordingly summoned to the Imperial Court to meet charges".* [19]

The emperor summoned the Gurū to his court in Lahore. Gurū Amar Dās Sāhib sent a trusted and able representative of the Gurū's Darbār in Rām Dās. This act alone shows the Gurū was not prepared to be summoned at the whim of an emperor of a temporal power structure. As Sache Pātshāh the Gurū did not submit to the writ of any worldly king but held the position with grace and respect. When Rām Dās arrived in Lahore, various Brahmins, Khatrīs, Pandits, Amīrs and Vazīrs were present, and after Akbar asked them to present their case, the Brahmins and Khatrīs argued the Sikhs had started their own Panth, rejected the Ved and Gīta and had begun reciting their own Banī.[20] Akbar then turned to Rām Dās and asked him to recite the Hindu scriptures since he had also been accused of not knowing what those scriptures said. Kavī Santokh Singh narrates Rām Dās not only recited but explained with great detail and then went on to explain 'Oankār'. There was no response from the

Brahmins and Khatrīs, who soon left the court in a state of utter embarrassment. Akbar is said to have recognised the Truth that came from Rām Dās, which marked the start of cordial relations between the Gurū's Darbār and the Mughal Court.

Emperor travelled to Goindvāl Sahib

The emperor was so impressed with the Gurū's emissary that he decided to pay homage to the Gurū himself. As such, the tradition of an emperor visiting the Gurū's Darbār continued with Gurū Amar Dās Sāhib. However, tradition holds that when the emperor travelled to the Gurū's Darbār the Gurū refused to meet him until he took part in Pangat. This signaled the Gurū's intent for all people, regardless of wealth and social status, to sit on a level platform and break bread with fellow humans. It also signified the importance of upholding the Gurū's authority and position as Sache Pātshāh of both worlds. The emperor obliged and after taking part in Pangat was allowed an audience with the Gurū. Interestingly, some of the Hill Rajas attended the Gurū's Darbār too, such as the Raja of Haripur Guler in Kangra. He irst took part in Pangat and then met the Gurū. Hari Ram Gupta also writes how he supplied timber for the Gurū's construction work at Goindvāl Sāhib.[21]

Standing for the people

Giānī Giān Singh narrates an episode in which Gurū Amar Dās, while travelling to Hardwār with a large contingent of Sikhs, was stopped and asked to pay a toll. The Gurū refused, and whilst the incident was reported to the authorities, no further charges were levied. Elsewhere we find an account of Emperor Akbar once stopping in Lahore and setting up an encampment with a large army for one year. This drove up trade prices, and the poor peasantry of Panjāb suffered greatly from the scarcity of grain. When Akbar was preparing to leave, the

ਪਾਤਿਸ਼ਾਹੀ ਮਹਿਮਾ – Revisiting Sikh Sovereignty

Gurū knew prices would suddenly fall, adversely affecting the peasantry since the year of scarcity had driven them into debt. The Gurū championed the people's voice by speaking directly with Akbar, who consented to lift land tax for a year. Gokul Chand Narang observes,

> "This timely intercession immensely increased the popularity of the Guru and made him an idol with the peasantry of Majha and Malwa, who in course of time provided almost all the fighting strength of [Guru] Govind [Singh]and ultimately transformed Sikhism into a military power."[22]

Not only did Gurū Amar Dās Sāhib stand in direct opposition to the regime in Delhi, but the Gurū also simultaneously challenged superstitious rituals such as Sati and Parda. Sati was the act performed by a widow that would self-immolate by throwing herself onto the funeral pyre of her deceased husband. This was commonplace amongst the people, but the Gurū disallowed the Sikhs from performing this ritual and stated,

> "Do not call them 'sati', who burns themselves along with their husbands' corpses. O Nanak, they alone are known as 'sati', who die from the shock of separation".[23]

In addition to condemning Sati, the Gurū also allowed remarriage, which offered a compassionate and practical solution to the problem that Sati had created. This demonstrates again how the Gurū was creating a new culture, a new way of existing that embodied the Divine attributes of the Creator and Creation.

Srī Gurū Amar Dās Sāhib jī Mahārāj

Passing of the Gurūship

Towards the latter years of Gurū Amar Dās Sāhib's reign, preparations were made to build a second town in which another centre of influence could be created. Despite all the sincere efforts to make Goindvāl Sāhib a major centre, some historians have noted how the physical locality of Goindvāl Sāhib had its limitations as it stood adjacent to the busy road later renamed the Grand Truck Road (GT Road), thus it was too close to the gaze of imperial officers. Rām Dās was commissioned to find a new site and thus began the search for a new location, which till this day is perhaps the most famous Sikh city in the world; Amritsar, which went on to become a sort of Sikh "capital".[24]

The decision to choose this area, again, demonstrates the socio-political foresight of the Gurū. It was neither too close nor too far from the hustle and bustle of the GT Road, and perhaps more importantly, it was situated on a cross-section between two commercial routes connecting Jalandhar with Eminabad, thus possessed the potential for rapid growth.

When the time came for Gurū Amar Dās Sāhib to leave this world, Rām Dās was appointed as the successor to Gurū Nānak Sāhib's Throne; having seen in Rām Dās what Gurū Angad Sāhib had seen in Gurū Amar Dās Sāhib. Rām Dās became Gurū Rām Dās Sāhib in the year 1574 and continued to build and evolve the Sikh movement.

NOTES

[1] Bhāī Nand Lal (1633-1713), *Ganjnama*, Kalaam-e-Goya, translated by Sardar Pritpal Singh Bindra, 2003, Institute of Sikh Studies, Chandigarh

[2] Dr Sarbjinder Singh, 2008, *Divine Revelation*, Sikh Foundation, Delhi, p28

[3] Pashaura Singh, 2000, *The Guru Granth Sahib*, Oxford University Press, p20

[4] Bhatt Nalh, Svaiyay Mehl 4, Gurū Granth Sāhib, Ang 1400

[5] Kavī Chūramanī Bhāī Santokh Singh, 1843, *Srī Gur Pratap Sūraj Granth*, Steek 3, Rās 1, Adhiāi 19, Line 28, Edited by Dr. Ajeet Singh Aulakh, 2014, 3rd Edition, p151

[6] Bhāī Gurdās, *Vārān*, Vār 1, Paurī 46, translated by Shamsher Singh Puri, 2009, Singh Brothers, Amritsar, 1st Edition, p157

[7] Kavī Chūramanī Bhāī Santokh Singh, 1843, *Srī Gur Pratap Sūraj Granth*, Steek 3, Rās 1, Adhiāi 19, Line 19, Edited by Dr. Ajeet Singh Aulakh, 2014, 3rd Edition, p150

[8] Kavī Chūramanī Bhāī Santokh Singh, 1843, *Srī Gur Pratap Sūraj Granth*, Steek 3, Rās 1, Adhiāi 19, Line 46, Edited by Dr. Ajeet Singh Aulakh, 2014, 3rd Edition, p153

[9] Bhāī Gurdās, *Vārān*, Vār 11, Paurī 16, translated by Shamsher Singh Puri, 2009, Singh Brothers, Amritsar, 1st Edition, p577

[10] Kavī Chūramanī Bhāī Santokh Singh, 1843, *Srī Gur Pratap Sūraj Granth*, Steek 3, Rās 1, Adhiāi 43, Line 1-43, Edited by Dr. Ajeet Singh Aulakh, 2014, 3rd Edition, p320-325,

[11] The author notes, it is likely this was the same Bhāī Būlla, the scribe, referred to by Bhāī Gurdās in Vār 11, Pauri 16

[12] Kavī Chūramanī Bhāī Santokh Singh, 1843, *Srī Gur Pratap Sūraj Granth*, Steek 3, Rās 1, Adhiāi 19, Line 20-25, Edited by Dr. Ajeet Singh Aulakh, 2014, 3rd Edition, p322-323

[13] Hari Ram Gupta, 1984, *History of the Sikhs, The Sikh Gurus 1469-1708,* Vol. 1, p.117

[14] ਰਤਨ ਸਿੰਘ ਭੰਗੂ, ਸ੍ਰੀ ਗੁਰ ਪੰਥ ਪ੍ਰਕਾਸ਼

Rattan Singh Bhangoo, 1841, *Sri Gur Panth Prakash*, (11:3) Translation by Gurtej Singh, 2015, Vol. 1, Singh Brothers, Amritsar, p49

[15] Giānī Giān Singh, 1878, *Sri Gur Panth Prakāsh*, edited Giānī Kirpāl Singh, p469; Giānī Kirpāl Singh provides 1878 as the date of publication for this granth.

[16] Sir Gokul Chand Narang, 1912, *Transformation of Sikhism*, Ripon Printing Press, Lahore, 3rd Edition, p65

[17] Kavī Chūrāmanī Bhāī Santokh Singh, 1843, *Srī Gur Pratap Sūraj Granth*, Steek 3, Rās 1, Adhiāi 43, Line 30, Edited by Dr. Ajeet Singh Aulakh, 2014, 3rd Edition, p324

[18] Kavī Chūrāmanī Bhāī Santokh Singh, 1843, *Srī Gur Pratap Sūraj Granth*, Steek 3, Rās 1, Adhiāi 43, Line 35-38, Edited by Dr. Ajeet Singh Aulakh, 2014, 3rd Edition, p324-325

[19] Professor Puran Singh, 1920, *The Book of The Ten Masters*, Singh Brothers, Amritsar, p61

Kavī Chūrāmanī Bhāī Santokh Singh, 1843, *Srī Gur Pratap Sūraj Granth*, Steek 3, Rās 1, Adhiāi 44, Line 16-19, Edited by Dr. Ajeet Singh Aulakh, 2014, 3rd Edition, p328

[21] Hari Ram Gupta, 1984, *History of the Sikhs, The Sikh Gurus 1469-1708*, Vol. 1, p.123

[22] Sir Gokul Chand Narang, 1912, *Transformation of Sikhism*, Ripon Printing Press, Lahore, 3rd Edition, p61

[23] *Gurū Amar Das*, Raag Soohee, Gurū Granth Sāhib, Ang 787

[24] Sir Gokul Chand Narang, 1912, *Transformation of Sikhism*, Ripon Printing Press, Lahore, 3rd Edition, p69-70

ਪਾਤਿਸ਼ਾਹੀ ਮਹਿਮਾ – Revisiting Sikh Sovereignty

Srī Gurū Rām Dās Sāhib Jī Maharaj

ਹਮ ਅਜ਼ ਸਲਤਨਤ ਹਮ ਜ਼ਿ ਫ਼ਰਕਸ ਨਿਸ਼ਾ
ਗਿਰਾਂਮਾਯਾ ਤਰ ਅਫ਼ਸਰਿ ਸਰਵਰਾਂ ॥ ੭੦ ॥

[Gurū Rām Dās] embraces both the temporal and celestial emblems, [Gurū Rām Dās] is the Emperor of emperors. 70.[1]

Gurū Rām Dās Sāhib wrote 638 Shabads that can be found in the Gurū Granth Sāhib[2] and started the system of preparing handwritten Gutkās. The Guru also formalised the Anand Karaj ceremony, which marks the union of two souls on Earth. Having been asked to establish a new town by Gurū Amar Dās Sāhib, Gurū Rām Dās Sāhib chose a new site surrounded by villages where the digging of a tank started in 1577.[3] This site eventually became known as Amritsar.

The Masand System

Building on Gurū Nānak Sāhib's Divinely inspired movement, Gurū Rām Dās Sāhib established the Masand system, which was essentially a network of individuals that acted as the Gurū's agents in administering various tasks on behalf of the Gurū. Thought to have come from the term *'masnad-i a-ala'* meaning 'His Excellency', a title often held by the Afghan nobles.[4] A part of the Masand's remit was to collect donations from the people that partially went towards the cost of excavating two reservoirs; one at Amritsar, then called Chak Gurū, Chak Rām Dās, or Rāmdāspur, and one at Santokhsar. Gurū Rām Dās invited individuals of 52 trades[5] to firstly take up their residence in Amritsar, and then to set up in Gurū ka Bazār, which generated a hub of trade activity. The Guru reinvested the revenue to expand the Sikh Panth. As well as collecting revenue on behalf of the Guru's Darbār, the Masands were also well-rehearsed in Gurmat and were thus responsible for disseminating Gurmat to the people.

The Bhatts

Historically originating from Rajasthan around the 9th century, the Bhatts attained the highest religious education available to the people of their time. When the glory of Gurū Nānak Sāhib reached the Bhatts, they immediately sang spontaneous praises of the Gurū Sāhibān; thus, their verses were included in the Gurū Granth Sāhib, a sign of the Gurū's sovereign authority and intent to reinvent religion and faith as it was then understood. There are writings of 15 different Bhatts included in the Gurū Granth Sāhib. Bhatt Nalh, who sang of the glory of Sikh sovereignty during the early years of the Gurū's Darbār has recorded the following Shabad in the Gurū Granth Sāhib,

ਰਾਜੁ ਜੋਗੁ ਤਖਤੁ ਦੀਅਨੁ ਗੁਰ ਰਾਮਦਾਸ ॥
ਪ੍ਰਥਮੇ ਨਾਨਕ ਚੰਦੁ ਜਗਤ ਭਯੋ ਆਨੰਦੁ ਤਾਰਿਨਿ ਮਨੁਖ੍ਯ ਜਨ ਕੀਅਉ ਪ੍ਰਗਾਸ ॥
ਗੁਰ ਅੰਗਦ ਦੀਅਉ ਨਿਧਾਨੁ ਅਕਥ ਕਥਾ ਗਿਆਨੁ ਪੰਚ ਭੂਤ ਬਸਿ ਕੀਨੇ ਜਮਤ ਨ ਤ੍ਰਾਸ ॥
ਗੁਰ ਅਮਰੁ ਗੁਰੂ ਸ੍ਰੀ ਸਤਿ ਕਲਿਜੁਗਿ ਰਾਖੀ ਪਤਿ ਅਘਨ ਦੇਖਤ ਗਤੁ ਚਰਨ ਕਵਲ ਜਾਸ ॥
ਸਭ ਬਿਧਿ ਮਾਨ੍ਯਿਉ ਮਨੁ ਤਬ ਹੀ ਭਯਉ ਪ੍ਰਸੰਨੁ ਰਾਜੁ ਜੋਗੁ ਤਖਤੁ ਦੀਅਨੁ ਗੁਰ ਰਾਮਦਾਸ ॥੪॥

> "Gurū Ram Das was blessed with the throne of worldly and spiritual rule. First came Guru Nanak who illuminated the world like the full moon and filled it with bliss. To carry humanity across Gurū bestowed their Radiance, and blessed Guru Angad with the treasure of spiritual wisdom, and the Unspoken Speech; They overcame the five demons [vices] and the fear of the Messenger of Death. The Great Guru, Guru Amar Das then preserved honour in the Dark Age of Kalijug. Seeing their lotus feet, sin and evil are destroyed. When

ਪਾਤਿਸ਼ਾਹੀ ਮਹਿਮਾ – Revisiting Sikh Sovereignty

Gurū was totally satisfied in every way, they bestowed upon Guru Ram Das the throne of political and spiritual sovereignty"[6]

Bhatt Nalh uses the term ਰਾਜੁ ਜੋਗੁ (Rāj Jog), which is appears frequently throughout the Gurū Granth Sāhib, used in particular by the Bhatts and Gurū Arjan Sāhib[7], as well as Bhāī Gurdās jī.[8] The phrase is a synonym for Mīrī-Pīrī and represents a state of union between both spiritual and worldly aspirations, one which the Gurū Sāhibān established. Bhāī Kahn Singh Nabha defines this phrase to describe a worldly ruler who has immersed themselves with Akāl,[9] which in many ways encapsulates the essence of sovereignty established by the Gurū Sāhibān. It is worth noting the choice of words Bhatt Nalh, and other contemporaries of the Gurū, such as Bhāī Gurdās jī[10], purposefully used to depict the customs of Gurū's Court.

Mahakavi Santokh Singh is another Sikh writer who describes the royal splendour of Gurū Ram Dās Sāhib's court, which is replete with symbols of sovereignty. He narrates;

ਦੋਹਰਾ - ਸਿੰਘਾਸਨ ਸੰਤੋਖ ਪਰ ਸੱਤਯ ਛਤਰ ਅਭਿਰਾਮੁ।
ਸੱਤਯਨਾਮ ਝੰਡਾ ਝੁਲਤਿ ਰਾਜਤਿ ਸਤਿਗੁਰੁ ਰਾਮ ॥੧॥

Gurū Ram Das is seated on the Throne of Compassion, under the beautiful Canopy of Truth. Here [at the Gurū's Darbār] is where the flags of the True Name fly.[11]

The Bhatts, Bhāī Gurdās jī, and later Bhāī Nand Lal jī, all of whom eulogise the Gurū's Court, all lived in Panjāb under the monarchical infrastructure referred to earlier. Yet they reject the authority of such worldly kings and accept only the Gurū Sāhibān as Sache Pātshah. Unlike the Mughal or Hindu kings, for the Sikhs, the Gurū Sāhibān were the true kings of both worlds. Gurū Nānak Sāhib's instruction that he alone sits on a throne who is worthy of the throne[12], and the reiteration of this by Gurū Amar Dās Sāhib[13], as well as Bhagat Kabir ji's earlier declaration that these worldly kings put on a false display and only last a few days, that there is no king equal to Vāhegurū[14], highlights the importance and centrality of the Gurū's Darbār within the Sikh world.

The Gurū Sāhibān were neither oppressive or greedy in the pursuit of worldly riches and power, nor were they renunciates like the *yogis* or *faqirs* like Sufi Muslims. They advocated and lived a householder's life but pioneered a new model of governance based on truth and compassion, which is what led Bhatts such as Kalh to write;

ਸਤਗੁਰ ਮਤਿ ਗੂੜ੍ਹ ਬਿਮਲ ਸਤਸੰਗਤਿ ਆਤਮੁ ਰੰਗਿ ਚਲੂਲੁ ਭਯਾ ॥
ਜਾਗ੍ਯਾ ਮਨੁ ਕਵਲੁ ਸਹਜਿ ਪਰਕਾਸ੍ਯਾ ਅਭੈ ਨਿਰੰਜਨੁ ਘਰਹਿ ਲਹਾ ॥
ਸਤਗੁਰਿ ਦਯਾਲਿ ਹਰਿ ਨਾਮੁ ਦ੍ਰਿੜ੍ਹਾਯਾ ਤਿਸੁ ਪ੍ਰਸਾਦਿ ਵਸਿ ਪੰਚ ਕਰੇ ॥
ਕਵਿ ਕਲੵ ਠਕੁਰ ਹਰਦਾਸ ਤਨੇ ਗੁਰ ਰਾਮਦਾਸ ਸਰ ਅਭਰ ਭਰੇ ॥੩॥

The true Gurū's understanding is deep and profound. The Sat Sangat is their pure congregation. They are drenched in the deep crimson colour of the *Akāl*. The Lotus of their mind remains awake and aware, illuminated with intuitive wisdom. In their own home, they have obtained the *Niranjan*. The Merciful True Gurū has implanted the Nām within me, and by their grace, I have overpowered the five thieves. So, speaks Kalh the poet: Guru Ram Das, the son of Har Das, fills the empty pools to overflowing.[15]

A new social order

Therein lies the importance of the Bhatts writings in Gurū Granth Sāhib. They showcase how the Gurū Sāhibān were fearless and completely different in stature, approach, and governance to the mundane kings who were susceptible to the five vices. Through the institute of Sangat, they galvanised the spirit of the people, uplifting them to create a better society for all. A new social order was created with the establishment of towns, as referred to in Gurū Granth Sāhib.

Gurū Ram Dās Sāhib has composed a Shabad in which they praise the founding of towns by the early Gurū Sāhibān:

ਪਉੜੀ ॥
ਗੁਰਿ ਸਚੈ ਬਧਾ ਥੇਹੁ ਰਖਵਾਲੇ ਗੁਰਿ ਦਿਤੇ ॥ ਪੂਰਨ ਹੋਈ ਆਸ ਗੁਰ ਰਚਨੀ ਮਨ ਰਤੇ ॥ ਗੁਰਿ ਕ੍ਰਿਪਾਲਿ ਬੇਅੰਤਿ ਅਵਗੁਣ ਸਭਿ ਹਤੇ ॥ ਗੁਰਿ ਅਪਣੀ ਕਿਰਪਾ ਧਾਰਿ ਅਪਣੇ ਕਰਿ ਲਿਤੇ ॥ ਨਾਨਕ ਸਦ ਬਲਿਹਾਰ ਜਿਸੁ ਗੁਰ ਕੇ ਗੁਣ ਇਤੇ ॥ ੨੨ ॥

"The True Gurū has established the town; the Gurū has appointed its guard and protectors. My hopes are fulfilled, and my mind is imbued with the love of the Gurū's feet. The Gurū is infinitely merciful; the Gurū has erased all my sins. The Gurū has showered me with Kirpā, and has made me their own. Nānak is forever a sacrifice to the Gurū, who has countless Virtues."[16]

According to the *Faridkot Teeka*, this is a reference to the founding of a town, established following orders from Gurū Angad Sāhib to Gurū Amar Dās Sāhib. The Shabad states how the Gurū sent protectors, and their hopes were realised. According to the Sampardai tradition, the context behind this Shabad is said to derive from Gurū Angad Sāhib's establishment of Goindvāl Sāhib and the order to send Gurū Amar Dās Sāhib as its protector, just like Gurū Nānak Sāhib established Khadūr Sāhib and sent Gurū Angad Sāhib as its protector.[17]

> *"In the search after purely religious matters, we often forget how much the Panjab owes to the Sikh Gurus for advancing trade and manufacture of the country. If the Mughal emperors were great builders, the Sikh Gurus were no less."*[18]

Within 100 years, empowered with the Pātshāhī of Gurū Nānak Sāhib, the Gurū's Darbār had founded new towns, established a new script, and challenged both the ruling elite and the religious leaders on social and political issues. When the time arose, Gurū Ram Dās Sāhib appointed Arjan Mal as the successor to the Gurū's Throne in 1581.

The Gurūs Darbār and Halemī Rāj

Before concluding this section, I would like to address some points made by Professor Louis Fenech in his book, *The Darbar of the Sikh Gurus*, first published in 2008. Professor Fenech's work mainly focuses on the court of Gurū Gobind Singh Sāhib and the life of Bhāī Nand Lal jī. However, he dedicates three chapters of his book to the earlier Gurū Sāhibān. In the first chapter Professor Fenech surmises that despite contemporary condemnation of the literature of Islamicate courts and eighteenth-century Sikh tradition's vehemence towards certain members of the court (for example, Aurangzeb), eighteenth-century Sikh writers in many ways appropriated and imposed the language and symbols of those courts when they describe the Darbārs of the Sikh Gurū Sāhibān. The absence of a comprehensive contemporary account of the early Gurūs, such as the ones that exist for Aurangzeb (Tarikh-I Dil-kusha), notes Professor Fenech, makes it difficult to be sure whether the Gurū Sāhibān possessed "a formal court with designated attendants, advisors, newswriters, agents, canopy-bearers, and so on, who were regularly in attendance and formed a hierarchy bound together by precise etiquette".[19]

Whilst Professor Fenech illustrates the lack of contemporary accounts that depict the courts of the early Gurū Sāhibān, he does refer to various contributions from Bhāī Gurdās jī and the Bhatts, whose writings are contained within the Gurū Granth Sāhib, which offer an unambiguous portrayal of the regal elements of the Darbār of the Gurū Sāhibān.

ਪਾਤਿਸ਼ਾਹੀ ਮਹਿਮਾ – Revisiting Sikh Sovereignty

On the one hand, he concludes, based on his reading of Bhāī Gurdās jī's Vaaran[20] and Gurū Nānak Sāhib's own writings[21], that the Sikh Darbār,

> *"was a more open, fluid court in the sense that Sikh values and standards of refinement, love, loyalty, beauty, service, etc. idealized by courtiers inhabiting other courts were to be cultivated by all Sikhs and potential gurmukhs alike in their self-fashioning and were not simply the prerogative of a restricted talented, well-born few who ultimately formed a powerful and prestigious elite."*[22]

However, he also goes on to state that these "circumstantial references to a Sikh court" were transformed into genuine ones by eighteenth-century Sikh writers whose texts were,

> *"...apocryphal attempts to demonstrate both the symbolic legitimacy of the sovereignty of the Sikhs under Bandā, the later Sikhs Misls, and, under Ranjīt Singh too".*[23]

He states writers such as Chibbar were the first to depict the earlier courts of the Gurū Sāhibān as,

> *"...grand and influential centres of largesse whose nobles were selfless Sikh warriors/servants fighting on behalf of their Guru and Master, and all of those threatened by oppression on the one hand, and pious and devoted Sikhs writing and reciting poetry, and singing shabads on the other, all of whom provided examples of the ideal Khalsa Sikh".*[24]

This type of conjecture is extended to contemporaries of the Gurū such as Bhāī Gurdās jī, and the Bhatts. In the second chapter, Professor Fenech writes,

Srī Gurū Rām Dās Sāhib jī Māhārāj

> *"There seems little doubt that both Bhai Gurdas and the bhatts did understand and help perpetuate an image of the early Gurus and their disciples as kings surrounded in their courts by poets and courtiers, but whether these hymns are descriptive or idealistic (at least in terms of outward appearance) remains unknown. So also unknown is whether the early Gurus understood themselves in the royal manner that the Bhatts describe".*[25]

 Notwithstanding the reference I have made to the Gurū's own Shabads, in which they praise the actions of earlier Gurū Sāhibān, the Bhatts writings consolidate the fact that the Gurū Sāhibān were of one single Light or one singular focus. Whilst they had different physical attributes and personalities, and perhaps even different physical manifestations of their Darbār, they were all working under the sovereign agency initiated by Gurū Nānak Sāhib, following the directive received from Akāl Purakh.

 Bhatt Kalh in particular sings of Gurū Nānak Sāhib's glory, proclaiming Gurū Nānak Sāhib had established both spiritual and worldly rule.[26] Notwithstanding Professor Fenech's claims that he was not a contemporary of the Gurū, we cannot overlook the fact that he would've met and conversed with significant personalities such as Bhāī Gurdās jī, Baba Buddhā jī, other Bhatts and of course Gurū Arjan Sāhib, who clearly attributed such statements to be the truth, in the act of firstly including them in Gurbānī and secondly, with the endorsement of Bhāi Gurdās jī' works. As Professor Pashaura Singh has said elsewhere, this single fact alone nullifies the argument of a lack of contemporaneous written accounts.

 Whilst Professor Fenech does go on to acknowledge that Gurū Arjan Sāhib was the ultimate authority, and saw "nothing untoward with such kingly associations", when the Gurū included the Bhatts writings in Gurū Granth Sāhib, he concludes the Bhatts writings were unlikely to be descriptive because,

ਪਾਤਿਸ਼ਾਹੀ ਮਹਿਮਾ – Revisiting Sikh Sovereignty

"...such an understanding would run counter to the overwhelming message of humility one regularly encounters within the entire Sikh canon".[27]

In essence, Professor Fenech surmises that how Bhāī Gurdās jī and the Bhatts depict the early Gurū Sāhibān, (presumably Gurū Nānak Sāhib, Gurū Angad Sāhib, and Gurū Amar Dās Sāhib), as worldly kings, goes against the notion of humility espoused in the Gurū Granth Sāhib. However, I would suggest the significance of their portrayal lies not in the literal depiction; rather, it lies in the fact that they're eulogizing Gurū Nānak Sāhib as having established both spiritual and political power. Whilst Gurū Nānak Sāhib does warn of the pitfalls of lavish and grand royal courts and the overindulgence of great armies, the Guru does not shun or disapprove of the necessity to maintain political power. Gurū Nānak Sāhib writes only those worthy of sitting on thrones are eligible to do so, and the criteria for that eligibility is Gurmat; those who have subdued the five vices.[28]

Gurū Amar Dās Sāhib reinforces this understanding in their Bānī going on to explain how mere worldly rulers suffer in the love of duality,[29] and Gurū Arjan Sāhib proclaims that the Sikh movement was built on the notion of Halemī Rāj, the rule of the meek/humble, a point that Professor Fenech too later acknowledges.

Furthermore, the decision taken by the Gurū Sāhibān to firstly adopt regal attire and hold court, then to approve the depiction of the Bhatts, Bhāī Gurdās, and Bhāī Nand Lāl in which they're shown to manifest emblems of sovereignty associated with Persian Islamicate traditions, demonstrates the overriding commitment to the establishment of Sikh sovereignty. Whilst Gurū Nānak Sāhib forewarned against the over-indulgence and egocentric nature of worldly kings, they initiated a new movement in Kartārpur Sāhib and paved the way for subsequent Gurū Sāhibān to build on the institute of Sangat, Pangat, and Gurū's Darbār.

Srī Gurū Rām Dās Sāhib jī Mahārāj

NOTES

[1] Bhāī Nand Lal (1633-1713), *Ganjnama, Kalaam-e-Goya*, translated by Sardar Pritpal Singh Bindra, 2003, Institute of Sikh Studies, Chandigarh

[2] Dr Sarbjinder Singh, 2008, *Divine Revelation*, Sikh Foundation, Delhi, p30

[3] Hari Ram Gupta, 1984, *History of the Sikhs, The Sikh Gurus 1469-1708*, Vol. 1, p.126

[4] J. S. Grewal & Irfan Habib, 2001, *Sikh History from Persian Sources*, Tulika Books, Delhi, p8

[5] Teja Singh and Ganda Singh, 1950, *A Short History of the Sikhs (1469-1765)*, Volume One, Sixth Edition, Publication Bureau, Punjabi University, Patiala, p25

[6] Bhatt Nalh, Gurū Granth Sāhib, Svaiyay Mehl 4, Ang 1399

[7] Gurū Arjan, Raag Gaurī, Gurū Granth Sāhib, Ang 188; and Ang 239

[8] See Bhāī Gurdās, *Vāran*, Vār 24, Paurī 14; Vār 25, Paurī 11; Vār 27, Paurī 8; Vār 29, Paurī 10 and 11, translated by Shamsher Singh Puri, 2009, Singh Brothers, Amritsar, 1st Edition, p1145, p1189, p1293, p1387-1389

[9] Bhāī Kahn Singh Nabha, 1930, *Gurshabad Ratankar Mahan Kosh*, Publication Bureau, Punjabi University, Patiala, Vol. 4, p2304

[10] Bhāī Gurdās, *Vāran*, Vār 1, Paurī 47, translated by Shamsher Singh Puri, 2009, Singh Brothers, Amritsar, 1st Edition, p159 - "ਬੈਠਾ ਸੋਢੀ ਪਾਤਿਸਾਹੁ ਰਾਮਦਾਸ ਸਤਿਗੁਰੂ ਕਹਾਵੈ"

[11] Kavī Chūrāmanī Bhāī Santokh Singh, 1843, *Srī Gur Pratap Sūraj Granth*, Steek 3, Rās 2, Adhiāi 2, Line 1, Edited by Dr. Ajeet Singh Aulakh, 2014, 3rd Edition, p536

[12] Gurū Nānak Sāhib, Raag Maroo, Gurū Granth Sāhib, Ang 1038

[13] Gurū Amar Dās Sāhib, Raag Maroo, Gurū Granth Sāhib, Ang 1088

[14] Bhagat Kabir ji, Raag Bilaaval, Gurū Granth Sāhib, Ang 856

[15] Bhatt Kalh, Swaiyay Mehl 4, Gurū Granth Sāhib, Ang 1396

[16] Gurū Rām Dās *Sāhib*, Raag Sorath, *Gurū Granth Sāhib*, Ang 653

[17] Sant Hari Singh Randhawa, Aad Srī Gurū Granth Sāhib ji da Sampardai Steek, Gurbānī Arth Bhandar, Pothi 6, Damdami Taksal, p452

[18] Teja Singh and Ganda Singh, 1950, *A Short History of the Sikhs (1469-1765)*, Volume One, Sixth Edition, Publication Bureau, Punjabi University, Patiala, p25

[19] Louis E Fenech, 2008, *The Darbar of the Sikh Gurus,* Oxford University Press, Delhi, p12

[20] Bhāī Gurdās, *Vārān*, Vār 6, Paurī 12, translated by Shamsher Singh Puri, 2009, Singh Brothers, Amritsar, 1st Edition, p351

[21] Gurū Nānak, Siree Raag, Gurū Granth Sāhib, Ang 21

[22] Louis E Fenech, 2008, *The Darbar of the Sikh Gurus,* Oxford University Press, Delhi, p13

[23] Louis E Fenech, 2008, *The Darbar of the Sikh Gurus,* Oxford University Press, Delhi, p16

[24] Louis E Fenech, 2008, *The Darbar of the Sikh Gurus,* Oxford University Press, Delhi, p18

[25] Louis E Fenech, 2008, *The Darbar of the Sikh Gurus,* Oxford University Press, Delhi, p59

[26] Bhatt Kalh, Svaiyay Mehl 1, Gurū Granth Sāhib, Ang 1389

[27] Louis E Fenech, 2008, *The Darbar of the Sikh Gurus,* Oxford University Press, Delhi, p59

[28] Gurū Nānak Sāhib, Raag Maroo, Gurū Granth Sāhib, Ang 1038

[29] Gurū Amar Dās Sāhib, Raag Maroo, Gurū Granth Sāhib, Ang 1088

ਪਾਤਿਸ਼ਾਹੀ ਮਹਿਮਾ – Revisiting Sikh Sovereignty

Srī Gurū Arjan Dev Sāhib Jī Maharaj

ਅਜ਼ੋ ਨਜ਼ਮ ਕਾਲਿ ਹੱਕ ਅਮਦੇਸ਼ਾ ਰਾ
ਬਦੋ ਨਸਕ ਇਲਮਿ ਯਕੀਂ-ਪੇਸ਼ਾ ਰਾ ॥ ੭੮ ॥

Celestial verses radiate through [Gurū Arjan Sāhib], all the enlightening discourses as well pertain to [Gurū Arjan Sāhib]. (78)[1]

The reign of Gurū Arjan Sāhib (1581-1606) was perhaps one of the most crucial periods of Sikh history. Gurū Arjan Sāhib completed the construction of Srī Harmandir Sāhib in Amritsar, which Gurū Rām Dās had started. Srī Harmandir Sāhib is completely unique in both layout and architecture. It was built with four openings, one on each side, to represent the notion that anyone was welcome in the Gurū's Darbār, to take part in Sangat, no matter their caste, colour, or creed. Unlike conventional centres of congregation, the steps leading to Srī Harmandir Sāhib were built down and not up. This was purposely built to signal that one must lower their ego and acquire an abundance of humility if one wishes to meet the Almighty. In contrast to the Hindu temples of the time, there were no stone images or idols placed inside Srī Harimandir Sāhib, a reflection of Gurmat, which condemned idol worship.

> *"Not only was the importance of the new town increased by [Guru] Arjun as the chief place of Sikh pilgrimage, but by transforming his headquarters to the place, he made it the centre of Sikh activity. It became, in fact, the capital and metropolis of the*

ਪਾਤਿਸ਼ਾਹੀ ਮਹਿਮਾ – Revisiting Sikh Sovereignty

infant commonwealth that the genius of [Guru] Arjun was gradually and peacefully building up."[2]

A "state within a state"

Gurū Arjan Sāhib continued the tradition of opposing the false religious doctrines of other traditions in his writings, and also set about changing the conventional design of places of worship. By this stage, Sikhī had broken people free from the yoke of the Brahmanical structures. Amritsar became a critical city for the Sikhs, cementing their position as sovereigns of the Gurū, as they became accustomed to a regular government, which Cunningham described as a "state within a state".[3]

While it ought to be evident to the reader by now that the Sikh Panth was more than what Cunningham implies, especially in relation to the term "state", his observation is none the less an important one. It demonstrates a degree of acknowledging the independence of the Gurū's Darbār, pointing towards the sovereignty that I maintain was an integral part of the Sikh movement.

In addition to completing the construction of Srī Harmandir Sāhib, Gurū Arjan Sāhib also renamed the town of Rāmdāspur to Amritsar and oversaw the establishment of Tarn Taran Sāhib, which is similar in design to Harmandir Sāhib; where a reservoir of water was built in the middle of the compound. Here the Gurū opened a centre to house and serve those who suffered from medical ailments such as leprosy.

The Gurū wrote 2312 Shabads that can today be found in the Gurū Granth Sāhib. Within the first century, having already announced its distinct worldview as espoused, by Gurū Nānak Sāhib and the following 3 Mahals, the Sikh movement under Gurū Arjan Sāhib was further refined as a movement independent of Brahmanical and Abrahamic influence.

Srī Gurū Arjan Dev Sāhib jī Mahārāj
Adi Granth Sāhib

Having built the towns and centres of Sikh significance in a distinct Sikh style, Gurū Arjan Sāhib next oversaw the collation of the writings of the previous Gurū Sāhibān and various others such as Bhagat Kabīr jī and Baba Farīd jī.

Sarūp Das Bhalla writes:

ਏਕ ਦਿਵਸ ਪ੍ਰਭ ਪ੍ਰਾਤਹਕਾਲ। ਦਾਇਆ ਭਰੇ ਪ੍ਰਭ ਦੀਨ ਦਇਆਲ।
ਜਹ ਮਨ ਉਪਜੀ ਪ੍ਰਗਟਿਓ ਜਗ ਪੰਥ। ਤਿਹ ਕਾਰਨ ਕੀਜੇ ਅਬ ਗ੍ਰੰਥ।੨।
ਭਾਈ ਗੁਰਦਾਸ ਕੋ ਆਗਿਆ ਕਰੀ। ਸਭ ਕਰੋ ਇਕਤ ਬਾਨੀ ਇਹ ਘਰੀ।
ਅਰੁ ਬਾਨੀ ਭਗਤਨ ਕੀ ਸਭ ਮੇਲੋ। ਸਾਚੀ ਰਾਖੋ ਝੂਠੀ ਪੇਲੋ।੩।
ਤਬ ਗੁਰਦਾਸ ਕਰੀ ਅਰਦਾਸ। ਸਭ ਪੋਥੀ ਸੰਸਰਾਮ ਕੇ ਪਾਸ।
ਮੋਹਨ ਮਸਤਾਨ ਸਾਹਿਬ ਕ ਪੂਤ। ਵੇ ਤਪ ਭਗਤ ਜੋਗ ਕਾ ਸੂਤ੍ਰ।੪।[4]

Early one morning, Gurū Sāhib, the compassionate and merciful declared, "As the Panth has been revealed to the world, so there must be the Granth too". (2)
Bhāī Gurdās jī was tasked with the duty of collating and preparing an authentic copy of the writings, including that of the Bhagats'. (3)
Bhāī Gurdās then initiates an Ardas and tells how all the Pothis are with Sahns Ram, son of Mohan Das (thus grandson of Gurū Amar Das). (4)

Sarūp Das Bhalla goes on to narrate how Sahns Ram had collated the writings during the time of Gurū Amar Dās Sāhib. His father, Mohan Dās, is also said to have had some Pothīs too. Gurū Arjan Sāhib travelled to Goindvāl Sāhib and met Mohan Dās themselves, and a Shabad was recited, which is contained within Gurū Granth Sāhib.[5] It is recorded that both Bhāī Gurdās jī and Baba Buddhā jī had made attempts to retrieve the Pothīs, but Mohan Dās was in deep meditation and had not complied. Gurū Arjan Sāhib themselves travelled to Goindvāl Sāhib and retrieved the Pothis. The context behind this Shabad is explained by Mahakavi Santokh Singh in Gurpartap Sūraj Granth[6], Sarūp Das Bhalla's Mehmā Prakāsh and by Bhagat Singh in Gurbilās Pātshahi 6.[7]

Whilst it was Gurū Arjan Sāhib who compiled the Adi Granth, the act of gathering the Divine compositions started with Gurū Nānak Sāhib.[8] We know that Gurū Nānak Sāhib had begun the preservation of their own writings, because Bhāī Gurdās jī narrates that Gurū Nānak Sāhib carried a Pothī, along with a water pot and prayer carpet, upon their visit to Mecca.[9] The Purātan Janamsākhī also narrates that it was during Gurū Nānak Sāhib's second journey towards the modern-day region of Srī Lanka, where companions Saido and Gheho recorded the Gurū's utterance of Maajh Di Vaar.[10] Throughout Gurū Sāhib's travels, he also collected the writings of other Bhagats and Saints, most notably Bhagat Kabīr jī and Bhagat Farīd jī. Their writings were included in the Adi Granth by Gurū Arjan Sāhib.

To assist in the task of compiling the Adi Granth, it is almost certain, as Professor Fenech too describes, Gurū Sāhib would have employed a team of skilled craftsmen including, but not limited to, papermakers, calligraphers, illuminators, gilders, ink mixers, and scribes.[11] It is likely Gurū Sāhib opened and ran workshops where the writing, editing, binding, and publishing of works took place. This would have been a close-knit operation since we know many adversaries tried to claim legitimacy as the rightful heirs of Gurū Nānak Sāhib's throne.

Kesar Singh Chibbar (1769) narrates that Prithi Chand, who was the Gurū's brother, along with his son Meharvan had compiled a granth of their own for the Minas, in which they had included compositions from the first four Gurū Sāhibān.[12] We'll come onto the Minas in a moment, but Meharvan was said to have been versed in Persian, Hindi, Sanskrit, and Gurmukhi, which gave him the tools to be able to compose poetry under the authorship of Gurū Nānak Sāhib. When news of this reached Gurū Arjan Sāhib, Chibbar writes that the Guru made an announcement to address the problem caused by their actions.

ਭਾਈ ਗੁਰਦਾਸ! ਗੁਰੂ ਦੀ ਬਾਣੀ ਜੁਦਾ ਕਰੀਏ ॥
ਮੀਨੇ ਪਾਂਦੇ ਨੇ ਰਲਾ, ਸੋ ਵਿਚ ਰਲਾ ਨ ਧਰੀਏ ॥ ੧੩

> Bhāī Gurdās! [Lets] separate the Gurū's compositions.
> The minas are mixing the compositions which should be set in order.

In fact, groups had begun to assemble false collections of Shabads attributed to Gurū Nānak Sāhib, "either for the purpose of promoting their own claims to be the true Sikhs or to bring the Gurū into disrepute",[14] during the Guruship of Gurū Amar Dās Sāhib. Perhaps this is why Gurū Amar Dās Sāhib asks the beloved Sikhs of Satgurū to sing the true Bani, as recorded in Anand Sahib.[15]

In the next *paurī*, Gurū Amar Dās Sāhib reiterates that without Satgurū, all other Bani is false. The instruction to the Sikhs was to become conscious of those imposters who utter false Bani, in a meaningless way; a direct challenge to individuals who were seeking to assert their influence and control of the Gurū's Darbār

Gurū Arjan Sāhib held counsel with Gursikhs such as Baba Buddhā jī and Bhāī Gurdās jī and discussed various matters such as where the Adi Granth should be enthroned and who should become the first custodian. Bhagat Singh narrates they chose Harmandir Sāhib, and Gurū Arjan Sāhib instructed the Sikhs to place Adi Granth on a raised throne, as they all slept on the floor.[16]

The next morning, they arose early, and Gurū Arjan Sāhib advised Baba Buddhā jī to place Adi Granth on his head as they walked towards Harmandir Sāhib, Gurū Arjan Sāhib waved the *Chaur Sāhib* during the first installment. After the first installment, Gurū Arjan Sāhib took a seat outside Harmandir Sāhib out of respect and to impart such knowledge amongst the Sikhs that they bow to Adi Granth.

The establishment of Sri Harmandir Sāhib and then the instruction to revere Adi Granth Sāhib with the utmost respect were two defining moments in the evolution of the Sikh movement. Harbans Singh notes,

> "both provided to be of great significance in moulding Sikh self-consciousness and in the reification of Sikh life and society. The Granth Sāhib was the permanent repository of the Gurus' message – the revealer of Divine truth, and was meant to be the spiritual and religious guide of Sikhs for all time to come. It was the source of their verbal tradition and it shaped their intellectual and cultural environment".[17]

The Adi-Granth was enthroned at Srī Harmandir Sāhib on 16th August 1604.[18] The Granth has served as the guiding light to Sikhs for centuries, as Sikhs became accustomed to bowing to the Granth from this point onwards, a tradition commonly associated with the events of 1708. Building on Harbans Singh's point above, Pashaura Singh writes,

> "The compilation of the Adi Granth was intimately linked with the process of Sikh self-definition. The Sikh Panth had indeed developed a strong sense of independent identity by the end of the sixteenth century."[19]

Distinct and independent

This move towards a distinct and stand-alone identity is evident in the Gurū's continued rejection of the pathways of Islam and Hinduism. Gurū Arjan Sāhib, for example, makes a direct assertion that defines Sikhs as separate from Hindus and Muslims, and indeed other structures.[20] Thus the idea of a separate Sikh identity was promoted by the Gurūs and is evident in Gurū Granth Sāhib today.

In Persian, the term 'Mahal' means 'castle', 'ward of the city' or 'palace', therefore the use of the word 'Mahal', or 'Mahala', by Gurū Arjan Sāhib to denote which of the Guru Sāhibān wrote a particular Shabad, carries a political connotation too. This provides great insight into Gurū Arjan Sāhib's vision and aspirations for the Sikh movement. The Gurū Sāhibān were one and the same in spirit, evident in the way in which each of the Gurūs referred to themselves in their writings as Nānak, and also how their actions complemented each other. Contrary to what writers, such as Ernest Trumpp and Hew McLeod have tried to propagate, there was no diversion in "ideology", from Gurū Nānak Sāhib to Gurū Gobind Singh Sāhib. Rather there was a natural flow of evolution from one Mahal to the next. Dr Trilochan Singh[21], in particular, has done a tremendous job in exposing the misconception of their claims, as has Professor Pashaura Singh, and Balbinder Singh Bhogal. The latter in particular writes,

> *"This assumption of a break in Sikh tradition operates on a simplistic and modern dichotomy that ignores the constant innovation of the Sikh tradition..."*[22]

Collection of *dasvandh* and founding of further towns

In addition to building institutions and increasing the number of Sikhs, the Gurū also started to collect *dasvandh* or *bhetā*, which many non-Sikh writers have referred to as a tax,

> *"In his reign, Arjan Mal appointed a person over the Sikhs of every city so that he might collect tax and tribute from them."*[23]

Cunningham too comments that once Gurū Arjan Sāhib had built Srī Harmandir Sāhib and installed the Adi Granth,

ਪਾਤਿਸ਼ਾਹੀ ਮਹਿਮਾ – Revisiting Sikh Sovereignty

> *"the Gooroo next reduced to a systematic tax the customary offerings of his converts or adherents, who, under his ascendency, were to be found in every city and province…the agents of Arjoon were spread over the country to demand and receive the contributions of the faithful, which they proceeded to deliver to the Gooroo in person at an annual assembly."*[24]

During the extensive travels to the Doaba and Majha regions, Gurū Arjan Sāhib also founded the towns of Kartārpur Sāhib (Jalandhar) and Srī Gobindpur Sāhib along the River Beas. Dr. Sangat Singh notes how the Lt Governor of Jalandhar Doab, Syed Azim Khan, incidentally a supporter of the Guru, played a pivotal role in establishing Sikh influence in Kartārpur Sāhib.[25] In this way, the Sikhs became accustomed to regular self-government. In addition to collecting *dasvandh*, Gurū Arjan Sāhib also adopted other means of acquiring resources and influence. Cunningham writes,

> *"…he dispatched his followers into foreign countries to be as keen in traffic as they were zealous in belief, and it is probable that his transactions as a merchant were extensive, although confined to the purchase of horses in Toorkistan."*[26]

Another writer, Sir Jadunath Sarkar also notes how,

> *"The number of Sikh converts greatly increased, and with them the Gurū's wealth. He organised a permanent source of income. A band of agents were stationed in every city from Kabul to Dacca where there was a Sikh, to collect the tithes and offerings of the faithful; and this spiritual tribute, so far as it escaped peculation by the agents, reached the central treasury at Amritsar".*[27]

He speaks about the Gurū's status as a king surrounded by a body of courtiers and ministers. The sheer extent of land on which the Gurū's emissaries were stationed, covering a distance of over 2000 miles from modern-day Afghanistan to Bangladesh, is quite remarkable. It is remarkable because one of the oldest and longest major roads, today known as the Grand Trunk Road, formerly Uttarapath, Sarak-e-Azam, Badshahi Sarak, and Sarak-e-Sher Shah, connected Kabul to Dacca. The Gurūs emissaries would therefore have made their way through major cities such as Peshawar, Rawalpindi, Gujranwala, Lahore, Amritsar, Panipat, Delhi, Benares, Patna, Kolkata, and of course Dhaka to collect *dasvandh*, which were brought back to Amritsar. The sole purpose of establishing this network of emissaries, which evolved from the Manjī system under Gurū Amar Dās Sāhib, was to build the reach of the Gurū's sovereignty and grow the Sikh Panth. In the Dabistan (1645), the author comments,

> *"In short, every mahal [each Gurū's reign], the Sikhs increased in numbers, till the reign of Arjan Mal, they became very numerous. Not many cities remained in the inhabited region, where the Sikhs had not settled in some number."* [28]

Military training and development

Gurū Arjan Sāhib enhanced the political standpoint of the Sikh Panth by adding to the growing number of institutions and cities. In acquiring horses from foreign lands, a clear message was sent out to the ruling elite; empowered by Nām, the Gurmukhs were rising and mobilizing under the sovereignty of Gurū Nānak Sāhib's Darbār.

This was not an incidental development; rather it was a primary objective of the Gurū, both intentional and purposeful, and symptomatic of the Gurū's writings. Gurū Arjan Sāhib ensured their son, Hargobind, was thoroughly trained in horse riding, swordsmanship, and warfare at the hands of Baba Buddhā jī. These were the tell-tale signs that the Gurū had the foresight to prepare for what lay in store for the Sikh Panth. Bhatt Sattā and Balvand notably describe the Gurū's Court:

ਤਖਤਿ ਬੈਠਾ ਅਰਜਨ ਗੁਰੂ ਸਤਿਗੁਰ ਕਾ ਖਿਵੈ ਚੰਦੋਆ ॥
ਉਗਵਣਹੁ ਤੈ ਆਥਵਣਹੁ ਚਹੁ ਚਕੀ ਕੀਅਨੁ ਲੋਆ ॥

"Gurū Arjan sits on the throne; the royal canopy waves over the True Gurū. From east to west, their Radiance illuminates all".[29]

The Gurū's Sikhiā was manifested by Divine revelation, and it was the intelligence and foresight with which the Gurū's spiritual revolution materialised for the common person that made it so unique. Not only did the Gurū continue to criticise the hypocrisy of emperors and religious leaders, but also offered a system of governance in which human values were promoted, based on a Divine connection of the soul with the ultimate soul. The Gurū was both compassionate and incisive in revealing this truth to the world.

Imperial threats and fines

It was clear that in the 100 or so years of the Gurūship period to this point, the Gurū had firmly asserted their authority, paying no heed to imperial forces. The Sikh uprising had alarmed the Mughal administration.

According to the author of the Dabistān, Mughal Emperor Jahangir was most displeased with the Gurū's rise in popularity. He was further infuriated in learning that the Gurū had assisted his son, Prince Khusrao, who had rebelled against the Mughal regime.[30] Writing in 1812, Malcolm also asserted,

> *"the jealousy of the Muhammedan government was excited, and he was made its sacrifice...his martyrdom, for such they term it, was caused by the active hatred of a rival Hindu zealot, Danichand*

Cshatriya, whose writings he refused to admit into the Adi-Granth, on the grounds that the tenets inculcated in them were irreconcilable to the pure doctrine of the unity and omnipotence of God taught in that sacred volume."[31]

Emperor Jahangir fined Gurū Arjan Sāhib 2 lakhs, however the Gurū refused to pay it. It is recorded that Prithi Chand, who was the eldest brother of Gurū Arjan Sāhib, and thus son of Gurū Rām Dās Sāhib, also colluded with the governor to ensure the Gurū was arrested. In his mind, Prithi Chand felt his father ought to have picked him over Gurū Arjan Sāhib in 1581. Like the previous Gurū's sons, Srī Chand, Lakhmī Dās (and his son Dharam Chand), Dāsū, Dātū, Mohan and Mohārī, all of whom had lived in close proximity to the Gurū, it was Prithi Chand's ego that did not allow him to be Gurū-like. Prithi Chand went on to found a dissident group that became known as the Minas, out of spite for not being chosen as the next Gurū.

The Minas

Kesar Singh Chibbar narrates how the Mina's literary publications were deemed a threat to the sanctity and sovereignty of the Gurū's Word, which as we have touched upon earlier, is what led Gurū Arjan Sāhib to compile the Adi Granth Sāhib.

Bhāī Gurdās jī too condemns the Minas who had turned their allegiance but sought to claim a place as heirs of Gurū Nānak Sāhib's throne. The entire 36th Vaar, with 21 Pauris, is written in no uncertain terms about the deceitful Minas. He writes,

ਸਤਿਗੁਰੁ ਸਚਾ ਪਾਤਿਸਾਹੁ ਮੁਹੁ ਕਾਲੇ ਮੀਣਾ।

The True Gurū is the True Emperor while the Minas are only disgraced.[32]

ਪਾਤਿਸ਼ਾਹੀ ਮਹਿਮਾ – Revisiting Sikh Sovereignty

In this Vaar, Bhāī Gurdās jī is advising the Sikhs against the dangers of such individuals, who ultimately are disgraced for their actions. Bhāī Gurdās jī goes on to warn the Sikhs not to associate themselves with the Minas, that, in essence, a fake and hypocritical leader will not lead one to salvation but only to further suffering; this is the boon of following fake god-men. Bhāī Gurdās jī tells us the Minas are false coins from a false mint and offers a whole range of different metaphors from the natural world to expound his case against the deceitful ways of the Minas. It is also worth noting here that approximately 150 years later, the Panth adopted an official position against the Minas, and other false groups, as captured in the Bhāī Chaupā Singh Rehatnama.

Kesar Singh Chibbar provides an extensive insight into the conflict that existed between the Gurū's Darbār and the Minas, providing reference to how Prithi Chand also tried to poison young Hargobind, Gurū Arjan Sāhib's only child. In fact, Gurū Arjan Sāhib makes references to these persons attacks in Gurū Granth Sāhib. There is a Shabad relating to an imperial petition brought against the Gurū[33], as well as one concerning the failed poison attempt, recorded in Gurū Granth Sāhib.[34] This Shabad was spoken in relation to Prithi Chand's failed attempt to kill young Hargobind, by way of bribing a Brahmin.[35] Giānī Gian Singh narrates how this was, in fact, a second failed attempt following the episode where a venomous snake was unleashed into young Hargobind's room as he played.[36] On the subject of failed assassination attempts, Gurū Arjan Sāhib also makes reference to the failed assassination attempt upon their own life by Mughal officer Sulhi Khan.[37]

Due to the collusion of Mughal officers, the Minas controlled Amritsar. Prithi Chand was succeeded by his son Meharvān who in turn was followed by an individual called Hariji. Hariji is the one who prevented Gurū Tegh Bahādur Sāhib from entering the city, but we'll touch upon that later in this chapter. Furthermore, Cunningham too writes,

"...he [Gurū Arjan Sāhib] is said to have refused to betroth his son to the daughter of Chundoo Shah, the finance administrator of the Lahore province; and he further appears to have been sought as a political partisan."[38]

Arrest and Imprisonment

Therefore, we know of many reasons why the Gurū was called to Lahore and imprisoned, but the refusal to pay the tax imposed by Jahangir appears to have been the main cause of concern within the Mughal establishment We shall see later how Gurū Hargobind Sāhib was imprisoned in Gwailor Fort too, perhaps for this unpaid tax, but at this point, it is important to note that it was the establishment of Sikh sovereign agency permeated from the Gurū's Darbār that posed a great threat to the Imperial establishment. Jahangir in his personal memoirs writes,

"He [Gurū Arjan Sāhib] was noised about as a religious and worldly leader. They called him Guru, and from all directions crowds of fools would come to him and express great devotion to him. This busy traffic had been carried on for three or four generations. For years the thought had been presenting itself to my mind that either I should put an end to this false traffic, or he should be brought into the fold of Islam."[39]

It is evident Jahangir was outraged at the rebellious nature of Gurū Arjan Sahib. Given the speed with which Gurū's Darbār had been established and the kind of mobilization taking place, specifically the founding new towns and cities. He goes on in his memoirs,

ਪਾਤਿਸ਼ਾਹੀ ਮਹਿਮਾ – Revisiting Sikh Sovereignty

"...When this matter was brought to the notice of this glorious court and I realised the full extent of his false conduct, I ordered that he be brought to my presence [at Lahore]. I gave over his homes and houses and children to Murtaza Khan [a minister in charge of awards and military contingents], confiscated his goods and ordered him to be capitally punished."[40]

Interestingly, Bhagat Singh, the author of Gurbilās Pātshāhī 6, offers another perspective that is more incriminating of Chandu Shah. He narrates Jahangir had invited Gurū Sāhib to Lahore and asked him many questions about who was greater, a Muslim or a Hindu.[41] To this, narrates Bhagat Singh, Gurū Sāhib recites Ramkalee Mahalā 5.[42] Perhaps this added to the discontent Jahangir had already amassed for the Gurū's Darbār.

Torture and assassination

In addition to various other sources, in a letter dated September 25th, 1606, written from Lahore by Father Jerome Xavier to the Jesuits' Provincial Supervisor of Goa, we come to know that before his martyrdom Gurū Arjan Sāhib went through a series of torture. This letter from Father Xavier is the first known account by a European who writes about Gurū Arjan Sāhib's "holy and saintly personality and his dignity and reputation".[43]

Jahangir's order was made to strike fear into the hearts of not only the Sikhs but non-Muslims generally. It was a statement of intent aimed at all disbelievers of Islam that Jahangir was prepared to rule with an iron fist and would impose the most barbaric penalties for those who chose to disobey the establishment. The Gurū's Darbār posed a direct threat to the reign of Jahangir, who unleashed unjust and brute force to stop the development of the Panth. The Gurū had not only amassed a large following but had awoken the common person. The people were beginning to break loose from their socio-political restraints imposed by the shackles of the ruling elite.

If we are to take a basic understanding of Gurmat to be what the Gurū said and did, then in the twenty-five years of Gurū Arjan Sāhib's rule, the Sikhs had become conscious of the reality that they were neither Muslims nor Hindus. Gurū Arjan Sāhib was very clear in his choice of words:

> "I do not keep the Hindu fast, nor do I observe the month of Ramadan. I serve only the One, who will protect me in the end. The One Lord of the World is my Allah. He administers justice to both Hindus and Muslims. I do not make pilgrimages to Mecca, nor do I worship at Hindu sacred shrines. I serve the One Lord, and not any other. I do not perform Hindu worship services, nor do I offer the Muslim prayers. I have taken the One Formless Lord into my heart; I humbly worship the One. I am not a Hindu, nor am I a Muslim".[44]

Add to this the political advances of the Gurū's movement, the building of towns, cities, collecting *dasvandh*, and the deployment of agents across the land, it becomes increasingly clear why the Imperial establishment targeted Gurū Arjan Sāhib. Cunningham notes how Gurū Arjan Sāhib had created a "state within a state", which naturally would've alarmed the establishment. This perspective is supported by the writings of early Sikh scholars and also, more importantly, evident from how the Gurū's Darbār and its royal insignia are described by the Bhatts in Gurū Granth Sāhib. As we have considered, there are at least three occasions within Gurū Granth Sāhib that Gurū Arjan Sāhib writes about the failed attempts on his and his family's life too.[45]

According to Sikh traditional accounts of history, Gurū Arjan Sāhib was made to sit on a hot iron plate whilst the torturers poured hot sand over their body and then boiled in a large cauldron. On May

30th, 1606, with hands and feet bound together and wounds blistering all over his body, Gurū Arjan Sāhib was thrown into the River Ravi.

Srī Gurū Arjan Dev Sāhib jī Māhārāj

NOTES

[1] Bhāī Nand Lal (1633-1713), *Ganjnama*, Kalaam-e-Goya, translated by Sardar Pritpal Singh Bindra, 2003, Institute of Sikh Studies, Chandigarh

[2] Sir Gokul Chand Narang, 1912, *Transformation of Sikhism*, Ripon Printing Press, Lahore, 3rd Edition, p67-68

[3] J. D. Cunningham, 1849, *History of the Sikhs*, Oxford University Press: Oxford, p49

[4] ਸਰੂਪ ਦਾਸ ਭੱਲਾ, ੧੭੭੬, ਮਹਿਮਾ ਪ੍ਰਕਾਸ਼

Sārūp Das Bhalla, 1776, *Mehmā Prakāsh*, Edited by Dr. Uttam Singh Bhatia, 1971, Bagh 2, Khand 1, Bhasha Vibhag, Panjab, p348

[5] Gurū Arjan, Raag Gauree, Gurū Granth Sāhib, Ang 248

[6] Kavī Chūrāmanī Bhāī Santokh Singh, 1843, *Srī Gur Pratap Sūraj Granth*, Steek 3, Rās 3, Adhiāi 34, Line 1, Edited by Dr. Ajeet Singh Aulakh, 2014, 3rd Edition, p490

[7] ਭਗਤ ਸਿੰਘ, ੧੭੧੮, ਗੁਰ ਬਿਲਾਸ ਪਾਤਸ਼ਾਹੀ ੬

Bhagat Singh, 1718, *Gurbilās Pātshahi 6*, Edited by Dr. Gurmukh Singh, 1997, Punjabi University, Patiala, Chapter 4, p90

[8] Teja Singh and Ganda Singh, 1950, *A Short History of the Sikhs (1469-1765)*, Volume One, Sixth Edition, Publication Bureau, Punjabi University, Patiala, p31

[9] Bhāī Gurdās, *Vārān*, Vār 1, Paurī 32, translated by Shamsher Singh Puri, 2009, Singh Brothers, Amritsar, 1st Edition, p128

[10] Bhāī Vir Singh, 1926, *Purātan Janam Sākhī*

Purātan Janam Sakhi (1588), edited by Bhāī Vir Singh, 1926, Sākhī 43

[11] Louis E Fenech, 2008, *The Darbar of the Sikh Gurus*, Oxford University Press, Delhi, p67

[12] ਭਾਈ ਕੇਸਰ ਸਿੰਘ ਛਿਬੱਰ, ੧੭੬੯, ਬੰਸਾਵਲੀਨਾਮਾ ਦਸਾਂ ਪਾਤਸ਼ਾਹੀਆਂ ਕਾ

Kesar Singh Chibbar, 1769, *Bansāvalīnāmā*, Edited by Piara Singh Padam, 1997, Singh Brothers, Amritsar, p80-81

[13] ਭਾਈ ਕੇਸਰ ਸਿੰਘ ਛਿਬੱਰ, ੧੭੬੯, ਬੰਸਾਵਲੀਨਾਮਾ ਦਸਾਂ ਪਾਤਸ਼ਾਹੀਆਂ ਕਾ

Kesar Singh Chibbar, 1769, *Bansāvalīnāmā*, Edited by Piara Singh Padam, 1997, Singh Brothers, Amritsar, p80-81

[14] W. Owen Cole and Piara Singh Sambhi, 1995, *The Sikhs and Their Religious Beliefs and Practices*, Second Edition, p47
[15] Gurū Amar Das, Raag Raamkali, Ang 920, Gurū Granth Sāhib
[16] ਭਗਤ ਸਿੰਘ, ੧੭੧੮, ਗੁਰ ਬਿਲਾਸ ਪਾਤਸ਼ਾਹੀ ੬
Bhagat Singh, 1718, *Gurbilās Pātshahi 6*, Edited by Dr. Gurmukh Singh, 1997, Punjabi University, Patiala, Chapter 5, p154
[17] Harbans Singh, 1982, *Gurū Tegh Bahadur*, Sterling Publishers, p17
[18] ਭਗਤ ਸਿੰਘ, ੧੭੧੮, ਗੁਰ ਬਿਲਾਸ ਪਾਤਸ਼ਾਹੀ ੬
Bhagat Singh, 1718, *Gurbilās Pātshahi 6*, Edited by Dr. Gurmukh Singh, 1997, Punjabi University, Patiala, Chapter 4, p90
[19] Pashaura Singh, 2000, *The Guru Granth Sahib, Canon, Meaning and Authority*, Oxford University Press, p174
[20] Gurū Arjan, Raag Bhairao, Gurū Granth Sāhib, Ang 1136
[21] Trilochan Singh, 1994, *Ernest Trumpp and W.H. McLeod As Scholars of Sikh History, Religion and Culture*, International Centre of Sikh Studies, Chandigarh
[22] Balbinder Bhogal, 2007, Text as sword Sikh religious violence taken for wonder, published in Religion and Violence in South Asia, p108
[23] Mobad, 1645-46, *Dabistān-i Mazāhib, Sikhism and the Sikhs*, translated by J. S. Grewal & Irfan Habib, 2001, *Sikh History from Persian Sources*, Tulika Books, Delhi, p66
[24] J. D. Cunningham, 1849, *History of the Sikhs*, Oxford University Press: Oxford, p49
[25] Dr Sangat Singh, 2014, *The Sikhs in History*, Singh Brothers, Amritsar, p32
[26] J. D. Cunningham, 1849, *History of the Sikhs*, Oxford University Press: Oxford, p49-50.
[27] Sir Jadunath Sarkar, 1930, *A Short History of Aurangzib*, M. C. Sarkar & Sons, Calcutta, p164
[28] Mobad, 1645-46, *Dabistān-i Mazāhib, Sikhism and the Sikhs*, translated by J. S. Grewal & Irfan Habib, 2001, *Sikh History from Persian Sources*, Tulika Books, Delhi,
[29] Bhatt Satta & Balvand, Gurū Granth Sāhib, Raag Raamkalee, Ang 968

[30] Mobad, 1645-46, *Dabistān-i Mazāhib, Sikhism and the Sikhs*, translated by J. S. Grewal & Irfan Habib, 2001, *Sikh History from Persian Sources,* Tulika Books, Delhi, p67

[31] John Malcolm, 1812, *Sketch of the Sikhs*, p32.

[32] Bhāī Gurdās, *Vāran*, Vār 36, Paurī 1, translated by Shamsher Singh Puri, 2009, Singh Brothers, Amritsar, 1st Edition, p1663

[33] Gurū Arjan Sāhib, Raag Gauree, Guru Granth Sāhib, Ang 199

[34] Gurū Arjan Sāhib, Raag Bhāīrao, Guru Granth Sāhib, Ang 1137

[35] ਸੰਤ ਹਰੀ ਸਿੰਘ 'ਰੰਧਾਵੇ ਵਾਲੇ', ੨੦੧੬, ਆਦਿ ਸ੍ਰੀ ਗੁਰੂ ਗ੍ਰੰਥ ਸਾਹਿਬ ਜੀ ਦਾ ਸੰਪ੍ਰਦਾਈ ਸਟੀਕ, ਗੁਰਬਾਣੀ ਅਰਥ-ਭੰਡਾਰ

Sant Hari Singh Randhawa, 2016, *Aad Srī Gurū Granth Sāhib ji da Sampardai Steek, Gurbānī Arth Bhandar*, Damdami Taksal

[36] Giānī Giān Singh, 1891, *Tvārīkh Guru Khālsā*, Chattar Singh Jeevan Singh, Amritsar, p306

[37] Gurū Arjan Sāhib, Raag Bilaaval, Guru Granth Sāhib, Ang 825

[38] J. D. Cunningham, 1849, *History of the Sikhs*, Oxford University Press: Oxford, p50.

[39] Jahangir, *Tuzuk-I Jahangiri*, as quoted by Teja Singh and Ganda Singh, 1950, *A Short History of the Sikhs (1469-1765)*, Volume One, Sixth Edition, Publication Bureau, Punjabi University, Patiala, p.34

[40] Jahangir, *Tuzuk-I Jahangiri*, edited by Saiyid Ahmad, Aligargh. 1864, p34 [Translated by Shireen Moosvi. J S Grewal & I Habib, Sikh History from Persian Sources, 2001. Tulika Books. p57

[41] ਭਗਤ ਸਿੰਘ, ੧੭੧੮, ਗੁਰ ਬਿਲਾਸ ਪਾਤਸ਼ਾਹੀ ੬

Bhagat Singh, 1718, *Gurbilās Pātshahi 6*, Edited by Dr. Gurmukh Singh, 1997, Punjabi University, Patiala, Chapter 7;290, p240

[42] Gurū Arjan Sāhib, Raag Raamkalee, Guru Granth Sāhib Ang 885

[43] Dr. Ganda Singh, 1962, *Early European Accounts of the Sikhs*, Firma K. L. Mukhopadhyaya, Calcutta, p48-49.

[44] Gurū Arjan Sāhib, Raag Bhāīrao, Guru Granth Sāhib, Ang 1136

[45] Raag Gauree, Ang 199; Raag Bhāīrao, Ang 1137; and Raag Bilaaval, Ang 825

Srī Gurū Hargobind Sāhib Jī Maharaj

ਹਮ ਅਜ਼ ਫ਼ਕਰ ਵ ਹਮ ਸਲਤਨਤ ਨਾਮਵਰ
ਬ-ਫ਼ਰਮਾਨਿ ਉ ਜੁਮਲਾ ਜ਼ੇਰੋਂ ਜ਼ਬਰ ॥ ੮੪ ॥

> [Gurū Hargobind Sāhib] is renowned through saintliness and regality, high and low remain under their command. 84.[1]

Gurū Hargobind Sāhib was bestowed with Guruship in 1606. Jahangir's scaremongering tactics failed to halt the Gurū's mission. Instead of laying low and retreating as Jahangir had hoped, Gurū Hargobind Sāhib rallied the Sikhs and initiated the next phase of Gurū Nānak Sāhib's mission. To advance the Sikh Panth and in the stand against oppression and injustice, the Sikh's martial prowess was nurtured, something which previous Gurū Sāhibān had initiated. Gurū Hargobind Sāhib took Sikhī to the next stage without compromising any of its core principles.

Rise of the Sikh warrior

Gurū Hargobind Sāhib wanted to know what Gurū Arjan Sāhib's final command was, so they asked the assembly of five Sikhs.[2] We learn from Kavi Santokh Singh that Bhāī Pirānā, a close associate of Gurū Arjan Sāhib, stated:

"ਕਰਹੁ ਨ ਸ਼ੋਕ ਗੁਵਿੰਦ ਗੁਨ ਗਾਵਹੁ । ਅਪਰ ਸਕਲ ਕੋ ਕਹੁ ਮਿਟਾਵਹੁ ।
ਸਾਯੁਧ ਹੋਹੁ ਤਖ਼ਤ ਪਰ ਰਾਜਹੁ । ਜਥਾ ਸ਼ਕਤਿ ਸੈਨਾ ਸੰਗ ਸਾਜਹੁ" ॥ ੨੦ ॥

Srī Gurū Hargobind Sāhib jī Mahārāj

Do not endure pain, [instead] sing the virtues of Gobind. Encourage others to do the same and relinquish the pain.
Adorn weapons and sit on the throne to rule, wield power and keep an army with you.[3]

At the centre of this mandate exists the perpetual spirit of Sikh sovereignty, which powered the Sikh movement during the period of the Gurū Sāhibān, The Gurū adorned two swords, one to represent their spiritual powers and the other as a sign of their temporal authority. The presence of the first sword is often overlooked, and Gurū Hargobind Sāhib is wrongly viewed as someone who just militarised the Sikhs. However, the fact that the first sword was identified as one which represented the Gurū Sāhib's spiritual power was indicative of their intentions. When they asked Baba Buddhā jī to then present the second sword, it signaled the intent to defend Gurū's Darbār and the fight against oppression with any means necessary.

Gurū Hargobind Sāhib's outward guise is often mistaken by many to represent a change or diversion in Gurmat. This is false; the Gurū continued along the same path of standing up and speaking out against injustice. The adorning of the swords was a message to the ruling elite that the Gurū would continue to defend the sanctity and sovereignty of the Gurū's Darbār and would do so with the sword. It was a timely statement of intent in which armed conflict was a necessary and liberating tool for the oppressed. As we shall see, it was not just to defend, but also to further the institute of Gurū's Darbār and the institutions of Sangat, Pangat, the Manjhī and Masand system.

Srī Akāl Takht Sāhib

We learn from Gurbilās Pātshahi 6, via the writings of Bhagat Singh that Gurū Sāhib announced the plans to build Srī Akāl Takht Sāhib, just twelve days after the Shaheedi of Gurū Arjan Sāhib. Many Sikhs had gathered from Khadūr Sāhib, Goindvāl Sāhib, and other areas from within Amritsar. Baba Buddhā jī led the recital of Gurū Granth Sāhib, as Bhāī Gurdās jī waved the Chaur Sāhib:

ਦੋਹਰਾ
ਲੈ ਆਗਯਾ ਸਭ ਕੀ ਤਬੈ ਬੁਢੇ ਪਾਯੋ ਭੋਗ।
ਰਾਗ ਮਾਲ ਪੜ ਪ੍ਰੇਮ ਸਿਉਂ ਗ੍ਰਿੰਥ ਗੁਰੁ ਜੀ ਜੋਗੁ ॥੧੩॥

Taking approval from everyone, Baba Buddha began the Bhog. Reading Raagmala with love, to complete the Paath.[4]

After this, the Masands presented the Gurū with the same offerings as the previous Gurū Sāhibān were presented – coconut, seli, etc. Gurū Sāhib stated that was no longer needed, now was the time to become armed, declaring:

"ਰਵਿ ਬੰਸੀ ਹਮ ਛਡੀ ਜਾਤਿ। ਹਮ ਕਉ ਸਦਹੀ ਜੁਧ ਸਹਾਤਿ।"

We belong to the warrior creed; our job is to wage war[5]

Bhagat Singh records, upon hearing this, Baba Buddhā jī is pleased and, following further instruction from Gurū Sāhib, places the five items in the treasury. Gurū Sāhib declares,

ਸ਼ਸਤ੍ਰ ਅਸਤ੍ਰ ਅਬ ਧਾਰਹੁੰ ਪਿਤ ਬਦਲੇ ਕੇ ਹੇਤੁ।
ਭੂਮਿ ਭਾਰ ਸਭ ਦੂਰ ਕਰਿ ਕਹਿ ਬਚ ਪ੍ਰਭ ਜਸ ਕੇਤ ॥੧੫॥

Now we are to adorn all types of weapons to deliver justice for the Shaheedi of our father. We will now ease the suffering upon this world.[6]

Gurū Sāhib is presented with a *dastaar*, and all those present offered many other gifts, as Anand Sāhib was recited and *Karah Prashad* was given. This alarmed the Masands who were present at the *Gurgaddhī* ceremony. They complained to the Gurū's mother, Mata Ganga, insinuating this signified a change from Gurū Nānak

Sāhib; however, Mata Ganga advised them to accept this declaration of war as Hukam of Akāl. This signifies the first moment the Masands changed.

Sikhs instructed to wage war

According to Bhagat Singh, Gurū Hargobind Sāhib issued Hukamnāmās the very next day for Sikhs across the lands to present weapons at the Guru's Darbār within fifteen days. The construction of Akāl Takht was then initiated:

> ਕਰ ਅਰਦਾਸ ਸ੍ਰੀ ਸਤਿਗੁਰੂ ਪੁਨ ਪ੍ਰਸਾਦਿ ਵਰਤਾਇ।
> ਪ੍ਰਿਥਮ ਨੀਂਵ ਸ੍ਰੀ ਗੁਰੂ ਰਖੀ ਅਬਚਲ ਤਖਤ ਸੁਹਾਇ॥੩੮॥
>
> Gurū Hargobind Sāhib completed an Ardas and Karah Prashad was distributed. The foundation stone was laid by Gurū Sāhib; the Akāl Takht was established.[7]

The entire throne was built by the hands of Gurū Hargobind Sāhib, Baba Buddhā jī, and Bhāī Gurdās jī. Kavī Santokh Singh too narrates how the Guru issued Hukamnāme for the Sikhs to arrive, specifically asking for them to bring an assortment of weapons and horses to Harmandir Sāhib, Amritsar:

> "ਜੋ ਸਿੱਖ ਆਨਹਿ ਸ਼ਸਤ੍ਰ ਤੁਰੰਗਾ। ਹੋਇ ਖੁਸ਼ੀ ਗੁਰ ਕੀ ਸੁਖ ਸੰਗਾ।
> ਸਭਿ ਆਵੈਂ ਦਰਸ਼ਨ ਹਿਤ ਕਰਿਬੇ। ਲਯਾਇਂ ਅਕੋਰ ਬਿਲਮ ਨਹਿੰ
> ਧਰਿਬੇ" ॥੧੯॥
>
> "If a Sikh wishes to visit, they should be certain to bring weapons and horses. They will obtain the Gurū's joy and remain happy. Those who come should not bring any other kind of offering or gift.[8]

Upon completing the construction of Akāl Takht, the Sikhs arrived as per the Hukamnāmā, accompanied by many weapons, horses, warriors, and war drums. Dhādīs, including the famed Abdul and Nathā, were soon invited who sang war ballads, and Gurū Sāhib was anointed with the two swords representing temporal and spiritual power.

ਦੋਹਰਾ

ਅਸਿ ਉਸਤਤਿ ਢਾਢੀ ਕਰੀ ਸੁਨ ਗੁਰ ਭਏ ਕ੍ਰਿਪਾਲ ॥
ਸ੍ਰੀ ਗੁਰ ਬਚ ਐਸੇ ਕਹੇ ਢਾਢੀ ਭਯੋ ਨਿਹਾਲ ॥੬੩॥

Gurū was pleased as the dhadhis sang the Gurū's praises. Gurū Sāhib then spoke the following, to which the dhadis felt exhalted.

ਚੌਪਾਈ

ਪੁਨ ਢਾਢੀ ਕਉ ਬਚਨ ਸੁਨਾਏ । ਰਹੋ ਨਿਕਟ ਹਮਰੇ ਸੁਖ ਪਾਏ ।
ਵਾਰ ਸਭੀ ਸੂਰਨ ਕੀ ਗਾਵਉ । ਠਾਢੇ ਆਗੇ ਨਿਤ ਸੁਨਾਵਉ ॥੬੪॥
ਸਤਿ ਬਚਨ ਢਾਢੀ ਮਨ ਲੀਨੇ । ਸੰਗਤ ਕਉ ਗੁਰੂ ਆਗਿਆ ਦੀਨੇ ।
ਹਮ ਹੁਮਾਇ ਸੰਗਤਿ ਸਭਿ ਆਈ । ਹੈ ਪਟ ਸ਼ਸਤ੍ਰ ਸੁ ਪੂਜ ਚੜਾਈ ॥੬੫॥

Gurū spoke, "You will now stay with us. You will sing war ballads of brave warriors. Standing close by. The dhadhis bowed in reverence. Gurū Sāhib gave Sangat permission, to come forward and present horses, weapons and fine clothing.[9]

For a full account of this episode, it would be wise for the reader to refer to Gurbilās Pātshahi 6. The author provides a wonderfully detailed account, including the arrival of 400 warriors from across Malwa, Majha, and Doab that offered their head at the Akāl Takht. Gurū Sāhib chose four Sikhs, four of the five that had travelled with Gurū Arjan Sāhib to Lahore – Bhāī Bidhī Chand, Bhāī Perra ji, Bhāī Pirānā ji and Bhāī Jetha ji, and made them Generals of a contingent of 100 warriors each, complete with weapons and horses, forming the elite fighting contingent of the Akāl Senā.[10]

As we have already seen, it was Gurū Nānak Sāhib who first established a town, that of Kartārpur Sāhib, and Gurū Hargobind Sāhib simply built upon this. The Akāl Takht was the Gurū's seat of temporal and spiritual power, and its construction in Amritsar was a manifestation of Gurū Nānak Sāhib's instruction that he alone sits on a throne who is worthy of the throne.[11] Gurū Nānak Sāhib has been referred to as a king of both the spiritual and temporal domains, in Gurū Granth Sāhib. Gurū Amar Dās Sāhib too reiterates this point in Raag Maru.[12]

Akāl within Kāl

It is worth emphasizing here that the Akāl Takht isn't just the political headquarters of the Sikh Panth. It is not that Akāl Takht represents the "political" or the "secular" and Harmandir Sāhib the "religion" or the "church". The root of that separation is grounded in what took place in Europe following the so-called Renaissance and Reformation, shaping modern forms of governance, which we shall consider in Part Three of the book. To use this European lens is to undermine the distinct and standalone praxis of Gurmat. The Akāl Takht stands in close proximity to Harmandir Sāhib to represent the Sikh centrality of Akāl within Kāl; Divine existence within the temporal structures of worldly governance. There is no hierarchy between the two, but instead, a fluid dynamism woven into the tapestry of the entire Srī Darbār Sāhib, reflecting how the Divine is at the nucleus of temporal Sikh thought and action. The greatness of the two structures in Sikhī is that they complement each other. It is not a mere unity of two separate institutions but a representation of Sikh agency, and it epitomises the concept of oneness that is a core aspect of the Sikh world view.

Young men were invited to bring horses and arms to be trained by the Gurū. The Gurū became the bane of tyrants and was both fearless and compassionate. Gurū Sāhib was a great warrior, a destroyer of armies but also highly benevolent in character.[13] Bhāī

Gurdās jī cemented the view that the Gurū's sovereignty was, is, and will always remain throughout all the Ages.[14] According to the Dabistan, Gurū Hargobind Sāhib kept,

> *"Seven hundred horses in his stable with three hundred battle-tested horsemen and sixty musketeers always in his service. Among them a set of persons occupied themselves in trade, service and work [on his behalf]."*[15]

Gurū Sāhib consolidated the work of the previous Gurū Sāhibān, adding to cities such as Kartārpur Sāhib, Khadūr Sāhib, Goindvāl Sāhib, Amritsar, Taran Tāran and Kartārpur Sāhib (Jalandhar) by further establishing Srī Hargobindpur and Kīratpur Sāhib. The transformation in Panjāb was a steady and gradual process, not least because the people had to be gradually awakened to the new paradigm created by Gurū Sāhib, but there also existed the firm opposition from one of the greatest empires of all times.

The Gurū's mission was to uplift everyone irrespective of caste and creed. The path of Sikh liberation was made available to everyone, and the Gurū led from the front. In keeping with the Sikhiā that Gurū Nānak Sāhib gave to the Siddhs, Gurū Hargobind Sāhib mobilised the Sikh within the world. Harbans Singh writes,

> *"The scriptural thesis had to be lived among the people and not in the seclusion of a monastery for the training of a few. Hence, the progress could only be gradual both in the education of the people and in the pace of the movement. The latter could not outstrip the former. The task was stupendous. For, it had to take place in the face of the understandable opposition of one of the greatest empires of all times."*[16]

Srī Gurū Hargobind Sāhib jī Mahārāj

The Gurū's activities were beginning to alarm the emperor, and it was at this point that Meharvān, son of Prithi Chand, the Gurū's paternal uncle, decided to take advantage of the situation and tried bringing an end to the Gurū's reign. Meharvān had previously staked a claim to the Gurūship, but his fallacious persistence to argue that Gurū Nānak Sāhib's path was merely about spirituality not only went against Gurū Nānak Sāhib's own writings but was also refuted by the socio-political achievements of Gurū Nānak Sāhib and the early successors. After being ousted, Meharvān had become bitter and jealous of Gurū Hargobind Sāhib's feats, therefore colluded with Chandu Shah and complained to the emperor that the Gurū had abandoned the way of previous Gurū Sāhibān by adorning the sword and training an army. They also informed the emperor that the Gurū had begun to dispose of judicial cases like the law-courts.

Gurū Hargobind Sāhib imprisoned

All of this, perhaps also the outstanding tax charge levied against the Gurū's father, contributed towards Gurū Hargobind Sāhib's arrest, and they were placed in Gwalior Fort along with other political prisoners. Amongst the prisoners were 52 kings of independent territories, whom Jahangir had imprisoned in order to tax their kingdoms.

Bhagat Singh offers the earliest account of the build-up to Gurū Sāhib's arrest. Writing in 1751, with the assistance of Shaheed Bhāī Mani Singh, he narrates that Chandu Shah, overcome with jealousy, had paid the royal court's astrologer to sow seeds of doubt into Jahangir's mind over his reign. In the Mughal courts, an astrologer was deemed a trustworthy counsel as they claimed to be able to tell the future. Chandu Shah advised the astrologer to create an atmosphere of uncertainty and doom by advising Jahangir there was an impending danger to his life. Chandu Shah felt Jahangir would inevitably ask how to avoid this. Therefore, Chandu Shah informed the astrologist to advise Jahangir to imprison Gurū Hargobind Sāhib at Gwalior Fort.[17] The astrologist did exactly this, telling Jahangir to imprison the Gurū for 40 days in Gwalior and conduct prayers for 40 days to prevent the impending doom. It is recorded that Gurū Sāhib agreed, as they knew the real culprit behind this was Chandu Shah, and actually had a greater motive to go to Gwalior.

Hardas, the Chief Warden of the fort, was a Sikh of the Guru and was overcome with joy upon hearing that the Gurū would be blessing him with their presence. Chandu Shah, unaware of Hardas' reverence for the Gurū, had dispatched a letter in which he asked him to poison the Gurū whilst they were in Gwalior. Hardas is said to have informed Gurū Hargobind Sāhib of this letter upon their arrival, and thus the Gurū's initial suspicions had been confirmed. Forty days passed without incident; in fact, Bhagat Singh records, the Gurū was in bliss, and the other prisoners developed an affection for the Gurū.

According to Irfan Habib's translation of the Dabistan, Mohsin Fani recorded that the Gurū was imprisoned for 12 years.[18] Historian Hari Ram Gupta suggests that the actual duration is unknown with some, including Giānī Giān Singh's Twarikh Gurū Khālsā recording it was in fact for a duration of only two months. This would bring it closer to the time suggested by Bhagat Singh in Gurbilās Pātshahi 6. Dr Sangat Singh contends it was a seven-year period.[19] Irrespective of the duration, what we know is Gurū Hargobind Sāhib was imprisoned due to their political mobilisation, which had caused a stir amongst the ruling elite, just as Sikh tradition holds that Gurū Nānak Sāhib had been incarcerated for his political dissent during the reign of Babur.

Bandi Chhor

Swarūp Singh Kaushish provides a detailed account of a conversation Gurū Sāhib has with their Sikh, Bhāī Nanoo, about the detainment in Gwalior. Whilst addressing the Sangat, Gurū Hargobind Sāhib describes how there were one-hundred-and-three detainees in the fort, of which fifty-two were kings serving long-term sentences. When news of Gurū Hargobind Sāhib's impending release reached them, Kaushish narrates how the kings, fearful they may be kept in the fort for the remainder of their lives, pleaded with the Gurū to also secure their release. The Gurū acted upon this by sending an ultimatum to Jahangir via Wazir Khan; that unless the other detainees were released, they would not leave the fort.

The order from Jahangir was two-fold; firstly, all those with a limited number of years remaining should be released, and secondly, for the long-term detainees, anyone who could hold onto the Gurū's coat would be allowed to leave. At this point, Gurū Sāhib had a special coat made with enough tassels to secure the release of the long-term prisoners.[20]

Interestingly, Kaushish narrates how the Gurū had stated there were one-hundred-and-three prisoners in the Fort of Gwalior and that Gurū Sāhib secured the release of them all. From this passage, Kaushish explicitly states fifty-two kings were serving long term sentences; it is assumed, therefore, that fifty-one of the inmates were serving short-term sentences,

Today, the episode concerning Gurū Hargobind Sāhib leaving the Fort of Gwalior is celebrated by Sikhs worldwide as "Bandi Chhor". As mentioned, the fort was also home to many other political prisoners of high status, including rebel princes of royal families. It is worth reiterating that upon their release from prison, the Gurū demanded the release of other political prisoners; thus, liberating many others, giving them the freedom to rule their own territories. The celebration of Bandi Chhor coincides with Diwali and has for Sikhs become a shining light of the Gurū's victory in liberating political prisoners. The significance of Gurū Sāhib's actions lies in the manner with which they outdid both Chandu Shah and Jahangir, with the former thinking the Gurū would never leave the fort alive, and the latter who had thought only a few would be released due to the conditions of his order.

ਪਾਤਿਸ਼ਾਹੀ ਮਹਿਮਾ – Revisiting Sikh Sovereignty

Battles with Mughal regime following imprisonment

The Gurū went to battle with the Mughal regime on a number of occasions, which led to their movement from Amritsar to Kartārpur Sāhib (Jalandhar) and Kīratpur Sāhib. The first, Battle of Amritsar (1634) was fought between Gurū Hargobind Sāhib with the Akāl Senā and the troops of Shah Jahan who had taken over the Mughal regime following the death of Jahangir. The build-up to the battle is of paramount importance because it provides an insight into the workings of Sikh sovereignty.

Shah Jahan was on a hawking expedition to the west of Amritsar, and the Gurū had entered the same area in pursuit of game. It so happened that the emperor was presented with a hawk, and eager to see what it could do, he released it in the hope that it would find its prey. The Gurū's Sikhs saw the hawk and took it into their possession. The two forces came to blows, which eventually resulted in defeat for the Mughal troops. A further battalion was sent, but the Akāl Senā inflicted heavy blows, which forced the Mughals to retreat.

During this battle, some seven hundred Sikhs of the Akāl Senā defeated an army of seven thousand imperial forces of the Mughal regime, including their commander Mukhlis Khan. The father and son duo of Bhatt Kirat and Bhatt Bhikka, the writings of whom are enshrined in the Gurū Granth Sāhib, were both present during this battle. Following the Battle of Amritsar, Gurū Hargobind Sāhib moved from Amritsar to Kartārpur Sāhib (Jalandhar) before eventually going to Kīratpur Sāhib.

Eight months later, the Gurū again was engaged in battle with the Mughal Governor of Lahore. The build-up to this battle is contained in the famous story narrated to Sikh children till this day, of Bidhī Chand, a most beloved and trustworthy companion of the Gurū. He was asked to retrieve two of the Gurū's finest horses, Dilbagh and Gulbagh, recently purchased by the Gurū's devoted Sikh, Sadh. He had travelled to Iraq to buy the horses, but upon his return journey to the Gurū's dominion, was stopped by Mughal officers in Lahore who seized the Gurū's war horses.

In time Bidhī Chand managed to free the horses and brought them to Gurū Hargobind Sāhib, but the Mughal forces soon attacked. They clashed with the Akāl Senā, who, led by the Gurū's Generals Bidhī Chand and Baba Gurditta, eventually defeated the enemy near Lahara Gaga, which is on the outskirts of Bathinda in Panjāb.

This battle was followed four months later with the Battle of Kartārpur (Jalandhar), April 1635. This was led by Paindah Khan, who was once an officer of the Akāl Senā. Both Paindah Khan and his deputy were defeated along with their forces. In Dabistan-I, Mazahib, the author narrates,

> *"From one [Sikh] named Sadh I heard that a man in that battle swung his sword towards the Gurū. The Gurū, turning to him, told the swordsman: "One does not wield the sword like this. This is how one strikes" – and with that stroke he finished off the foe. One of the Gurū's companions asked this writer, "What is the reason that the Gurū, while giving the strokem said, "See, this is how one strikes!"? I replied, "it seems to me that the Gurū's striking with the sword was only by way of instruction, since an instructor is called Gurū; it was not by way of anger [that he said so], since that would be unworthy".* [21]

In this Battle of Kartārpur (Jalandhar), the Gurū's youngest son, Tegh Bahādur Sāhib, was commended for showing remarkable bravery and fighting prowess on the battlefield.

Gurū Hargobind Sāhib engaged in seven battles with troops of the Mughal regime, and won every battle. This may explain the evident omission of reference to Gurū Hargobind Sāhib in any Persian work on Shah Jahan, whose administration perhaps downplayed the confrontation as local or regional conflicts between the Akāl Senā and provincial governors of the Mughal empire. However, from a Sikh perspective, the Gurū went on the offensive with the first confrontation over the hawk and continued to wreak havoc against the Mughal government. The underlying motive was to further the Sikh cause. The Sikh movement grew in numbers and popularity from each battle, which gave a new lease of freedom for the land's inhabitants.

The Gurū's Victory

Bhāī Gurdās jī describes Gurū Hargobind Sāhib as a great warrior; a destroyer of various armies who was also highly benevolent of character:

ਦਲਭੰਜਨ ਗੁਰ ਸੂਰਮਾ ਬਢ ਜੋਧਾ ਬਹੁ ਪਰਉਪਕਾਰੀ।

The great warrior Gurū, destroyer of armies, was also highly benevolent of character. [22]

The above description from a contemporary of the Gurū is echoed by later writers such as Kavī Santokh Singh, who provides a vivid depiction of Gurū Sāhib in battle, as well as the Gurū's Darbār of Kartārpur Sāhib (Jalandhar):

ਪਾਤਸ਼ਾਹੁ ਸਾਚਾ ਜਗਤ ਹੁਇ ਅੰਤ ਸਹਾਈ।
ਸੋਢੀ ਬੰਸ ਸਮੁੰਦ੍ਰ ਮਹਿੰ ਬਿਦਤ ਨਿਸਰਾਈ।
ਦੇਗ ਤੇਗ ਪੂਰੋ ਧਨੀ ਬਡ ਡੀਲ ਬਿਸਾਲਾ।
ਫਤੇ ਕਰਤਿ ਅਨਗਨ ਰਿਪੁਨਿ ਰਣ ਕਰਮ ਕਰਾਲਾ ॥੧੪॥ [23]

As with many early writers, Gurū Sāhib is referred to by Kavī Santokh Singh as Sache Pātshāh, the True Sovereign, who is like the moon on a dark night. Establishing both Degh and Tegh, Gurū Sāhib is strong and powerful; remaining victorious over countless enemies on the battlefield. Elsewhere Kavī Santokh Singh describes how

Kīrtan is sung in Rāg, Nagāray can be heard, and all the Sangat in attendance at the Kartārpur Darbār, are overcome with bliss.

Meanwhile, he narrates how the worldly kings are trembling at the thought of the Gurū's Darbār, with many thinking of running away after hearing about the Gurū's power. Both Delhi and Lahore are riddled with shame and fear; they only open the gates to their forts on certain days:

ਪਰੀ ਧਾਕ ਚਹੁੰ ਦਿਸ਼ਨਿ ਮਹਿੰ ਕੰਪੇ ਗਨ ਰਾਜੇ।
ਸੁਨਿ ਪ੍ਰਤਾਪ ਭਾਜਨਿ ਚਹਤਿ ਸਭਿ ਤਜਹਿ ਸਮਾਜੇ।
ਦਿੱਲੀ ਲਵਪੁਰਿ ਆਦਿ ਗਛ ਤ੍ਰਾਸਤਿ ਧਰਿ ਲਾਜੇ।
ਬਾਜੇ ਬਾਜੇ ਦਿਨ ਬਿਥੈ ਖੋਲਤਿ ਦਰਵਾਜੇ ॥੧੨॥ [24]

Kings on all four sides trembled upon hearing about Guru Sāhib's strength. Delhi and Lahore are fearful, they only open their forts on certain days.

When Gurū Sāhib moved from Kartārpur Sāhib (Jalandhar) to Kīratpur Sāhib, they consolidated the Sangat and sent trusted Sikhs, such as Bidhī Chand, to spread the Gurū's Wisdom. Kīratpur Sāhib now became the central point of attraction for the Sikhs, with groups travelling from far-off regions. Kaushish writes,

> "News of the arrival of Guru Hargobind Jee from Kartarpur brought supporters from far and near. From the village of Ramdas, Bhana of Budha's lineage came along with a multitude of followers. From Alipur Shamali, Bhāī Ballo's Mai Das came, accompanied by the people of Multan. From Duburjee came Anmbiye's Kaula. From (village) Bhāī-Ke-Fafeyan, Behlo came, along with the people of Sialkot. Raja Kalyan Chand came from Kahlur. Accompanied by the son Tara Chand from Handoor,

Himat Chand came and brought Diwan Chand along with him. Sikhs from Chamba arrived. They all presented their offerings and had darshan, the glimpse, of the Guru."[25]

Sovereign Sikh agency

The Gurū's cousin Meharvān, son of Prithi Chand had co-opted with the imperial regime, to take occupation of Srī Darbār Sāhib in 1635, but in building and establishing the Darbār of Kīratpur Sāhib, Gurū Sāhib demonstrated they were the sole authority responsible for, and capable of administering sovereign Sikh agency. It is a testament to the power and pull of Gurū Sāhib that so many individuals, and houses from across the region, came to Kīratpur Sāhib. Bhāī Gurdās provides an extensive list of names and describes their traits and professions. From readers of Shabad such as Itta Rora Awal and Nihalu to craftsmen carpenters such as Dhingar and Maddu and former inmates at Gwalior such as Bhai Tiratha Lashkar and Hardas[26], it is clear the Gurū attracted a wealth of talented, experienced, and politically active individuals with skills in all manners of work to provide the best opportunities for the Sikhs to develop and flourish. The Gurū's fame spread far and wide,

"...many men came to enlist under the Gurū's banner. They said that no one else had power to contend with the emperor".[27]

Passing of the Gurūship

When the time came, Gurū Hargobind Sāhib chose Har Rāi as the successor to Gurū Nānak Sāhib's Throne; thus began the reign of Sache Pātshāh Srī Gurū Har Rāi Sāhib jī Maharaj.

NOTES

[1] Bhāī Nand Lal (1633-1713), *Ganjnama*, Kalaam-e-Goya, translated by Sardar Pritpal Singh Bindra, 2003, Institute of Sikh Studies, Chandigarh

[2] Kavī Chūrāmanī Bhāī Santokh Singh, 1843, *Srī Gur Pratap Sūraj Granth*, Steek 5, Rās 4, Adhiāi 40, Line 18, Edited by Dr. Ajeet Singh Aulakh, 2014, 3rd Edition, p17

[3] Kavī Chūrāmanī Bhāī Santokh Singh, 1843, *Srī Gur Pratap Sūraj Granth*, Steek 5, Rās 4, Adhiāi 40, Line 18, Edited by Dr. Ajeet Singh Aulakh, 2014, 3rd Edition, p18

[4] ਭਗਤ ਸਿੰਘ, ੧੭੧੮, ਗੁਰ ਬਿਲਾਸ ਪਾਤਸ਼ਾਹੀ ੬

Bhagat Singh, 1718, *Gurbilās Pātshahi 6*, Edited by Dr. Gurmukh Singh, 1997, Punjabi University, Patiala, Chapter 8;13, p249

[5] ਭਗਤ ਸਿੰਘ, ੧੭੧੮, ਗੁਰ ਬਿਲਾਸ ਪਾਤਸ਼ਾਹੀ ੬

Bhagat Singh, 1718, *Gurbilās Pātshahi 6*, Edited by Dr. Gurmukh Singh, 1997, Punjabi University, Patiala, Chapter 8;21, p250

[6] ਭਗਤ ਸਿੰਘ, ੧੭੧੮, ਗੁਰ ਬਿਲਾਸ ਪਾਤਸ਼ਾਹੀ ੬

Bhagat Singh, 1718, *Gurbilās Pātshahi 6*, Edited by Dr. Gurmukh Singh, 1997, Punjabi University, Patiala, Chapter 8;25, p250

[7] ਭਗਤ ਸਿੰਘ, ੧੭੧੮, ਗੁਰ ਬਿਲਾਸ ਪਾਤਸ਼ਾਹੀ ੬

Bhagat Singh, 1718, *Gurbilās Pātshahi 6*, Edited by Dr. Gurmukh Singh, 1997, Punjabi University, Patiala, Chapter 8;38, p251

[8] Kavī Chūrāmanī Bhāī Santokh Singh, 1843, *Srī Gur Pratap Sūraj Granth*, Steek 5, Rās 4, Adhiāi 42, Line 18, Edited by Dr. Ajeet Singh Aulakh, 2014, 3rd Edition, p31

[9] ਭਗਤ ਸਿੰਘ, ੧੭੧੮, ਗੁਰ ਬਿਲਾਸ ਪਾਤਸ਼ਾਹੀ ੬

Bhagat Singh, 1718, *Gurbilās Pātshahi 6*, Edited by Dr. Gurmukh Singh, 1997, Punjabi University, Patiala, Chapter 8;63-65, p254

[10] ਭਗਤ ਸਿੰਘ, ੧੭੧੮, ਗੁਰ ਬਿਲਾਸ ਪਾਤਸ਼ਾਹੀ ੬

Bhagat Singh, 1718, *Gurbilās Pātshahi 6*, Edited by Dr. Gurmukh Singh, 1997, Punjabi University, Patiala, Chapter 8;75-76, p255

[11] Gurū Nānak Sāhib, Raag Maroo Gurū Granth Sāhib, Ang 1038

[12] Gurū Amar Dās, Raag Maroo, Gurū Granth Sāhib, Ang 1088

[13] Bhāī Gurdās, *Vārān*, Vār 1, Paurī 48, translated by Shamsher Singh Puri, 2009, Singh Brothers, Amritsar, 1st Edition, p161

[14] Bhāī Gurdās, *Vārān*, Vār 15, Paurī 1, translated by Shamsher Singh Puri, 2009, Singh Brothers, Amritsar, 1st Edition, p739

[15] Mobad, 1645-46, *Dabistān-i Mazāhib, Sikhism and the Sikhs*, translated by J. S. Grewal & Irfan Habib, 2001, *Sikh History from Persian Sources*, Tulika Books, Delhi, p69

[16] Harbans Singh, 1992, *The Encyclopaedia of Sikhism*

[17] ਭਗਤ ਸਿੰਘ, ੧੭੧੮, ਗੁਰ ਬਿਲਾਸ ਪਾਤਸ਼ਾਹੀ ੬

Bhagat Singh, 1718, *Gurbilās Pātshahi 6*, Edited by Dr. Gurmukh Singh, 1997, Punjabi University, Patiala, Chapter 8; 428-432, p290

[18] Mobad, 1645-46, *Dabistān-i Mazāhib, Sikhism and the Sikhs*, translated by J. S. Grewal & Irfan Habib, 2001, *Sikh History from Persian Sources*, Tulika Books, Delhi, p68

[19] Dr Sangat Singh, 2014, *The Sikhs in History*, Singh Brothers, Amritsar, p41

[20] ਭਾਈ ਸਰੂਪ ਸਿੰਘ ਕੌਸ਼ਿਸ, ੧੭੯੦, ਗੁਰੂ ਕੀਆਂ ਸਾਖੀਆਂ

Bhai Swarup Singh Kaushish, 1790, *Guru Kīān Sākhīān*, Sākhī 1, edited by Piara Singh Padam, 1986, Singh Brothers, Amritsar, p38

[21] Mobad, 1645-46, *Dabistān-i Mazāhib, Sikhism and the Sikhs*, translated by J. S. Grewal & Irfan Habib, 2001, *Sikh History from Persian Sources*, Tulika Books, Delhi, p68

[22] Bhāī Gurdās, *Vārān*, Vār 1, Paurī 48, translated by Shamsher Singh Puri, 2009, Singh Brothers, Amritsar, 1st Edition, p161

[23] Kavī Chūrāmanī Bhāī Santokh Singh, 1843, *Srī Gur Pratap Sūraj Granth* Steek 6, Rās 7, Adhiāi 61, Line 14, edited by Dr. Ajeet Singh Aulakh, 2014, 3rd Edition, p614

[24] Kavī Chūrāmanī Bhāī Santokh Singh, 1843, *Srī Gur Pratap Sūraj Granth* Steek 6, Rās 7, Adhiāi 61, Line 17, edited by Dr. Ajeet Singh Aulakh, 2014, 3rd Edition, p615

[25] ਭਾਈ ਸਰੂਪ ਸਿੰਘ ਕੌਸ਼ਿਸ, ੧੭੯੦, ਗੁਰੂ ਕੀਆਂ ਸਾਖੀਆਂ
Bhai Swarup Singh Kaushish, 1790, *Guru Kīān Sākhīān*, Sākhī 1, edited by Piara Singh Padam, 1986, Singh Brothers, Amritsar, p37

[26] Bhāī Gurdās, *Vārān*, Vār 11, Paurī 29-31, translated by Shamsher Singh Puri, 2009, Singh Brothers, Amritsar, 1st Edition, p603-607

[27] Sir Jadunath Sarkar, 1930, *A Short History of Aurangzib*, M. C. Sarkar & Sons, Calcutta, p165

Srī Gurū Har Rāi Sāhib jī Maharaj

ਗਰਦਨ-ਜ਼ਨਿ ਸਰਕਸ਼ਾਂ ਗੁਰੂ ਕਰਤਾ ਹਰਿ ਰਾਏ
ਯਾਰਿ ਮੁਤਜ਼ੱਰਆਂ ਗੁਰੂ ਕਰਤਾ ਹਰਿ ਰਾਏ ॥੯੧॥

> Gurū Har Rai is the annihilator of the rebellious and arrogant.
> Gurū Har Rai is the shelter of the weak. 91.[1]

Gurū Har Rāi Sāhib succeeded Gurū Hargobind Sāhib in 1644 and oversaw a period of the Sikh movement that was relatively peaceful but not without political activity. The basis for Sikh political mobilization, conduct, and agency was guaranteed by the Gurū's sovereignty. They did not accept the governance of the Mughal regime and remained a separate and independent entity. Gurū Har Rai Sāhib built upon the fiscal policies of Gurū Amar Das Sāhib and Gurū Ram Das Sāhib; the development of Sikh trade under Gurū Arjan Sāhib and the battle success of the Akāl Senā under Gurū Hargobind Sāhib. In light of the close counsel of Sikhs we find reference to during the reign of each of the previous Gurū Sāhibān, Gurū Har Rāi Sāhib would likely have maintained the same.

The Gurū's Army

The Gurū kept a cavalry of 2200 trained Sikh fighters who were ever ready to ensure the sanctity and sovereignty of the Gurū's Darbār were preserved. They functioned as the vanguard to the Gurū's Darbār, and Gurū's Sangat who had developed a unique sense of belonging and togetherness by attuning their consciousness to the Gurū's Shabad. As mentioned, there were no battles fought between the Gurū's Darbār and the imperial forces, or indeed the Hill Rajas, during the time of Gurū Har Rāi Sāhib. Despite this, the Gurū continued to maintain and train the Sikh army, promote horse riding and hunting, as well as developing the Darbār on other fronts. This demonstrates the proactive nature of the Sikh resistance to tyranny and oppression during the Gurū period. Peacetime did not mean they abandoned their weapons; on the contrary, it was a time of consolidation and further expansion.

Growing the Panth

The Gurū was able to open and provide safe sanctuaries for wildlife and, following in the footsteps of other Gurū Sāhibān, preserved medicinal herbal gardens for those in need of medical attention. With no immediate armed threat, Gurū Sāhib refocused on growing the Panth, travelling far and wide to places such as Kashmīr[2] and developing cordial relations with the Raja of Bilaspur[3] and Shah Jahan after the Gurū supplied medicine to the Mughal emperor's son, Dara Shikoh[4].

Dara Shikoh has been described as being similar in character and nature to the likes of Mughal emperors Akbar and Khusrao that came before him. However, following the wars of succession within the Mughal empire, Aurangzeb came out on top. He killed his brother Dara Shikoh and imprisoned his father, Shah Jahan.

Emperor Aurangzeb summons Gurū Har Rāi Sāhib to Delhi

Once he had ascended to the imperial throne and neutralised the threat of internal dissidents, Aurangzeb turned his attention to the growing influence of Gurū Har Rai Sāhib's Darbār. Sikh history records that he summoned the Gurū to Delhi. It is said that Gurū Har Rāi Sāhib penned a letter in which they confirmed the association with Dara Shikoh and that they would be sending their son Rām Rāi to Delhi as an emissary to address any concerns Aurangzeb may have. Some may ask why the Gurū didn't attend in person; however, as

ਪਾਤਿਸ਼ਾਹੀ ਮਹਿਮਾ – Revisiting Sikh Sovereignty

Sache Pātshāh, Gurū Sāhib could not be summoned at the whim of a temporal king. Moreover, it would have been counterproductive to accept the invitation given the hostilities developing within the Mughal administration. This was a power play on behalf of the Gurū, demonstrating that Gurū's Darbār was completely sovereign and answerable only to the Court of Akāl Purakh.

Gurū Sāhib's response and brief to Rām Rāi

In Tvārīkh Gurū Khālsā, Giānī Gian Singh narrates the contents of the initial letter Gurū Har Rāi Sāhib sent to Aurangzeb;

> "...we are not under your landlordship nor are we your servants. We are not interested in any of your wealth, if we happen to be in Delhi we'll come and see you ourselves".[5]

This was not received well in the imperial echelons of power, and it is recorded that Aurangzeb made three attempts to send a garrison of troops to the Gurū; however, each convoy failed to complete the mission.

Precolonial texts are fairly unanimous on how Gurū Sāhib prepared Rām Rāi for the meeting with Aurangzeb. Whilst preparing his son, Kaushish writes that Gurū Har Rai Sāhib explained, "I am with you, *ang-sang*, do not be fearful of anything and speak with conviction."[6] Kavī Santokh Singh writes he was instructed to speak the truth contained within Gurbānī and to remember to uphold the ideals of Gurū Nānak Sāhib;

> *"Fearlessly interpret the Gurū's Word and history of the great Gurū Sāhibān. Do not consider anything more previous than the great spiritual gifts which you have already received from Gurū Nānak and fear not to uphold the dignity and grandeur of Gurū Nānak's Darbār".*[7]

The authors of Mehmā Prakāsh[8] and Tvārīkh Gurū Khālsā[9], both offer similar accounts in which Rām Rāi was to entertain no fear or intimidation of the Mughal emperor. So long as he remembered the great Gurū Nānak Sāhib and represented Sikh ideals truthfully, there could be no one more powerful than him at that point. Giānī Giān Singh states the overriding instruction was to uphold and assert the grandeur and truth of Sikhī, not to submit to threat and coercion but be as firm as a rock in both faith and conviction.

However, not long after arriving in the Mughal court, whether through intimidation or to appease the men of the imperial capital, Rām Rāi seemed to forget the Gurū's orders and began to show miracles for the emperor's enjoyment and also misquoted a Shabad of Gurū Nānak Sāhib in which he replaced the word 'Muslim' with 'faithless', which changed the meaning of the Shabad[10]. This went against the Gurū's specific orders, for which Kaushish narrates Gurū Har Rāi Sāhib stated, "you no longer deserve my affection, and this blunder of yours cannot be forgotten".[11]

Gurū Sāhib's position

Sikh accounts record that Gurū Har Rai Sāhib was deeply hurt by the compromising actions of Rām Rāi, who went against the Gurū's specific instructions,

> "Ram Rai should have even taken the risk of sacrificing his life to read and interpret the text of Gurū Nānak's Shabad. He should not have cared whether the interpretation pleased the emperor and his Islamic theologians. The Gurū's Word explains the Truth, which no sensible man can deny. Instead of humiliating himself by submitting to fear and dread of the emperor, Ram Rai should have shown the fearlessness and courage which all disciplined Sikhs are expected to have. He would then have been

worthy of my love, my favour and blessings. I wrote to him to leave the court after the first five or six meetings with the emperor, but he disregarded my orders and followed Aurangzeb like a lackey to Agra and other places during the past few months. Let him now enjoy the patronage and favours of the Mughal court. I have decided to disown and disinherit him". [12]

This is quite a fascinating response from the Gurū because it illustrates the Gurū's intention to place the welfare of the Sikh movement, the Sikh Panth, before their own familial and worldly attachments, a feature of the Gurū-ship period that is often only attributed to Gurū Gobind Singh. However, as we've seen, each of the Gurū Sāhibān, including Gurū Har Rai Sāhib, placed allegiance to the Sikh movement above all other commitments. Kavi Santokh Singh also provides more context to this episode by narrating how Gurū Har Rāi Sāhib referred to the resilience and resistance shown by Gurū Nānak Sāhib during the Udassīs; that despite encountering the most bloodthirsty rulers of various kingdoms, and the miracle-working yogis, mullahs, and qazis, from Dacca in the East to Mecca and Medina in the West, he fearlessly asserted the truth of Gurmat.

Similarly, Gurū Arjan Sāhib refused either to show miracles or compromise on any issue with his imperial torturers.[13] But Rām Rāi "danced attendance on Aurangzeb like a loyal Mughal courtier and followed him wherever he went". He was disowned and left to enjoy royal favours and privileges of the Mughal Darbār. Kavī Santokh Singh narrates how the Gurū stated he should not even return to the country:

"ਛੋਰਹਿ ਅਬਿ ਤੇ ਮੇਲ ਹਮਾਰੋ। ਕਰਿ ਐਸ਼ਰਜ ਕੋ ਰਹੋ ਸੁਖਾਰੋ।
ਧਰਸਹਿ ਨਹਿੰ ਦਰਸਾਵਹਿ ਦਰਸ਼ਨ। ਕਰਹੁ ਤੁਰਕ ਲਛਮੀ ਜੁ
ਸਪਰਸ਼ਨ ॥ ੩੦ ॥

Srī Gurū Har Rāi Sāhib jī Mahārāj

ਇਤਿ ਮੁਖ ਕਰਿ ਇਸ ਦੇਸ਼ ਨ ਆਵਹੁ। ਉਤ ਹੀ ਬਸਿ ਕਰਿ ਬੈਸ ਬਿਤਆਵਹੁ।
ਅਪਰਾਧੀ ਸ੍ਰੀ ਨਾਨਕ ਕੇਰ। ਹਮ ਸੋਂ ਨੇਰ ਹੋਇ ਕਿਮ ਫੇਰ" ॥੩੧॥

"Now he should not meet me, he should remain happy with his wealth [acquired from the Delhi Darbar]. I will not visit him anymore; he should remain with the wealth and money provided by the Turks.
He should not turn this way and come to this country, rather he should live out his life there. That person who turns away from Srī Gurū Nānak, how can he be considered close to me?"[14]

Kavi Santokh Singh's choice of words, particularly "country", demonstrates a sense of separateness between Delhi and the Gurū's Darbar in Kīratpur Sāhib, Panjāb, to the extent that they were perceived as separate political dominions. We shall see this remained a constant reality for the Sikhs throughout the Gurū period and the 150 years leading up to the colonial encounter. Pre-colonial texts show those who had pledged their allegiance to the institute of Gurū Granth and Gurū Panth always united on matters relating to the political sovereignty of the Sikh Nation. They understood it was of utmost importance, and they recognised the Gurū's Darbār as a separate political dominion to Delhi and any otherworldly power structure.

Rām Rāi shows remorse

It should be noted that Rām Rāi is said to have shown great remorse, sending a letter to Gurū Har Rāi Sāhib admitting his grave errors in disregarding the Gurū's instructions. He is said to have shown sincere repentance over what he had done in the court of Aurangzeb and that he was willing to accept any punishment from his father. The Gurū, however, remained firm on his position; that Rām Rāi had demonstrated he was not fit to remain in the Gurū's Darbār, let alone be in contention to take on the Guruship. This illustrates the consequences of compromising on Gurmat, which is of utmost importance in the Sikh world.

Sikh history then records how Rām Rāi turned to his uncle, Dhīr Mal, elder brother of Gurū Har Rāi Sāhib, for support. He penned a letter to Dhīr Mal in which he details his mistake and gives an ultimatum of sorts in which he referred to the decision taken by Gurū Rām Dās Sāhib to ignore his eldest son Prithī Chand and bestow Gurūship to Gurū Arjan Sāhib. If you recall, we considered Prithī Chand earlier in this section; he founded the Mīnās. Rām Rāi inferred this was a wrong choice because of the conflict it caused with the family and ultimately led to the martyrdom of Gurū Arjan Sāhib, thus trying to draw parallels in an attempt to convince Dhīr Mal that he should be forgiven.[15] Dhīr Mal accepted Rām Rāi's request and, along with his mother, went to visit his younger brother, Gurū Har Rāi Sāhib.

Gurū Sāhib's position reaffirmed

Kavī Santokh Singh again provides a very vivid depiction of the response that came from Gurū Har Rāi Sāhib. It is worth referring to this here. He narrates,

> *"Gurū Nānak Sāhib ignored their otherwise noble and virtuous sons, and appointed their most devoted and enlightened disciple Angad, as the successor. Gurū Angad's sons abandoned themselves to yogic centres of influence. They were disregarded as incompetent and unsuitable to either grasp the inner depths of Sikh mysticism or to shoulder the heavy responsibilities of the Sikh Sangat. Gurū Angad bestowed Gurūship on his 70-year-old disciple Amar Dās. Gurū Amar Das ignored their son Mohan because he was such an intoxicated contemplative, that he was too unworldly and too*

egoistic, spiritually, to shoulder the burden of Guru Nānak's faith and institutions. Prithi Chand the eldest son of Guru Ram Das, was disobedient, haughty, over-ambitious for material gains and powers. He befriended and sought the patronage of the Mughal governor and commanders of Lahore. All these things, which Prithi Chand considered his special virtues disqualified him from the right to deserve Guruship. Subsequent history tells us how far they drifted from Sikhī. They have unashamedly compiled their own granth, captured with the political support of Mughal officers, the administration of Srī Darbār Sāhib. They have not only compromised with the Mughal rulers on the political and cultural plane, but they call themselves Bhaktias (Vaishnava Hindus). How correct Guru Ram Dās was in ignoring Prithi Chand and selecting their youngest son is proved by subsequent history. The peerless Guru Arjan was selected because they alone had the fearlessness, the purity of heart, the dynamic wisdom and courage of conviction, and the fortitude to suffer for the unshakable ideas of Sikhī. They refused to show any miracles and accepted the cup of martyrdom because to abide by the Will of Akāl and stand for Truth and conviction was the highest stage of spirituality in Sikhī. Guruship in the past has always gone to the perfect soul, the most Divinely illumined, and above all the most deserving. So, it will in the future".[16]

Kavi Santokh Singh narrates how Guru Sāhib went on to conclude that if Rām Rāi is forgiven just because he is the Guru's son, it would set the most dangerous precedent in Sikh history, and it will become impossible for future generations to preserve the sanctity and immutability of the Guru Granth Sāhib. The overall message was that the sacred Word of the Gurū cannot be altered to suit the whims of the present and future rulers, otherwise, there would be no end to the degradation that may set in. Rām Rāi had to face the consequences of his misdemeanor. This carries an enormous political connotation in that Gurū Sāhib recognised from Rām Rāi's actions that he was not capable of upholding the sanctity and sovereignty of Gurū Nānak's Darbār. Whilst Rām Rāi may in theory have understood the ramifications of Aurangzeb, or indeed any other ruler or king, imposing his political power over the Sikhs, he was heavily misled by the Masands who had ulterior motives.

Aurangzeb infiltrates the Masands and Amritsar

It was during this time that Aurangzeb and his agents began to infiltrate the various institutions set up by the Gurū Sāhibān, including the network of Masands, who were now showing signs of turning their backs on the Gurū's Darbār. There was also the emergence of Dhīr Mal, the Gurū's brother and the Mīnās (previously founded by Prithī Chand), who were working against the socio-political advancement of the Sikh movement. Both felt they ought to have succeeded to the Throne of Gurū Nānak Sāhib and colluded at varying degrees with the imperial government.

As the Gurū was based in Kīratpur Sāhib, Sri Darbār Sāhib remained under the temporal control and influence of the Mīnās and Meharvān, followed by his son Harji for a period of about 60 years from 1635 to 1695. The Mīnās wreaked havoc as they tried to distort Gurmat, introducing mythology into the teachings of Gurmat with the help of Mughal collusion. This was a major concern for the Gurū, who worked to disassociate the Sikh community from the influence of the Minas by training and dispatching new Masands, tasked with the job of spreading Gurmat. Despite the occupation of anti-Gurmat forces within Amritsar, the Gurū continued forth with the expansion of the Sikh Panth and established new Manjhīs.

Gurū Sāhib establishes 360 new Manjhīs

Gurū Har Rāi Sāhib also made various expeditions throughout Panjāb which saw an increase in people from all backgrounds seek sanctuary within the Gurū's Darbār. We learn from Sarūp Dās that Bhagat Bhagwan and Bhāī Feru, two Sikhs of Gurū Har Rai Sāhib, were instrumental in spreading Sikhī. In an effort to counter the growing influence of Minas, it is recorded that Bhagat Bhagwan, under the stewardship of Gurū Har Rai Sāhib, established a further three-hundred and sixty centres or Manjhīs in and around Gaya and Patna, in the Bihar region. Bhāī Feru was sent in the opposite direction to the South of Lahore in modern-day Pakistan to organise the Sikhs in the same way. On the one hand, Gurū Sāhib was growing the Sikh movement, and on the other, their persona made even the biggest of egoist bow in reverence at the Gurū's Darbār in Kīratpur, including kings from the Northern regions.[17] The decision to establish new centres at this stage, despite growing tensions from the Minas and Dhirmals, demonstrates the Gurū's commitment to maintain sovereignty and continue growing the Sikh Panth.

The feats of Gurū Har Rāi Sāhib are recorded within the Persian works of Muhammad Qāsim "Ibrat" too, a translation of which is presented by Irfan Habib. Within this text, the author, who was a native of Lahore, writes,

> *"Group upon group of people bent their necks to follow and obey him, and glorified him through a thousand ways of giving him respect and honour".[18]*

Elsewhere, with the help of Aurangzeb, Rām Rāi had also succeeded in winning over a section of Sikhs to his side. Aurangzeb provided the resources he needed, including a piece of land to build a centre of influence. This piece of land was the foundation of present-day Dehradun in Panjāb. The descendants of Rām Rāi came to be known as Rām Rāiyas. They, alongside the Minas and descendants of Prithi Chand, are considered Bemukhs for betraying the Gurū and Sikh ideals.

Passing of the Gurūship

Gurū Har Rai Sāhib did not compose any Shabads, but as the seventh light of Gurū Nānak Sāhib, he held the utmost regard for Shabad and encouraged the Sikhs to live by the teachings espoused by the earlier Gurū Sāhibān. Sikh tradition holds that the Gurū was once asked whether there was any value to reciting Gurbānī without understanding the Shabad; the reply was yes, whether you comprehend it or not, the word bears the fruit of liberation. The metaphor he used was fragrance, how perfume persists in the broken pieces even after the vase that contained it has been shattered.

Dr Sangat Singh notes how traditional Sikh chroniclers do not provide any specific cause for the death of Gurū Har Rāi Sāhib, who left this world at the age of 31. He states how some have concluded that Gurū Har Rai Sāhib was poisoned by agents of the Mughal regime, at the behest of Aurangzeb.[19] This area requires more research but it would not be unbecoming of the Mughals, who had recognised the threat of Sikh sovereignty under the Gurū's reign.

Kavi Santokh Singh narrates the scene in which Gurū Har Krishan Sāhib took to the throne in 1661. Flags of the Gurū were hoisted high; guns were loaded and fired to mark the event, and joyous war cries were roared into the skies by the Gurū's beloved.[20] Thus Gurū Har Krishan Sāhib bowed before Gurū Har Rāi Sāhib and swore allegiance to uphold the sovereign seat of Gurū Nānak Sāhib and never to submit to the authority and threats of any worldly rulers.

NOTES

[1] Bhāī Nand Lal (1633-1713), *Ganjnama, Kalaam-e-Goya*, translated by Sardar Pritpal Singh Bindra, 2003, Institute of Sikh Studies, Chandigarh

[2] ਭਾਈ ਸਰੂਪ ਸਿੰਘ ਕੌਸ਼ਿਸ਼, ੧੭੯੦, ਗੁਰੂ ਕੀਆਂ ਸਾਖੀਆਂ
Bhai Swarup Singh Kaushish, 1790, *Gurū Kīān Sākhīān*, Sākhī 6, edited by Piara Singh Padam, 1986, Singh Brothers, Amritsar, p44

[3] Kaushish narrates how Rājā Deep Chand of Bilāspur felt obliged to visit the Gurū, since his grandfather, Kalyān Chand, had been emancipated by Gurū Hargobind Sāhib from the Fort of Gwalior, and they had a good relationship with the House of Gurū Nānak, narrating how he himself would visit the Gurū in Kīratpur with his father Rājā Tārā Chand. Sakhī 13, p56.

[4] Giānī Giān Singh, 1878, *Sri Gur Panth Prakāsh*, edited Giānī Kirpāl Singh, p121 and Satbir Singh, 1957, *Sada Itihas Life Story of Ten Masters*, 7th Edition, 1991, p296

[5] Giānī Giān Singh, *Tvārīkh Gurū Khālsā*, Chattar Singh Jeevan Singh, Amritsar, p480

[6] ਭਾਈ ਸਰੂਪ ਸਿੰਘ ਕੌਸ਼ਿਸ਼, ੧੭੯੦, ਗੁਰੂ ਕੀਆਂ ਸਾਖੀਆਂ
Bhai Swarup Singh Kaushish, 1790, *Gurū Kīān Sākhīān*, Sākhī 7, edited by Piara Singh Padam, 1986, Singh Brothers, Amritsar, p46

[7] Kavī Chūrāmanī Bhāī Santokh Singh, 1843, *Sri Gur Pratap Sūraj Granth*, Steek 7, Rās 9, Adhiāi 37, Line 1, Edited by Dr. Ajeet Singh Aulakh, 2014, 3rd Edition, p242

[8] ਸਰੂਪ ਦਾਸ ਭੱਲਾ, ੧੭੭੬, ਮਹਿਮਾ ਪ੍ਰਕਾਸ਼
Sārūp Das Bhalla, 1776, *Mehmā Prakāsh*, Edited by Dr. Uttam Singh Bhatia, 1971, Bagh 2, Khand 2, Sākhī 18, Bhasha Vibhag, Panjab, p576

[9] Giānī Giān Singh, *Tvārīkh Gurū Khālsā*, Chattar Singh Jeevan Singh, Amritsar, p481

[10] Gurū Nānak Sāhib, Raag Aasaa, Guru Granth Sahib, Ang 466 –
ਮਿਟੀ ਮੁਸਲਮਾਨ ਕੀ ਪੇੜੈ ਪਈ ਕੁਮ੍ਹਿਆਰ ॥
ਘੜਿ ਭਾਂਡੇ ਇਟਾ ਕੀਆ ਜਲਦੀ ਕਰੇ ਪੁਕਾਰ ॥

[11] ਭਾਈ ਸਰੂਪ ਸਿੰਘ ਕੌਸ਼ਿਸ਼, ੧੭੯੦, ਗੁਰੂ ਕੀਆਂ ਸਾਖੀਆਂ
Bhai Swarup Singh Kaushish, 1790, *Guru Kīān Sākhīān*, Sākhī 8, edited by Piara Singh Padam, 1986, Singh Brothers, Amritsar, p49

[12] ਸਰੂਪ ਦਾਸ ਭੱਲਾ, ੧੭੭੬, ਮਹਿਮਾ ਪ੍ਰਕਾਸ਼
Sārūp Das Bhalla, 1776, *Mehmā Prakāsh*, Edited by Dr. Uttam Singh Bhatia, 1971, Bagh 2, Khand 2, Sākhī 18, Bhasha Vibhag, Panjab, p576-590; translation taken from Trilochan Singh, *Life of Gurū Har Krishan*, p73

[13] Kavī Chūrāmanī Bhāī Santokh Singh, 1843, *Srī Gur Pratap Sūraj Granth*, Steek 7, Rās 9, Adhiāi 58, Line 23, Edited by Dr. Ajeet Singh Aulakh, 2014, 3rd Edition, p371

[14] Kavī Chūrāmanī Bhāī Santokh Singh, 1843, *Srī Gur Pratap Sūraj Granth*, Steek 7, Rās 9, Adhiāi 58, Line 31, Edited by Dr. Ajeet Singh Aulakh, 2014, 3rd Edition, p372

[15] Kavī Chūrāmanī Bhāī Santokh Singh, 1843, *Srī Gur Pratap Sūraj Granth*, Steek 7, Rās 10, Adhiāi 19 Edited by Dr. Ajeet Singh Aulakh, 2014, 3rd Edition, p500-505

[16] Kavī Chūrāmanī Bhāī Santokh Singh, 1843, *Srī Gur Pratap Sūraj Granth*, Steek 7, Rās 10, Adhiāi 20, Edited by Dr. Ajeet Singh Aulakh, 2014, 3rd Edition, p505; translation taken from Trilochan Singh, *Life of Gurū Har Krishan*, p79

[17] ਸਰੂਪ ਦਾਸ ਭੱਲਾ, ੧੭੭੬, ਮਹਿਮਾ ਪ੍ਰਕਾਸ਼
Sārūp Das Bhalla, 1776, *Mehmā Prakāsh*, Edited by Dr. Uttam Singh Bhatia, 1971, Bagh 2, Khand 2, Sākhī 15, Bhasha Vibhag, Panjab, p563

[18] Gurū Nānak, Guru Gobind Singh and the Revolt under Banda Bahādur 1709-10 & 1713-16, from Muhammad Qāsim "Ibrat", Ibratnama, translated by J. S. Grewal & Irfan Habib, 2001, *Sikh History from Persian Sources*, Tulika Books, Delhi, p112

[19] Dr Sangat Singh, 2014, *The Sikhs in History*, Singh Brothers, Amritsar, p51

[20] Kavī Chūrāmanī Bhāī Santokh Singh, 1843, *Srī Gur Pratap Sūraj Granth*, Steek 7, Rās 10, Adhiāi 27, Line 28-29, Edited by Dr. Ajeet Singh Aulakh, 2014, 3rd Edition, p551

Srī Gurū Har Krishan Sāhib Jī Maharaj

ਤੁਫ਼ੈਲਸ਼ ਦੋ ਆਲਮ ਬਵਦ ਕਾਮਯਾਬ
ਜ਼ਮੀਨੋ ਜ਼ਮਾਂ ਜਮਲਾ ਫ਼ਰਮਾਂਬਰਸ਼ ॥ ੯੬ ॥

> Due to [Gurū Har Krishan Sāhib's] goodwill both the worlds succeed. Due to this goodwill, even an iota attains sun-like splendour (96)[1]

The eighth light of Gurū Nānak Sāhib, Gurū Har Krishan Sāhib, led the Sikh movement for a short duration before his departure at the tender age of nine. Despite only ruling for just under three years, Gurū Sāhib was both mature and wise in his conduct and upheld the integral ideals of Sikh sovereignty throughout his Gurūship. It is likely that the Masands and other adversaries of the Gurū's Darbār would have succeeded in their mission to deliver fatal ideological blows to Gurmat if it were not for the leadership qualities of Gurū Har Krishan Sāhib. Not only did the Gurū keep the Masands and Minas at bay, but they further solidified the Sikh movement by upholding the traditions and customs of the earlier Gurū Sāhibān.

Astute leadership

Much like Gurū Har Rāi Sāhib, Gurū Har Krishan Sāhib oversaw a period of the Sikh movement in which there was no confrontation on the battlefield. That being said, the animosity from groups such as the Minas and Masands still existed, but the Gurū led the Sikhs wisely. This was the need of the time due to the tactics of the Masands and other agents of the imperial regime who were seeking to dilute and distort the Gurū's revolutionary way.

> *"With cautious and enlightened foresight, Gurū Har Krishan ignored the self-propagated popularity of Aurangzeb and Ram Rai and won the hearts of Hindus, Muslims and Sikhs alike by his matchless humanity and spirituality".*[2]

Bhāī Nand Lal jī, the court poet of Gurū Gobind Singh, writes, the distance separating Gurū Har Krishan Sāhib and Akāl Purakh is but the thickness of a leaf.[3] This sheds much light on the personality and character of Gurū Har Krishan Sāhib. Age has no value in this situation because the Divine Jot of Gurū is at work.

Gurū's Darbār at Kiratpur Sāhib

According to Dr. Trilochan Singh, Gurū Har Krishan Sāhib's rule can be divided into two distinct periods. The first period covers the duration of Gurū Sāhib's residence in Kīratpur Sāhib when people came from far and wide places such as Patna, Dacca, Kabul, and Peshawar, to share an audience with Sache Pātshāh. The Sikhs would bring news about the activities of Rām Rāi's followers and the Masands, who at this stage were doing their best to confuse the masses into believing Rām Rāi was the true heir to Gurū Nānak Sāhib's Throne.

The Gurū's instruction to the Sikhs was to ignore Rām Rāi and not associate with those who sought the patronage of Mughal rulers. Gurū Har Krishan Sāhib would advise those who had committed to uphold the ideals espoused by Gurū Nānak Sāhib to assemble in Kīratpur Sāhib and take guidance and instruction from the Gurū on how best to move forward. During this period, Gurū Sāhib approved copies of Adi Granth, which were presented to him by calligraphists and scribes. Gurū Sāhib also sent a Hukamnāmā to the Sikhs in

Srī Gurū Har Krishan Sāhib jī Mahārāj

Patna, an English translation of which was presented by Dr. Trilochan Singh in his 1981 work on Gurū Sāhib:

> *"Srī Gurū Har Krishan has ordered us [the Scribes of the Gurū's Darbār] to write to Bhāī Ani Rai, Bhāī Jas, Bhāī Ranga, Bhāī Hazuri, Bhāī Nehchal and the whole Sangat of Patna. Srī Gurū [Har Krishan] ji has received all the offerings and tithes of the congregation (Sangat) sent by hand with Bhāī Banno. Gurū ji is pleased and sends their blessings to the Sangat of Patna. Akāl shall fulfill the desires of all, and the Gurū will bless and pray for the fulfilment of the laborious and noble aspiration of all. Please continue to send the tithes. Always attend and participate in the congregation. Recite daily Arti and Sohila. Srī Gurū [Har Krishan Sāhib] is graciously pleased with the Sangat of Patna. Gurū ji will always come to the aid of those who seek his grace and blessings. Srī Gurū Har Krishan blesses you all."*[4]

Dr. Gandā Singh also referenced this Hukamnāmā in his work published in the 1960s.[5] He included a photocopy of the Hukamnāmā, which at the time was kept in the Sikh Reference Library, Amritsar. In this way, the Gurū spent time in Kīratpur Sāhib offering advice and guidance to the Sikh Sangat, received financial support to further the Sikh movement, and upheld the sovereignty of the Gurū's Darbār by not allowing the efforts of individuals such as Rām Rāi to go unchallenged.

Travelling to Delhi

The second period covers the duration of some five months before the Gurū's departure from this world, in which Gurū Sāhib travelled to

Delhi following an invitation from Rajput Prince, Mirza Raja Jai Singh, who sent an envoy bearing gifts as a mark of respect for the Gurū's Darbār.

Kavi Santokh Singh narrates this episode and notes that the envoy was welcomed with open arms and offered robes of honour and gifts to be sent back to Raja Jai Singh, along with the message that Gurū Har Krishan Sāhib would reach Delhi in two to three weeks. It is important to note here, that whilst Aurangzeb had tried many times to summon the Gurū to Delhi, the Gurū had refused to go, on the same basis as Gurū Har Rāi Sāhib, that they would not be used as a political tool in the hands of the Mughal rulers. In fact, as we have discussed in this section, all of the Gurū Sāhibān refused to attend the Mughal Court when summoned in a manner intended to subdue or indeed assert a degree of authority over the Gurū.

This tradition followed Gurū Nānak Sāhib's own declaration that in this Age of Kaljug, kings and rulers were tigers and their courtiers, dogs, who would harass the people as they slept, and pierced their nails into the bodies to suck their blood; a metaphor to highlight the extent of exploitation and falsehood prevalent in other worldly courts.

Gurū Har Krishan Sāhib left a large group of advisors and military guards in Kiratpur Sāhib, which perhaps indicates that the Gurū did not envisage a confrontation with the imperial forces of Delhi. It was during the Gurū's travels to Delhi that they encountered the proud Brahmin who, unable to comprehend the young Gurū's status as Sache Pātshah, began to question Gurū Sāhib about their knowledge of Hindu scripture.

It is quite a famous incident from Sikh history, so I shall not go into detail; however, the lesson for us here is in the Sikhīa that Gurū Sāhib imparted on the proud Brahmin. He was taught the true meaning of Brahmin, as told by Gurū Arjan Sāhib in Salok Sehaskriti[6], that only he is a true Brahmin who has the knowledge of Akāl Purakh. The writings of true Brahmins, such as Bhagat Kabīr ji, Bhagat Ravi Das ji, and Bhagat Nām Dev ji are included in the Gurū Granth Sāhib because they exemplified the true essence of the word Brahmin. Such were the blessings of the Gurū that even during their travels, the Gurū would impart profound knowledge on the most ignorant and ego-ridden individuals of the land.

Meeting with the emperor

There appears to be some conflict as to whether Gurū Har Krishan Sāhib met Aurangzeb or not. Dr. Trilochan Singh accepts that scholar Sarūp Das Bhalla, author of the 18th-century Mehima Prakāsh, depicts a meeting between Gurū Sāhib and Aurangzeb. (Not to be confused with Kripal Singh's Mehima Prakāsh Vartak, written in 1741.) Sarūp Das Bhalla is said to have been a ninth-generation descendent of Gurū Amar Dās Sāhib.

Sārūp Das Bhalla narrates how Raja Jai Singh met Aurangzeb. He details the meeting at some length in his third story related to Gurū Har Krishan Sāhib entitled 'Sākhī Aurangzeb Baadshah se milaap ki":

ਪੁਨ ਰਾਜਾ ਬਾਦਸਾਹ ਪੈ ਗਏ।
ਬਾਦਸਾਹ ਜਹ ਪੂਛਤ ਭਏ।
ਗੁਰੂ ਹਰਿ ਕ੍ਰਿਸਨ ਹੈ ਬਾਲਕ ਰੂਪ।
ਕਹੋਂ ਸਿਫਤ ਸਭ ਅਮਿਤ ਅਨੂਪ।੨।
ਤਬ ਰਾਜੇ ਮਹਮਾ ਗੁਰ ਕੀ ਕਰੀ।
ਕਰ ਸਿਫਤ ਬ੍ਰਿਤੰਤ ਸਭ ਮੁਖੋਂ ਉਚਰੀ।
ਤਬ ਸੁਨ ਨੋਰੰਗਸਾਹ ਭਏ ਨਰਮ।
ਦੇਖਨ ਕੋ ਭਈ ਉਲਫਤ ਗਰਮ।੩।[7]

Sarūp Dās Bhalla describes how Aurangzeb questioned why a child was sat on the throne of Gurū Nānak Sāhib, but Raja Jai Singh responded to the questions by singing of the Gurū's glory. Seemingly impressed with the responses, Aurangzeb declared he wished to meet the Gurū and asked the Raja to convey that message to Gurū Sāhib. He provided gifts to be sent with Raja Jai Singh as an offering for the Gurū. Sarūp Das then narrates the part that Dr Trilochan Singh refers to:

ਰਾਜਾ ਗਏ ਸਤਗੁਰ ਕੇ ਪਾਸ।
ਹਾਥ ਜੋੜ ਕੀਨੀ ਅਰਦਾਸ।
ਬਾਦਸਾਹ ਮਿਲਨੇ ਕੋ ਚਹੈ।
ਜੋ ਆਗਿਆ ਹੋਏ ਸੋਈ ਹਮ ਕਹੈ।੮।੮

> Raja Jai Singh then went to see Gurū Har Krishan Sāhib. Clasping his palms in reverence he informed Gurū Sāhib; "the emperor wishes to meet you; whatever was asked of me I have delivered".

According to Sārūp Das Bhalla, Gurū Har Krishan Sāhib offered a wry smile and agreed to proceed to meet Aurangzeb with both Raja Jai Singh and Rām Rāi. The author narrates the questions Aurangzeb asked about why Gurū Har Krishan Sāhib was chosen as the successor of Gurū Har Rai Sāhib, and not Rām Rāi, even though Rām Rāi was the elder son.[9]

Rām Rāi then answers that Gurū Har Krishan Sāhib is the rightful heir to Gurū Nānak Sāhib's Throne because they were chosen as such by Gurū Har Rai Sāhib, and refers to his own disobedience. Despite Dr Trilochan Singh's reliance on Mehima Prakāsh, he refutes the meeting took place. He appears to cite a passage not in the edition referred to in this book, in which he quotes the Gurū as having stated they will not go to the court to meet the emperor.[10] Dr Trilochan Singh also states that no other historical record shows a meeting between Gurū Har Krishan Sāhib and Aurangzeb.

On the contrary, I have found another account that is an almost identical depiction of the meeting described by Sarūp Das Bhalla. This account is held by the author of Guru Kīan Sākhīa, Swarūp Singh Kaushish, who compiled his work in 1790. He narrates the account in section 18 entitled, "ਸਾਖੀ ਗੁਰੂ ਹਰਿਕ੍ਰਿਸ਼ਨ ਜੀ ਕੀ ਸ਼ਾਹੀ ਦਰਬਾਰ ਮੇਂ

ਜਾਨੇ ਕੀ" - Story related to Gurū Har Krishan Sāhib's visit to the court [of Aurangzeb]:[11]

> ਬਾਦਸ਼ਾਹ ਨੇ ਬਾਲਾ ਗੁਰੂ ਜੀ ਕਾ ਸਤਿਕਾਰ ਕੀਆ। ਬਾਦ ਮੇਂ ਸ੍ਰੀ ਰਾਮ ਰਾਜਾ ਜੀ ਸੇ ਪੂਛਨਾਂ ਕੀ, ਪੀਰ ਜੀ! ਹਮਾਰੀ ਸ਼ੰਕਾ ਕੋ ਨਿਵਿਰਾ ਕਰੀਏ। ਦੇਖੀਏ ਆਪ ਬਡੇ ਥੇ, ਤੁਮੇਂ ਜਿਹ ਪਦਵੀ ਕਿਉਂ ਨਾ ਦਈ ਗਈ। ਆਪ ਇਸ ਮੇਂ ਮੇਰੀ ਨਿਸ਼ਾ ਕਰੀਏ। ਕਿਆ ਆਪ ਕਾ ਅਪਮਾਨ ਨਹੀਂ ਹੁਆ?

"The emperor welcomed the young Gurū with respect. He then turned to Rām Rāi and asked, "Pir ji, please eliminate my doubts; you were older, so why were you not bestowed with this throne, please enlighten me, don't you think you've been disrespected?""

Kaushish presents a very similar account of the line of questioning as portrayed by Sarūp Dās Bhalla. In response to the above, Kaushish narrates that Rām Rāi spoke and answered as such:

> ਬਾਦਸ਼ਾਹ ਗੁਰਿਆਈ ਕਿਸੇ ਕੀ ਮਲਕੀਤੀ ਵਸਤੁ ਨਹੀਂ, ਪਿਤਾ ਜੀ ਸਰਬ-ਕਲਾ ਸੰਪੂਰਨ ਥੇ। ਮੁਝੇ ਉਨੈ ਜਹਾਂ ਭੇਜ ਦੀਆ ਥਾ, ਹਮ ਉਨ ਕੀ ਅਗਿਆ ਪਾਇ ਜਹਾਂ ਆਇ ਗਏ ਸੀ। ਉਪਰੰਤ ਉਨੈ ਇਸੇ ਸਹੀ ਅਧਿਕਾਰੀ ਦੇਖ ਇਨ ਕੋ ਗੁਰਤਾ ਦੇ ਦਈ ਹੈ। ਮਰਜਾਦਾ ਅਨੁਸਾਰ ਹੁਣ ਇਹ ਗੁਰੂ ਨਾਨਕ ਜੀ ਕੀ ਗਾਦੀ ਤੇ ਇਸਥਿੱਤ ਹੈ, ਹਮ ਅਬ ਇਨ ਕੇ ਬਚਨੋਂ ਕੇ ਅਧੀਨ ਹੈਂ।

"Emperor, the Gurgaddi is not an individual's domain My father possessed all virtues. My father asked me to come here, and obeying this order, I came here. Above all, deeming [Gurū Har Krishan Sāhib] to be competent, my father endowed the Gurgaddi to them. As per tradition, they are now seated on the throne of Gurū Nānak. I am now under their command".

Kaushish then narrates how Aurangzeb, seemingly pleased with the meeting, suggested they rest, perhaps in view of Guru Sāhib's illness, with the intent of having further discourse in the following days. However, Kaushish notes that Gurū Sāhib's health began to deteriorate that evening as the onset of smallpox started to take its toll on Gurū Sāhib's body.

Purpose of visiting Delhi

As mentioned, other historians such as Puran Singh[12] and before him writers such as Kavī Santokh Singh in Gur Pratap Suraj Granth and Kesar Singh Chibbar in Bansāvalīnāmā suggest that no meeting took place. Notwithstanding the apparent uncertainty expressed by some historians about whether an actual meeting took place or not, the significance of Gurū Har Krishan Sāhib's visit to Delhi lies in the fact that Gurū Sāhib arrived in Delhi as a guest of Raja Jai Singh. Kavi Santokh Singh records Gurū Har Krishan Sāhib had expressed great joy in the invitation from Raja Jai Singh.[13]

Furthermore, Gurū Sāhib did not hide the fact that they went to Delhi partly in acceptance of the invitation from Raja Jai Singh, but also to address the Sikh community in Delhi, who had been misguided by Rām Rāi and the Masands. With Amritsar also still under the control of the Mīnās, it was an opportunity to reassert the sanctity and sovereignty of Gurū's Darbār, under attack from various adversaries in Delhi.

We must also consider the actions of the Gurū in Delhi, that during the health pandemic ravaging the city at the time, they remained on the front line to offer support and counsel to the grief-stricken residents. Giānī Gian Singh notes how one of Gurū Sāhib's officials, Bhāī Gurbaksh, was charged with the duty of dispensing herbal medicine and offering Charan Amrit of the Gurū to combat the disease, which saved many lives.[14]

Therefore, Gurū Har Krishan Sāhib was following in the examples set by Gurū Har Rai Sāhib. Dr Trilochan Singh provides great clarity when he states,

"... Aurangzeb and Ram Rai had combined their forces for political control of Guruship of the Sikhs, while Guru Har Krishan was determined to preserve the moral and spiritual integrity of his position even at the cost of his life. While the common man who sympathised with the Child-Guru was panic-stricken at the very thought of what might happen. Guru Har Krishan alone grasped the truth and reality of the situation and remained cheerfully calm and courageously composed. He alone was able to visualise the infinite power sustaining his soul. He reacted with kingly dignity, forethought and independence of mind at all the sinister moves of Ram Rai and Aurangzeb". [15]

Passing of the Gurūship

Kaushish narrates a very important episode, which revealed Gurū Har Krishan Sāhib's appointment of the next Gurū. In their last moments, surrounded by their counsel of Sikhs, Kaushish narrates;

"ਸਤਿਗੁਰੂ ਆਂਖ ਉਘੇੜ ਇਨ ਕੀ ਤਰਫ ਦੇਖਾ, ਧੀਮੀ ਅਵਾਜ਼ ਸੇ ਬਚਨ ਹੋਆ – ਪਾਂਚ ਪੈਸੇ ਨਲੀਏਰ ਲੈ ਆਉ। ਬਚਨ ਪਾਇ ਨਿਕਟ ਬੈਠੇ ਦੀਵਾਨ ਦਰਘਾ ਮੱਲ ਜੀ ਗੁਰਿਆਈ ਕੀ ਸਮੱਗਰੀ ਲੈ ਆਏ। ਗੁਰੂ ਜੀ ਨੇ ਇਸੇ ਹਾਥ ਛੁਹਾਇ ਤੀਨ ਦਫਾ ਦਾਈਂ ਭੁਜਾ ਹਿਲਾਇ ਕੇ ਕਹਾ – 'ਹਮਾਰੇ ਪੀਛੇ ਸਿੱਖ ਸੰਗਤਾ ਕਾ ਗੁਰੂ ਮੇਰਾ ਬਾਬਾ, ਬਕਾਲਾ ਨਗਰੀ ਮੇਂ ਹੈ, ਉਨ ਕਾ ਦਰਸ਼ਨ ਪਾਈਏ! ਦੀਵਾਨ ਜੀ! ਇਹ ਗੁਰਿਆਈ ਕੀ ਸਮੱਗਰੀ ਬਕਾਲਾ ਗਾਊਂ ਮੇਂ ਲੈ ਜਾਇ ਕੇ ਬਾਬਾ ਸ੍ਰੀ ਤੇਗ ਬਹਾਦਰ ਜੀ ਆਗੇ ਭੇਟਾ ਕਰ ਦੇਨੀ। ਉਸਬ ਕੇ ਬਾਦ ਆਜ ਸੇ ਸਿੱਖ ਸੰਗਤਾ ਕਾ ਸਤਿਗੁਰ ਬਕਾਲਾ ਨਗਰੀ ਵਾਲਾ ਬਾਬਾ ਜੀ ਹਨ। ਸੰਗਤਾ ਜਾਇ ਕੇ ਉਨਾਂ ਕੇ ਦਰਸ਼ਨ ਪਾਵਣ'। ਇਤਨਾ ਬਚਨ ਕਹਿ ਕੇ

ਗੁਰੂ ਜੀ ਕੀ ਲਿਵ ਉਸ ਨਿਰੰਕਾਰ ਗੈਲ ਲਗ ਗਈ, ਸ਼ਬਦ ਕੀਰਤਨ ਹੋਨੇ ਲਾਗਾ"।

"Satguru opened their eyes and looked towards them and, in very low tone, remarked, "Bring five paise (coins) and a coconut." From those who were sitting beside him, Durgah Mal went and brought the items requested for bestowing Guruship. Guru Ji touched it and said, "After me, the Guru for the Sikh Congregations will be my Baba, who is at the town of Bakālā, have his darshan. Diwan Jee, you better take this material to the village Bakālā and present it before Srī Guru Tegh Bahādur Ji. From now on the Satguru of the Sikhs is Baba Ji at the town of Bakālā. People should go and have his darshan." And after saying so, Guru Ji was immersed within Nirankar, Shabad Kirtan resounded."16

This is perhaps one of the most interesting accounts found in the writings of Kaushish because Gurū Har Krishan Sāhib is said to have explicitly stated "my Baba", literally their grandfather's brother, Gurū Tegh Bahādur Sāhib, as the rightful heir to Gurū Nānak Sāhib's Throne. There is no ambiguity in their choice of words; the Sikh Sangat in attendance were told exactly who in Bakālā the Gurū was referring to. It is a little surprising to note Dr. Trilochan Singh omits this reference in his otherwise splendid work on Gurū Har Krishan Sāhib. He instead opted to cite Parchian Patshahi Das, Mehmā Prakāsh and Kavi Santokh Singh's Gurpratap Sūraj Granth, all of whom can be said to offer less certainty over the exact person Gurū Har Krishan Sāhib had chosen, merely stating "the Baba resides in Bakālā". Thus, another example of how Kaushish' Gurū Kīan Sākhīān contains valuable accounts, not available anywhere else.

Srī Gurū Har Krishan Sāhib jī Māhārāj

NOTES

[1] Bhāī Nand Lal (1633-1713), *Ganjnama, Kalaam-e-Goya*, translated by Sardar Pritpal Singh Bindra, 2003, Institute of Sikh Studies, Chandigarh

[2] Dr. Trilochan Singh, Life of Gurū Har Krishan, 1981, p93

[3] Bhāī Nand Lal (1633-1713), *Ganjnama, Kalaam-e-Goya*, translated by Sardar Pritpal Singh Bindra, 2003, Institute of Sikh Studies, Chandigarh, p177

[4] Dr. Trilochan Singh, 1981, *Life of Gurū Har Krishan*, Introduction, pxvi

[5] Dr. Ganda Singh, 1967, *Hukamname Sikh Guru, Mata Sahiban, Baba Banda Singh and Guru Ke Khalse De*, 1967, Baldev Singh, Kapurthala, New Revised Edition, 2015, p.74-75

[6] Guru Arjan Sāhib, Salok Sehaskriti, Guru Granth Sāhib, Ang 1360

[7] ਸਰੂਪ ਦਾਸ ਭੱਲਾ, ੧੭੭੬, ਮਹਿਮਾ ਪ੍ਰਕਾਸ਼

Sārūp Das Bhalla, 1776, *Mehmā Prakāsh*, Edited by Dr. Uttam Singh Bhatia, 1971, Bagh 2, Khand 2, Sākhī 3, Bhasha Vibhag, Panjab, p613

[8] ਸਰੂਪ ਦਾਸ ਭੱਲਾ, ੧੭੭੬, ਮਹਿਮਾ ਪ੍ਰਕਾਸ਼

Sārūp Das Bhalla, 1776, *Mehmā Prakāsh*, Edited by Dr. Uttam Singh Bhatia, 1971, Bagh 2, Khand 2, Sākhī 3, Bhasha Vibhag, Panjab, p614

[9] ਸਰੂਪ ਦਾਸ ਭੱਲਾ, ੧੭੭੬, ਮਹਿਮਾ ਪ੍ਰਕਾਸ਼

Sārūp Das Bhalla, 1776, *Mehmā Prakāsh*, Edited by Dr. Uttam Singh Bhatia, 1971, Bagh 2, Khand 2, Sākhī 3, Bhasha Vibhag, Panjab, p615

[10] Dr. Trilochan Singh, 1981, *Life of Gurū Har Krishan*, p150

[11] ਭਾਈ ਸਰੂਪ ਸਿੰਘ ਕੌਸ਼ਿਸ਼, ੧੭੯੦, ਗੁਰੂ ਕੀਆਂ ਸਾਖੀਆਂ

Bhai Swarup Singh Kaushish, 1790, *Gurū Kīan Sākhīān*, Sākhī 1, edited by Piara Singh Padam, 1986, Singh Brothers, Amritsar, p63

[12] Professor Puran Singh, 1920, *The Book of The Ten Masters*, Singh Brothers, Amritsar, p97

[13] Kavī Chūrāmanī Bhāī Santokh Singh, 1843, *Srī Gur Pratap Sūraj Granth*, Steek 7, Rās 10, Adhiāi 33 to 36, Edited by Dr. Ajeet Singh Aulakh, 2014, 3rd Edition, p587-609

[14] Giānī Giān Singh, 1891, *Tvārīkh Gurū Khālsā*, Chattar Singh Jeevan Singh, Amritsar, p495

[15] Dr. Trilochan Singh, 1981, *Life of Gurū Har Krishan*, p136

[16] ਭਾਈ ਸਰੂਪ ਸਿੰਘ ਕੌਸ਼ਿਸ਼, ੧੭੯੦, ਗੁਰੂ ਕੀਆਂ ਸਾਖੀਆਂ Bhai Swarup Singh Kaushish, 1790, *Gurū Kīān Sākhīān*, Sākhī 18, edited by Piara Singh Padam, 1986, Singh Brothers, Amritsar, p64

Srī Gurū Tegh Bahādur Sāhib jī Maharaj

ਅਨਵਾਰਿ ਹੱਕ ਅਜ਼ ਵਜੂਦਿ ਪਾਕਿਸ਼ ਰੌਸ਼ਨ
ਹਰ ਦੋ ਆਲਮ ਜ਼ਿ ਫ਼ੈਜ਼ਿ ਫ਼ਜ਼ਲਸ਼ ਰੌਸ਼ਨ ॥ ੧੦੦ ॥

The rays of truth sparkle through [Gurū Tegh Bahādur Sāhib's] entity, both the worlds are illuminated due to [Gurū Tegh Bahādur Sāhib's] kindness. 100.[1]

Gurū Tegh Bahādur Sāhib, the ninth light of Gurū Nānak Sāhib, was born on 1 April 1621 and bestowed with Gurūship on 11 August 1664 following the departure of Gurū Har Krishan Sāhib. The responsibility of furthering the Sikh identity and movement that had been nurtured by the previous 8 Gurū Sāhibān, now rested with Gurū Tegh Bahādur Sāhib.

Gurū Tegh Bahādur Sāhib was the youngest of the five sons of Gurū Hargobind Sāhib, the sixth light of Gurū Nānak Sāhib. The author of Gurbilās Pātshahi 6 narrates that upon seeing young Gurū Tegh Bahādur Sāhib for the first time, Gurū Hargobind Sāhib declared they would take the office of Gurū one day, to protect the weak and relieve their distress.

Expanse of sovereign Sikh spaces

Let's consider for a moment the expanse of Gurū Sāhib's reign by this stage. Towns and sovereign Sikh spaces established by the Gurū Sāhibān included Kartārpur Sāhib, Khadūr Sāhib, Goindvāl Sāhib, Amritsar Sāhib, Tarn Tāran Sāhib, Kartārpur Sāhib (Jalandhar) and

ਪਾਤਿਸ਼ਾਹੀ ਮਹਿਮਾ – Revisiting Sikh Sovereignty

Kīratpur Sāhib. In addition to the physical establishment of Sikh centres, the decision to establish the network of Manjhīs under Gurū Amar Dās Sāhib and later their evolution into the Masands under Gurū Ram Dās Sāhib had a radical impact upon the dissemination of Gurmat to the people across Panjāb, and the neighbouring regions. Whilst Sikhī was growing, and the Gurū's appointed emissaries were travelling far and wide, the central base of operation remained in Panjāb. During the reign of Gurū Tegh Bahādur Sāhib's father, Gurū Hargobind Sāhib, the City of Amritsar served as the capital, which is where Gurū Tegh Bahādur Sāhib spent the majority of his early years.

They would have experienced the city's magnificence as Sikhs, from far and wide, would travel and assemble to pay their respects to Gurū Hargobind Sāhib. Gifts of weapons and horses were especially brought here during the gatherings during the months of Vaisākhī and Bandi Chorr Divas. Harbans Singh notes,

> "... In front of the Akal Takht, an edifice erected by Guru Hargobind, were held contests in martial skills. Here the bards, Abdullah and Nattha, recited heroic poetry. At the Akal Takht, Guru Hargobind sat in state and convened assemblies of Sikhs and delivered sermons. As Bhai Buddha managed the Harmandir, Bhai Gurdas managed the Akal Takht. Bhai Gurdas ranked with the former in Sikh hierarchy. He was a man of wide learning and wrote elegant verse both in Braj and Punjabi. He was learned in ancient texts and had calligraphed the first copy of the Adi Granth at the dictation of Guru Arjun. He chronicled in poetry events from the lives of the preceding Gurus and their Sikhs and gave exposition of the Sikh doctrine. In this city of Amritsar, permeated with a fresh spiritual leaven and with a fervent spirit of devotion and moral vigour."[2]

Thus, under Gurū Sāhib's reign, Amritsar was a lively and cultured place for Sikhs to exist. However, this experience was short-lived for Gurū Tegh Bahādur Sāhib due to the invasion by the Mughal emperor's army and the occupation of the Mīnās that we discussed previously. Gurū Tegh Bahādur Sāhib moved to Goindvāl Sāhib where he was raised under the guidance and tutelage of Baba Buddhā jī, who trained him in archery and horsemanship, and Bhāī Gurdās jī who supervised languages and poetry.

Early involvement within Gurū's Darbār

According to Gurbilās Pātshahi 6, Gurū Tegh Bahādur Sāhib married Mata Gujri jī on 4th February 1633. Sikhs congregated in Kartārpur Sāhib (Jalandhar), travelling from Goindvāl Sāhib, Khadūr Sāhib, Amritsar, Mandiali, Batala, Kangar, and other places. Elsewhere, Kavi Santokh Singh also narrates how Gurū Tegh Bahādur Sāhib's mother, Mata Nānaki jī, would often ask their husband, Gurū Hargobind Sāhib, how they felt their son could attain the rank of Gurū, because they were quiet and humble in demeanour, seemingly devoid of worldly ambition. Kavi Santokh Singh notes Gurū Hargobind Sāhib's response,

> *"Tegh Bahadur can suffer what none other can. His forbearance is unsurpassed. He is master of many Virtues. Without a peer is he in this world. This is one reason which entitles him to acknowledgement. Secondly, a son will be born to him who will be mighty of limb and be the vanquisher of foes. He will take part in many a battle. He will excel in both valour and compassion. He will bring fame to the House of Guru Nanak, the world-teacher".[3]*

As mentioned earlier, Gurū Hargobind Sāhib went to war with Mughal forces on several occasions, and Gurū Tegh Bahādur Sāhib, at the age of 14, was involved in the Battle of Kartārpur, April 1635, caused by Paindah Khan. The training that Gurū Tegh Bahādur Sāhib had received in their formative years was put to the test, and Kavi Santokh Singh records how they made bold charges against the enemy in all directions. When they were asked to fall back, it is recorded that Gurū Tegh Bahādur Sāhib, like their brothers, answered it was unrighteous to turn one's back on the battlefield.[4]

Whilst the two leading stalwarts of the Gurū's Darbār, Baba Buddhā jī and Bhāī Gurdās jī had both passed on by this stage, following the Battle of Kartārpur, Gurū Hargobind Sāhib shifted to Kīratpur Sāhib where they spent the last nine years of their life. Harbans Singh notes one noteworthy absentee, Dhīr Mal, the elder son of Baba Gurditta jī, thus the grandson of Gurū Hargobind Sāhib. He remained in Kartārpur Sāhib (Jalandhar) and refused to part with the Adi Granth Sāhib, which had come into his possession. If you recall, we briefly considered Dhīr Mal in the section pertaining to Gurū Har Rai Sāhib. He was not happy about seeing his younger brother take the Throne of Gurū Nānak Sāhib and thus sought refuge and support from the Mughal regime, who helped him infiltrate the various institutions set up by the Gurū Sāhibān, including the network of Masands. In 1643 he received a revenue-free grant and propped himself up as an heir to the throne of Gurū Nānak Sāhib. Following the passing of Gurū Har Krishan Sāhib, Dhīr Mal even shifted to Bakālā in the hope of being selected for succession to the throne.

Time in Bakālā

The town of Bakālā, located in the district of Amritsar, had become a second home for Gurū Tegh Bahādur Sāhib, since they moved there from Kīratpur Sāhib, following the passing of Gurū Hargobind Sāhib. Sukha Singh, the author of Gurbilās Pātshahi 10, describes Bakālā as a prosperous town with many beautiful pools, wells, and *baolis*. This is where Gurū Tegh Bahādur Sāhib spent most of their time in contemplation but was by no means a recluse. They attended to family responsibilities and remained engaged in horse riding and training. They were also kept informed about the happenings in the Gurū's Darbār, under Gurū Har Rai Sāhib and Gurū Har Krishan Sāhib. It is from Bakālā that Gurū Tegh Bahādur Sāhib also travelled eastward to spread the Gurū's wisdom. Harbans Singh narrates how following his journey to the east, Gurū Tegh Bahādur Sāhib arrived in Delhi,

> "...when he heard the news of Guru Har Krishan's having been summoned by Emperor Aurangzeb. The next day, he called at the house of Raja Jai Singh in Raisina to condole with Guru Har Krishan on the death of his father. Tegh Bahadur did not stay in Delhi much longer and resumed his journey back to the Punjab. As he reached Bakala, Sikhs swarmed from all sides to see him. The town was in bustle once again".[5]

Remaining active in promoting and growing the Sikh Panth while the Guruship rested with Gurū Har Rāi Sāhib and Gurū Har Krishan Sāhib, Gurū Tegh Bahādur Sāhib was involved from a distance but when the time came, was ready to take on the Gurūship.

Assassination attempt from Dhīr Mal

Despite the explicit nature of Gurū Har Krishan Sāhib's nomination, as depicted by Kaushish, several claimants had arrived in Bakālā, following the revelations from Gurū Har Krishan Sāhib that the next Gurū would be found there. Leading the group of impostors was Dhīr Mal, who put up an otherwise convincing claim as he also possessed the original copy of the Adi-Granth Sāhib. Kavi Santokh Singh narrates the episode in which Dhīr Mal conspired with his Masand, Shihan, to attack the Gurū. The attack occurred as Gurū Sāhib was

ਪਾਤਿਸ਼ਾਹੀ ਮਹਿਮਾ – Revisiting Sikh Sovereignty

on horseback, riding back into the town of Bakālā. Santokh Singh narrates muskets were fired, but they missed the Gurū.[6]

Dhīrmal and Rām Rāi are said to have exchanged letters in a bid to conspire against Gurū Tegh Bahādur Sāhib[7], with the intent to remove Gurū Sāhib from the Throne of Gurū Nānak Sāhib.

Tours across Panjāb and to the East

As we have seen, the doctrine of Sikh sovereignty encompassed every aspect of the Sikh movement under the Gurū period, and the reign of Gurū Tegh Bahādur Sāhib was no different. Kaushish narrates how Gurū Tegh Bahādur Sāhib, along with a contingent of prominent Sikhs, arrived in Amritsar in November 1664. They set up camp near the Akāl Bunga of Gurū Hargobind Sāhib. The news of Gurū Tegh Bahādur Sāhib's arrival spread quickly, and Sikhs began to congregate at Srī Harmandir Sāhib. Following their visit to Amritsar, the contingent travelled with Gurū Sāhib to Tarn Tāran Sāhib, Khadūr Sāhib, and other towns throughout December. Gurū Sāhib is said to have spent two months in the Majha region of Panjāb, that is the territory between Rivers Beas and Ravi, before embarking upon the towns of Jeera, Moga, and others, spreading Gurmat.

Kaushish narrates how Gurū Sāhib rested in Sabo-ki-Talwandi, a major town in the forest of Lakhi Jungle. Today this lies in the district of Bathinda in East Panjāb. The farmers of this place served the Gurū, and the following year, Gurū Sāhib celebrated the festival of Vaisākhī, during which times the local farmers came forward and mentioned there was a shortage of water and no waterholes, which meant their cattle would go thirsty, preventing the farmers from earning a living. Under the lead of Gurū Sāhib, a pool was excavated within ten days, which Gurū Sāhib named as Gurū Sar (Gurū's Pool).[8] Today Gurdwara Srī Gursarovar Sāhib stands in this place, within the vicinity of Takht Srī Damdama Sāhib.

Since Bakālā was close to Kartārpur Sāhib (Jalandhar), where Dhīr Mal had established his base, and also close to another adversary of the Gurū's Darbār, Meharvān who had taken over Amritsar, Gurū Tegh Bahādur Sāhib did not adopt Bakālā as the headquarters of their reign but instead relocated to Kīratpur Sāhib. If you recall, this is where Gurū Hargobind Sāhib had resided for many years, and also where Gurū Har Rāi Sāhib had stayed. However, this did not prove to be a permanent home for the Gurū either, since their brother Sūraj Mal had set up there.[9]

Gurū Sāhib founded the town of Chak Nānaki, which went on to become Srī Anandpur Sāhib, near the banks of the Satluj. At Chak Nānaki, there was a small settlement on a hillock, where young Gobind Rai was married to Mata Jeeto; the place became known as 'Gurū Ka Lahore.' Gurū Sāhib did not stay at Chak Nānaki for long periods, as they also began an extensive tour of the east to meet Sikh Sangat, consolidate their position with the old congregations, and build new centres of Sikh influence. The Gurū issued Hukamnāmās (decrees) as they addressed the Sikh Sangat. Some of the decrees from the 1660s have survived.[10] They refer to offerings of various kinds, including money for the Gurū's cause. They also indicate that Gurū Tegh Bahādur Sāhib's stay at Monghyr in Bihar was fairly long and that the Sangat in both Benares and Patna reaffirmed their allegiance to the Darbār of Gurū Nānak Sāhib under the reign of Gurū Tegh Bahādur Sāhib.

Aurangzeb's policy to suppress Sikhs from Delhi

Around about the same time, Aurangzeb had issued several decrees to enforce his interpretation of Islam. He prevented the construction of new places of worship and ordered the execution of his brother, Dara Shikoh. From Aurangzeb's viewpoint, no other faith could be equated with his own. In April 1669, he issued a general order to demolish "the schools and temples of the infidels" and to put down their "teachings and religious practices".[11] In January 1670, he ordered the city of Mathura to be renamed Islamabad, following the destruction of significant temples.[12]

ਪਾਤਿਸ਼ਾਹੀ ਮਹਿਮਾ – Revisiting Sikh Sovereignty

According to the Ahkam-I Alamgiri (Orders of Aurangzeb), preserved by his Secretary, Inayatullah Khan Ismi, the emperor had ordered the destruction of a Sikh "place of worship" and replaced it with a mosque.[13] As well as religious persecution, Aurangzeb also imposed heavy economic pressure on non-Muslims. The imposition of *jazia* tax, which if you recall was abolished by Gurū Amar Dās Sāhib, was now once again levied against non-Muslims for choosing to live in his Islamic State. There was also the abolishment of a customs duty for Muslim traders, but no such relief was given to non-Muslims. In 1671 an order was issued in which it was told only Muslims were to be appointed rent collectors in the land of the Mughal Crown.[14] All these measures were adopted to drive out, or convert, non-Muslims.

While many will be familiar with the religious intolerance of Aurangzeb, it would be prudent to briefly explain the general administrative system of Mughal rule under Aurangzeb. The system was such that he was Commander-in-Chief, ruling what was essentially a military government dependent upon the absolute authority of his decree. He had no regular council of ministers. The Wazīr or Dīvan was the highest officer below him, and other ministers were also inferior to him.[15] Sir Jadunath Sarkar writes,

> *"The Emperor was theoretically the highest judge in the realm, and used to try cases personally... The imperial Qazi always accompanied the Emperor, and appointed and dismissed the local Qazis of the cities and villages in every province... The administrative agency in the provinces of the Mughal empire was an exact miniature of the Central Government"*[16]

This was a marked deviation from the "fairly high degree of decentralisation"[17] in the governance that came before him, and indeed the Mughal empire. The centralised governance model was later reintroduced through the colonial encounter, firstly by the structure of colonial administration and, secondly, by the Indian

National Congress. On both accounts, the Sikhs vehemently opposed this centralised model of governance. We will touch upon this later in the book.

Aurangzeb's attitude towards Gurū's Darbār

Aurangzeb's attitude towards the Gurū's Darbār has been recorded by Rattan Singh Bhangoo. He narrates how the general relationship between the Gurū's Darbār and the imperial court, prior to Aurangzeb, was sometimes cordial and at other times hostile. When Aurangzeb took office, his fanatical ways would not be tolerated by the Gurū. They opposed one another, which escalated following the Gurū's decision to assist those facing persecution from Aurangzeb. It was at Chak Nānakī where the Gurū was visited by residents from Kashmir who entered the Gurū's Darbār and made their appeal seeking protection against Aurangzeb. Bhangoo narrates:

ਤੇਗ ਬਹਾਦਰ ਬਡਬਲ ਧਾਰੀ, ਪ੍ਰਗਟ ਭਾਈ ਗਲ ਦੁਨੀਆ ਸਾਰੀ।
ਜਾਂ ਪੈ ਆਇ ਮਰੈ ਕੋ ਦੁਖ, ਪਰੈ ਚਰਨ ਮੈਂ ਹੋਵੈ ਸੁਖ ॥੫॥
ਦੁਨੀਆ ਮਤਲਬ ਸੁਖ ਕੀ ਸਾਰੀ, ਆਵੈ ਸ਼ਰਨੀ ਜਿਹ ਬੈ ਭਾਰੀ।
ਲਗਤ ਚਰਨ ਹੁਇ ਤੁਰਤ ਸੁਖਾਰੈ, ਪ੍ਰਗਟ ਭਈ ਜਹ ਗਲ ਜਗ ਸਾਰੈ ॥੬॥

The whole world recognised Guru Tegh Bahādur Sāhib as a great repository of power. Whosoever was troubled by pain sought refuge at their feet and became happy. (5)
The whole world is motivated by pleasure. He who was terrified would take refuge with the Gurū. It became known to the entire world that he who seeks refuge at the Gurū's feet, at once becomes happy. (6)[18]

Bhangoo describes, in some detail, the context behind their ordeal, how Aurangzeb had promised to locate and convert everyone to Islam throughout the twenty-two provinces. As the imperial forces started to identify and convert non-Muslims, many decided to place the responsibility upon the Brahmins, to whom they were subservient. Their logic was that if the Brahmins could be converted, then they were ready to accept Islam. Bhangoo narrates how they won respite for themselves and deflected the evil onto the Brahmins, who in turn had no solution. They exhausted all their praying and austerities but were unable to prevent Aurangzeb from increasing his reign of terror in Kashmir:

ਅਹਦੀਏ ਦੁੜਾਏ ਵਲ ਕਸ਼ਮੀਰ, ਹੁਕਮ ਸੁਣੇ ਤਿਨ ਕਰੀ ਨ ਧੀਰ।
ਤੁਰਫ ਫੜੇ ਥੇ ਦੇ ਕੇ ਤਾਣ, ਸਭ ਹਿੰਦੂ ਕੀਏ ਮੁੱਸਲਮਾਨ ॥੧੭॥
ਹਿੰਦੂ ਬਚੈਂ ਲੁਕ ਬਤੇਰਾ ਕਰੈਂ, ਔਰ ਲਏ ਸਭ ਮੁਸਲੈ ਕਰੈ।
ਯੌਂ ਸਭ ਜਗ ਸੁਨ ਭਯੋ ਤਰਾਸ, ਤਬ ਬਿਪ ਆਏ ਸਤਿਗੁਰੂ ਪਾਸ ॥੧੮॥

He [Aurangzeb] dispatched messengers towards Kashmir. They received the orders and left without delay. Hindus were forcibly rounded up and were all converted to Islam. 17.
Hindus tried to save themselves by hiding. All others were converted to Islam. On hearing this, fear paralyzed the entire world. Then the Brahmins came to the True Gurū [Gurū Tegh Bahādur Sāhib].18.[19]

The Brahmins came from Kanshi (Benares), the Ganges, Kurukshetra, and other places to plead with the Gurū. Bhangoo states they even declared, "you are a warrior, pick up your sword"[20], and that they were prepared to follow the Gurū into battle. Gurū Sāhib's response was a measured but unprecedented one. The Gurū advised the Brahmins to go back and inform Aurangzeb that if he could convert Gurū Tegh Bahādur Sāhib, all the people of the land were willing to convert to Islam. The Brahmins did just that, and Sikh tradition records that Gurū Sāhib travelled to Delhi voluntarily. In should be pointed out that both Kaushish and Bhalla, offer a slightly different narrative in so much as Gurū Tegh Bahādur Sāhib was escorted to Delhi, along with their close Counsel of five Sikhs, Bhāī Mati Das, Bhāī Sati Das, Bhāī Daggo, Bhāī Dyal Das and Bhāī Sangat.

Srī Gurū Tegh Bahādur Sāhib jī Mahārāj

Gurū Sāhib's defiance

Gurū Tegh Bahādur Sāhib was imprisoned and tortured but did not accept any of the imperial court's conditions. The Mughal torturers berated the Gurū to show a miracle to prove they were Sache Pātshāh. The torturers also taunted the Gurū about how Rām Rāi had been turned in the imperial court. Bhangoo narrates Gurū Tegh Bahādur's response:

ਤਬ ਸਤਿਗੁਰੁ ਫਿਰ ਇਮ ਕਹਯੋ, ਨਹਿੰ ਅੱਛਾ ਕੀਅ ਰਮਰਾਇ।
ਆਪ ਬੜਾਈ ਸੈ ਗਇਓ, ਗਲ ਪਿਛਲਨ ਪਾਇ ਬਲਾਇ॥ ੪੦॥

The True Gurū then spoke like this: "Ram Rai did not do well. He walked off with adulation but has unleashed the devil for those coming after him. 40.[21]

A truly remarkable show of strength, power, and defiance amid horrendous torture and imminent death. The Gurū demonstrated, as Sache Pātshāh, they could not be converted or subdued. The Gurū continued to challenge the tormentors, as well as the Mughal establishment, and remained undefeated even in death. This account is also found in Gurū Kīān Sākhīā by Kaushish[22], which was published some fifty years before Bhangoo's Panth Prakāsh. The Gurū's courage to resist oppression is found not only in their actions whilst in Delhi, but also in their own Words, as preserved in the Shabads that reside in Gurū Granth Sāhib. There was no victory for Aurangzeb. Defeated and engrossed by his own ego, he ordered the execution of Gurū Tegh Bahādur Sāhib.

Saināpatī provides another excellent commentary on the martyrdom of Gurū Tegh Bahādur Sāhib. He writes:

ਪ੍ਰਗਟ ਭਏ ਗੁਰ ਤੇਗ ਬਹਾਦਰ। ਸਗਲ ਸ੍ਰਿਸਟਿ ਪੈ ਜਾਕੀ ਚਾਦਰ।
ਕਰਮ ਧਰਮ ਕੀ ਜਿਨਿ ਪਤਿ ਰਾਖੀ। ਅਟਲ ਕਰੀ ਕਲਿਜੁਗ ਸੈ ਸਾਖੀ॥ ੧੪॥

Then appeared Gurū Tegh Bahādur on the firmament, who sheltered the whole Creation with his grace. The Gurū upheld the right to religious freedom and deeds, which immortalised their Saga in the age of Kaljug.[23]

Saināpatī, much like Bhangoo, narrates how the Gurū's sacrifice came to be praised throughout the world and beyond. He goes on to expressly state that the right to wear a *Tilak* and *Janeu* remained in practice. We saw earlier in this chapter how Gurū Nānak Sāhib had profusely argued against the wearing of the *Janeu*, so it is important to note here that Gurū Tegh Bahādur Sāhib was upholding the religious freedom of Brahmins to have a right to practice their way of life; they were not condoning such a practice, rather protecting their right to it.

Gurū Tegh Bahādur Sāhib's martyrdom at Chandni Chowk opposite the Red Fort in Delhi took place on 11th November 1675. In Bachittar Natak, it is recorded as such:

ਤਿਲਕ ਜੰਞੂ ਰਾਖਾ ਪ੍ਰਭ ਤਾ ਕਾ ॥ ਕੀਨੋ ਬਡੋ ਕਲੂ ਮਹਿ ਸਾਕਾ ॥
ਸਾਧਨ ਹੇਤਿ ਇਤੀ ਜਿਨਿ ਕਰੀ ॥ ਸੀਸੁ ਦੀਆ ਪਰ ਸੀ ਨ ਉਚਰੀ ॥੧੩॥
ਧਰਮ ਹੇਤਿ ਸਾਕਾ ਜਿਨਿ ਕੀਆ ॥ ਸੀਸੁ ਦੀਆ ਪਰ ਸਿਰਰੁ ਨ ਦੀਆ ॥
ਨਾਟਕ ਚੇਟਕ ਕੀਏ ਕੁਕਾਜਾ ॥ ਪ੍ਰਭ ਲੋਗਨ ਕਹ ਆਵਤ ਲਾਜਾ ॥੧੪॥

[Gurū Tegh Bahādur] protected the bearers of the Tilak and Janeo, which marked a great event in the Age of Kaljug. For the sake of the pious, the Gurū laid down their head but not their resolve. For the sake of Dharam, they sacrificed themselves. The Gurū laid down their head but not their creed. The saints of Akāl abhor the performance of miracles and malpractices.

ਦੋਹਰਾ
ਠੀਕਰਿ ਫੋਰਿ ਦਿਲੀਸਿ ਸਿਰਿ ਪ੍ਰਭ ਕੀਆ ਪਯਾਨ ॥
ਤੇਗ ਬਹਾਦਰ ਸੀ ਕ੍ਰਿਆ ਕਰੀ ਨ ਕਿਨਹੂੰ ਆਨ ॥੧੫॥

Srī Guru Tegh Bahādur Sāhib jī Mahārāj

ਤੇਗ ਬਹਾਦਰ ਕੇ ਚਲਤ ਭਯੋ ਜਗਤ ਕੋ ਸੋਕ ॥
ਹੈ ਹੈ ਹੈ ਸਭ ਜਗ ਭਯੋ ਜੈ ਜੈ ਜੈ ਸੁਰ ਲੋਕ ॥੧੬॥

Breaking the potsherd of the body head of the king of Delhi (Aurangzeb), they left for the abode of Akal.
None could perform such a feat as that of Tegh Bahādur.
The whole world bemoaned the departure of Tegh Bahādur. While the world lamented, the heavens hailed their arrival.[24]

It is important to read this passage from Bachitar Natak, along with the works of Bhangoo and Saināpatī, because today, the opening lines are often taken out of context to the rest of the passage and mistakenly interpreted as the Guru having given their head for Hinduism. In a world built on colonial logic, this narrative emboldens Indian nationalists who deem Sikhī to be an offshoot of Hinduism. Bachitar Natak and Saināpatī's work predates the formation of the Indian state by 250 years; Bhangoo's work does so by hundred years, so it is ludicrous to make this inference. In addition to the depiction provided by Bhangoo, it is imperative to appreciate that Bachitar Natak also explicitly states Guru Tegh Bahādur Sāhib gave their head for Dharam, which is more reflective of the ideals of the Sikh movement under the Guru Sāhibān. We already know how critical the Guru was of the Brahmin, and in Bachitar Natak, it is clear that it was for the sake of the pious.

"Hind di Chadar" is another phrase used to describe Guru Tegh Bahādur, but Saināpatī uses "Srist ki Chadar", meaning protector of the whole of creation, which is perhaps more representative of Gurmat. In any event, it must be noted here 'Hind' is a reference to the land east of the River Indus, rather than a reference to the Hindu religion, which is how this episode has been represented by Indian nationalists and revisionists.

ਦੋਹਰਾ ॥
ਤੇਗ ਬਹਾਦਰ ਧਰਮ ਧੁਜ ਹਰਤਾ ਤੁਰਕਨ ਮੂਲ ॥

ਚਰਨ ਸ਼ਰਨ ਤਾਰਨ ਤਰ ਨਮੋ ਹੋਇ ਅਨਕੂਲ ॥੨੧॥

Gurū Tegh Bahādur Sāhib is the flag of righteousness, the One to rip up the roots of the Mughals. The Gurū's feet are the boat to carry us across this world ocean, to the Gurū I pay my salutations having entered their sanctuary.[25]

Passing of the Gurūship

Before departing for Delhi on 8th July 1675, Gurū Tegh Bahādur Sāhib as appointed their son Gobind Rai as the next Gurū. Gobind Rai was adorned with weapons before a descendent of Baba Buddhā jī completed the ceremony.[26]

Srī Gurū Tegh Bahādur Sāhib jī Māhārāj

NOTES

[1] Bhāī Nand Lal (1633-1713), *Ganjnama, Kalaam-e-Goya*, translated by Sardar Pritpal Singh Bindra, 2003, Institute of Sikh Studies, Chandigarh

[2] Harbans Singh, 1982, *Gurū Tegh Bahadur*, Sterling Publishers, p22

[3] Kavī Chūrāmanī Bhāī Santokh Singh, 1843, *Srī Gur Pratap Sūraj Granth*, Steek 6, Rās 8 Adhiāi 43, Edited by Dr. Ajeet Singh Aulakh, 2014 3rd Edition, p886-891

[4] Kavī Chūrāmanī Bhāī Santokh Singh, 1843, *Srī Gur Pratap Sūraj Granth*, Steek 8, Rās 11 Adhiāi 32, Edited by Dr. Ajeet Singh Aulakh, 2014 3rd Edition, p197-203

[5] Harbans Singh, 1982, *Gurū Tegh Bahadur*, Sterling Publishers, p46

[6] Kavī Chūrāmanī Bhāī Santokh Singh, 1843, *Srī Gur Pratap Sūraj Granth*, Steek 8, Rās 11 Adhiāi 32, Edited by Dr. Ajeet Singh Aulakh, 2014 3rd Edition, p197-203,

[7] Kavī Chūrāmanī Bhāī Santokh Singh, 1843, *Srī Gur Pratap Sūraj Granth*, Steek 8, Rās 11 Adhiāi 32, Edited by Dr. Ajeet Singh Aulakh, 2014 3rd Edition, p197-203

[8] ਭਾਈ ਸਰੂਪ ਸਿੰਘ ਕੌਸ਼ਿਸ, ੧੨੯੦, ਗੁਰੂ ਕੀਆਂ ਸਾਖੀਆਂ
Bhai Swarup Singh Kaushish, 1790, *Gurū Kīān Sākhīān*, Sākhī 21, edited by Piara Singh Padam, 1986, Singh Brothers, Amritsar, p69

[9] J.S.Grewal, 1994, *The Sikhs of the Punjab*, Cambridge university Press, Delhi, p69

[10] ਗੰਡਾ ਸਿੰਘ, ੧੯੬੭, ਹੁਕਮਨਾਮੇ ਸਿੱਖ ਗੁਰੂ, ਮਾਤਾ ਸਾਹਿਬਾਨ, ਬਾਬਾ ਬੰਦਾ ਸਿੰਘ ਅਤੇ ਗੁਰੂ ਕੇ ਖਾਲਸੇ ਦੇ
Dr. Ganda Singh, 1967, *Hukamname Sikh Guru, Mata Sahiban, Baba Banda Singh and Guru Ke Khalse De*, 1967, Baldev Singh, Kapurthala, New Revised Edition, 2015, p78-85

[11] Sir Jadunath Sarkar, 1930, *A Short History of Aurangzib*, M. C. Sarkar & Sons, Calcutta, p155

[12] Sir Jadunath Sarkar, 1930, *A Short History of Aurangzib*, M. C. Sarkar & Sons, Calcutta, p156

ਪਾਤਿਸ਼ਾਹੀ ਮਹਿਮਾ – Revisiting Sikh Sovereignty

[13] Ahkam-I Alamgiri, 1703-07, translated by J. S. Grewal & Irfan Habib, 2001, *Sikh History from Persian Sources,* Tulika Books, Delhi, p97

[14] Sir Jadunath Sarkar, 1930, *A Short History of Aurangzib*, M. C. Sarkar & Sons, Calcutta, p157

[15] Sir Jadunath Sarkar, 1930, *A Short History of Aurangzib*, M. C. Sarkar & Sons, Calcutta, p483

[16] Sir Jadunath Sarkar, 1930, *A Short History of Aurangzib*, M. C. Sarkar & Sons, Calcutta, p484-485

[17] Pritam Singh, 2008, *Federalism, Nationalism and Development, India and the Punjab economy*, Routledge, Oxon, p56-57

[18] ਰਤਨ ਸਿੰਘ ਭੰਗੂ, ੧੮੪੧, ਸ੍ਰੀ ਗੁਰ ਪੰਥ ਪ੍ਰਕਾਸ਼
Rattan Singh Bhangoo, 1841, *Sri Gur Panth Prakash*, (12:6) Translation by Gurtej Singh, 2015, Vol. 1, Singh Brothers, Amritsar, p51

[19] ਰਤਨ ਸਿੰਘ ਭੰਗੂ, ੧੮੪੧, ਸ੍ਰੀ ਗੁਰ ਪੰਥ ਪ੍ਰਕਾਸ਼
Rattan Singh Bhangoo, 1841, *Sri Gur Panth Prakash*, (12:18) Translation by Gurtej Singh, 2015, Vol. 1, Singh Brothers, Amritsar, p53

[20] ਰਤਨ ਸਿੰਘ ਭੰਗੂ, ੧੮੪੧, ਸ੍ਰੀ ਗੁਰ ਪੰਥ ਪ੍ਰਕਾਸ਼
Rattan Singh Bhangoo, 1841, *Sri Gur Panth Prakash*, (12:25) Translation by Gurtej Singh, 2015, Vol. 1, Singh Brothers, Amritsar, p55

[21] ਰਤਨ ਸਿੰਘ ਭੰਗੂ, ੧੮੪੧, ਸ੍ਰੀ ਗੁਰ ਪੰਥ ਪ੍ਰਕਾਸ਼
Rattan Singh Bhangoo, 1841, *Sri Gur Panth Prakash*, (12:40) Translation by Gurtej Singh, 2015, Vol. 1, Singh Brothers, Amritsar, p57

[22] ਭਾਈ ਸਰੂਪ ਸਿੰਘ ਕੌਸ਼ਿਸ਼, ੧੭੯੦, ਗੁਰੂ ਕੀਆਂ ਸਾਖੀਆਂ
Bhai Swarup Singh Kaushish, 1790, *Gurū Kīān Sākhīān*, Sākhī 29, edited by Piara Singh Padam, 1986, Singh Brothers, Amritsar, p81

[23] Saināpatī, 1711, *Srī Gur Sobha*, translation by Prof. Kulwant Singh, Institute of Sikh Studies, Chandigarh, p7

[24] Gurū Gobind Singh, *Bachittar Natak*, Dasam Granth, Ang 131

[25] Kavī Chūrāmanī Bhāī Santokh Singh, 1843, Srī Gur Nānak Prakāsh, translated by Resham Singh & Jīvanpal Singh, 2019 p81

[26] ਭਾਈ ਸਰੂਪ ਸਿੰਘ ਕੌਸ਼ਿਸ਼, ੧੭੯੦, ਗੁਰੂ ਕੀਆਂ ਸਾਖੀਆਂ
Bhai Swarup Singh Kaushish, 1790, *Gurū Kīān Sākhīān*, Sākhī 28, edited by Piara Singh Padam, 1986, Singh Brothers, Amritsar, p79

ਪਾਤਿਸ਼ਾਹੀ ਮਹਿਮਾ – Revisiting Sikh Sovereignty

Srī Gurū Gobind Singh Sāhib Ji Maharaj

ਹੱਕ ਹੱਕ ਆਗਾਹ ਗੁਰ ਗੋਬਿੰਦ ਸਿੰਘ ॥
ਸ਼ਾਹਿ ਸ਼ਹਨਸ਼ਾਹ ਗੁਰ ਗੋਬਿੰਦ ਸਿੰਘ ॥੧੦੭॥

> Gurū Gobind Singh is the knower of Truth.
> Gurū Gobind Singh is the sovereign of sovereigns. 107[1]

Following the martyrdom of Gurū Tegh Bahādur Sāhib, Gurū Gobind Singh's immediate focus was on growing the Sikh movement and evolving both the literary and the martial tradition founded by the previous Gurū Sāhibān.

The Anandpur Darbār

Not only was Gurū Sāhib a warrior and prolific writer, but the Gurū's Darbār of Anandpur Sāhib in the late 17th to early 18th century was also home to the most skilled fighters and writers. Kaushish writes how the Gurū issued Hukamnāme in all four directions asking Sikhs to present themselves with books, horses, and weapons.[2] Copies of the Hukamnāme are preserved in Dr. Ganda Singh's work.[3]

As I mentioned in the introduction, the Gurū's Darbār was a centre of both the armed and the learned because where the Darbār was adorned with weapons meant for the destruction of oppressive forces, the Gurū gave equal importance to the dissemination of knowledge and literature to increase the Sangat's understanding and power.[4] Chibbar also writes Gurū Sāhib had issued Hukamnāme in 1677 to the Sikhs and summoned other writers from across the land to join them. No costs were spared in ensuring only the best arrived:

ਪਾਤਿਸ਼ਾਹੀ ਮਹਿਮਾ – Revisiting Sikh Sovereignty

> ਲਿਖ ਹੁਕਮਨਾਮੇ ਸਿਖਾਂ ਨੂੰ ਭਿਜਵਾਏ ।੫੫।
> "ਜੋ ਬ੍ਰਹਮਨ ਵਿਦਿਆਵਾਨੁ ਹੈ ਚੰਗਾ, ਸੋ ਭਿਜਵਾਣਾ।
> ਜੋ ਖਰਚ ਲਗੇ, ਸੋ ਗੁਰੂ ਕੇ ਘਰੋਂ ਲਾਣਾ ।"[5]

Hukamnāme were issued to the Sikhs
"Those [other learned] scholars should also arrive, whatever the cost, the Gurū's House shall cover".

Poets and writers soon arrived, and the Anandpur Darbār came into its own. Within three years, renowned writers such as Lakhan Rai (1680) and Tansukh (1683) completed translations of texts such as 'Hitopadesh'. Even when the Gurū was based at Poantā Sāhib, a grand Darbār of poets was held on the banks of the river Jamunā.[6]

> ਦੋਹਰਾ
> ਬਾਵਨ ਕਵੀ ਹਜ਼ੂਰ ਗੁਰ ਰਹਿਤ ਸਦਾ ਹੀ ਪਾਸ।
> ਆਵੈਂ ਜਾਹਿੰ ਅਨੇਕ ਹੀ, ਕਹਿ ਜਸ, ਲੈਂ ਧਨ ਰਾਸ ॥੧॥[7]

Fifty-two poets always remained with Gurū Sāhib in the Darbār. Many more would come and visit the Gurū, speak [their] praise and gain much wealth.

Such was the standard of literature produced at the Anandpur Darbār that writers of all backgrounds travelled from far and wide to join the Gurū in Anandpur Sāhib. Of the first poets and writers that arrived, many were overwhelmed with the caliber of literature being produced from Gurū's Darbār that they called upon others to join them and truly experience first-hand the greatness and uniqueness of the Gurū's Darbār.[8]

Gurū Gobind Singh provided the space for poets from different backgrounds and cultures to write freely. The Anandpur Darbār also allowed dedicated students to dedicate themselves to intensive study. All of their day-to-day needs and requirements were provided for by the Gurū's Darbār. Such was the value placed on the production of literature from Anandpur Sāhib that the Gurū would provide costly shawls and gold as incentive and reward for their creative work. Dr. Sukhdial Singh notes how Kavi Darbārs were held on the night of Pūranmāshī, when it was a full-moon. Dr. Sukhdial Singh writes,

> "In the light of the moon and under the patronization of the Guru, the poets recited their poems to the Sikh congregation and it applauded them with the Jaikaras. In these Kavi Darbars, the Sikhs heard ballads extolling the deeds of warriors of the times of their sixth Guru who had defied tyranny with the force of arms,"[9]

Kavī Santokh Singh provides some context to understand the sheer volume of literature produced about one particular granth[10] He states the pages upon which the poets produced their fine writings weighed ੩ ਮਣ (1 mn = 37kg, so that is approximately 330kg). They were compiling a literary work, which they lovingly referred to as 'Vidhia Dhar', also known as 'Vidhia Sagar', and 'Samund Sagar'. In addition to Kavī Santokh Singh's work, we know of at least two other Precolonial sources that refer to this monumental granth being created at Anandpur Sāhib, namely Mehmā Prakāsh[11] and Bansāvalīnāmā. Unlike Srī Dasam Granth, which was preserved by Shaheed Bhāī Manī Singh following the Battle of Chamkaur Sāhib (1704), in which countless handwritten works were lost, it appears no one could preserve or indeed reproduce the compositions contained within Vidhia Sagar.[12]

The achievements of the Anandpur Darbār were many. Gurū Gobind Singh ended the stranglehold of the Brahmanical classes in literary composition and knowledge production. The "high-born" classes no longer had a monopoly over the ownership and dissemination of knowledge and creative expression. Those whom society had deemed the lowest of the low were able to attend the Anandpur Darbar, learn and engage with the poets and writers.

ਪਾਤਿਸ਼ਾਹੀ ਮਹਿਮਾ – Revisiting Sikh Sovereignty

Persian writer Muhammed Qāsim "Ibrat" provides a detailed account of how the Gurū's Darbār was also noted by the Mughal regime. Writing about Gurū Gobind Singh in 1723, he notes,

> "The magnificence of his state grew to such an extent that he was not behind the nobles of 5,000 [zāt] or even rulers of principalities in anything concerned with greatness of splendour or accumulation of resources...the inclination to serve him on the part of all kinds of people exceeded every limit and there was no month or year when the roads were not filled by caravans of people carrying offerings to him."[13]

Ibrat continues that due to the Gurū's radical and rebellious ways, many others refused to pay tax and tributes to the Mughal regime and also established "unprecedented innovations in cities and villages". He also makes reference to the ultimatum sent to Gurū Sāhib, that if the Gurū continued to mobilise in this way, the Imperial forces would attack and seek to remove the Gurū from those territories upon which the Gurū's Darbār had been established.

Founding of Poanta Sāhib

With the expansion of the Gurū's movement came the founding of Poanta Sāhib, but adversaries of the Gurū's Darbār were also growing, both internal and external. On the one hand, Kalgīdhar Pātshāh was leading a resurgence of literature production from Anandpur Sāhib, and on the other, they were readying the Sikhs for battles to preserve and further Sikh sovereignty. The chiefs of the Sivalik Hills, who were subordinate to the Mughal administration, formed an integral part of the Mughal regime. They would soon collude as enemies of the Gurū's Darbār. As subordinates to the Mughal administration, they used Mughal coinage, had to pay annual tribute, and were expected to provide military support for the

Mughal's imperial campaigns. As the head of the imperial regime, the Mughal emperor claimed a right to oversee the ratification of any succession to their thrones. The Hill Chiefs thus had little sovereign agency of their own but, in return, "relied on Mughal support against acts of war".[14]

The battles Gurū Sāhib waged are chronicled by 18th-century Sikh writers, including Saināpatī, Koer Singh Kalāl, Kesar Singh Chibbar, and Swarūp Singh Kaushish. The first battle, the Battle of Bhangani, takes place on 18th September 1688. The Gurū's Darbār in Poanta Sāhib, as a hub of military and martial activity, had alarmed Fateh Shāh, one of the neighbouring Hill Chiefs.

Battle of Bhangani, 1688

A detailed account of the build-up to this battle is provided by Kaushish, including the context behind Gurū Sāhib composing Krishan Avtar, found in Srī Dasam Granth[15] It is here, after learning about the impending invasion that Gurū Gobind Singh is recorded to have said;

ਛੱਤ੍ਰੀ ਕੋ ਪੂਤ ਹੌਂ ਬਾਹਮਨ ਕੋ ਨਾਹਿ ਕੈ ਤਪੁ ਆਵਤ ਹੌਂ ਜੁ ਕਰੋਂ।
ਅਰ ਔਰ ਜੰਜਾਰ ਜਿਤੇ ਗ੍ਰਿਹ ਕੋ ਤੁਹਿ ਤਿਆਗ ਕਹਾਂ ਚਿੱਤ ਤਾ ਮੈਂ ਧਰੋਂ।
ਅਬ ਰੀਝ ਕੈ ਦੇਹੁ ਵਹੈ ਹਮ ਕੋ ਜੋਉ ਹਉਂ ਬੇਨਤੀ ਕਰ ਜੋਰ ਕਰੋਂ।
ਜਬ ਆਉ ਕੀ ਆਉਧ ਨਿਧਾਨ ਬਨੈ ਅਤਿ ਹੀ ਰਨ ਮੈ ਤਬ ਜੂਝ ਮਰੋਂ।੨੪੮੯।

> I'm a Kshatri's son, not of a Brahmin that I may get panicky. Many are there, domesticated affairs, should I abandon all and just put mind in You? Now, gratify and endow me, as I am earnestly beseeching You. So that, when the life's end approaches, I revel in the war (struggle), and die (sacrifice) in glory.

Gurū Sāhib completed Krishan Avtār, found in Srī Dasam Granth, during this stay at Paonta Sāhib. Compositions from Krishan

Avtar were sung in the Gurū's Darbār in preparation for war with Fateh Shah;

ਗੰਨ ਜੀਓ ਤਿਹ ਕੂ ਜਗ ਮੋ ਮੁਖ ਤੇ ਹਰਿ ਚਿੱਤ ਮਹਿ ਜੁਗ ਬੀਚਾਰੈ।
ਦੇਹ ਅਨਿੱਤ ਨ ਨਿੱਤ ਰਹੈ, ਜਸ ਨਾਵ ਚੜੈ ਭਵ ਸਾਗਰ ਤਾਰੇ।
ਧੀਰਜ ਧਾਮ ਬਨਾਇ ਇਹੈ ਤਨ ਬੁਧਿ ਸੁ ਦੀਪਕ ਜਿਉਂ ਉਜੀਆਰੈ।
ਗਯਾਨਹਿ ਕੀ ਬਢਨੀ ਮਨੋ ਹਾਥ ਲੈ ਕਾਤਰਤਾ ਕੁਤਵਾਰ ਬੁਹਾਰੈ।੨੪੯੧।

> Auspicious is one who, keeping God's Name on lips, remembers in heart the war (struggle). Because the body is destructible, not immortal and one climbs into the boat to go across the sea. "One should make the heart a domain of patience and enlighten it with the lamp of intellect, And, taking the broom of knowledge in his hand, Clean up all the litter and sweepings. 2491.

In addition to Kaushish, Chibbar[16] too provides a similar account of the battle; however, for a full account of the battle, it would be wise to refer to Saināpatī's detailed account.[17] Saināpatī describes how Gurū Gobind Singh marched to the battlefield with Nishaan Sāhibs hoisted high above. Upon reaching the battlefield, Gurū Sāhib examined the enemy's position and then deployed their Misls to take up their positions around the enemy.[18] From his work we learn there were in fact, eleven Misls under the command of Gurū Gobind Singh, four of whom were headed up by the Gurū's own cousins, Sango Shah, Jitmal, Sangat Rai, and Hari Chand – sons of Bibī Viro jī (sister of Gurū Tegh Bahādur Sāhib). Gulab Rai, the great-grandson of Gurū Hargobind Sāhib, was the head of a fifth Misl. Five further Misls were under the command of Pir Budhu Shah and his four sons, and the eleventh Misl was under the direct command of Gurū Gobind Singh. The formation of the Misls was such that Gurū Gobind Singh led from the centre, with their five cousins leading their units from the right-wing, and Pir Budhu Shah and his sons leading the left-wing.

Fateh Shah of Srī Nagar was joined by other prominent Hill Chiefs such as Hari Chand Handooria and Bhim Chand of Bilaspur, as well as Mughal troops under Najabat Khan and Bhikham Khan. On the Gurū's side, in addition to the names mentioned above, other warriors including his maternal uncle Kirpal Das and Lāl Chand, who according to Giānī Giān Singh in Twarikh Gurū Khālsā was the son of Bidhī Chand, the beloved Gursikh of Gurū Hargobind Sāhib, were also present. In his account, Saināpatī provides a graphic but masterful depiction of the battle, in poetic verse, praising the Gurū's timely battle stratagem and the bravery of the mighty Sikh warriors engaged in pitched battles that ultimately ended in victory for the Gurū and the Sikhs.

Because the allied forces of the Hill Chiefs and Mughal regime had attacked the Gurū to suppress the mobilization of Sikhs at Poanta Sāhib, this victory sent a resounding message; that the Gurū was committed to founding new towns and cities, and would defend any attack or invasion that infringed the sovereignty of the Gurū's Darbār.

Battle of Nadaun, 1691

Gurū Sāhib's next battle took place on 20th March 1691, against the Mughal forces of Alaf Khan, an acclaimed warrior. Gurū Gobind Singh took part in this battle in support of Bhim Chand, who by this time had sought Gurū's refuge following Aurangzeb's demands for tributes from the Hill Chiefs. Despite the previous clash with Bhim Chand, the Gurū's decision to stand with Bhim Chand exemplifies the magnanimity of Gurū Sāhib's cause, that the perpetual aim was always to fight oppression, exploitation, and tyranny in all forms. A fierce battle took place, again masterfully told by the likes of Saināpatī, but expanded upon in Bachitar Natak. The battle ended in defeat for the Mughal forces, and Gurū Gobind Singh is said to have returned to Anandpur Sāhib. There is a period of several years where no battles occur, but the Gurū spends time nurturing the Sangat and growing Sikhī through visiting various adjoining towns and cities.

ਪਾਤਿਸ਼ਾਹੀ ਮਹਿਮਾ – Revisiting Sikh Sovereignty

Gurū Gobind Singh Sāhib's writings

The Gurū also penned many compositions that reflected their political endeavours, providing an insight into the Gurū's worldview. They can be found in the writings contained in *Srī Dasam Granth*. In *Jaap Sāhib*, Gurū Gobind Singh writes about the attributes of the Creator, stating the Creator has no visible mark or sign, neither caste nor lineage. The critique of other religions and practices that propagated falsehood by advocating for idol worship, and asceticism, is a hallmark of Gurū Sāhib's writings. The nature of this overt critique by Gurū Gobind Singh reflects the denunciation of Brahmanism, Islam, and other structures, that we also find in Shabads contained within Gurū Granth Sāhib, which would no doubt have alarmed the Hill Chiefs and their Mughal superiors in Delhi.

Benti Chaupai, a composition penned by Gurū Sāhib around 1690, is equally compelling. It evokes the power that created Brahma, Vishnu, and Mahesh (Shiva). Gurū Sāhib reaffirms the pledge of allegiance to Akāl and expressly states their renunciation of other traditions or religions. In *Chandī di Vār*, Gurū Gobind Singh builds on the themes discussed in Bentī Chaupaī, by informing the Sikhs that there is only one power that manifested and sustained entities such as Brahma, Vishnu, Shiva, Durga, Rama, and Krishna. Gurū Sāhib is not praising them, as many Indian or Hindu revisionists would like to suggest, rather the Gurū explicitly narrates how they bow only to the power behind their creation. This is a revolutionary composition, at a time when Gurū Sāhib was waging war with people who held such deities in the highest regard.

Vaisākhī of 1695

During the Vaisākhī of 1695, Kaushish narrates a rather interesting account of what took place in the Gurū's Darbār. He states that Gurū Gobind Singh ordained for all Sikhs to wear a *sarbloh kara* (iron bracelet) in the right hand and also to start keeping their hair intact[19].

This is another one of Kaushish's unique contributions. It certainly tallies up within the context of Gurū Sāhib's vision to prepare the Sikhs for the pending transformation in 1699. In the same way, Sikhs had become accustomed to bowing in reverence to the Adi Granth Sāhib, since the time of Gurū Arjan Sāhib, this account from Kaushish is not unbecoming of the character of Gurū Sāhib to prepare the Sikhs for a new tradition in the evolution of the Sikh movement.

Attack on Anandpur, 1696

The next battle took place on 20th March 1696, as Aurangzeb's army commander Dilawar Khan sent his son Rustam Khan (Khanzada) to attack the Gurū at Anandpur. As he prepared his troops, an informer conveyed this message to the Gurū, who made immediate plans to prepare for battle. The intelligence Gurū Sāhib received speaks volumes of the growing appeal Gurū's Darbār was having on the villagers. When Rustam Khan's imperial forces saw the battle-hardened warriors of Gurū Gobind Singh, they absconded.[20] A second force was brought by Dilawar Khan's subordinate, Hussain Khan. He decided to invade the Hill Chiefs instead of Anandpur Sāhib. Despite the Hill Chiefs consolidating their armies, they could not sustain the attack from Hussain Khan and collaborated with him, including Bhim Chand. It is said Hussain Khan merged the whole valley into Mughal territory.[21] He soon surrounded the capital of the state of Raja Gaj Singh Gopal of Guler. The siege went on for approximately fifteen days. Raja Gopal sent his minister to Anandpur Sāhib, asking for the Gurū's support. Despite the Gurū's efforts to resolve the matter through diplomacy, both sides eventually engaged in a fierce battle. It is said that Hussain Khan was renowned as a great fighter of the Imperial army. Galloping his horse, he fiercely jumped into the battlefield. Upon seeing him, Gurū Sāhib ordered Bhāī Sangat Singh and other Sikhs to march forward and face him. Hussain Khan met his death. The battle continued to rage, and Bhāī Sangat Singh, along with other Gursikhs, were martyred.[22] The battle eventually ended in victory for the Gurū's warriors, who retreated to Anandpur Sāhib.

Decree to dissolve the Masand system

In a little over two decades following the martyrdom of Gurū Tegh Bahādur Sāhib, with the battle victories under Gurū Gobind Singh we see the rising power of Gurū's Darbar. It is during this time that Gurū Sāhib dissolved the Masand system. As we have seen already in this chapter, they were initially a body of agents that worked to further the Gurū's mission, however, over time, they became corrupt and declined in both character and integrity, seeking the companion of both Hill Chiefs and the Mughal administration to undermine the Gurū's authority. Following several complaints to the Gurū, the control once vested to the Masand system was stripped away as the Gurū took full control and ordered the Sikhs to renounce the Masands. It was declared that no Sikh should listen to the Masands claiming to represent the Gurū, rather only accept the Gurū's instruction from those with a handwritten Hukamnāmā or letter from the Gurū.[23] The Sikhs were even ordered to refuse any offerings from the Masands, to the extent that if they saw a Masand approaching from the side and an elephant charging from the other side, they were to meet the elephant head on than keep any company with the Masands.[24] Saināpatī records;

ਜਗਤ ਉਧਾਰਨ ਕਾਰਨੇ ਸਤਿਗੁਰੁ ਕਿਯੋ ਬਿਚਾਰ।
ਕਰ ਮਸੰਦ ਤਬ ਦੂਰ ਸਬ ਨਿਰਮਲ ਕਰ ਸੰਸਾਰ ॥ ੧੫ ॥ ੧੩੧ ॥

Reflecting upon the necessary cause of action needed for emancipating humanity.
Satgurū, turned out all the Masands, with the aim of cleansing the whole system. 15.131.[25]

Srī Gurū Gobind Singh Sāhib jī Māhārāj

Creation of the Khālsā, 1699

The decision to remove the influence of the Masands was not standalone. The timing of this decision coincided with the revelation of the Khālsā; that the Sikhs were to accept the Khālsā as representatives of the Gurū, in place of the Masands. Sarūp Das Bhalla narrates:

ਲਿਖ ਹੁਕਮ ਨਾਮੇ ਸਭ ਦੇਸ ਪਠਾਏ। ਜੋ ਕੋ ਮੇਰਾ ਸਿਖੁ ਕਹਾਏ।
ਅਬ ਮਸੰਦ ਮੈ ਕੀਨੇ ਦੂਰਿ। ਸਭ ਕੀਆ ਖਾਲਸਾ ਮਿਲੇ ਹਜੂਰ।੬੨।[26]

Hukamname were issued all over the land. Whosoever called themselves a Sikh of the Guru, should distance themselves from the Masands, and greet the Khalsa instead. 62.

Saināpatī too provides a detailed but poetic narration of what the Gurū said about the creation of the Khālsā. The Khālsā was created with a very specific and purposeful aim; "to decimate the demonic and annihilate the wicked. The Gurū established the Khālsā to eradicate of human suffering".[27]

Gurū Gobind Singh created the Khālsā as a vehicle to continue the Sikh mission, as Sardar Jagjit Singh notes, "... with the deliberate plan that the downtrodden, including the outcastes, should capture political power",[28] thus demonstrating the distinct nature of the Gurū's movement in which the lowest of the low according to Brahmin estimation were made equal co-sharers of that authority. It was at this juncture when the tenth Gurū then knelt before the authority of the Khālsā, in the same way Gurū Nānak Sāhib had bowed before Bhāī Lehna two centuries earlier, a feat unparalleled in world history. This moment in which the Gurū asked the Khālsā for Amrit marked a seismic shift in both the minds and bodies of the downtrodden members of society who, empowered by the Gurū's sovereignty, transformed from sparrows into hawks.

Sarūp Das Bhalla provides a fascinating account of a conversation that took place during the first Amrit initiation. He narrates:

ਉਪਰੰਤ ਇਨ ਪਾਂਚੋਂ ਕੋ ਲੈ ਕੇ ਦੀਵਾਨ ਅਸਥਾਨ ਤੇ ਆਏ, ਦਖਨੇ ਵਾਲੇ ਚਕ੍ਰਿਤ ਰਹਿ ਗਏ। ਗੁਰੂ ਜੀ ਨੇ ਬੈਠੀ ਸਿੱਖ ਸੰਗਤ ਤਰਫ ਦੇਖਾ, ਬਚਨ ਹੋਆ – "ਭਾਈ ਸਿੱਖੋ! ਜਿਥੇ ਪਹਿਲੇ ਸਤਿਗੁਰਾਂ ਸਿੱਖੀ ਕੀ ਪਰਖ ਕੀ ਤਾਂ ਉਸ ਸਮੇਂ ਪਰਖ ਬੀਚ ਇਕੇਲਾ ਭਾਈ ਲਹਿਣਾ ਹੀ ਸਾਬਤ ਨਿਕਲਾ ਥਾ। ਸਤਿਗੁਰਾਂ ਉਸੇ ਆਪਨੇ ਅੰਗ ਕੇ ਗੈਲ ਲਗਾਇ ਉਸ ਕਾ ਨਾਉਂ ਅੰਗਦ ਰਾਖਾ ਥਾ। ਅਬ ਕੀ ਵਾਰ ਪਾਂਚ ਮਰਜੀਵੜੇ ਸਿਖ ਪਰਖ ਮੇਂ ਸਾਬਤ ਨਿਕਲੇ ਹੈਂ, ਮੈਂ ਇਨ ਕੋ 'ਪਾਂਚ ਪਿਆਰੇ' ਕੀ ਪਦਵੀ ਦੇਤਾ ਹੂੰ। ਜਬ ਤੀਕ ਸੂਰਜ ਤੇ ਚਾਂਦ ਧਰਤੀ ਅਸਮਾਨ ਰਹੇਂਗੇ ਇਨ ਕਾ ਨਾਉਂ ਰਹਿੰਦੀ ਦੁਨੀਆਂ ਤਕ ਰਹੇਗਾ।

Gurū Ji looked at the audience and expounded, "Bhāī Sikho, when the first Satgurū performed a trial, only one, Bhāī Lehna, triumphed through. Satgurū took Bhāī Lehna as a part of themselves and gave the name of Angad (a part of their own body). This time five self-sacrificing personalities have emerged out of the test. I endow them the status of Panj Pyare (the Five-beloved Ones). Till the time sun and the moon remain in the skies, and the earth sustains existence, their name will prevail in the universe."[29]

Gurū Sāhib then added that their names would forever be remembered in a Sikh's *Ardas* and when *Karrah Parshad* is prepared, the names of these five will be recalled, and their share will be taken out after us. The Gurū then instructed Bhāī Chaupat to retrieve water from the River Satluj in preparation of Amrit made using the double-edged sword.

Gurū Gobind Singh's reference to Gurū Nānak Sāhib, at the time of creating the Khālsā, demonstrates the oneness of Gurū's Light, and just how far the Sikhs had come in 200 years. The concept of giving one's head was not a new one but had been there from the offset, with Gurū Nānak Sāhib first declaring:

ਜਉ ਤਉ ਪ੍ਰੇਮ ਖੇਲਣ ਕਾ ਚਾਉ ॥ ਸਿਰੁ ਧਰਿ ਤਲੀ ਗਲੀ ਮੇਰੀ ਆਉ ॥
ਇਤੁ ਮਾਰਗਿ ਪੈਰੁ ਧਰੀਜੈ ॥ ਸਿਰੁ ਦੀਜੈ ਕਾਣਿ ਨ ਕੀਜੈ ॥੨੦॥

If you desire to play this game of love, then step onto my path with your head in hand. When you place your feet on this Path, give me your head, and pay no any attention to public opinion.[30]

Besides meaning pure, the word Khālsā is a Persian term meaning free or autonomous. Historically it was the term used for a particular section of land under direct control and ownership of the Mughal emperor. All revenue contributions from this type of land were sent directly to the Mughal treasury without interference from the Jagirdars or revenue collectors. The use of the term Khālsā by Guru Gobind Singh was a direct challenge to Mughal power and authority; it was reminiscent of Guru Amar Das' decision to create 22 Manjhīs to reflect the 22 states under Mughal rule. It was the creation of a parallel power structure, one which reported directly to the Gurū, safe from the deceitful ways of the Masands, to enhance the sovereignty and authority of the Gurū's Darbār.

Deployment of the Khālsā

Rattan Singh Bhangoo offers an array of powerful and mesmerizing couplets and verses on the creation of the Khālsā. He narrates how Guru Gobind Singh decentralised and delegated their temporal power to the Khālsā and placed them in positions of power in every sphere of activity. Following the creation of the Khālsā, Guru Gobind Singh deployed the newly appointed emissaries in all four directions.[31] From Anandpur Sāhib, Gurū Sāhib travelled to Amritsar and Patna, as well as several other places of the Gurū Darbār's influence. In light of the influence of Masands, this was a bold and revolutionary new move to oust the corrupt Masands and reestablish the sanctity and sovereignty of the Gurū's Darbār. The young Gursikhs were dispatched with full powers to initiate others into the Khālsā Panth.

From the writings of precolonial texts, we find that the significance of administering Amrit was that it was an initiation ceremony, not a baptism that carries a Christian connotation. The

ਪਾਤਿਸ਼ਾਹੀ ਮਹਿਮਾ – Revisiting Sikh Sovereignty

creation of the Khālsā was about empowering the individual Sikh to oppose falsehood, tyranny, and oppression. That empowerment came directly from the Gurū as they bestowed sovereignty on each individual Sikh, and the Khālsā collective, before kneeling and asking for Amrit too.

Gurū Gobind Singh assigned such symbols to every member of the Khālsā that they became a living insignia, distinguishable from a distance, of the open revolution Gurū Sāhib had launched. It was a direct confrontation between Khālsā and the Imperial regime. There were no illusions on either side; the Sikhs knew there could be no compromise between their revolution and the established order it was mandated to overthrow.

Koer Singh offers a unique and mesmerizing insight into the five Kakkar. Ordinarily, they are known as Kes (uncut hair); Kanga (comb); Kachera (undergarment), Kirpan (dagger or sword); and Kara (iron bracelet). However, writing in 1751, Koer Singh narrates the five main attributes of the Khālsā were (i) Kes; (ii) Kanga; (iii) Kachera; (iv) Kard (small dagger); and (v) the love for weapons and Shabad[32]. There is no mention of Kara. Perhaps because historically, a Kara would've been considered a weapon for both offensive and defensive use, falling within the broader instruction of bearing arms.

Following the creation of the Khālsā, there was strong opposition from both the Mughal regime and Hill Chiefs and some of the Sikh followers who had not quite shaken off the stranglehold of the Brahmanical caste order. Saināpatī provides a thorough insight into the development of the opposition, which created social divisions and boycotts from within Sikh society. His writings amplify the importance of Khālsā Rehat (discipline), both as a means of actualizing the ideals and conduct of the Khālsā and as an identifying characteristic of the Khālsā. Kaushish also dedicates an entire Sākhī to the importance of Rehat.

The creation of the Khālsā and its immediate deployment all over the land saw a radical expansion of the Sikh Panth; however, Gurū Sāhib's headquarters remained in Anandpur Sāhib.

Hindu Hill Chiefs attack

In 1700, the Hill Chief of Kahloor, which today lies in Himachal Pradesh, claimed the land of Anandpur Sāhib and threatened to wage war with the Gurū if he did not vacate the territory. The Gurū chose to remain in Anandpur Sāhib and duly accepted the challenge. This decision carries an incredibly important lesson for Sikhs today. This was territory belonging to the Gurū's Darbār, to the Gurū's Khālsā, and they had every intention of defending their territory, signifying the importance of preserving and defending sovereign Sikh land. This was the battle in which Sāhibzada Baba Ajit Singh first displayed exemplary courage and great military prowess in the clash that lasted four whole days, resulting in victory for the Gurū's forces. Unable to penetrate the Gurū's forces defending from the seven forts at Anandpur Sāhib, the Hill Chiefs retreated but soon hatched a plan to send an intoxicated elephant to break down the barricade outside Fort Lohgarh. However, they were met by the Gurū's brave and courageous Khālsā, including the legendary Bhāī Bachittar Singh, who delivered a fatal blow to the charging intoxicated elephant. The Khālsā remained victorious, and the Hill Chiefs were forced to retreat once again. They suffered some large blows in this series of battles, including the death of Raja Kesrī Chand, whose head was severed by the sword of Bhāī Uday Singh, before he presented it at the feet of Gurū Gobind Singh.[33]

With no other option left, the Hill Chiefs led by Raja Ajmer Chand met and consoled one another. They drafted a letter, tied it to a cow, and left it outside the Fort of Anandgarh. In the letter, they acknowledged their mistakes and swore on the cow (whom they deemed holy) and the Hindu sacred thread that they would never raid Anandpur Sāhib again. They also lamented that they were ashamed to show their faces to the hill people, but if the Gurū left the Fort of Anandgarh just once and came back later, it would help them restore some dignity.[34]

ਪਾਤਿਸ਼ਾਹੀ ਮਹਿਮਾ – Revisiting Sikh Sovereignty

Sikh history records that Gurū Sāhib did not trust their oaths of swearing on the cow or Hindu sacred thread, but accepted their mercy petition. The Gurū moved to a hilltop in the valley of Nirmoh, which was just south of Kīratpur. However, the moment Gurū Sāhib and the Khālsā forces retreated, the Hill Chiefs broke all their pledges and took occupation of all the villages surrounding Anandpur Sāhib. Raja Ajmer Chand addressed the other Hill Chiefs and conspired to attack the Gurū and Khālsā forces at Nirmoh, whom he thought would not be able to defend themselves without the protection of any fort. The plan was to surround Gurū Sāhib and either kill or capture them and present to the Mughal Suba of Sirhind. Some of the Hill Chiefs did not agree to the plan; however, the majority felt it was the best course of action to cement their control and influence over the region. They attacked Nirmoh on 8th October 1700, however they met firm resistance from the Gurū's encampment.

Unable to penetrate Sikh fortifications, Raja Ajmer Chand, the son of Bhim Chand, sent a letter through his Minister Parma Nand to the Governor of Sirhind, asking for back-up forces to be deployed. The Mughal Governor sent Rustam Khan, who, if you recall, was the commander who had failed to break through the Gurū's forces at Anandpur five years earlier. As it transpired, the Governor of Sirhind, in choosing to send Rustam Khan, had effectively signed his death warrant as he was killed by an arrow fired by the Gurū, and his brother Nasir Ali Khan was killed similarly by an arrow fired by the Gurū's formidable General, Bhāī Uday Singh.[35] The Battle of Nirmohgarh is narrated in epic style and much detail by Saināpatī, who uses an array of metaphors and similes that capture the unrelenting bravery and battle prowess for which the Khālsā warriors became famous.

This was the second battle of the Khālsā, but the seventh time Gurū Gobind Singh had led the Sikh warriors into battle. There were a further three encounters with the Hindu Hill Chiefs during the Gurū's tenure at Basali, a locality found in the present-day district of Ropar before the Gurū returned to Anandpur Sāhib in late 1700.

Upon returning to Anandpur Sāhib, Gurū Sāhib initiated a phase of fortifying the territory that had become a citadel of Sikh power. Anandpur Sāhib was turned into a town of bliss with its inhabitants singing of the blissful glory that prevailed at Anandpur. In March 1701, Baba Ajit Singh and Bhāī Uday Singh along with other Khālsā warriors were deployed by the Gurū to assist the Sikh Sangat that had been attacked by the Rangars and Gujars of Kamlot on route to Anandpur Sāhib.[36]

Saināpatī's unique portrayal of Gurū Sāhib's victorious battles sheds much light on the expansive rise of Sikh power under Gurū Gobind Singh. From the initial challenges of Gurū Nānak Sāhib to the martyrdom of Gurū Arjan Sāhib, the powerbrokers of South Asia were conscious of the growing rise of the Sikh movement. Ever since Gurū Hargobind Sāhib's decision to adorn two swords, one representing rule over the temporal and one over the spiritual, which represented the next phase of Gurū Nānak Sāhib's revolution, the Mughal empire began to feel the effects of Sikh warfare, and that was extended to the Hill Chiefs. The manner with which Gurū Sāhib galvanised the Sikhs, following the martyrdom of Gurū Tegh Bahādur Sāhib, the second such ordeal the Sikhs endured that century, speaks volumes about the Gurū's radiant glory and captivating appeal.

Writ of the Khālsā

By 1704, the Gurū had strengthened the Sikh stronghold in Anandpur Sāhib, and the Khālsā's writ ran large over the surrounding region. The fame and popularity that permeated from Anandpur Sāhib only heightened discontent within the ranks of the Hill Chiefs, who conspired to attack Anandpur Sāhib again. They were badly beaten in the initial skirmishes, so they approached the support of Mughal authorities in Sirhind and Lahore. Saināpatī narrates how the Khālsā remained victorious at Anandpur Sāhib despite the combined effort of Mughal, Pathan, and Hindu Hill Chiefs.[37]

ਪਾਤਿਸ਼ਾਹੀ ਮਹਿਮਾ – Revisiting Sikh Sovereignty

Dr. W. L. M'Gregor, writing in 1846, also provides an insight into the attitude of the Hindu Hill Rajas during the establishment of Sikh sovereignty in Anandpur. He notes,

> *"in the course of two years [Guru] Govind subdued the country around him, extending his conquests as far as Roopar, on the left bank of the Sutlej. He took possession of the whole tract of country thus obtained and the hill Rajahs being unable to oppose Govind, they became alarmed lest he should expel them from their dominions, and seize their country. They therefore addressed a letter to the emperor, complaining of the encroachments of the Gooroo, and requesting aid in order that they might oppose his further aggressions".*[38]

In June 1705, the combined forces of the Mughal regime and the Hill Chiefs laid siege upon Anandpur Sāhib again; this time the siege lasted months. Later reports from Bahādur Shah's Court record,

> *"He [Gurū Gobind Singh] exercised dominance and authority in the submontane tract of the Kahlur Hills. When his friendship with the mountain Rajas was disrupted, imperial forces from Lahore, Jammu and Sahrind and all the Rajas came and besieged him".*[39]

Siege of Anandpur

There were some small skirmishes, but the real damage was done when food supplies and water from all sides were cut off. Many people inside Anandpur Sāhib started to die from starvation and thirst, and in a state of desperation, began to leave the city. Amongst those who left were the famous forty, who, having approached the Gurū to leave, were asked to sign a letter simply stating they were no longer the

Guru's Sikhs. We'll consider them again shortly. On the cold night of 5th December 1705, Gurū Gobind Singh departed from Anandpur Sāhib, along with their family and the devout Khālsā.

The Gurū's two youngest sons, Sāhibzada Zorawar Singh and Sāhibzada Fateh Singh, were separated from the Gurū as they crossed the Sirsa River. They went with their grandmother, Mata Gujri jī, whilst Gurū Gobind Singh's two eldest sons, Sāhibzada Ajit Singh and Sāhibzada Jujhar Singh accompanied the Gurū and the small unit of Khālsā to the town of Chamkaur Sāhib. Here a bloody battle took place, perhaps one of the most famous battles in Sikh history.

Battle of Chamkaur Sāhib, 1705

Both Saināpatī and Kavi Santokh Singh provide a masterful depiction of the Battle of Chamkaur, in which 40 or so Khālsā withstood the combined military might of 22 royal principalities of the Hill Chiefs and the Mughal forces led by Wazir Khan. Their account narrates soldiers within the Mughal ranks from as far as Europe, Uzbekistan, and Afghanistan, numbering 1.8 million. In the Zafarnamah, according to the translation provided by Prof. Surinderjit Singh, Gurū Gobind Singh refers to their forty famished men that were suddenly attacked by a million enemy troops.[40] In this eye-witness account, Gurū Gobind Singh reiterates the significant gulf in numbers, that even with the bravery of the forty Khālsā, the attack of countless adversaries took its toll. The strategic deployment and superior military prowess of the Khālsā are displayed throughout this battle. As tempting as it may be, it is not within the scope of this book to provide an in-depth commentary of the battle, but suffice to say, it is full of feats of Sikh bravery, courage, and resistance. Three of the original five that gave their head in 1699, Bhāī Mohkam Singh, Bhāī Himmat Singh, and Bhāī Sāhib Singh attained martyrdom, as did the Gurū's two elder sons, Sāhibzādā Ajit Singh and Sāhibzādā Jujhar Singh, and 30 or so other devout Khālsā warriors. Elsewhere, the

Guru's two youngest sons, Sāhibzādā Zorawar Singh and Sāhibzādā Fateh Singh were captured by Mughal forces and taunted with threats of death if they did not embrace Islam. The two young sons of the Gurū remained steadfast in their Sikhī and remained loyal to the Guru's Darbār. Following in the footsteps of their grandfather, Guru Tegh Bāhādur Sāhib, they embraced death over enslavement. They were mercilessly bricked alive. Within a short span, Gurū Gobind Singh lost their four sons, their mother, and many of the Khālsā from Anandpur Sāhib.

Battle of Muktsar Sāhib, 1705

Following this heavy loss, Gurū Gobind Singh regrouped and in the Battle of Muktsar Sāhib, repulsed another attack from Mughal forces under the leadership of Wazir Khan. It was in this battle that the forty who abandoned the Gurū in Anandpur Sāhib during the siege returned to serve the Gurū's Darbār. Under the inspired leadership of Bibi Bhag Kaur, sister to Bhag Singh and Dilbagh Singh, and wife of Nidhan Singh, just three of those men who had abandoned the Gurū, they fought valiantly in the Battle of Muktsar Sāhib, in which Bibi Bhag Kaur was injured too. In their dying wish to the Gurū, they asked the Gurū to tear up their signed letter. The Gurū duly accepted and endowed them with the honorific title '40 liberated ones' on 28 December 1705.[41] Following this battle, Gurū Gobind Singh penned the famous "Epistle of Victory", the Zafarnama, in Persian and sent it with Bhāī Daya Singh to Aurangzeb[42]. It is said upon reading the letter, Aurangzeb was greatly distressed and wanted to conciliate with the Gurū; however, he died before any meeting between the two took place.

Regrouping and mobilization in Malwa

Within Sri Gur Sobha, we learn that Gurū Gobind Singh fought a total of eleven battles with the Hindu Hill Rajas and six with the

Mughal forces. In some of those battles, the two enemy forces had colluded and combined their forces, but in a lot of them, the Hindu Hill Rajas had asked the Mughal regime for assistance because they were unable to defeat the Gurū and the Khālsā. This was the case with the Siege of Anandpur Sāhib.

Having relinquished Anandpur Sāhib in the manner described above, Gurū Gobind Singh spent almost a year in the Malwa region surrounding Muktsar Sāhib. The stay was most fruitful, with hundreds of thousands from Malwa joining the ranks of the Khālsā. It is during this time the Gurū worked with Shaheed Bhāī Mani Singh in preparing the Gurū Granth Sāhib and also collected their own writings, which formed the Srī Dasam Granth. Gurū Sāhib is said to have moved southward and was soon engaged in battles. There was the Battle of Baghaur (1706) and also the Battle of Jajau (1707).[43] The former was fought against Rajput Hill Chiefs, and the latter, following Aurangzeb's death, was a battle for the Mughal throne, as Tara Azam and Bahādur Shah, two of Aurangzeb's four sons, clashed on the battlefield near Agra.

Battle of Jajau, 1707

In the same way Emperor Humayun had sought the refuge of Gurū Angad Sāhib, Bahādur Shah had sought the assistance of Gurū Gobind Singh, and according to Kaushish, Gurū Sāhib dispatched Bhāī Daya Singh along with twenty-five other Khālsā to form a military allegiance with Bahādur Shah's troops, before joining the battle. Tara Azam and his son lost their lives, and with Gurū Sāhib's assistance, Bahādur Shah achieved the victory. As a result, there were cordial relations between the Mughal regime and the Gurū's Darbār.[44] Saināpatī too states that the Gurū offered moral support but does not provide as much detail as other Sikh sources. Kavi Santokh Singh narrates a very detailed account of the relationship between Gurū Gobind Singh and Bahādur Shah, which we'll cover shortly.

Another detailed account is found in the writings of Giānī Giān Singh. It is worth revisiting this account in some detail here. He describes how Bhāī Nand Lāl jī was instrumental in negotiating the terms of Gurū Sāhib's military allegiance with Bahādur Shah in the Battle of Jajau. After Bahādur Shah accepted the conditions, namely to honour his word unlike his father, Gurū Sāhib deployed Bhāī Daya Singh and Bhāī Dharam Singh along with a contingent of elite Khālsā warriors, with the specific task of remaining near Bahādur Shah. The plan was for Gurū Sāhib to enter the battlefield and kill Tara Azam. As both sides prepared for battle, Gurū Sāhib called Khālsā warriors to Agra, and Bahādur Shah grew more confident of victory upon seeing the arrival of the famed battle-hardened Khālsā. Battle commenced and many valiant soldiers fought bravely as the deafening sound of gunfire from the array of weapons echoed throughout the battlefield. Hundreds of horsemen clashed, and the ground was soon soaked crimson red from the blood of wounded and killed warriors.

This continued for three whole days. On the fourth, it is recorded, Bahadar Shah became quite anxious and approached Bhāī Nand Lal jī to seek reassurance that the Gurū would enter the battlefield. He was reminded to uphold his word to the Gurū and is said to have a signed a letter to that effect. Kavi Santokh Singh narrates a similar account; in fact, he states that it was the Gurū who insisted on receiving this in writing.

ਤਾਰਾ ਆਜ਼ਮ ਕੋ ਹਮ ਮਾਰੈਂ। ਤਖਤ ਬਹਾਦਰ ਸ਼ਾਹ ਬਿਠਾਰੈਂ।
ਪੀਛੇ ਤੇ ਕਰਿ ਪੂਰਨ ਸਵਾਲ। ਲਗੀ ਬਲਮ ਜਾਂ ਤੇ ਨੰਦ ਲਾਲ!

I shall kill Tara Azam, and place Bahādur Shah on the throne. As long as Bahādur Shah upholds his word, this is why it is taking time, O' Nand Lal.[45]

Bhāī Nand Lal jī, in his role as Gurū Sāhib's emissary, relayed this message to Bahādur Shah, who recognised instantly the Gurū knew exactly what his intentions were, so he sent an official with his handwritten letter confirming he would uphold his end of the deal. As the official delivered the letter, the battle continued to rage, and Bahādur Shah became fearful it would be his last day on Earth. He confided in Bhāī Dharam Singh, who had seen the fear in his eyes. Bahādur Shah bemoaned his predicament as his brother's forces, which outnumbered his own, gathered momentum and closed in on his position. He asked when Gurū Gobind Singh would arrive, asking Dharam Singh to do an Ardas for the Gurū to arrive soon. He is even recorded to have lost hope in the Gurū, becoming doubtful of the Gurū's promise, that perhaps Gurū Sāhib had lured him into this battle to ensure he met his end as revenge for what Aurangzeb had done to his sons. As Bahādur Shah began to lose faith, Dharam Singh is said to have reassured him that the Gurū would deliver on his word.

No sooner had Dharam Singh said this, Gurū Gobind Singh rode their horse into battle, fully-armed and accompanied by his Shaheed Fauja, whose battle insignia could be seen by Bahādur Shah as he sat on his elephant:

ਇਤਨੇ ਮਹਿੰ ਗੁਰ ਦਈ ਦਿਖਾਈ। ਸੰਗ ਸ਼ਹੀਦਨ ਦਲ ਸਮੁਦਾਈ ॥੨੪॥
ਬ੍ਰਿੰਦ ਨਿਸ਼ਾਨਨ ਫਰਰੇ ਛੁਟੇ। ਏਕੈ ਬਾਰਿ ਬਾਜ ਜਨੁ ਟੁਟੈ।

At that moment the Gurū appeared, riding into the battle with his army of martyrs. Their Nishan Sāhibs could be seen everywhere, as he pounced on the enemy forces.[46]

Bahādur Shah was instantly calmed and felt victory would soon be his, with the Gurū on his side. Giānī Gian Singh narrates how it was an arrow fired from the Gurū's personal quiver, unleashed with such ferocity that it penetrated Tara Azam's skull, killing him instantly. The Gurū and the Khālsā continued to fight in the battle and killed many more enemy troops. Soon enough, they secured victory for Bahādur Shah and retreated to Agra.[47]

Some may raise question marks over the credibility of this source; after all, Kavi Santokh Singh is writing in the mid-19th century, and Giānī Gian Singh is relying on the oral tradition, writing in the 1890s, approximately 180 years after the battle. However, Koer Singh Kalaal provides an almost identical account, some 150 years earlier, in his Gurbilās Pātshahi 10, penned in 1751.[48] This is a primary source on the life of Gurū Gobind Singh; in places, the works are more detailed than Sainapatī's Gursobha, Bachitar Natak, and even Bhāī Nand Lal jī's works, which are more about the praise and glory of Gurū Gobind Singh, less about his life and actions. Koer Singh also describes how Bahādur Shah had become fearful of losing the battle and relied heavily on the Gurū's intervention. He states how it was an arrow fired by Gurū Gobind Singh that killed Tara Azam.

In the aforementioned sources, Bahādur Shah is said to have retrieved the arrow that killed his brother and announced a large reward for the arrow's owner. Many warriors presented themselves; however, the arrow did not match the arrows in their possession. The Amirs and Vazirs proclaimed the arrow belonged to a Divine being, but he did not belong to the Mughal army. Bhāī Dharam Singh is said to have informed the Mughal court that the arrow belonged to Gurū Gobind Singh, which Bahādur Shah immediately verified by sending an attendant with Bhāī Nand Lal jī. The arrow was presented before Gurū Gobind Singh, who picked it up and placed it with the rest in their quiver, and no one could tell them apart. As a result, Bahādur Shah bowed in reverence to the Gurū and proclaimed his victory was possible only with the blessing of Gurū Gobind Singh. He invited Gurū Sāhib and respectfully honoured the Gurū. Persian sources of reports from Bahādur Shah's Court record that the Gurū arrived in the court fully armed and was presented with various expensive gifts, including a robe of honour and "medallion set with precious stones".[49]

Gurū Gobind Singh and Bahādur Shah

The relationship between Gurū Gobind Singh and Bahādur Shah is an intriguing one, much like the relationship between the latter's uncle Dara Shikoh and Gurū Har Rai Sāhib. Perhaps the Gurū assisted Bahādur Shah because of the latter's decision to show some consideration to the Gurū during the earlier battles with the Hindu Hill Chiefs.

The Gurū had delivered on their side of the deal by ensuring victory for Bahādur Shah in the Battle of Jajau; now, it was on Bahādur Shah to deliver on his promise. He arrived at the Gurū's Darbār with an offering of gifts, and remembering his promise to the Gurū, he asked how he could be of service. The Gurū handed Bahādur Shah a document, which had a list of seventeen names, including the likes of Wazir Khan, Suchanand, Nazam Din, Karam Chand Choudhry, and Raja Ajmer Chand; primary adversaries of the Gurū's Darbār who had inflicted crimes against the Panth. The request was to hand them over to the Gurū so they could be dealt with accordingly.

This seemed a relatively reasonable request given how the Gurū had personally assisted Bahādur Shah in ascending to the Mughal throne; however, Bahādur Shah's response was wholly unsatisfactory. According to Giānī Giān Singh, he asked the Gurū to wait five to seven years whilst he fully established his rule, and in the meantime offered any land of the Gurū's liking to settle upon. As a gesture of goodwill, he also offered to repatriate what the Gurū had lost in Anandpur Sāhib, including *Jagirs* for the Khālsā Singhs.

The Gurū listened and responded,

> *"Bahādur Shah you speak of delivering upon your promise in 5 to 7 years, but with the support of Akāl, I shall send one Bandā, who will bring all those I have listed to justice within 5 to 7 months! He shall punish those corrupt and oppressive officials of the Mughal dynasty. As for your offering to repatriate what I lost in Anandpur, you do not have the power to compensate me for what I once had in Anandpur. In the same vein, your proposal to offer Jagir to my Khālsā; let me tell you as sovereigns they are very much capable of capturing land themselves. I do not wish to ask for anything of you. My Khālsā will*

ਪਾਤਿਸ਼ਾਹੀ ਮਹਿਮਾ – Revisiting Sikh Sovereignty

achieve it all with their own strength and power of will".[50]

Kavi Santokh Singh mentions the duration Bahādur Shah asked for was one year, but the Gurū's response was similar. At the nucleus of Gurū Sāhib's response, as recorded in the pre-colonial accounts, is the notion of Sikh sovereignty. Gurū Sāhib gives Bahadur Shah the opportunity to honour his word; however, when he is unwilling to do so, the Gurū does not petition him any further. A line is drawn, and the task is then handed to the Khālsā. Shortly after this exchange, the Gurū travelled South, and the emperor continued with his mission to consolidate power by subduing the advances of his other brother.

Mandate to Banda Singh Bahādur

Gurū Gobind Singh travelled to Nanded, where the famous meeting takes place with Madho Das, who becomes Bandā Singh Bahādur. Bandā Singh was dispatched to Panjāb where he delivered on the Gurū's Hukam to bring justice and establish Khālsā Raj, which we will visit in the next chapter. Gurū Sāhib remained in Nanded, where people flocked to see them. During this time, an assassin was sent, purportedly by Wazir Khan, to kill the Gurū. The assassin, Jamshed Khan, succeeded in wounding Gurū Gobind Singh but was killed by the Gurū.[51] An entry exists in Mughal Court records of the incident, following which a robe of honour was bestowed upon the assassin's son[52], which suggests Bahādur Shah held the assassin in higher regard, thus exposing his true character.

Passing of the Gurūship

Whilst the wound healed, a few days later, Gurū Gobind Singh announced to the Khālsā that they would soon be leaving this world. According to Sainapatī, the Sikhs were keen to learn who the next Gurū would be:

ਵਾਹਿ ਸਮੈ ਗੁਰੂ ਬੈਨ ਸੁਨਾਯੋ । ਖਾਲਸ ਅਪਨੋ ਰੂਪ ਬਤਾਯੋ ।
"ਖਾਲਸ ਹੀ ਸੋ ਹੈ ਮਮ ਕਾਮਾ । ਬਖਸ ਕਿਯੋ ਖਾਲਸ ਜੋ ਜਾਮਾ ॥ ੪੧ ॥ ੮੦੬ ॥
ਖਾਲਸ ਮੇਰੇ ਰੂਪ ਹੈ, ਹੋ ਖਾਲਸ ਕੇ ਪਾਸ ।
ਆਦਿ ਅੰਤ ਹੀ ਹੋਤ ਹੈ, ਖਾਲਸ ਹੀ ਮੈ ਬਾਸ ॥ ੪੨ ॥ ੮੦੭ ॥

At that moment the Divine Guru had remarked that the Khalsa was the embodiment of them. "I devote the whole of my life to the Khalsa, so I now endow the Khalsa with my own form". 41.806.
"As the Khalsa bears my own identity, so am I with the Khalsa each and every moment. So have I been since the beginning till eternity, in the Khalsa commonwealth does my spirit reside". 42. 807.[53]

It is interesting to note Sainapatī, who remember is writing between 1701-1711, does not state anywhere that Gurū Gobind Singh passed on Gurūship to the Granth. In fact, no contemporary source does this. Bhagat Singh's Gurbilās Pātshahi 6 (1718) is perhaps the first early text that refers to the Granth as Gurū.[54] Koer Singh's Gurbilās Pātshahi 10, written in 1751, also mentions the Granth in this light.[55]

Contemporary omission is perhaps explained by the fact Sikhs had become accustomed to bowing to the Adi Granth, as we discussed earlier, since the time of Gurū Arjan Sāhib, and therefore, writers such as Sainapatī deemed it necessary to emphasise the importance of the creation of the Gurū Panth. As well as referring to the Granth, writers such as Bhagat Singh and Koer Singh maintain the same degree of importance on the passing of Gurū's temporal power to the Khālsā. Koer Singh writes that whilst in Nanded, Gurū Gobind Singh urged the Sikhs to have full faith in the Gurū Granth Sāhib:

ਤਾਂ ਤੇ ਜੋ ਮੁਹ ਸਿਖ ਸੁਜਾਨਾ ।
ਮਾਨੇ ਗੁਰੂ ਗ੍ਰੰਥ ਭਗਵਾਨਾ ।

Those who speak of themselves as Sikh,
Must accept the Guru Granth. [56]

ਪਾਤਿਸ਼ਾਹੀ ਮਹਿਮਾ – Revisiting Sikh Sovereignty

Kesar Singh Chibbar (1769), also records the significance of Gurū Granth Sāhib following the departure of Gurū Gobind Singh. He states:

ਦੋਇ ਜਾਮ ਰੈਨਿ ਗਈ ਤਾਂ ਬਜਾਈ। ਸਿੱਖਾਂ ਹੱਥ ਜੋੜਿ ਕਰਿ ਬੇਨਤੀ ਪੁਛਾਈ:
"ਗਰਬਿ ਨਿਵਾਜ਼! ਸਿੱਖ-ਸੰਗਤਿ ਹੈ ਤੇਰੀ, ਇਸ ਦਾ ਕੀ ਹਵਾਲੁ।
ਬਚਨ ਕੀਤਾ, "ਗ੍ਰੰਥ ਹੈ ਗੁਰੁ, ਲੜ ਪਕੜੋ ਅਕਾਲ"। ੬੭੯।
ਗੁਰੁ ਹੈ ਖਾਲਸਾ, ਅਤੇ ਖਾਲਸਾ ਹੈ ਗੁਰੁ।
ਗੋਦੀ ਸ੍ਰੀ ਸਾਹਿਬ ਦੇਵੀ ਮਾਤਾ ਦੀ ਪਾਏ, ਭਜਨ ਕਰਨਾ ਸ਼ੁਰੂ।
ਆਪਸ ਵਿਚਿ ਕਰਨਾ ਪਿਆਰ, ਪੰਥ ਦੇ ਵਾਧੇ ਨੂੰ ਲੋਚਨਾ।
ਆਗਿਆ ਗ੍ਰੰਥ ਸਾਹਿਬ ਕੀ ਕਰਨੀ, ਸ਼ਬਦ ਦੀ ਖੋਜਣਾ। ੬੮੦।[57]

The Sikhs, with folded hands, asked: "O Gareeb Nivaz, what will come of this Sikh Sangat of yours"?
The Gurū spoke, "the Granth is Guru, adjoin to Akāl". 679
The Gurū is the Khālsā, the Khālsā is the Gurū.
Placed with Mata Sāhib Devi, start
Love each other and deliver on your promise to the Panth.
Listen to the Granth and contemplate on the Shabad. 680.

From precolonial texts, there is no ambiguity over the equal importance placed upon the institute of both Gurū Granth and the Gurū Panth. As mentioned above, the Sikhs had become accustomed to bowing to the Granth since the times of Gurū Arjan Sāhib, and this tradition was forever immortalised by the passing of Gurūship to the Granth by Gurū Gobind Singh.

However, Sikhī would not be what it is today without the Gurūs' temporal endeavours and the passing of their political responsibility unto the Khālsā. What sets the Gurūs' Sikhī apart from all other movements and ideologies that came before it is that in the space of 200 years or so, the Gurūs nurtured Sangat into the Panth, then bowed in reverence before the Panth. Powered by the Truth of Gurbānī, this nurturing of the Panth is a defining aspect of the Sikh revolution. Without the Panth, there is no means by which the Sikhs can continue the Gurūs' movement; there is no Bandā Singh, Kapur Singh, Jassa Singh, Sada Kaur, Ranjīt Singh, Hari Singh, and so forth. There are no movements for sovereignty or the establishment of political structures that redefined Panjāb.

Gurū Khālsā Panth

Within the creation of the Khālsā Panth is the making of a new identity based on the Truth espoused in Gurbānī, an identity which stands distinct against other prevalent traditions, customs, and norms that the Gurūs spoke out against. The Gurmukh, one who speaks like the Gurū, or simply Gurū-oriented as I've described elsewhere in this book, is the embodiment of that new identity. Contrary to the narrative presented by those who have taken a position to study and present Sikhī through the imposition of Western notions of religiosity, the emergence of the collective Gurmukhs, under the sovereign leadership and guidance of the Gurū Sāhibān and then the Khālsā Panth, is perhaps the single greatest transformation of a people. The Gurū does not speak of a Gurmukh within the bounds of Western notions of religiosity, and neither do other contributors to the Gurū Granth Sāhib. We also see this evident in the writings of the 17th, 18th and 19th century Sikh writers. Instead, the emphasis is on those who have find Satgurū and walk on the Gurū ordained path towards Nām and realizing Khālsā Raj.

The advent of Gurū Nānak Sāhib was the signal of a new awakening, an awakening so powerful that it changed everything. The Gurū Sāhibān carried the torch of this revolutionary enlightenment through many dark periods, awakening princes and paupers alike to the Truth of Creation that sits within. Despite relentless persecution, torture, death, and destruction, the Gurū Sāhibān stood firm, never wavering from their Divine wisdom and vision. They went toe-to-toe with many ego-fueled rulers in all social and political arenas. In a little over 200 years, through ten human forms, the Gurū Sāhibān demonstrated how those who based their actions on temporal laws of the land, written by egoic men, actually held no real jurisdiction or indeed power, over those Divine beings who rule both the spiritual and temporal worlds. Despite the Gurū Sāhibān facing direct attacks in the form of imprisonment, assassination, or attempted assassination, the Sikh movement continued to go from strength to strength, eventually realizing its objective with the manifestation of the Gurū' Khālsā Panth.

The establishment of the Gurū Khālsā Panth is testament to the enduring spirit of Sikh resistance and empowerment that is synonymised with the political actions of the Gurū Sāhibān, and the Panth's existence today is testament to the unwavering spirit of resistance of the Gurū's beloved Gurmukhs who have defended and furthered the sovereignty and sanctity of the Gurū's Panth with any means necessary. Central to all of the Panth's achievements and enduring struggles is the distinct identity and firm determination to remain distinct like the lotus flower who stays true to its nature, even though it may be surrounded by muddied waters. Remaining separate and sovereign from both Brahmanism's overarching influence and control, as well as the Mughal imperial regime, was key. This was only made possible due to the sovereignty of the Gurū's Darbār; perhaps the single greatest factor in the long road to the Sikh-led liberation for the people of Panjāb, and beyond.

Srī Gurū Gobind Singh Sāhib jī Māhārāj

NOTES

[1] Bhāī Nand Lal (1633-1713), *Ganjnama*, Kalaam-e-Goya, translated by Sardar Pritpal Singh Bindra, 2003, Institute of Sikh Studies, Chandigarh

[2] ਭਾਈ ਸਰੂਪ ਸਿੰਘ ਕੌਸ਼ਿਸ਼, ੧੭੯੦, ਗੁਰੂ ਕੀਆਂ ਸਾਖੀਆਂ
Bhai Swarup Singh Kaushish, 1790, *Guru Kīān Sākhīān*, Sākhī 37, edited by Piara Singh Padam, 1986, Singh Brothers, Amritsar, p91

[3] ਗੰਡਾ ਸਿੰਘ, ੧੯੬੭, ਹੁਕਮਨਾਮੇ ਸਿੱਖ ਗੁਰੂ, ਮਾਤਾ ਸਾਹਿਬਾਨ, ਬਾਬਾ ਬੰਦਾ ਸਿੰਘ ਅਤੇ ਗੁਰੂ ਕੇ ਖਾਲਸੇ ਦੇ
Dr. Ganda Singh, 1967, *Hukamname Sikh Guru, Mata Sahiban, Baba Banda Singh and Guru Ke Khalse De*, 1967, Baldev Singh, Kapurthala, New Revised Edition, 2015, p150

[4] ਪ੍ਰੋ. ਪਿਆਰਾ ਸਿੰਘ ਪਦਮ, ਸ੍ਰੀ ਗੁਰੂ ਗੋਬਿੰਦ ਸਿੰਘ ਜੀ ਦੇ ਦਰਬਾਰੀ ਰਤਨ
Professor Piara Singh Padam, 1974, *Sri Guru Gobind Singh Ji De Darbari Ratan*, Singh Brothers, p33

[5] ਭਾਈ ਕੇਸਰ ਸਿੰਘ ਛਿਬੱਰ, ੧੭੬੯, ਬੰਸਾਵਲੀਨਾਮਾ ਦਸਾਂ ਪਾਤਸ਼ਾਹੀਆਂ ਕਾ
Kesar Singh Chibbar, 1769, *Bansāvalīnāmā*, Edited by Piara Singh Padam, 1997, Singh Brothers, Amritsar, p130

[6] ਪ੍ਰੋ. ਪਿਆਰਾ ਸਿੰਘ ਪਦਮ, ਸ੍ਰੀ ਗੁਰੂ ਗੋਬਿੰਦ ਸਿੰਘ ਜੀ ਦੇ ਦਰਬਾਰੀ ਰਤਨ
Professor Piara Singh Padam, 1974, *Sri Guru Gobind Singh Ji De Darbari Ratan*, Singh Brothers, p27

[7] Kavī Chūrāmanī Bhāī Santokh Singh, 1843, *Srī Gur Pratap Sūraj Granth*, Steek 8, Rut 5 Adhiāi 52, edited by Dr. Ajeet Singh Aulakh, 2014, 3rd Edition, p834

[8] ਪ੍ਰੋ. ਪਿਆਰਾ ਸਿੰਘ ਪਦਮ, ਸ੍ਰੀ ਗੁਰੂ ਗੋਬਿੰਦ ਸਿੰਘ ਜੀ ਦੇ ਦਰਬਾਰੀ ਰਤਨ
Professor Piara Singh Padam, 1974, *Sri Guru Gobind Singh Ji De Darbari Ratan*, Singh Brothers, p28

[9] Dr Sukhdial Singh, 2007, *Origin and Evolution of the Khālsā Commonweatlh*, Chattar Singh Jiwan Singh, Amritsar, p57

[10] Kavī Chūrāmanī Bhāī Santokh Singh, 1843, *Srī Gur Pratap Sūraj Granth*, Steek 8, Rut 5 Adhiāi 52, edited by Dr. Ajeet Singh Aulakh, 2014, 3rd Edition, p834

[11] Sarūp Das Bhalla, Mehima Prakāsh, Bagh 2, Khand 2, Sakhi 11, p769

[12] ਪ੍ਰੋ. ਪਿਆਰਾ ਸਿੰਘ ਪਦਮ, ਸ੍ਰੀ ਗੁਰੂ ਗੋਬਿੰਦ ਸਿੰਘ ਜੀ ਦੇ ਦਰਬਾਰੀ ਰਤਨ
Professor Piara Singh Padam, 1974, *Sri Guru Gobind Singh Ji De Darbari Ratan*, Singh Brothers, p54

[13] Gurū Nānak, Guru Gobind Singh and the Revolt under Banda Bahādur 1709-10 & 1713-16, from Muhammad Qāsim "Ibrat", Ibratnama, translated by J. S. Grewal & Irfan Habib, 2001, *Sikh History from Persian Sources*, Tulika Books, Delhi, p113

[14] S.A.A. Rizvi, *The Wonder that was* India, Volume II, p172

[15] ਭਾਈ ਸਰੂਪ ਸਿੰਘ ਕੌਸ਼ਿਸ਼, ੧੭੯੦, ਗੁਰੂ ਕੀਆਂ ਸਾਖੀਆਂ
Bhai Swarup Singh Kaushish, 1790, *Guru Kīān Sākhīān*, Sākhī 43 and 44, edited by Piara Singh Padam, 1986, Singh Brothers, Amritsar, p98

[16] Kesar Singh Chibbar, Bansāvalīnāmā, p146

[17] Saināpatī, 1711, *Srī Gur Sobha*, translation by Prof. Kulwant Singh, Institute of Sikh Studies, Chandigarh, p19

[18] Saināpatī, 1711, *Srī Gur Sobha*, translation by Prof. Kulwant Singh, Institute of Sikh Studies, Chandigarh, p20

[19] ਭਾਈ ਸਰੂਪ ਸਿੰਘ ਕੌਸ਼ਿਸ਼, ੧੭੯੦, ਗੁਰੂ ਕੀਆਂ ਸਾਖੀਆਂ
Bhai Swarup Singh Kaushish, 1790, *Guru Kīān Sākhīān*, Sākhī 53, edited by Piara Singh Padam, 1986, Singh Brothers, Amritsar, p112

[20] Saināpatī, 1711, *Srī Gur Sobha*, translation by Prof. Kulwant Singh, Institute of Sikh Studies, Chandigarh, p49

[21] ਭਾਈ ਸਰੂਪ ਸਿੰਘ ਕੌਸ਼ਿਸ਼, ੧੭੯੦, ਗੁਰੂ ਕੀਆਂ ਸਾਖੀਆਂ
Bhai Swarup Singh Kaushish, 1790, *Guru Kīān Sākhīān*, Sākhī 53, edited by Piara Singh Padam, 1986, Singh Brothers, Amritsar, p114

[22] ਭਾਈ ਸਰੂਪ ਸਿੰਘ ਕੌਸ਼ਿਸ਼, ੧੭੯੦, ਗੁਰੂ ਕੀਆਂ ਸਾਖੀਆਂ
Bhai Swarup Singh Kaushish, 1790, *Guru Kīān Sākhīān*, Sākhī 53, edited by Piara Singh Padam, 1986, Singh Brothers, Amritsar, p114

[23] Sarūp Das Bhalla, Mehima Prakāsh, Bagh 2, Khand 2, p778

[24] ਭਾਈ ਸਰੂਪ ਸਿੰਘ ਕੌਸ਼ਿਸ਼, ੧੭੯੦, ਗੁਰੂ ਕੀਆਂ ਸਾਖੀਆਂ
Bhai Swarup Singh Kaushish, 1790, *Guru Kīān Sākhīān*, Sākhī 58, edited by Piara Singh Padam, 1986, Singh Brothers, Amritsar, p120

[25] Saināpatī, 1711, *Srī Gur Sobha*, translation by Prof. Kulwant Singh, Institute of Sikh Studies, Chandigarh, p63

[26] ਸਰੂਪ ਦਾਸ ਭੱਲਾ, ੧੭੭੬, ਮਹਿਮਾ ਪ੍ਰਕਾਸ਼
Sārūp Das Bhalla, 1776, *Mehmā Prakāsh*, Edited by Dr. Uttam Singh Bhatia, 1971, Bagh 2, Khand 2, Bhasha Vibhag, Panjab, p779

[27] Saināpatī, 1711, *Srī Gur Sobha*, translation by Prof. Kulwant Singh, Institute of Sikh Studies, Chandigarh, p61

[28] Jagjit Singh, 1981, *Percussions of History, The Sikh Revolution & in the Caravan of Revolutions*, The Nanakshahi Trust, Panjab, p125

[29] ਭਾਈ ਸਰੂਪ ਸਿੰਘ ਕੌਸ਼ਿਸ, ੧੭੯੦, ਗੁਰੂ ਕੀਆਂ ਸਾਖੀਆਂ
Bhai Swarup Singh Kaushish, 1790, *Gurū Kīān Sākhīān*, Sākhī 58, edited by Piara Singh Padam, 1986, Singh Brothers, Amritsar, p121

[30] Gurū Nānak Sāhib, Salok Vārān Thay Vadheek, Gurū Granth Sāhib, Ang 1412

[31] ਰਤਨ ਸਿੰਘ ਭੰਗੂ, ੧੮੪੧, ਸ੍ਰੀ ਗੁਰ ਪੰਥ ਪ੍ਰਕਾਸ਼
Rattan Singh Bhangoo, 1841, *Sri Gur Panth Prakash*, (2:35), edited by Kulwant Singh, IOSS, p89

[32] ਖੁਇਰ ਸਿੰਘ, ੧੭੫੧, ਗੁਰਬਿਲਾਸ ਪਾਤਸ਼ਾਹੀ ੧੦
Koer Singh, 1751, *Gurbilās Pātshahi Dasve*, edited by Shamsher Singh Ashok, 1999, Panjabi University, Patiala, p111

[33] ਭਾਈ ਸਰੂਪ ਸਿੰਘ ਕੌਸ਼ਿਸ, ੧੭੯੦, ਗੁਰੂ ਕੀਆਂ ਸਾਖੀਆਂ
Bhai Swarup Singh Kaushish, 1790, *Gurū Kīān Sākhīān*, Sākhī 68, edited by Piara Singh Padam, 1986, Singh Brothers, Amritsar, p136

[34] ਭਾਈ ਸਰੂਪ ਸਿੰਘ ਕੌਸ਼ਿਸ, ੧੭੯੦, ਗੁਰੂ ਕੀਆਂ ਸਾਖੀਆਂ
Bhai Swarup Singh Kaushish, 1790, *Gurū Kīān Sākhīān*, Sākhī 69, edited by Piara Singh Padam, 1986, Singh Brothers, Amritsar, p136

[35] ਭਾਈ ਸਰੂਪ ਸਿੰਘ ਕੌਸ਼ਿਸ, ੧੭੯੦, ਗੁਰੂ ਕੀਆਂ ਸਾਖੀਆਂ
Bhai Swarup Singh Kaushish, 1790, *Gurū Kīān Sākhīān*, Sākhī 70, edited by Piara Singh Padam, 1986, Singh Brothers, Amritsar, p139

[36] ਭਾਈ ਸਰੂਪ ਸਿੰਘ ਕੌਸ਼ਿਸ, ੧੭੯੦, ਗੁਰੂ ਕੀਆਂ ਸਾਖੀਆਂ
Bhai Swarup Singh Kaushish, 1790, *Gurū Kīān Sākhīān*, Sākhī 72, edited by Piara Singh Padam, 1986, Singh Brothers, Amritsar, p142

[37] Saināpatī, 1711, *Srī Gur Sobha*, translation by Prof. Kulwant Singh, Institute of Sikh Studies, Chandigarh, Chapter 11

[38] W. L. M'Gregor, 1846, *The History of the Sikhs*, Vol.2, James Madden, London, p85

[39] AkhbHarat-I Darbār-I mu'alla, 25 Rabi I, R.Y.1 (24 May 1710), translated by J. S. Grewal & Irfan Habib, 2001, *Sikh History from Persian Sources*, Tulika Books, Delhi, p107

[40] Gurū Gobind Singh, *Zafarnama*, translated by Prof. Surinderjit Singh, 2010, Third Edition, Singh Brothers, Amritsar, p44

[41] ਭਾਈ ਸਰੂਪ ਸਿੰਘ ਕੌਸ਼ਿਸ਼, ੧੭੯੦, ਗੁਰੂ ਕੀਆਂ ਸਾਖੀਆਂ

Bhai Swarup Singh Kaushish, 1790, *Gurū Kīān Sākhīān*, Sākhī 92, edited by Piara Singh Padam, 1986, Singh Brothers, Amritsar, p188

[42] ਖੁਇਰ ਸਿੰਘ, ੧੭੫੧, ਗੁਰਬਿਲਾਸ ਪਾਤਸ਼ਾਹੀ ੧੦

Koer Singh, 1751, *Gurbilās Pātshahi Dasve*, edited by Shamsher Singh Ashok, 1999, Panjabi University, Patiala, p202; AND ਭਾਈ ਖੇਸਰ ਸਿੰਘ ਛਿਬੱਰ, ੧੭੬੯, ਬੰਸਾਵਲੀਨਾਮਾ ਦਸਾਂ ਪਾਤਸ਼ਾਹੀਆਂ ਕਾ

Kesar Singh Chibbar, 1769, *Bansāvalīnāmā*, Edited by Piara Singh Padam, 1997, Singh Brothers, Amritsar, stanza 587-605

[43] ਭਾਈ ਸਰੂਪ ਸਿੰਘ ਕੌਸ਼ਿਸ਼, ੧੭੯੦, ਗੁਰੂ ਕੀਆਂ ਸਾਖੀਆਂ

Bhai Swarup Singh Kaushish, 1790, *Gurū Kīān Sākhīān*, Sākhī 104, edited by Piara Singh Padam, 1986, Singh Brothers, Amritsar, p188

[44] ਭਾਈ ਸਰੂਪ ਸਿੰਘ ਕੌਸ਼ਿਸ਼, ੧੭੯੦, ਗੁਰੂ ਕੀਆਂ ਸਾਖੀਆਂ

Bhai Swarup Singh Kaushish, 1790, *Gurū Kīān Sākhīān*, Sākhī 104, edited by Piara Singh Padam, 1986, Singh Brothers, Amritsar, p189

[45] Kavī Chūrāmanī Bhāī Santokh Singh, 1843, *Srī Gur Pratap Sūraj Granth*, Ayan 1, Adhiāi 41, Edited by Dr. Ajeet Singh Aulakh, 2014, 3rd Edition, p337

[46] Kavī Chūrāmanī Bhāī Santokh Singh, Srī Gur Pratap Sūraj Granth (1843), Steek 8, Ayan 1, Adhiāi 42, Edited by Dr. Ajeet Singh Aulakh, 2014, 3rd Edition, p343

[47] Giānī Giān Singh, 1891, *Tvārīkh Guru Khālsā*, Chattar Singh Jeevan Singh, Amritsar, p822

[48] ਖੁਇਰ ਸਿੰਘ, ੧੭੫੧, ਗੁਰਬਿਲਾਸ ਪਾਤਸ਼ਾਹੀ ੧੦

Koer Singh, 1751, *Gurbilās Pātshahi Dasve*, edited by Shamsher Singh Ashok, 1999, Panjabi University, Patiala, p230

[49] Akhbharat-I Darbār-I mu'alla, 5 Jumada I, R.Y.1 (4 August 1707), translated by J. S. Grewal & Irfan Habib, 2001, *Sikh History from Persian Sources,* Tulika Books, Delhi, p106

[50] Giānī Giān Singh, 1891, *Tvārīkh Gurū Khālsā*, Chattar Singh Jeevan Singh, Amritsar, p828

[51] Saināpatī, 1711, *Srī Gur Sobha*, translation by Prof. Kulwant Singh, Institute of Sikh Studies, Chandigarh, Chapter 18, p315

[52] Akhbharat-I Darbār-I mu'alla, 24 Sha'ban, R.Y. 2 (8 November 1708; and 25 Rabi'I, R.Y.4 (24 May 1710) translated by J. S. Grewal & Irfan Habib, 2001, *Sikh History from Persian Sources,* Tulika Books, Delhi, p107

[53] Saināpatī, 1711, *Srī Gur Sobha*, translation by Prof. Kulwant Singh, Institute of Sikh Studies, Chandigarh, Chapter 18, p323

[54] ਭਗਤ ਸਿੰਘ, ੧੭੧੮, ਗੁਰ ਬਿਲਾਸ ਪਾਤਸ਼ਾਹੀ ੬

Bhagat Singh, 1718, *Gurbilās Pātshahi 6*, Edited by Dr. Gurmukh Singh, 1997, Punjabi University, Patiala, Chapter 7, p240

[55] ਖੁਇਰ ਸਿੰਘ, ੧੨੫੧, ਗੁਰਬਿਲਾਸ ਪਾਤਸ਼ਾਹੀ ੧੦

Koer Singh, 1751, *Gurbilās Pātshahi Dasve*, edited by Shamsher Singh Ashok, 1999, Panjabi University, Patiala, p111

[56] ਖੁਇਰ ਸਿੰਘ, ੧੨੫੧, ਗੁਰਬਿਲਾਸ ਪਾਤਸ਼ਾਹੀ ੧੦

Koer Singh, 1751, *Gurbilās Pātshahi Dasve*, edited by Shamsher Singh Ashok, 1999, Panjabi University, Patiala, p264

[57] ਭਾਈ ਖੇਸਰ ਸਿੰਘ ਛਿਬੱਰ, ੧੭੬੯, ਬੰਸਾਵਲੀਨਾਮਾ ਦਸਾਂ ਪਾਤਸ਼ਾਹੀਆਂ ਕਾ

Kesar Singh Chibbar, 1769, *Bansāvalīnāmā*, Edited by Piara Singh Padam, 1997, Singh Brothers, Amritsar, p189

Part 2: Rise of the Khālsā and Pursuit of Rāj

Part 2 Rise of the Khālsā and Pursuit of Rāj

RISE OF THE KHĀLSĀ AND PURSUIT OF RĀJ

In Part One, we considered how the political accomplishments of the Gurū Sāhibān were guaranteed by the Divine sovereign agency of the Gurū's Darbār. Within the Sikh worldview, Mīrī is inseparable from Pīrī, which signifies the uniqueness of the Sikh movement; namely, the dual approach of liberation initiated by the Gurū Sāhibān, who illuminated a world engulfed in darkness, both in the spiritual and temporal sense. We considered how the establishment of the Akāl Takht within the Parikarma of Srī Darbār Sāhib in Amritsar, was in itself a reflection of the inseparability of Miri and Piri. Where they revealed the Shabad as a means of connecting the soul back with the Divine and emancipating the mind, the Gurū Sāhibān also actively engaged in challenging and defying the ego-centric power structures responsible for the suppression of mind and body.

As we have established, this began with Gurū Nānak Sāhib and the founding of Kartārpur Sāhib. However, in a post-1947 world, the temporal liberation is often solely attributed to Gurū Hargobind Sāhib or Gurū Gobind Singh. Rarely does one attribute physical liberation from oppressive structures of control and exploitation to the actions of Gurū Amar Dās Sāhib or Gurū Har Krishan Sāhib. Most historians appear to skim over, or even dilute the revolutionary aspects of their lives and contributions to Sikh Sangarsh. Furthermore, the actions of Gurū Gobind Singh are re-presented within the revisionist works of Indian nationalists that carry an Islamophobic rhetoric which reduces the Gurū's mobilization to an act of "Indian" patriotism. The fact that Gurū Gobind Singh waged more battles against the Hindu Hill kings is purposefully overlooked. The

ਪਾਤਿਸ਼ਾਹੀ ਮਹਿਮਾ – Revisiting Sikh Sovereignty

irony here, of course, is the fact that the same erroneous depiction can be traced back to the Persian accounts who, in order to justify the Imperial regime's oppressive ways, write that Gurū Nānak Sāhib was merely a *fakir*, but the later Gurū's introduced new customs which is why the Mughal forces were charged with orders to remove them.[1]

Western scholarship

Following the efforts of Hew McLeod, a lot of Western scholarship on "Sikh studies" has taken this position, a narrative that seeks to show a kind of 'break' in the Gurū's ideology[2], from a non-violent, pacifist movement to a militant and fundamental one. McLeod's modern narrative is built on the works of East India Company employees such as George Forster (1783), who described Gurū Gobind Singh as having deviated,

> *"From the ordinances of his predecessors, [and] imparted a strong military spirit to his adherents, whose zealous attachment enabled him to indulge the best of a fierce and turbulent temper."*[3]

Darshan Singh notes how these early European accounts associate the Sehajdhārīs with Gurū Nānak Sāhib and the Kesādhārdīs with Gurū Gobind Singh.[4] In most early European accounts, much like the Mughal accounts in relation to Gurū Nānak Sāhib referred to above, the diversion is attributed to the specific moment of the bearing of arms and raising armies. When the Gurūs exercised their Pātshāhī and sought to liberate the people from oppressive governance with the use of arms, that was the moment they established a parallel military force with the will to stand against other regimes. The early Gurū Sāhibān are painted differently altogether, despite the fact they readied the ground for the mobilisation that occurred later. These narratives and terms used by the British writers, arrive within a very specific context and geographical location. They are born from the imagination of

Part 2 Rise of the Khālsā and Pursuit of Rāj

Europeans who, having begun what decolonial scholarship terms both, their genocide and epistemicide[i] in the 16th century were engaged in their own mission of creating a new global order. We will look at this in more depth in the Part 3; however, it is important to remember that their narratives are often projected against the backdrop of Christianity, and the so-called Renaissance and Protestant Reformation in Europe, or as Darshan Singh has noted, on a superficial understanding of the Sikh tradition, which assumes that the Gurūs were reformists, or that Sikhs were an offshoot of Hinduism, or the product of some attempt to amalgamate and "reconcile the warring religions of Hinduism and Islam."[5]

One Light Ten Bodies

As we have seen, seven of the ten Gurū Sāhibān faced direct action from the imperial regime, whether through imprisonment, assassination, or attempted assassinations. The other three also had some kind of run-in with the Mughal establishment, albeit in a lesser confrontational manner. This is because the Gurū Sāhibān were politically active in building and furthering Sangarsh, by building parallel power structures through the sovereignty of the Gurū's Darbār. The obvious oneness of the Gurūs is evident in their own Words and their actions, as well as being evident in earlier pre-colonial Sikhs texts,

---

[i] I am referring here to the specific body of work of decolonial thinkers, in particular Anibal Quijano and Ramon Grosfoguel, the former who characterised the global, capitalist, colonial, modern system of power as beginning in the 16th century, and the latter who built on this work by contextualising the "Four Genocides/Epistemicides of the Long 16th Century" and thus critiqued the basis of the system that privileges as superior Western white male knowledge production, and inferiorises knowledges that are non-Western.

ਪਾਤਿਸ਼ਾਹੀ ਮਹਿਮਾ – Revisiting Sikh Sovereignty

ਗੁਰੂ ਗੋਬਿੰਦ ਸਿੰਘ ਗੁਰੂ ਨਾਨਕ ਮੈ ਭੇਦ ਨ ਰਾਈ।
ਜਾਮੇ ਦਸ, ਇਕ ਜੋਤਿ ਸਮਾਈ।
ਜੇ ਕੋਈ ਪੰਥ ਤਵਨ ਕੇ ਆਇਆ।
ਤਿਨ ਅਪਨਾ ਕੁਲ ਬੰਸੁ ਤਰਾਇਆ।੨੩੦।[6]

Do not differentiate between Gurū Gobind Singh to Gurū Nānak.
They were but one Light in 10 bodies.
Whosoever joined the Panth, they saved their entire family lineage.

There is constant reference to the Oneness of the Gurū Sāhibān included in the writings of precolonial texts The spiritual light, Shabad, that powered the accomplishments of all the Gurū Sāhibān was infused into the Gurū Granth Sāhib, and its eternal glow was forever placed within the bodies of the Khālsā. Thus, the responsibility of carrying the light that dispelled the darkness of Kaljug was bestowed upon the collective of Gurmukhs, who pledged to accept the Shabad as their spiritual guide and uphold the Gurū-inspired movement for Khālsā Rāj. Following the departure of Gurū Gobind Singh in 1708, the movement, or Sangarsh, has taken many forms and many names, which we shall now consider, from the campaigns of Bandā Singh Bahādur; to the guerrilla units of the Misl period; to the resistance of Sikh rulers and rebels during colonial occupation; to the present-day movement for liberation initiated in 1986 with the Declaration of Khālistān.

Sikh Sangarsh

As we have seen in Part One, the Sikh Sangarsh initiated by the Gurū Sāhibān was built on the foundations of Truth; unique from other political establishments built on ego and devoid of any notion of Hukam or Nām. This applies to both the imperial empire that governed Panjāb and the surrounding region, as well as the structures of power elsewhere in the world. Sikh sovereignty was at

Part 2 Rise of the Khālsā and Pursuit of Rāj

the nucleus of the movement initiated by Gurū Nānak Sāhib, actualised by the Gurū's Darbār and in the second half of this book, which is divided into Parts Two, Three and Four, we shall consider how the accomplishments of the Sikhs following the Gurū's departure in 1708, inspired by Gurmat, built on the movement initiated by the Gurū Sāhibān. We will consider the rise and fall of Rāj under Bandā Singh, the Misl Sardārs and Ranjīt Singh before looking at the advent of European colonization, which marked the start of Panjāb's current predicament in which the British violently gained control of wealth and resources for their own personal and imperial needs; a legacy continued by the neocolonial state of India. Sikh Sangarsh was present long before the events of 1984, 1978, 1947 or 1849. The trajectory of the idea of Khālistān, as encapsulated in the Declaration of Khalistan[7], was set by the founding of Kartārpur Sāhib by Gurū Nānak Sāhib. The Gurūs carved out new towns and territories from the established landscape under Mughal rule and, as we've seen, went to war over that territory, which signified governance based on the ideals enshrined within Gurū Granth Sāhib. The Sikhs have been on this path of establishing a home in which they can realise the Gurū's vision of an egalitarian society, for the betterment of all, for five centuries.

It can be tempting to analyze or present Sikh political events in isolation of four specific periods; 1469-1708; 1708-1849; 1849-1984; and 1984-present. While this approach, or some slight variation of it, allows one to consider significant moments in the history of the Sikhs, it can also sometimes be wrongly inferred as a break or diversion in the political aspirations of the Sikh movement. It can also entrap important discourse and debate within a historicised perspective of the Gurū Sāhibān and the Khālsā. It is therefore important that any such examination of the rise of the Khālsā and pursuit of Rāj, be considered, firstly within the scope of Mīrī-Pīrī, and secondly, within the wider context of the Age of Kaljug; the cycle of time, heavily discussed and explained in the Gurū Granth Sāhib. This is an approach I have tried to incorporate within the various chapters of this book.

While the Sangarsh began with the arrival of Gurū Nānak Sāhib, let us now consider how the Gurū-inspired awakening seeded revolution after revolution.

Part 2 Rise of the Khālsā and Pursuit of Rāj

NOTES

[1] See for example AkhbHarat-I Darbār-I mu'alla, 25 Rabi I, R.Y.1 (24 May 1710), and and Gurū Nānak, Gurū Gobind Singh and the Revolt under Banda Bahādur 1709-10 & 1713-16, from Muhammad Qāsim "Ibrat", Ibratnama, translated by J. S. Grewal & Irfan Habib, 2001, *Sikh History from Persian Sources,* Tulika Books, Delhi, p110

[2] For example see W.H. McLeod (1984), Textual Sources for the Study of Sikhism, Manchester University Press; T.N. Madan (1994), 'The Double-Edged Sword: Fundamentalism and the Sikh Religious Tradition', in Fundamentalisms Observed, Martin E. Marty and R. Scott Appleby, University of Chicago Press, p594-627; L.Fenech (2000), Martyrdom in the Sikh Tradition: Playing the 'Game of Love', Oxford University Press; and H.S. Syan, 2013, Sikh Militancy in the Seventeenth Century, Religious Violence in Mughal and Early Modern India, I.B. Tauris, London

[3] George Forster, 1783, *A Journey from Bengal to England*, London, p309-310

[4] Darshan Singh, 1999, *Western Perspective on the Sikh Religion*, Singh Brothers, Amrtisar, p135

[5] Darshan Singh, 1999, *Western Perspective on the Sikh Religion*, Singh Brothers, Amrtisar, p132

[6] ਭਾਈ ਖੇਸਰ ਸਿੰਘ ਛਿਬੱਰ, ੧੭੬੯, ਬੰਸਾਵਲੀਨਾਮਾ ਦਸਾਂ ਪਾਤਸ਼ਾਹੀਆਂ ਕਾ

Kesar Singh Chibbar, 1769, *Bansāvalīnāmā*, Edited by Piara Singh Padam, 1997, Singh Brothers, Amritsar, p194

[7] See - "Panthic Dastavej", edited by Narayan Singh Chuaura and Journalist Karamjit Singh - https://sikhsiyasat.net/wp-content/uploads/2015/12/Resolutions-of-the-Sarbat-Khalsa-1986.compressed.pdf; and 1984Tribute.com Team, *The Sikh Martyrs*, Volume 1, p251-256

ਪਾਤਿਸ਼ਾਹੀ ਮਹਿਮਾ – Revisiting Sikh Sovereignty

Bandā Singh Bahadur and the Khālsā Republic

The rise of the Khālsā, as a Gurū-empowered sovereign entity, continues to be a great source of inspiration for Sikhs across the globe. Sikh interaction, organization, activism and struggle for independence continues to be built around the actions of the Khālsā. The Gurū's Khālsā is one who does not bow to the authority of any worldly king or queen, empire or government. Khālsā only accepts the authority of Akāl and seeks to establish Rāj bestowed upon it by the Pātshāhī of Gurū Nānak Sāhib.

Gurū Gobind Singh's mandate to Bandā Singh

Following the Gurū period, the Sikhs immediately set out to deliver on the mandate to punish oppressors and establish political power for the Khālsā. This was the primary objective of the mandate Gurū Gobind Singh gave to Bandā Singh Bahādur in 1708. It was to lead the Khālsā, as an equal amongst the Khālsā; sovereigns empowered by the authority of the Gurū, to uproot oppression and establish Khālsā rule. Khālsā rule not for the purpose of replacing one empire with another, but creating radical change by building new structures of governance that built on the foundations of the Gurū-period.

Bandā Singh Bahādur was like a wild storm that gathered momentum as he moved from the south, travelling north, destroying all oppressive structures in its path. The system of landlords that were agents of oppressive Mughal governance was abolished by the Khālsā under Bandā Singh's leadership. Whilst his tenure was short-lived, the ramifications of his Gurū-inspired movement were far-reaching. The political achievements of the first, post-Guru movement for Sikh sovereignty paved the way for the creation of the Sikh Misls, who continued the tradition of either seeking to establish Sikh Rāj or fighting until death for its establishment. The 18th century is littered with countless stories of Sikh resistance and victory.

It had been almost a decade since the creation of the Khālsā, an event in which the institution of the Masands was replaced. As discussed, this organizational restructuring also signaled the dawn of a new era within the Gurū's Darbār. Whilst the Gurū Granth Sāhib remained the permanent spiritual guide for the Sikhs, the temporal powers of the Gurū were now vested in the Khālsā, under the collective leadership of the five-beloved ones (Panj Pyar-e). Bandā Singh Bahādur was hand-picked by Gurū Gobind Singh to be the first executive head of the Khālsā Collective. Along with Bandā Singh, the Panj Pyar-e, and 25 other Khālsā were dispatched to Panjāb from Nanded after Gurū Gobind Singh anointed them with weapons and battle standards.

Bandā Singh Bahādur

Sikh tradition records that Bandā Singh was given a mandate always to seek the wise counsel of the Panj Pyar-e, who at the time were Bhāī Binod Singh, Bhāī Kahan Singh, Bhāī Baaj Singh, Bhāī Daya Singh, and Bhāī Ram Singh. They were both custodians of the Gurū's temporal power and battle-hardened warriors. Sarūp Das Bhalla[1], Rattan Singh Bhangoo[2] and Giānī Giān Singh[3] are unanimous with the first three names. They differ slightly on the other two names; Bhangoo states it was Daya Singh and Nain Singh, whilst Giānī Giān Singh states it was Ram Singh and Bijay Singh.

Bandā Singh himself is generally known to have been from an ascetic background, previously known as Madho Das. This is the impression one takes from reading early texts such as Kaushish's Gurū Kīan Sākhīa, Chibbar's Bansāvalīnāmā, and even earlier, Dadhi Nath Mal's Amarnāmāh, said to be an eye-witness account

ਪਾਤਿਸ਼ਾਹੀ ਮਹਿਮਾ – Revisiting Sikh Sovereignty

recorded by the bard Nath Mal, who was there during Gurū Sāhib's appointment of Bandā Singh. Sardar Gurtej Singh writes how the text was originally recorded in Persian, and found appended to a copy of Srī Gur Sobhā[4], transcribed in Gurmukhi, but later rendered into the original Persian by Dr Ganda Singh in 1953.

Bandā Singh and his background

Despite these contemporary and near contemporary accounts, as well as Dr Ganda Singh's well-researched 1935 work on Bandā Singh[5], some historians have raised questions over Bandā Singh's background. Dr. Sukhdial Singh has suggested the manner with which Bandā Singh moved from Nanded, was like an experienced military General. To overcome the terrain and conquer large regions with such relative ease could not have been accomplished by a life-long ascetic. Dr Sukhdial Singh states,

> "Banda Singh's military consciousness had considered North-India, the weakest point of the Mughal Empire. Therefore, he started his armed struggle from the area, lying between Sonepat and Rohtak. This was neither the task of a clever Bairagi saint nor could be the ask of a person who had recently joined the Sikh religion. To take up arms against the mightiest Empire of the world, could be done only by a leader of the masses or by a trained army General."[6]

Dr Sukhdial Singh goes on to question how an ascetic could strategically attack specific military posts with such precise planning that within a few months, some of the most heavily fortified Mughal posts were decimated. He offers another perspective – that Bandā Singh was, in fact, a former Commander of a Sikh Regiment in the Mughal Army. The basis of this assertion is in reference to the existence of such a regiment mentioned by Kesar Singh Chibbar in

Bansāvalīnāmā and a Hukamnāmā addressed to those who served under Prince Azim-ud din (Muazzam, Bahādur Shah), issued by Gurū Gobind Singh Sāhib. The assumption is that Bandā Singh was, in fact, a tested and faithful devotee of Gurū Gobind Singh, for it was he who in 1698 had prevented Mughal forces from attacking the Gurū's Sikhs, as they attacked other Hill Rajas. This is a bold assertion to make; one would assume if he were a Commander of a Mughal regiment, there would be some mention of it within their records, if not within the writings of our own scholars from the 18th century.

Bandā Singh's previous life engagements have also been considered by various other writers. Early European writers such as James Browne (1770), and after him J.D. Cunningham (1849) offer their own views. The former maintains Bandā Singh was born in Jalandhar, whilst the latter states "he was a native of South India".[7] Hari Ram Gupta (1952)[8] believes he belonged to a District in modern-day Himachal Pradesh, and he too maintains Bandā Singh was known to Gurū Gobind Singh before the Gurū met him in Nanded. Gupta suggests the Gurū must have met Bandā Singh during the stay at Poanta Sāhib (1685 to 1688) when out on a hunting expedition. He offers other similar arguments later presented by Dr. Sukhdial Singh, such as Bandā Singh's knowledge of Panjāb and the decision to choose the battle stratagem that he did. However, I have not found reference to a contemporary account that records the Gurū's prior knowledge of Bandā Singh, or indeed of any such meeting during a hunting expedition.

Nonetheless, the main point about an ascetic lacking the military experience to move through the Mughal strongholds with such relative ease and precision is interesting. What Dr. Sukhdial Singh has suggested therefore appears to hold some weight, until that is we look at who Bandā Singh was with. One must remember Bandā Singh was not alone; he was riding with the wise counsel of the Gurū's Panj Pyar-e, who knew the political landscape having fought many battles under the Gurū. They were, in essence, the military brains behind the armed struggle, which propelled Bandā Singh to lead and liberate

Kaithal, Sonepat, Samana, Kapuri, Shahbad, Sadhuara, and Banur in 1709, before liberating Sarhind in 1710. Their constant guidance and counsel, based on years of military experience, fighting under Gurū Gobind Singh Sāhib, is what led to the founding of Khālsā Raj, in which sovereign flags and mints of the Khālsā Panth were established from the Satluj to the Jamuna River.

The Panj Pyar-e

The military prowess and trustworthiness of the Panj Pyar-e that accompanied Bandā Singh is well documented. The Khālsā was organised into Misls and used the same military formation set by Gurū Gobind Singh. Bandā Singh was in the middle, with Baaj Singh, Ram Singh, Fateh Singh, Ali Singh, and Mali Singh heading up fighting units on the right-flank, and Binod Singh, Kahan Singh, Miri Singh, Bijai Singh, and Gulab Singh taking up units on the left-flank.

The voluminous works of Rattan Singh Bhangoo attest to this fact. Regarded as one of the most authoritative accounts of the Khālsā Panth, Bhangoo's accounts detail the early political successes of the Khālsā. Empowered by the Pātshāhī of Gurū Sāhib, Bhangoo narrates many important and famous accounts from Sikh history with great fondness and appreciation for the Gurū's Darbār. In relation to the selection of Panj-Pyar-e that accompanied Bandā Singh, he narrates:

ਸਿੰਘ ਮਡੈਲਨ ਲਈ ਬੁਲਾਇ, ਉਨ ਕੋ ਮੁਹਰੇ ਲੀਜੇ ਲਾਇ।
ਓਇ ਹੈਂ ਮਹਾ ਸੂਰ ਅਤਿ ਹਠੀ, ਉਨ ਤੇ ਫੌਜ ਤੁਰਕ ਜਾਇ ਨਥੀ ॥੧੬॥
ਓਇ ਹੈਂ ਸੂਰ ਮਹਾਂ ਬਲਵਾਨ, ਉਨ ਪੈਂ ਹੈ ਸਤਿਗੁਰੂ ਮਿਹਰਵਾਨ।
ਓਇ ਹੈਂ ਗੁਰ ਨਿਜ ਪ੍ਰਣ ਕੇ ਪੂਰੇ, ਓਇ ਸੂਰਨ ਮੈਂ ਹੈਂ ਅਤਿ ਸੂਰੇ ॥੧੭॥
"ਓਇ ਨਿਜ ਅਪਨੇ ਗੁਰ ਕੇ ਭਗਤ, ਉਨ ਮੈਂ ਹੈਂ ਸਭ ਹਮਰੀ ਸ਼ਕਤਿ।
ਉਨਕੋ ਹਮ ਬਖ਼ਸ਼ੀ ਗੁਰਿਆਈ, ਹਮ ਬਖ਼ਸ਼ੀ ਉਨ ਲਈ ਸੱਚਈ ॥੧੮॥
ਹਮ ਮੈਂ ਉਨ ਮੈਂ ਭੇਦ ਕਿਛੁ ਨਾਹਿ, ਉਨ ਮੈਂ ਹਮ ਓਇ ਹਮਰੇ ਮਾਂਹਿ"।

ਐਸੇ ਬੰਦਾ ਦਯੋ ਸਮਝਾਇ, ਚੰਗੀ ਵਿਧ ਵਹਿ ਚਲੈ ਕਮਾਇ ॥ ੧੯ ॥ [9]

Inviting the Singhs of Majha, they were put in the forefront. They are very brave and steadfast warriors, upon seeing them the army of the Turks will soon flee. They are brave and very strong warriors. Satgurū is particularly fond of them. They are the bravest of the brave, like the Guru they are faithful to the pledged word. "They are the admirers of their Guru; All my powers rests with them. I have bestowed Guru-ship upon them and they have taken it over. Between them and me there is no difference, they inhere in me and I abide in them". In this way Bandā was instructed, and desired to comply fully and in a proper manner.

Bhangoo goes on to write respected elders Binod Singh and Kahan Singh were two of those Singhs from Majha that rode with Bandā Singh[10], thus demonstrating my earlier point that Bandā Singh's immediate counsel included some of the most trusted and knowledgeable members of the Gurū Khālsā Panth. Baaj Singh of Mirpur Patti is another that Bhangoo mentions by name, describing him amongst the most devoted and trusted Sikhs. As mentioned earlier, Bhangoo states the other two were Daya Singh and Nain Singh, describing them as *bhujangis* (young ones) from within the Gurū's close circle.

Road to victory

As they rode for Panjāb, Bandā Singh issued a directive for letters to be sent to all known Singhs in Panjāb. In the letters, Bandā Singh details his intent to deliver on the Gurū's mandate; namely to liberate the country by destroying the oppressive power in Sarhind.[11] The letters were also delivered as far as Kabul, Kandhar, and Bhakkar. Bhangoo narrates:

ਜੋ ਖਾਲਸੇ ਮੌਂ ਆ ਰਲੇ, ਪਤਿਸ਼ਾਹੀਓਂ ਵੱਡਾ ਹੋਇ।
ਜੋ ਖਾਲਸੈ ਸੌਂ ਨਹਿਂ ਮਿਲੈ, ਰਹਿ ਪਛਤਾਵਤ ਓਰਿ ॥ ੬ ॥ [12]

ਪਾਤਿਸ਼ਾਹੀ ਮਹਿਮਾ – Revisiting Sikh Sovereignty

"He who comes and joins the Khālsā, will be raised above the kings, and those who do not will ever regret."

Many answered Bandā Singh's call, those who could not afford the journey alone met up with other Singhs and shared their resources; some even raised loans and offered body, mind, and money to the cause. Bhangoo records some of the first to join were roaming tradesmen with well loaded bullocks and spears in hand. Singhs from Malwa soon joined, but those in parts of the Majha region found it difficult to get past the encampment of Turks. They reached Kīratpur Sāhib and camped there, informing Bandā Singh, who advised them to stay there until further orders arrived. Aali Singh and Mali Singh soon joined Bandā Singh's ranks, as well as other Singhs from Bhasaur. Bandā Singh nominated Fateh Singh from Malwa as a Commander following the victory in Samana, which was the town in which the executioners of Gurū Tegh Bahādur Sāhib and the two younger Sāhibzade of Gurū Gobind Singh lived.[13]

Victory here was swiftly followed by the victory in Sadhaura. The ruler of Sadhaura was Osman Khan, the individual responsible for torturing to death Budhu Shah. Budhu Shah was the Muslim saint who had assisted Gurū Gobind Singh in the Battle of Bhangani. Bandā Singh then sent for the contingent of Singhs encamped near Kīratpur Sāhib, news of which infuriated the Mughal officer Wazira who dispatched his Malerkotla armies. A large battle then ensued, with the Khālsā taking some big losses, however remaining steadfast, victory soon arrived. Baaj Singh was designated Minister of Finance by Bandā Singh, as well as giving control of fifty-two towns to him and Ram Singh, Koer Singh, and Shyam Singh, with Aali Singh designated to deputise, collecting revenue.[14] Malerkotla was next to face the Khālsā under Bandā Singh, followed by Kaithal, Jind, Panipat, Moonak, and Karnal. The region of Doab was liberated too. Wherever they marched, sovereign flags of the Khālsā were erected, and mints were established to issue coinage in the name of the Gurū.

Bandā Singh Bahādur and the Khālsā Republic

The impact of Bandā Singh's revolution was felt across the twenty-two provinces:

ਬੰਦੈ ਗਰਦੀ ਪਰੀ ਪੰਜਾਬ, ਧਾਕੇ ਪਰੀ ਬਾਈ ਸੂਬੇ ਤਾਕ।
ਮਧ ਕਾਬਲੈ ਸੋਚਾਂ ਕਰੈਂ 'ਮਤ ਹਮ ਪਰ ਬੰਦਾ ਆਇ ਪਰੇ' ॥ ੧੦ ॥ [15]

Bandā's revolution struck the Panjāb, and its impact was felt in all the twenty-two provinces. Even in Kabul it was thought, 'Bandā may come and fall upon us'.

The Expanse of Khālsā Republic

Under Bandā Singh Bahādur, the Khālsā ruled over all of Doābā, including Jalandhar, Hoshiārpur, Nawānshahr, Kapūrthalā, and Rupnagar, unfurling and then planting sovereign flags of the Gurū. The position in Lahore was an interesting one, in so much as Aslam Khān occupied the city. However, up until the gardens of Shalamar, which lay approximately 5km northeast of the city, Sikhs were vying for power. Khālsā rule was extended from the River Ravi to the Yamuna River, and Lahore, Kasūr, Bathindā, Panīpat and to the mountain ranges.[16]

Baaj Singh was placed in charge of Sirhind and his brother in Doaba. Forts were constructed from Panipat in modern-day Haryana right up to Pathankot in modern-day Himachal Pradesh. Just as Gurū Gobind Singh had informed Bahadur Shah, Panthic enemies such as Wazīr Khān and Suchā Nand were brought to justice, following the victory in the Battle of Chapparchirī (1710). The Khālsā's victory here marked the creation of the Khālsā Republic. It is important to note that although battles had been waged ever since the 11th-century invasions of Mahmud of Ghazni began, this was the first Republic of any kind in Panjāb. Bandā Singh set up the Capital at Lohgarh Fort, and the Sikhs referred to Bandā Singh as Baadshāh.

However, everything Bandā Singh established and acquired was placed at the feet of the Khālsā and in the name of the Gurū. He struck coinage upon which was inscribed, "Coin struck in both the worlds by the guarantee of Gurū Nānak's sword – By the grace of the True Sovereign, victory to Gurū Gobind Singh, the Kings of kings", and on the reverse, it read, "Minted in the age of Peace by the blessed fortune of the Khālsā – Sanctioned by the glorious Throne in the City. Year 2."

The Sikhs had established their own country, complete with a throne, a Capital, coins, sovereign seal, flags, and an army. The only difference was that whilst other sultanates ruled under their own name or family lineage, Bandā Singh's Rāj was all under the name of the Gurū.[17] Chibbar records that Bandā Singh would refer to the Gurmat imparted by Gurū Granth Sāhib, namely that a ruler must be just, not indulge in sin or unjust actions.[18]

Response from the Imperial government

Imperial officers in Delhi and Lahore came under great pressure; none dared to cross the boundaries drawn by Bandā Singh's encampments. Bahādur Shāh was notified of Bandā Singh's movement in May 1710, and he dispatched various contingents who marched against Bandā Singh and the Khālsā. As mentioned earlier, Bandā Singh did not stop there. Having liberated Panjāb in the name of the Khālsā, Bandā Singh turned his attention to the Hills region and established a cantonment near Kīratpur Sāhib and Anandpur Sāhib.

Despite Bahādur Shāh issuing edicts which directed his officers to "kill the worshippers of Nanak wherever they were found", upon reading the Persian accounts, such as *Akhbar-i-Darbar-i-Mualla*, we come to know a little about the kind of Khālsā Rāj Bandā Singh had established. He had around five thousand Muslim soldiers in his army, provided them a fixed wage, allowances and encouraged them to read their prayers. One of the reports written sometime before the Battle of Sirhind, from the Imperial news writer, Bhagwati Das, *harkarah*, through Hidaytuliah records,

Bandā Singh Bahādur and the Khālsā Republic

"The wretched Nanak-worshipper has his camp in the town of Kalanaur upto the 19th instant. During this period, he has promised and proclaimed, 'I do not oppress the Muslims'. Accordingly for any Muslim who approaches him, he fixes a daily allowance and wages, and looks after him. He has permitted them to read khutba and namaz. As such five thousand Muslims have gathered round him. Having entered into his friendship, they are free to shout and call their prayers in the army of the wretched (Sikhs)."[19]

The above account demonstrates the inclusive nature of the Khālsā Republic established by Bandā Singh. While the Mughal regime was vying for the death of all Sikhs, Bandā Singh promoted diversity and respected the individual rights of everyone irrespective of religion or cultural background, as per the Gurū's instruction.

Following the victory in Sirhind, Bandā Singh continued to lead the Khālsā into battle against other rulers of Saharanpur, Nanauta, and Jalalabad, the Rām Rāiyas of Ghudani, and the Faujadars of Batala and Sultanpur. This illustrates his mission wasn't simply about seeking revenge for the murder of the Gurū's young Sāhibzade. Delivering justice was most certainly a part of Bandā Singh's mission, however, once that justice was delivered, the Khālsā were to continue to wage war wherever there was oppression and tyranny, to liberate the people of the land, and establish Khālsā Raj.

From 1708 till the present day, the beloved Khālsā of the Gurū have either established Sikh sovereignty or sacrificed their lives in the pursuit of establishing it. The 18th and 19th-century pursuit and establishment of Sikh sovereignty is well documented. It is important to note Bandā Singh's Republic (1710-1716) sent shockwaves throughout the Mughal establishment. It was due to Sikh Rāj in Panjāb, alongside the rise of the Marathas under Sivaji in the late 17th century, that caused the inevitable demise of the Mughal empire.

ਪਾਤਿਸ਼ਾਹੀ ਮਹਿਮਾ – Revisiting Sikh Sovereignty

The Sikh and Maratha movements inspired others in Bengal, Uttar Pradesh, and the Deccan to "elevate their status from one of viceroyalty to kingship".[20] On the actions of Bandā Singh, writer Rajinder Singh states,

> *"He [Banda Singh] gave the Punjab a clean administration, rooted out corruption, inefficiency and extortion. He finished landlordism and established peasant-proprietorship in land. By dint of his military exploits and efficient administration he conclusively proved that the Sikhs were not only redoubtable soldiers, but also competent administrators. He enabled them to rise to their full stature and gave them a taste of running a government."*[21]

Siege of Gurdas Nangal and martyrdom

Bandā Singh's resilience and commitment to the Sikh cause, and of those Khālsā warriors that fought alongside, continued to emanate from their bodies even when death was imminent following the siege of Gurdās Nangal, which led to the eventual arrest and imprisonment of Bandā Singh. British bureaucrats John Surman and Edward Stephenson, who penned a letter to the Governor of Fort William and Council in Bengal, Robert Hedges, on 10th March 1716,

> *"...Some days ago they entered the city laden with fetters, his whole attendants which were left alive being about seven hundred and eighty all severally mounted on camels which were sent out of the City for that purpose, besides about two thousand heads stuck upon poles, being those who died by the sword in battle. He was carried into the presence of the king, and from thence to a close prison. He at*

present has his life prolonged with most of his mutsuddys in the hope to get an Account of his treasure in the several parts of his Kingdom, and of those that assisted him, when afterwards he will be executed, for the rest there are 100 each day beheaded. It is not a little remarkable with what patience they undergo their fate, and to the last it has not been found that one apostatised from his new formed religion.[22]

Notwithstanding the limits of colonial logic that referred to Sikhi as a "religion", which we shall consider in the coming chapters, the above account sheds light on how much Bandā Singh and the Khalsā had achieved in the space of just six years. Not only that but their commitment and dedication to Gurū Sāhib's mandate to establish Khālsā Rāj. Sikhs today recount the glorious stand of defiance made by the Gurū's Beloved at the time of death. Following the gruesome torture and execution of Bandā Singh, others who were awaiting their own death did not deter or flinch from the executioner's sword. One particular story is that of the Sikh youth who was the only son of a widowed mother. Upon hearing about his death sentence, the mother approached the officials and pleaded for his immediate release, stating he had been misled by the Sikhs and was caught up in the wrong company. Dr. Ganda Singh writes how the mother was able to secure his release; however, when she arrived at the cell and her son was brought out, the young boy refused and loudly cried, "My mother is a liar. I am heart and soul a devoted follower of the Gurūs. Send me quickly after my companions."[23]

Mughal accounts, such as Tarikh-i-Muhammad Shahi, record that no number of tears from the mother or persuasion from the Mughal officers could shake the young boy's faith and allegiance to the Gurū. He stepped back, turned towards the place of execution, and calmy bowed his head. The executioner's sword was as true as the

ਪਾਤਿਸ਼ਾਹੀ ਮਹਿਮਾ – Revisiting Sikh Sovereignty

Sikh youth's defiance, and he joined the countless other martyrs of the Sikh Panth.

Another eye-witness account is provided by Mirzā Muhammad, who belonged to a family of officials and entered imperial service in 1703. In his Ibratnama, which is a narrative of political events from 1703 until 1719, he writes,

> "On this day [of their arrival] I went to the Salt Market to witness the event and accompanied them from there to the Imperial Fort. Of the people of the city there were few who did not come to see the humbling of those rebels. Large crowds gathered in every lane and market such as had seldom appeared before. The Muslims were in a happy and festive mood. Yet many of those ill-fated ones [the Sikhs], who had come as prisoners in this condition, insisted on standing fast by their villainy. There was no sign of humility and submission on their faces. Rather most of them, riding on the camels' backs kept singing and reciting melodious verses. If anyone in the lanes and bazar reminded them of the cruelties they had committed, which brought them to this condition, they gave immediate and manly retorts, and attributed their capture and humiliation to the doings of fate. If anyone told them that they would now be executed, they replied, "Let them kill us! We do not fear death. Had we feared it, how could we have fought so many battles with you? We have fallen in your hands only because of hunger and lack of provisions; otherwise, you would have come to know of our bravery far more than has been witnessed till now."[24]

Another account is given by Sarūp Das in relation to Baaj Singh. The Mughal Emperor Farrukh Siyar, having heard about the courageous and daring actions of Baaj Singh during the establishment of Khālsā Rāj, and following the execution of Bandā Singh and many of the remaining Sikh prisoners, proclaimed, "I have heard a lot about this Baaj Singh, that he is brave and was favoured by the Gurū; which one of you is he?" Upon hearing this, Baaj Singh stood up and declared, "I am Baaj Singh," to which the emperor taunted him by saying, "I thought you were a great warrior, but now you are unable to do anything." Baaj Singh replied, "Remove these chains off me, and I'll show what I can do." The emperor obliged, and no sooner was Baaj Singh able to move his legs freely, he swooped upon the emperor's men like a hawk and killed three soldiers, even though he was still tightly handcuffed. He then turned towards a Nawab, however before he could get to him, the emperor's reinforcements surrounded him, and he was martyred.[25]

Although the Khālsā Republic established by Bandā Singh was short-lived due to the "inexhaustible temporal resources of the then greatest Empire in the world"[26], the post-Gurū movement to establish Sikh sovereignty remained an ever-present objective of the Khālsā throughout the 18th century and beyond. In the next two chapters, we shall look at the rise of the Misls, the Dal Khālsā, and Ranjīt Singh's Rāj.

NOTES

[1] ਸਰੂਪ ਦਾਸ ਭੱਲਾ, ੧੭੭੬, ਮਹਿਮਾ ਪ੍ਰਕਾਸ਼
Sārūp Das Bhalla, 1776, *Mehmā Prakāsh*, Edited by Dr. Uttam Singh Bhatia, 1971, Bagh 2, Khand 2, Bhasha Vibhag, Panjab, p865

[2] ਰਤਨ ਸਿੰਘ ਭੰਗੂ, ੧੮੪੧, ਸ੍ਰੀ ਗੁਰ ਪੰਥ ਪ੍ਰਕਾਸ਼
Rattan Singh Bhangoo, 1841, *Sri Gur Panth Prakash*, Translation by Gurtej Singh, 2015, Vol. 1, Singh Brothers, Amritsar, p173

[3] Giānī Giān Singh, 1891, *Tvārīkh Gurū Khālsā*, Chattar Singh Jeevan Singh, Amritsar, Bagh 1, p844

[4] Gurtej Singh, 2000, *Web of Indian Secularism; Chakravyuh*, p3. Amarnāmāh is a document of great importance.

[5] Dr Ganda Singh, 1935, *Life of Bandā Singh Bahadur*, Publication bureau, Punjabi University, Patiala

[6] Dr Sukhdial Singh, 2007, *Origin and Evolution of the Khālsā Commonweatlh*, Chattar Singh Jiwan Singh, Amritsar, p107

[7] J. D. Cunningham, 1849, *History of the Sikhs*, Oxford University Press: Oxford, p77

[8] Hari Ram Gupta, 1952, *History of the Sikhs*, Vol. 2, Munshiram Manoharlal, Delhi, p3

[9] ਰਤਨ ਸਿੰਘ ਭੰਗੂ, ੧੮੪੧, ਸ੍ਰੀ ਗੁਰ ਪੰਥ ਪ੍ਰਕਾਸ਼
Rattan Singh Bhangoo, 1841, *Sri Gur Panth Prakash*, (32:16-19) Translation by Gurtej Singh, 2015, Vol. 1, Singh Brothers, Amritsar, p171

[10] ਰਤਨ ਸਿੰਘ ਭੰਗੂ, ੧੮੪੧, ਸ੍ਰੀ ਗੁਰ ਪੰਥ ਪ੍ਰਕਾਸ਼
Rattan Singh Bhangoo, 1841, *Sri Gur Panth Prakash*, (32:22), Translation by Gurtej Singh, 2015, Vol. 1, Singh Brothers, Amritsar, p173

[11] ਰਤਨ ਸਿੰਘ ਭੰਗੂ, ੧੮੪੧, ਸ੍ਰੀ ਗੁਰ ਪੰਥ ਪ੍ਰਕਾਸ਼
Rattan Singh Bhangoo, 1841, *Sri Gur Panth Prakash*, (36:3), Translation by Gurtej Singh, 2015, Vol. 1, Singh Brothers, Amritsar, p187

[12] ਰਤਨ ਸਿੰਘ ਭੰਗੂ, ੧੮੪੧, ਸ੍ਰੀ ਗੁਰ ਪੰਥ ਪ੍ਰਕਾਸ਼
Rattan Singh Bhangoo, 1841, *Sri Gur Panth Prakash*, (36:6), Translation by Gurtej Singh, 2015, Vol. 1, Singh Brothers, Amritsar, p187

[13] Dr Ganda Singh, 1935, Life of Bandā Singh Bahadur, Publication bureau, Punjabi University, Patiala, p26

[14] ਰਤਨ ਸਿੰਘ ਭੰਗੂ, ੧੮੪੧, ਸ੍ਰੀ ਗੁਰ ਪੰਥ ਪ੍ਰਕਾਸ਼
Rattan Singh Bhangoo, 1841, *Sri Gur Panth Prakash*, (44:4), Translation by Gurtej Singh, 2015, Vol. 1, Singh Brothers, Amritsar, p217

[15] ਰਤਨ ਸਿੰਘ ਭੰਗੂ, ੧੮੪੧, ਸ੍ਰੀ ਗੁਰ ਪੰਥ ਪ੍ਰਕਾਸ਼
Rattan Singh Bhangoo, 1841, *Sri Gur Panth Prakash*, (47:10), Translation by Gurtej Singh, 2015, Vol. 1, Singh Brothers, Amritsar, p225

[16] ਗਿਆਨੀ ਸੋਹਣ ਸਿੰਘ ਸੀਤਲ, ੧੯੫੦, ਸਿੱਖ ਰਾਜ ਕਿਵੇਂ ਬਣਿਆ?
Giānī Sohan Singh Seetal, 1950, Sikh Rāj Kive Baniyā, Lahore Book Shop, Ludhiana, p27

[17] ਗਿਆਨੀ ਸੋਹਣ ਸਿੰਘ ਸੀਤਲ, ਸਿੱਖ ਰਾਜ ਕਿਵੇਂ ਬਣਿਆ? Giānī Sohan Singh Seetal, 1950, Sikh Rāj Kive Baniyā, Lahore Book Shop, Ludhiana, p27

[18] ਭਾਈ ਖੇਸਰ ਸਿੰਘ ਛਿਬੜ, ੧੨੬੯, ਬੰਸਾਵਲੀਨਾਮਾ ਦਸਾਂ ਪਾਤਸ਼ਾਹੀਆਂ ਕਾ
Kesar Singh Chibbar, 1769, *Bansāvalīnāmā*, Edited by Piara Singh Padam, 1997, Singh Brothers, Amritsar, p199

[19] Dr. Ganda Singh's paper "The Punjab News in the Akhbar-I-Darbar-I-Mualla", Indian Historical Records Commission Proceedings of Meetings Vol. XXIV. Jaipur, February 1948 - https://issuu.com/sikhdigitallibrary/docs/the_punjab_news_in_the_akhbar-i-dar

[20] Khushwant Singh, 1963, *A History of the Sikhs*, Vol. 1, Second Edition, Oxford University Press, p115

[21] Rajinder Singh, 1988, *Five Hundred Years of Sikhism*, Amritsar Chief Khalsa Diwan, Department of History, Panjab University, Patiala, p16-17

[22] John Surman and Edward Stephenson, 1715-1719, *Madras Diary and Consultation Book*, 87 Range 239, edited by Amandeep Singh Madra & Parmjit Singh, 2004, "Sicques, Tigers or Thieves": Eyewitness Accounts of the Sikhs (1606-1809), Palgrave Macmillan, p47

[23] Dr Ganda Singh, 1935, Life of Bandā Singh Bahadur, Publication Bureau, Punjabi University, Patiala, p153

[24] Banda Bahadur's Rebellion, 1710-16 from Mriza Muhammad, Ibratnama, translated by J. S. Grewal & Irfan Habib, 2001, *Sikh History from Persian Sources*, Tulika Books, Delhi, p140-141

[25] ਸਰੂਪ ਦਾਸ ਭੱਲਾ, ੧੭੭੬, ਮਹਿਮਾ ਪ੍ਰਕਾਸ਼

Sārūp Das Bhalla, 1776, *Mehmā Prakāsh*, Edited by Dr. Uttam Singh Bhatia, 1971, Bagh 2, Khand 2, Bhasha Vibhag, Panjab, p866

[26] Dr Ganda Singh, 1935, Life of Bandā Singh Bahadur, Publication Bureau, Punjabi University, Patiala, p169

Dal Khālsā and the Sikh Misl Confederacy

Following the execution of Bandā Singh and seven hundred Khālsā in the space of a week, Panjāb entered a period of struggle and hardship in which the Sikhs had to retreat in order to survive. However, even in those moments, the spirit of actualizing the political ambitions of the Khālsā was an ever-present force, one, in fact, that was prioritised over everything else.

Rattan Singh Bhangoo narrates how Captain Murray, the British officer who enquired about the origins of Sikh sovereignty, was quite inquisitive about the whereabouts of the Khālsā following Bandā Singh's execution.[1] While some Sikhs took up employment, received land grants, were permitted to occupy Dharamshals and Bungas, others, writes Bhangoo, kept the resistance going at the cost of great personal hardship in which they had to live in exile amongst the jungles. They endured poverty, hunger, and displacement but kept the Sangarsh alive.

Leadership roles of Mata Sundri and Mata Sāhib Devi

It is evident from the Hukamnāme[2] attributed to both Mata Sundri jī (a total of nine between 1717 and 1730) and Mata Sāhib Devi (a total of nine between 1726 and 1734) that they both assumed leaderships roles following the martyrdom of Bandā Singh. The short period of internal disagreement in Amritsar that occurred between the Bandāi Khālsā and the Tat Khālsā was resolved following intervention from Mata Sundri jī, who in 1721 instructed Shaheed Bhāī Manī Singh to take charge of matters in Amritsar.[3] The Hukamnāme issued between

1717 and 1734 are addressed to Sikhs across the land, and they cover various matters pertaining to the Panth, in particular, the financial upkeep of the Gurū's Darbār, further construction and expansion works and also more specific requests such as delivering Khālsāi justice. They indicate that the Sikhs within and outside of Panjāb accepted the authority of Mata Sundri jī and Mata Sāhib Devi during this time. The institution of Langar was maintained as evidenced by the requests for Sikhs to provide provisions. Chibbar provides a fascinating insight into the setup within the Panth during this time in which he dedicates a chapter to Mata Sāhib Devi and writes that she they on the throne within Gurū's Darbār, with Sikhs arriving from far and wide.[4]

We also learn from Chibbar about Mata Sāhib Devi's decision to stop the bi-annual gatherings that had begun to take place in Delhi. Thinking of their safety and welfare during that time and following a discussion with prominent Sikhs, a Gurmatā was passed for the meetings to reconvene in Amritsar. Mata Sāhib Devi nominated a group of Sikhs who left for Amritsar and made the necessary arrangements for the bi-annual meetings to continue there, thus directing the Sikhs back to Sri Darbār Sāhib. The Sarbat Khālsā gatherings started to galvanise small units of guerillas with appointed Jathedārs who slowly began retaking villages.

Jathedār Bhāī Tārā Singh

One such Jathedār was Bhāī Tārā Singh who, having previously fought under Bandā Singh[5], led one of the units that were a part of the guerilla warfare of that period. As a Panth Dardhī Gursikh who had bowed his allegiance to the Khālsā Panth, he built himself a *bunga* and continued to wage war with the Mughal establishment under the sovereign flags of the Khālsā. Keeping the Khālsā discipline intact, Bhangoo narrates that he wore blue dress and anointed himself with various weapons of war. He exemplified the Sikh attribute of *tyār-bar-tyār*, always ready to answer the call of the Khālsā. He is recorded to have stated:

ਦੰਗੈ ਹੀ ਤੇ ਪਯਾਗ ਪਤਿਸ਼ਾਹੀ, ਦੰਗੈ ਹੀ ਤੇ ਹੋਗ ਸੀਸ ਲਾਈ।
ਬਿਨ ਦੰਗੈ ਕੋਊ ਪੁਛੈ ਨ ਬਾਤ, ਹਮ ਸੰਗੋਂ ਹਚਾਵੈਂ ਜੋ ਲਖ ਘਾਤ॥੧੧॥ [6]

"It is through guerilla warfare alone that sovereignty is obtained. It affords an opportunity for dying meaningfully. Without resorting to such warfare, we get no hearing. Therefore, we resort to warfare a million times over."

In 1726, Bhāī Tara Singh's encampment was attacked by Mughal forces because the Singhs had taken Mughal horses; however, they resisted with such ferocity that the Mughals were forced to retreat. We learn from Bhangoo that one Baghel Singh led the initial defense single-handedly as he was outside the main encampment when the Mughals attacked. Daringly, Baghel Singh attacked one soldier with a spear and another with the sword causing them to fall off their horses. He was eventually fired upon; the sound of the shots alerted the others to reach the battle. They fought off the Mughals' advances, who then proceeded to petition the provincial Governor, Zakariya Khan. Faujdar Momman Khan was dispatched to attack Bhāī Tara Singh with 2200 cavalrymen along with forty camel guns, five elephant guns, and four light cannons.[7]

Both sides clashed, with the Mughals taking large casualties. Further reinforcements were called, and they mounted a new attack on the Sikhs encamped with Bhāī Tara Singh. Whilst the leaders of the two contingents were killed by the Singhs, along with others, as day broke, the Mughals were able to overcome the lesser contingent of remaining Singhs, and thus Bhāī Tara Singh was killed alongside the other twenty-two Singhs.[8]

The martyrdom of Bhāī Tārā Singh, who was well-loved and respected amongst the Khālsā, only served to motivate the Sikhs, who daringly attacked convoys carrying Mughal treasure. They continued to resist by acquiring horses and weapons signaling their intent to reestablish Khālsā Rāj.

Jathedār Bhāī Darbārā Singh

The continued resistance and defiance from the guerilla units eventually led the provincial Governor to attempt to reconcile matters with the Sikhs. He offered some land and money as a peace offering, with hopes of finally subduing the resistance of the Khālsā that had caused his administration much distress. The offer was presented before the Khālsā via Subeg Singh, who advised the Sikhs to accept the money and use it to protect the weak. They accepted this advice as a mark of denigration of the Mughal administration. However, on matters pertaining to the land and the Nawabī, Jathedar Darbāra Singh, having recognised this offer as a move to subdue the Khālsā's sovereignty, asked the other Sikh leaders, "When did we aspire to acquire the status of a Nawabship? The Gurū had decreed sovereignty for us. It appears to be within reach". He went on:

"ਹਮ ਰਾਖਤ ਪਤਿਸ਼ਾਹੀ ਦਾਵਾ, ਜਾਂ ਇਤਕੋ ਜਾਂ ਅਗਲੇ ਪਾਵਾ।
ਜੋ ਸਤਿਗੁਰ ਸਿੱਖਨ ਕਹੀ ਬਾਤ, ਹੋਗ ਸਾਈ ਨਹਿਂ ਖਾਲੀ ਜਾਤ" ॥੩੨॥

"We lay claims to sovereignty. Either we attain it or those coming after us will. Whatever the True Gurū has decreed for the Sikhs will come to pass it; it shall not remain unfulfilled.[9]

In fact, most of the Sikhs spoke in this manner, personifying the very essence of Sikh sovereignty. Amongst those who were present were revered Sikh personalities such as Kapūr Singh, Harī Singh Hazūrī, Deep Singh Shaheed, Jassā Singh Rāmgharīā, Karam Singh, Buddha Singh Sukherchakīā and Garjā Singh[10]. It had been approximately 18 years since the fall of Bandā Singh's Khālsā Republic, in which there had been many bloody clashes, but still the desire of establishing Khālsā Raj remained the foremost goal of the Khālsā. The Singhs agreed that Guru Gobind Singh had bestowed them with sovereignty and argued that they had no desire to secure their safety within the sovereignty of Mughal rule. However, they took the offer of land, appointed Kapūr Singh as the Nawab, and used the collection of revenue to rebuild the movement to establish Khālsā Rāj.

Formation of the Dal Khālsā

Since the desire to follow Gurū Gobind Singh's command was an ever-present force, under Nawab Kapūr Singh, the Sikhs were able to reorganise and re-establish themselves into two distinct groups, the Buddhā Dal and the Tarnā Dal. These two groups were both further divided into five units, each with a separate flag representing the sovereignty of the Khālsā Panth. Nawab Kapūr Singh assumed overall command as well as leading his own Misl. In doing so, he established 11 Misls, as was the case during the battles waged by Gurū Gobind Singh and Bandā Singh.

The Khālsā continued to clash with oppressive forces for the remainder of the 18th century. It would be wise for the reader to consult the writings of Rattan Singh Bhangoo and Giānī Giān Singh or other more contemporary accounts that provide ample details of the battles, the persecution, and the executions. During this period, notes Hari Ram Gupta,

> "The Sikhs never lost sight of their political ideal, and they concentrated their attention chiefly on Sarhind province. This was due to the fact this region had been the avenue of activities of seventh, eighth, ninth and tenth Gurus, as well as of Bandā Bahadur".[11]

From the clashes with the Afghan invaders such as Nadir Shāh (1738), Ahmad Shāh Abdāli (1747), and Ahmad Shāh Durrānī (1762) to the continued confrontations with officers of the Mughal administration such as Massā Rangar (1740); the Khālsā remained defiant in the pursuit of preserving Sikh sovereignty. Not only were the Sikhs the only notable force to continue attacking the Afghan rulers as they departed with loot, but they also contended with the likes of Zakariya Khān who had submitted before the Afghan invaders. Relying on a Muslim account, Malcolm writes,

> "Sikh horsemen were seen riding at full galop towards their favourite shrine of devotion. They were often slain in the attempt and sometimes taken prisoners; but they used, such occasions, to seek instead of avoiding, the crown of martyrdom: and the same authority states, that an instance was never known of a Sikh, taken his way to Amritsar, consenting to abjure his faith."[12]

The death-defying actions of revered Sikh martyrs such as Bhāī Mani Singh, Bhāī Taru Singh, Bhāī Bota Singh, and Bhāī Garja Singh, and Bhāī Sukhā Singh and Bhāī Mehtāb Singh, are a testament to the enduring spirit of Sikh resistance that defined the 18th century. Despite efforts to annihilate the Sikhs through systematic killing sprees, the Sikhs remained steadfast. According to conservative figures, close to a quarter-million Sikhs were killed between 1705 and 1767. Again, Hari Ram Gupta notes,

> "Just realise the immensity of sacrifice in human blood made by the Sikhs to gain mastery over their own homeland. At the most modest estimate it may be pointed out that Gurū Gobind Singh in several battles against him by the Mughals [and Hindu Hill Rajas], lost about five thousand [of] his newly created Khālsā. Under Bandā Bahādur at least twenty-five thousand Sikhs laid down their lives in the national cause. After Bandā's execution in June 1716, Abdus Samad Khan, Governor of Panjāb, 1713-26, killed

Dal Khālsā and the Sikh Misl Confederacy

not less than twenty thousand Sikhs. His son and successor Zakriya Khan, 1726-45, was responsible for the death of an equal number. His son Yahiya Khan, 1746-47 destroyed about ten thousand Sikhs in one campaign called the Chhota Ghallughara His brother Shahnawaz Khan in 1747 assasinated nearly one thousand Sikhs. He was a tyrant. This small number was due to his short tenure of office as well as to the influence of his Chief Minister Kauramal called Mithamal by the Sikhs. Yahiya's brother-in-law Muin-ul-Mulk, 1748-53 slaughtered more than thirty thousand. They were all Turks from Central Asia. Adina Beg Khan, a Panjābi Arain, in 1758 put to death at least five thousand. Ahmad Shah Abdali and his Afghan governors, 1753 to 1767, butchered around sixty thousand. Abdali's deputy Najob-ud-daulah, also an Afghan, slew nearly twenty thousand. Petty officials and public must have cut to pieces four thousand." [13]

Gupta's estimates for the number of Sikhs killed during this period make for grim reading. In relation to this specific period, he states around 200,000 Sikhs lost their lives due to the genocidal campaign of the Mughal regime. Through sheer resolve and faith in the words and actions of the Guru Sahibān, Sikhs endured the onslaught, reemerging time and time again in their perpetual struggle to deliver on the Guru's mandate and establish Rāj. Sangarsh was an inextricable part of Sikh existence for the Khālsā.

1st **Sikh Genocide**

Nawab Kapūr Singh and others including Jassā Singh Ahluwaliā, Jai Singh Kanhayā, Hari Singh Bhangi, and Naudh Singh of Sukerchakia had instructed commoners to withhold payments of revenue to the government officials, which led to the clashes with Jaspat Rai, resulting in his death at the hands of Nibhao Singh.

Jaspat Rai and Lakhpat Rai were two brothers, employed as principal officers under Shah Nawaz, the Governor of Panjāb, and it is recorded when Lakhpat Rai heard of his brother's death at the hands of the Khālsā, he is said to have thrown his turban on the ground and vowed not to retrieve it until he had killed all the Sikhs.[14] He launched a countrywide attack against both the active Khālsā and the Sikhs who were not engaged in the resistance. From Multan to Kasur to Attock to the whole of the Doaba region, Lakhpat Rai's men were ordered to hunt and kill the Sikhs. Thousands were butchered, *saroops* of Gurū Granth Sāhib were thrown into rivers, and mass atrocities were widespread. Despite the countrywide assault, the Khālsā fought back, offering stern resistance in places; however, they were eventually forced to retreat.

The Khālsā regroups

One of the main reasons the Khālsā survived those turbulent times is perhaps found in how they constantly reorganised and reformed their military activities. In 1748, at a Sarbat Khālsā, a resolution was passed in which the band of Sikhs were reorganised again. By this time, the original eleven units had grown into sixty-six[15], so Nawab Kapur Singh realigned the units to number 11 once again and placed Jassa Singh Alhuwalia in overall command.

The mass killing of Sikhs that ensued did not deter the Khālsā from rebuilding the movement for sovereignty. Whilst internal conflicts within the Mughal ranks erupted, the Khālsā recouped their strength. During Ahmad Shah Abdali's first invasion into Panjāb, in which the Mughals eventually compelled the Afghans to retire in March 1748, the Khālsā continued to evolve and adapt in readiness to take any opportunity that came their way. As mentioned above, Jassa Singh Ahluwalia took the reins as Commander-in-Chief of the independent units of the Khālsā Army, which were merged into the

Dal Khālsā comprising of 11 Misls. Six of these Misls made up the Buddha Dal, including Ahluwalia, Dallewalia, Faizullahpuria (Singhpuria), Karorasinghia, Nishanwala, and Shaheeda. The Taruna Dal included the remaining five Misls, Bhangi, Kanaiya, Nakai, Ramgharia and Sukarchakia. There was a 12th Misl too, the Phoolkia under Ala Singh of Patiala; however, they did not pledge full allegiance to the Dal Khālsā and on occasions acted against their best interests.[16]

2nd Sikh Genocide

For the next twenty or so years, Ahmad Shah Abdali continued to invade Panjāb, including his sixth invasion in 1762, which marked the second and larger Sikh Genocide. Having taken occupation of Lahore, he had received intelligence that a large number of Sikhs were moving southward, so he immediately set out with a large army and soon caught the Sikhs. The Khālsā who were with them, including the Misl chiefs, are said to have formed a large circle around those who were unarmed, including children and the elderly, as they fought off the attack. They sustained multiple injuries but continued fighting. Bhangoo narrates that Jassa Singh sustained twenty-two wounds[17], and others like Charat Singh of the Sukerchakiā Misl were wounded with strikes from arrows, spears, and swords, the amount of which could not be counted.[18] He emerged as a real war hero of that relentless attack by Ahmad Shah Abdali. Although tens of thousands perished, Bhangoo narrates how the non-combatants that made it to safety all sung Charat Singh's praises[19]. Ala Singh of the Phulkīān Misl was expected to reach them and offer support, he never arrived.[20]

Rise of the Sikh Misl Confederacy

Between 1747 and 1769, Ahmad Shah Abdali had invaded Panjāb a total of nine times. He had clashed with the Sikhs on each occasion, who were relentless in resisting his persecution and destruction.

ਪਾਤਿਸ਼ਾਹੀ ਮਹਿਮਾ – Revisiting Sikh Sovereignty

Taking inspiration from the political accomplishments of the Gurū Sāhibān, and those of Bandā Singh, the Sikhs became rulers of Panjāb during the Misl period.

From the mountains through which the Yamunā river passed in East Panjāb, to the regions of Sindh and Attock in West Panjāb, south toward Multān and north to Jammū[21], Sikh flags of sovereignty flew to the winds of freedom. Writing in 1849, Cunningham notes,

> "the native possessions of the Bunghees extended north, from their cities of Lahore and Amritsir, to the Jehlum, and then down that river. The Kuneias dwelt between Amritsar and the hills. The Sookerchukeeas lived south of the bunghees, between the Chenab and Ravee. The Nukeias held along the Ravee, south-west of Lahore. The Feizoolapooreeas possessed tracts along the right bank of the Beeas and of the Sutlej, below its junction. The Ahloowaleeas similarly occupied the left bank of the former river. The Dullehwalas possessed themselves of the right bank of the Upper Sutlej, and the Ramgurheeas lay in between these last two, but towards the hills. The Krora Singheeas also held lands in the Jalundhur Dooab, The Phoolkeeas were native to the country about Soonam and Bhuttinda, to the south of the Sutlej, and the Shuheeds and Nishaneeas do not seem to have possessed any villages which they did not hold by conquest; and thus these two Misls, along with those of Manjha who captured Sirhind, viz. the Bhunghees, the Alhoowaleeaas, the Dullehwalas, the Ramgurheeas, and the Krora Singheeas, divided among themselves the plains lying south of the Sutlej and under the hills from Feerozpoor to Kurnal, leaving to their allies, the Phoolkeeas, the lands

between Sirhind and Delhi, which adjoined their own possessions in Malwa".22

It was reserved for the Kanahīyā and Bhangī Misls to ensure a steady flow of minting coins, even during the defense of Lahore against attacks from Afghan invaders. In 1772, the Khālsā minted coins after taking Multān, and for the very first time, minted coins in Amritsar in 1775.[23] The Khālsā established permanent Mints at Amritsar, Lahore, and Multan, where coins were struck in praise of the Gurū Sāhibān.

Under the stewardship of Sardār Baghel Singh, the Khālsā entered Delhi and raised the sovereign flags of the Gurū on three occasions between January 1774 and March 1783. Cunningham states that the number of horsemen the Sikh forces could galvanise was estimated at anywhere between 70,000 and 280,000, which is a remarkable feat given the amount of death and destruction Sikhs endured during the two genocidal campaigns.

In 1962, Dr. Ganda Singh noted that another European writer had documented that the Sikh forces could be estimated between two and three-hundred-thousand.[24] This was the estimate provided by George Forster, a civil servant on the Madras establishment of the East India Company, who travelled across Panjāb in 1783 during his overland journey to England. Having encountered a Sikh contingent of 200 horsemen, Forster provided a first-hand account of what he experienced. In a document entitled, "from George Forster to Mr. Gregory at Lucknow, dated in Kachmere, 1783", he writes,

> *"a Seick Horseman is armed with a Matchlock and a sabre, both in their kind, excellent. In this matter I speak from a real knowledge, for in the course of my travels, I had twice an opportunity of meeting with their Parties, each of which might consist of 200 men. The Horses were better than any I had ever seen either amongst the Hindoo or Mussalman Troops in the Eastern parts of India. The*

men were well clothed, chiefly in white lamahs, and their arms, together with their accoutrements, which consisted of priming horns and Ammunition Pouches, were in good order. The latter were mostly covered with our scarlet cloth and ornamented with gold lace. From the great predilection which the Seicks have for firearms, and the constant use which they make of them, their mode of attack and defense, is different from that of any other Cavalry in Asia".[25]

Such praise was indicative of the military prowess that became a defining aspect of sovereign Sikh governance in Panjāb during the Misl period. This dominance came to a head in early 1783 when Sardars Jassa Singh Ahluwalia and Baghel Singh led a 60,000 strong contingent to to secure victory in Ghaziabad, some 20 kilometers south of Delhi, and other surrounding regions. Despite their internal grievances, on matters pertaining to the pursuit and establishment of Sikh sovereignty, the Misl Sardars were united.

Sardār Baghel Singh and the capture of Delhi

Bhangoo provides an intriguing account of Sardār Baghel Singh's arrival into Delhi. He narrates how the Mughal king in Delhi, Shah Alam II, was so petrified at the prospect of the Sikhs turning their attention to Delhi that he considered abandoning the city.[26] His advisors consoled him, suggesting he consult Begum Sumroo, leader of Sardhana, in modern-day Uttar Pradesh, just 85 kilometers northeast of Delhi. Sumroo was married to German adventurer Walter Reinhardt Sombre, and following his death in 1778, had assumed control over Sadhaura. According to Hari Ram Gupta, she headed up a force that consisted of "five battalions of infantry, a body of irregular horse, and about 300 European officers and gunners with forty cannons".[27] Gupta notes that Sumroo had pledged her political allegiance to the Mughal regime and had also pledged her devotion to

Dal Khālsā and the Sikh Misl Confederacy

the British, thus becoming a key negotiator between the Mughal and Sikh Misls.[28]

Begum Sumroo met Sardār Baghel Singh outside Delhi in March 1783 and negotiated that Shah Alam II pay Sardār Baghel Singh six annas in every rupee (16 annas) of the revenue and allow the Sikhs to construct seven Gurdwaras across Delhi.[29] Sardār Baghel Singh remained in the capital with 4000 troops but sent the other Sikh forces home to Panjāb. He remained in control of Delhi for eight months, during which time Gurdwaras were built at places to commemorate Mata Sundri jī, Mata Sāhib Devi, Gurū Har Krishan Sāhib, and Gurū Tegh Bahādur Sāhib. It is worth noting, the Mughals had erected two mosques at the sites related to Gurū Tegh Bahādur Sāhib; one where the Gurū Sāhib was beheaded, and the other where the Gurū's headless body was cremated by Lakhi Banjara. Gupta again records Sardār Baghel Singh obtained written consent from both the emperor and Muslim leaders (who initially opposed the plans) before demolishing the mosques and building the Gurdwaras.[30]

The tax that Sikh leaders imposed upon Delhi had a great impact on the riches of Panjāb. Forster notes that Panjāb was a wealthy nation under the Sikhs,

> *"From their being possessed of an ample, and fertile Territory, and being when not occupied in Military service, much attached to the Business of Agriculture, and well skilled in it, it must be supposed that the revenues of the Seicks are very considerable, tho it would be presumptuous in me to attempt at ascertaining the amount. The Subah of Lahor in the Reign of Aurangzebe produced the annual revenue to Government according to Mr. Bernier of 246 Lacks and 95 thousand Rupees; and from the general character of the Seicks [Sikhs] for their knowledge in the cultivation of Lands, I should imagine that there*

had been no decrease in the Revenue, since the country has been in their possession."[31]

This provides some insight into the amount of combined wealth held by the Sikh Nation under the rule of the Misl Confederacy in Panjāb towards the end of the 18th century. Having endured the struggle and hardship of barbaric policies from successive regimes in Delhi and foreign lands, the Sikhs had cemented their position as true sovereigns under the banner of the Gurū's Khālsā Panth. Forster goes on to write,

> *"Their Military Force also must be great, but I am little enabled to reduce that point to any certainty as to fix the amount of their Revenue. A Seick [Sikh] will say that his Country can furnish 4 to 500,000 Horsemen, and to authenticate his story, he tells you, that every person, even in the possession of a trifling property keeps a Horse, Matchlock and Side Arms. In which case, and if we can believe that they can produce when in unity 200,000 Horse, their force in Cavalry must be greater, than that of any power now existing in Hindostan".[32]*

Thus, the expanse and power of Sikh Rāj in the Country of Panjāb, before the establishment of Ranjīt Singh's Empire in 1799, was not only documented by Sikh writers such as Rattan Singh Bhangoo and Giānī Gian Singh, but also well documented by contemporary European writers. Francklin is another, writing in 1794, he states,

> *"At Pattiali they make excellent cloth, and firearms superior to most parts of Hindostaun. The collected force of the Seiks is immense, they being able to bring into the field an army of 250,000* men, a force apparently terrific, but from want of union*

Dal Khālsā and the Sikh Misl Confederacy

among themselves, not much to be dreaded by their neighbours".[33]

Francklin uses an asterisk next to the figure because he also provides a table denoting the number of Sikhs in each Misl. They were as follows:

Misl leader	Total
Beejee Singh [Baghel Singh]	12000
Tarah Singh	22000
Jessah Singh	14000
Kurrum Singh (of Shahabad)	12000
Jessah Singh (of Ramghur)	12000
Jundut Singh [Charat Singh Bhangi] (of Amritsar)	24000
Khosal Singh (of Fuzoolah Pore)	22000
Herri Singh (on the confines of Moultan)	40000
Runjet Singh (of Loeh Ghur)	70000
Shahur Singh [Sāhib Singh] (of Pattiali), Lall Singh, Juswaunt Singh (of Nawbeh) [Nabha], Gujput Singh (of Chunda) [Sind], and other chiefs	20000
Total	248,000

Francklin provides a detailed account of the Sikhs, documenting their lifestyle, habits, trade, and military might. In his writings, he concludes,

> *"this nation, so obscure as hardly to be mentioned, even as a tribe, at the beginning of the present century, have within the last 30 years, raised themselves in such reputation, as not only to attract the notice but excite the alarm of their neighbours, on both sides of their government".*[34]

ਪਾਤਿਸ਼ਾਹੀ ਮਹਿਮਾ – Revisiting Sikh Sovereignty

A testament to the enduring spirit of Sikh resilience and empowerment bestowed upon them by the Pātshāhī of the Gurū Sāhibān.

While these accounts demonstrate the extent and might of Sikh Rāj in the 18th century, they also reveal how weary the British were becoming of Sikh governance in Panjāb. We have a plethora of accounts written by British agents or civil servants that show their eagerness to understand Sikh polity, particularly the origins of Sikh sovereignty. While it was Captain Murray who asked Rattan Singh Bhangoo to document this comprehensively in the mid-19th century, others before him such as John Malcolm (1812); William Francklin (1798); James Browne (1788); Warren Hastings (1784); George Forster (1783); and Robert Orme (1760) had provided their own intel on the political endeavours of the Sikh Panth. Other European accounts from the likes of Antoine Louis Henri Polier (1787 and 1776); Francis Xavier Wendel (1768); and perhaps the earliest European account by Father Jerome Xavier (1606), also shed some light on the early understanding Europeans had of the Sikhs, the Khālsā, and the rise of Sikh power in Panjāb.

The Misls are often criticised today for being a group of wild fighters, constantly at loggerheads with one another; however, this is an unfair accusation. Notwithstanding the endurance and resilience with which they reestablished Sikh sovereignty, one fact remained apparent throughout their existence; when an external attack threatened Panjāb, they would always unite and die fighting on the battlefield together. Their love and allegiance to the Khālsā Panth took precedence, and they always endeavoured to uphold the sanctity and sovereignty of the Khālsā Panth.

NOTES

[1] ਰਤਨ ਸਿੰਘ ਭੰਗੂ, ੧੮੪੧, ਸ੍ਰੀ ਗੁਰ ਪੰਥ ਪ੍ਰਕਾਸ਼
Rattan Singh Bhangoo, 1841, *Sri Gur Panth Prakash*, (79:1) Translation by Gurtej Singh, 2015, Vol. 1, Singh Brothers, Amritsar, p379

[2] Dr. Ganda Singh, 1967, *Hukamname Sikh Guru, Mata Sahiban, Baba Banda Singh and Guru Ke Khalse De*, 1967, Baldev Singh, Kapurthala, New Revised Edition, 2015, p.198-233

[3] ਗਿਆਨੀ ਸੋਹਣ ਸਿੰਘ ਸੀਤਲ, ੧੯੫੦, ਸਿੱਖ ਰਾਜ ਕਿਵੇਂ ਬਣਿਆ?
Giānī Sohan Singh Seetal, 1950, *Sikh Rāj Kive Baniyā*, Lahore Book Shop, Ludhiana, p36

[4] ਭਾਈ ਕੇਸਰ ਸਿੰਘ ਛਿਬੱਰ, ੧੭੬੯, ਬੰਸਾਵਲੀਨਾਮਾ ਦਸਾਂ ਪਾਤਸ਼ਾਹੀਆਂ ਕਾ
Kesar Singh Chibbar, 1769, *Bansāvalīnāmā*, Edited by Piara Singh Padam, 1997, Singh Brothers, Amritsar, p214

[5] ਗਿਆਨੀ ਸੋਹਣ ਸਿੰਘ ਸੀਤਲ, ੧੯੫੦, ਸਿੱਖ ਰਾਜ ਕਿਵੇਂ ਬਣਿਆ?
Giānī Sohan Singh Seetal, 1950, *Sikh Rāj Kive Baniyā*, Lahore Book Shop, Ludhiana, p39

[6] ਰਤਨ ਸਿੰਘ ਭੰਗੂ, ੧੮੪੧, ਸ੍ਰੀ ਗੁਰ ਪੰਥ ਪ੍ਰਕਾਸ਼
Rattan Singh Bhangoo, 1841, *Sri Gur Panth Prakash*, (93:11) Translation by Gurtej Singh, 2015, Vol. 2, Singh Brothers, Amritsar, p447

[7] ਰਤਨ ਸਿੰਘ ਭੰਗੂ, ੧੮੪੧, ਸ੍ਰੀ ਗੁਰ ਪੰਥ ਪ੍ਰਕਾਸ਼
Rattan Singh Bhangoo, 1841, *Sri Gur Panth Prakash*, (94:11) Translation by Gurtej Singh, 2015, Vol. 2, Singh Brothers, Amritsar, p457

[8] ਰਤਨ ਸਿੰਘ ਭੰਗੂ, ੧੮੪੧, ਸ੍ਰੀ ਗੁਰ ਪੰਥ ਪ੍ਰਕਾਸ਼
Rattan Singh Bhangoo, 1841, *Sri Gur Panth Prakash*, (95:49) Translation by Gurtej Singh, 2015, Vol. 2, Singh Brothers, Amritsar, p469

[9] ਰਤਨ ਸਿੰਘ ਭੰਗੂ, ੧੮੪੧, ਸ੍ਰੀ ਗੁਰ ਪੰਥ ਪ੍ਰਕਾਸ਼
Rattan Singh Bhangoo, 1841, *Sri Gur Panth Prakash*, (100:37) Translation by Gurtej Singh, 2015, Vol. 2, Singh Brothers, Amritsar, p505

[10] ਗਿਆਨੀ ਸੋਹਣ ਸਿੰਘ ਸੀਤਲ, ੧੯੫੦, ਸਿੱਖ ਰਾਜ ਕਿਵੇਂ ਬਣਿਆ?
Giānī Sohan Singh Seetal, 1950, *Sikh Rāj Kive Baniyā*, Lahore Book Shop, Ludhiana, p46

[11] Hari Ram Gupta, 1952, *History of the Sikhs*, Vol. 4, Munshiram Manoharlal, Delhi, p13

[12] John Malcolm, 1812, *Sketch of Sikhs*, p88

[13] Hari Ram Gupta, 1952, *History of the Sikhs*, Vol. 2, Munshiram Manoharlal, Delhi, p255

[14] ਰਤਨ ਸਿੰਘ ਭੰਗੂ, ੧੮੪੧, ਸ੍ਰੀ ਗੁਰ ਪੰਥ ਪ੍ਰਕਾਸ਼

Rattan Singh Bhangoo, 1841, *Sri Gur Panth Prakash*, (131;4), Translation by Gurtej Singh, 2015, Vol. 2, Singh Brothers, Amritsar, p731

[15] ਗਿਆਨੀ ਸੋਹਣ ਸਿੰਘ ਸੀਤਲ, ੧੯੫੦, ਸਿੱਖ ਰਾਜ ਕਿਵੇਂ ਬਣਿਆ?

Giānī Sohan Singh Seetal, 1950, *Sikh Rāj Kive Baniyā*, Lahore Book Shop, Ludhiana, p113-115

[16] Khushwant Singh, 1963, *A History of the Sikhs*, Vol. 1, Second Edition, 2004, Oxford University Press, p128

[17] ਰਤਨ ਸਿੰਘ ਭੰਗੂ, ੧੮੪੧, ਸ੍ਰੀ ਗੁਰ ਪੰਥ ਪ੍ਰਕਾਸ਼

Rattan Singh Bhangoo, 1841, *Sri Gur Panth Prakash*, (152;89), Translation by Gurtej Singh, 2015, Vol. 2, Singh Brothers, Amritsar, p881

[18] ਰਤਨ ਸਿੰਘ ਭੰਗੂ, ੧੮੪੧, ਸ੍ਰੀ ਗੁਰ ਪੰਥ ਪ੍ਰਕਾਸ਼

Rattan Singh Bhangoo, 1841, *Sri Gur Panth Prakash*, (152;148), Translation by Gurtej Singh, 2015, Vol. 2, Singh Brothers, Amritsar, p893

[19] ਰਤਨ ਸਿੰਘ ਭੰਗੂ, ੧੮੪੧, ਸ੍ਰੀ ਗੁਰ ਪੰਥ ਪ੍ਰਕਾਸ਼

Rattan Singh Bhangoo, 1841, *Sri Gur Panth Prakash*, (152;150), Translation by Gurtej Singh, 2015, Vol. 2, Singh Brothers, Amritsar, p893

[20] Khushwant Singh, 1963, *A History of the Sikhs*, Vol. 1, Second Edition, 2004, Oxford University Press, p147

[21] ਗਿਆਨੀ ਸੋਹਣ ਸਿੰਘ ਸੀਤਲ, ੧੯੫੦, ਸਿੱਖ ਰਾਜ ਕਿਵੇਂ ਬਣਿਆ?

Giānī Sohan Singh Seetal, 1950, *Sikh Rāj Kive Baniyā*, Lahore Book Shop, Ludhiana, p219

[22] J. D. Cunningham, 1849, *History of the Sikhs*, Oxford University Press: Oxford, p108-109

[23] Patwant Singh and Jyoti M. Rai, 2008, *Empire of the Sikhs, The Life and Times of Maharaja Ranjit Singh*, Peter Owen Publishers, London, p187

[24] George Forster, 1793, *Travels*, edited Dr. Ganda Singh, 1962, *Early European Accounts of the Sikhs*, Firma K. L. Mukhopadhyaya, Calcutta, p90

[25] George Forster, 1793, *Travels*, edited Dr. Ganda Singh, 1962, *Early European Accounts of the Sikhs*, Firma K. L. Mukhopadhyaya, Calcutta, p89

[26] ਰਤਨ ਸਿੰਘ ਭੰਗੂ, ੧੮੪੧, ਸ੍ਰੀ ਗੁਰ ਪੰਥ ਪ੍ਰਕਾਸ਼

Rattan Singh Bhangoo, 1841, *Sri Gur Panth Prakash*, (177:44) Translation by Gurtej Singh, 2015, Vol. 2, Singh Brothers, Amritsar, p1077,

[27] Hari Ram Gupta, 1952, *History of the Sikhs*, Vol. 3, Munshiram Manoharlal, Delhi, p165

[28] Hari Ram Gupta, 1952, *History of the Sikhs*, Vol. 3, Munshiram Manoharlal, Delhi, p166

[29] ਰਤਨ ਸਿੰਘ ਭੰਗੂ, ੧੮੪੧, ਸ੍ਰੀ ਗੁਰ ਪੰਥ ਪ੍ਰਕਾਸ਼

Rattan Singh Bhangoo, 1841, *Sri Gur Panth Prakash*, (177:51) Translation by Gurtej Singh, 2015, Vol. 2, Singh Brothers, Amritsar, p1077

[30] Bhangoo, Vol. 2, p1079; see also Hari Ram Gupta, 1952, *History of the Sikhs*, Vol. 3, Munshiram Manoharlal, Delhi, p169

[31] George Forster, 1793, *Travels*, edited Dr. Ganda Singh, 1962, *Early European Accounts of the Sikhs*, Firma K. L. Mukhopadhyaya, Calcutta, p82

[32] George Forster, 1793, *Travels*, edited Dr. Ganda Singh, 1962, *Early European Accounts of the Sikhs*, Firma K. L. Mukhopadhyaya, Calcutta, p82

[33] William Francklin, 1974, *The Sikhs and their Country*, edited Dr. Ganda Singh, 1962, *Early European Accounts of the Sikhs*, p99

[34] William Francklin, 1974, *The Sikhs and their Country*, edited Dr. Ganda Singh, 1962, *Early European Accounts of the Sikhs*, p106

ਪਾਤਿਸ਼ਾਹੀ ਮਹਿਮਾ – Revisiting Sikh Sovereignty

Ranjīt Singh and Darbār-e Khālsā

Ranjīt Singh's consolidation of the Misls is well documented, and the glorious expanse of Sikh Rāj that followed under his leadership in Panjāb is best exemplified by the fact that he is remembered as Sher-e-Panjāb, the Lion of Panjāb. However, for the purpose of this book, I wish to revisit some of the decisions that, whether through his own volition or by treachery, caused the inevitable demise of his empire.

Unification of Panjāb and establishing the monarchy

In late 1798, as head of the Sukerchakia Misl, Ranjīt Singh marched towards the advances of Zaman Shah Durrani, Ahmad Shah Durrani's grandson, who was leading his fourth invasion of Panjāb. Rānī Sadā Kaur, Ranjīt Singh's mother-in-law who was instrumental in the rise of Ranjīt Singh, was also marching with him. Ultimately the Shah failed to proceed past Lahore and was forced to retreat, chased all the way to Attock by Ranjīt Singh's forces.

In the first few months of 1799, with the formidable support of the Khālsā, Ranjīt Singh took control of Lahore and on 7th July 1799, having neutralised the advances of other chiefs, became the undisputed ruler of all Panjāb. Lieut. Colonel Steinbach writes,

> *"Runjeet Singh exercised an absolute and arbitrary sway over the people, constituting himself chief judge and referee in questions of importance, collecting and appropriating the revenue, appointing and removing all the state officers at will, personally regulating all political negotiations, and exercising*

the royal prerogative of coining money and making war".[1]

Whilst some have praised Ranjīt Singh for unifying Panjāb, others such as Sardār Kapūr Singh have highlighted the cost of this unification. He writes, in creating the monarchy, Ranjīt Singh effectively,

> *"...sabotaged the natural development of the whole Sikh polity, behind which lay the traditions of the people, of many millennia past, and which was purified and sanctified by the Sikh Gurus themselves".[2]*

We will consider what Sardār Kapūr Singh may have meant by this in the next chapter, however let us first briefly revisit the period between 1799 and 1839.

Ranjīt Singh's expansion and Treaties

Cognizant of Sikh victory in Panjāb, Afghan leader Zaman Shah, appeared to have accepted the establishment of a new political reality in the region by sending various gifts to the Lahore Darbār. Ranjīt Singh accepted and returned this gesture of goodwill by sending gifts of his own. Amongst them were some pieces of cannon, which the Shah had lost in the rivers during his hurried retreat to Afghanistan. Contrary to the earlier writings of Prinsep, Cunningham, Wade, Griffin, Latif, and Sinha, writes Kushwant Singh, there is little doubt this gift was made after the new leader of Panjāb took control of Lahore.[3] This exchange demonstrates Ranjīt Singh's intent on developing cordial relations with foreign neighbours.

In January 1806, Ranjīt Singh signed a treaty of friendship with the East India Company, which stipulated that the British remove their encampment on the River Beas and not commit an act of hostility towards Panjāb on the premise that Ranjīt Singh refrained

ਪਾਤਿਸ਼ਾਹੀ ਮਹਿਮਾ – Revisiting Sikh Sovereignty

from offering any support to the enemies of the British government, mainly the Marathas. Soon enough, with the might of the Khālsā, Ranjīt Singh neutralised the threat from both the north-western and north-eastern frontiers of Panjāb. In relation to the Cis-Sutlej States, in 1809 Ranjīt Singh signed another treaty with the British, the Treaty of Lahore, in Amritsar, in which he affectively ceased control of this region to the British. The area included modern-day districts of Chandigarh, Patiala, Mohali, Mansa, Barnala, Sangrur, Jalandhar, Muktsar, Hoshiarpur, Bathinda, Ludhiana, Firozpur, Ambala, Faridkot, Moga, Fatehgarh, Jind, Fazilka, Panchkula, Rupnagar, and Yamunanagar. This Treaty was in many ways a watershed moment, much to the disapproval of Akali Phula Singh and Mohkam Chand, two staunch commanders of the Lahore Darbār since it marked the beginnings of the annexation of Mālwā.

During the second decade of Ranjīt Singh's rule, with formidable Khālsā warriors such as Rānī Sadā Kaur, Harī Singh Nalwā, Akālī Phūlā Singh, and Shām Singh Attārīvālā, he consolidated power with victories over Attock (July 1813), Kashmīr (July 1814, and 1819) and Multān (June 1818). Soon after, in the spring of 1822, Jean Baptiste Ventura and Jean Francois Allard, two officers of Napoleon's recently disbanded army, reached Lahore and were enlisted into the Sikh army. They joined the likes of English deserter Price, who had joined the Sikh army in 1809.

Within a few years, following the passing of army commanders such as Akali Phūla Singh, Mokham Chand, and Dewan Chand, the Darbār under Ranjīt Singh became more reliant on European generals such as Ventura. It is noted the Panjābi contingent amongst Ranjīt Singh's army developed a distrust of the British from this point forward.

Over the next few years, Ranjīt Singh maintained Sikh Rāj with a watchful eye on both the Afghans and Pathans in the west and the British along the south-east frontier. Expansion across the Indus Valley into the Khyber Pass was led by the legendary Sikh general, Harī Singh Nalwā, perhaps the most famous of Sikh generals during this period. Nalwā fought in most of the major battles during Sikh Rāj of Ranjīt Singh, from the Battle of Kasūr (1807) to the Battle of Jamrūd (1837). Of the several expeditions Ranjīt Singh dispatched against Multān up until 1818, Nalwā, notes Dr. Gurbachan Singh Nayyar,

> "...seems to have participated in almost all, albeit, his contribution in the last incursion, when Multan was annexed to the kingdom of Lahore, was great which considerably enhanced his prestige".[4]

Hari Singh Nalwā

Nalwā was appointed Governor of Peshawar in 1822 and remained so until his death. During the victory over Kashmir in 1819, historians have noted that Nalwa's fighting contingent was responsible for defeating prominent Afghan chiefs, which led to Sikh Rāj in the region. This appeared to become a formality, right up until Nalwā's final battle at Jamrūd in 1837.

Dost Muhammed, the Emir of Afghanistan, had dispatched a large contingent of 7000 horsemen, armed with matchlocks and guns, under the command of Muhammad Akhbar Khan who was accompanied by around 20,000 others.[5] It is said Nalwa, who was ill at this time, was at Peshawar, a region he had recaptured a year earlier, which was approximately 15km east of Jamrud. Giānī Gian Singh states the number of Afghan troops from Kabul was in the region of 10,000.[6]

The Sikh forces inside Jamrud numbered around 800, led by Hari Singh Nalwa's son, Māhā Singh. The Afghans managed to tear down one side of the fort, but, narrates Giānī Gian Singh, they did not enter the fort immediately. Māhā Singh was stationed inside with the Sikh forces. Eventually, the Afghans decided to enter but were met with a barrage of bullets and cannon fire, in which five hundred of them fell in one confrontation. Hearing of the situation at Jamrud, Nalwa is said to have risen off his sickbed, and despite no sign of reinforcements from Lahore, galvanised his garrison and marched straight to the battlefield. Most of the Afghans were forced to retreat in the night, leaving behind many of their possessions. One contingent remained and managed to fire a shot, which delivered a fatal blow to Nalwa. Historian Khushwant Singh notes,

> *"An account of the battle was sent by an Englishman, Dr. Wood, from Rohtas to the governor general (PC 59 of 29.5.1837). He wrote that in the great slaughter of the Afghans, Mohammed Afzal, the eldest son of Dost Mohammed, had been killed. According to Punjabi accounts they lost 6000 men; the Afghans, who outnumbered them, left about 11,000 men dead on the field. Of the death of Nalwa, Dr. Wood wrote: "He received four wounds, two sabre cuts across his breast; one arrow was fixed in his breast, which he deliberately pulled out himself, and continued to issue his orders as before until he received a gunshot wound in the side, from which he gradually sank and was carried off the field to the fort, where he expired, requesting that his death should not be made known until the arrival of the Maharajah's reliefs".*[7]

The account provided by Giānī Giān Singh is similar to this, in that the Sikhs mounted Nalwa onto an elephant and took him inside the fort. He writes how Maha Singh instructed the Sikhs to take Nalwa's body into another room, and if anybody asked about him, they were to say that he was better than before. The reason for this was two-fold; firstly, to ensure the remaining Sikhs did not become disheartened at the loss of such a great general and remained focused on the task at hand, and secondly to ensure the enemies, who were unnerved just by hearing Nalwa's name, did not garner the courage to attack again.[8]

Ranjīt Siṅgh's death and rise of the Dogrās

At the end of the following year, Ranjīt Siṅgh fell ill and remained bedridden for the last six months of his life. He passed away on 27th June 1839. Before passing away, Ranjīt Siṅgh summoned his closest advisors, ministers, generals, and warriors and reminded them of the need to remain unified in the face of inevitable attacks. Sikh writer Giānī Sohan Siṅgh Seetal narrates the riling speech Ranjīt Siṅgh is said to have given at this time:

"ਮੈਥੋਂ ਜੋ ਪੁੱਜ ਸਰ ਆਈ ਏ, ਤੁਹਾਡੀ ਸੇਵਾ ਕਰ ਚੱਲਿਆ ਹਾਂ। ਹੌਣੇ-ਹੌਣੇ ਦੀ ਸਰਦਾਰੀ ਦੇ ਮਣਕੇ ਭੰਨ ਕੇ ਇਕ ਕੈਂਠਾ ਬਣਾ ਦਿੱਤਾ ਹੈ, ਪਰ ਲੜੀ ਵਿਚ ਪਰੁੱਚੇ ਰਿਹੋ। ਮਿਲੇ ਰਹੋਗੇ, ਤਾਂ ਬਾਦਸ਼ਾਹ ਬਣੇ ਰਹੋਗੇ, ਨਿਖੜ ਜਾਉਗੇ, ਤਾਂ ਮਾਰੇ ਜਾਉਗੇ। ਤੁਹਾਡੇ ਪਰਤਾਪ ਦੇ ਸਾਮੁਣੇ ਖ਼ੈਬਰ ਦੀਆਂ ਪਹਾੜੀਆਂ ਕੰਬ ਰਹੀਆਂ ਹਨ। ਤੁਹਾਡੇ ਇਕਬਾਲ ਅੱਗੇ ਅਸਮਾਨ ਥਰ-ਥਰ ਕੰਬ ਰਿਹਾ ਹੈ। ਤੁਹਾਡੀ ਤੇਗ ਦੀ ਧਾਂਗ ਸਾਰੀ ਦੁਨੀਆਂ ਵਿਚ ਪਈ ਹੋਈ ਹੈ। ਡਰ ਹੈ, ਤਾਂ ਏਸ ਗੱਲ ਦਾ, ਕਿਤੇ ਇਹ ਤੇਗ ਤੁਹਾਡੇ ਆਪਣੇ ਘਰ ਵਿਚ ਨਾ ਖੜਕਣ ਲੱਗ ਪਵੇ। ਤੁਹਾਡੇ ਬਰਿਛਾਂ ਦੀ ਪਾਣ, ਤੁਹਾਡੇ ਆਪਣੇ ਲਹੂ ਵਿੱਚ ਨਾ ਉਤਰਨ ਲੱਗ ਪਵੇ। ਖ਼ਾਲਸਾ ਜੀ! । ਤੁਸੀਂ ਅੰਮ੍ਰਿਤਧਾਰੀ ਸਿੱਖ ਹੋ। ਅੰਮ੍ਰਿਤ ਵਿੱਚ ਅਕਾਲੀ ਬਾਣੀ ਦੇ ਨਾਲ ਨਾਲ ਦੋ ਚੀਜ਼ਾਂ ਹੋਰ ਵੀ ਖ਼ਾਸ ਹਨ: ਇਕ ਪਤਾਸੇ ਤੇ ਇਕ ਲੋਹੇ ਦਾ ਖੰਡਾ। ਬੱਸ, ਏਸੇ ਵਿਚ ਜ਼ਮਾਨੇ ਦੀ ਨੀਤੀ ਛਿਪੀ ਹੋਈ ਹੈ। ਜੇ ਲੋੜ ਹੋਵੇ, ਤਾਂ ਪਤਾਸਿਆਂ ਵਾਂਗ ਖੁਲ ਮਿਲ ਜਾਇਓ, ਆਪਾ ਮਿਟਾ ਕੇ ਦੂਜੇ ਦਾ ਰੂਪ ਬਣ ਜਾਇਓ, ਜਿਥੇ ਭਰਾਂ ਦਾ ਮੁੜਕਾ ਡੁੱਲੇ, ਓਥੇ ਲਹੂ ਵਹਾਂ ਦਿਓ। ਤੇ ਜੇ ਸਮਾਂ ਆ ਬਣੇ, ਤਾਂ ਖੰਡੇ ਵਾਂਗ ਸਖ਼ਤ ਤੇ ਤੇਜ਼ ਵੀ ਹੋ ਜਾਇਓ। ਗਰੀਬ-ਦੁਖੀਏ ਦੀ ਢਾਲ ਤੇ ਜ਼ਾਲਮ ਦੇ ਸਿਰ ਉੱਤੇ ਤਲਵਾਰ ਬਣ ਕੇ ਚਮਕਿਓ।"[9]

I will provide a summary of the above. Giānī Sohan Siṅgh Seetal writes that, in an almost prophetic manner, Ranjīt Siṅgh spoke of the manner in which the different Misls had been forged to create one powerful force. He is said to have forewarned the members of the Darbār to be mindful of the forces that surrounded them and make

ਪਾਤਿਸ਼ਾਹੀ ਮਹਿਮਾ – Revisiting Sikh Sovereignty

sure the weapons of the Sikh army did not turn on themselves. The analogy to Amrit, of becoming either sugar granules and reforming, or if the need arose, being stern and defiant like the double-edged Khaṇḍā, was a reminder of their overriding pledge to the sovereignty of the Khālsā, no matter what the personal cost. Perhaps, when death was staring him straight in the face, Ranjīt Singh had realised the gravity of his political mistakes.

Having harnessed Sikh ideals and principles to cement his Kingdom, he had continuously ignored the advice of his Governors, such as Nalwā, who had been a staunch critic of Ranjīt Singh's decision making. When he had come to know of Ranjīt Singh's intentions, before he fell on the battlefield, Nalwa had taken a public stand against the decision to pass the throne to Kharak Singh, who according to historian Gopal Singh, had declared,

> *"...this state belongs not to an individual, but to the Khalsa commonwealth. It is the sacrifices of a whole people over a century, blessed by the Guru's Grace, that we have won an empire. Its leadership belongs to where it belongs – to the whole Sikh people. Let them choose who shall lead them by consensus (Gurmattā). Kharak Singh is my friend but not able to bear this burden. Let's not fail our people when they need our dispassionate lead most".*[10]

However, as history tells us, such advice was ignored by Ranjīt Singh at the time. He had already begun vesting power to the Dogrās and Brahmins who did not have the best interests of the Panth at hand; Gulāb Singh intended to become ruler of Jammū, Kashmīr, and the eastern region, while Dhiān Singh's ambitions were to occupy Lahore and the rest of Panjāb.[11] Ranjīt Singh's eldest son Kharak Singh was anointed as the ruler of Panjāb, with Dhiān Singh Dogrā as the Chief Minister.[12]

Kharak Singh's reign

Often described as a weak and unfit king by historians, Kharak Singh's tenure as ruler was short-lived. Despite the character assassination of Kharak Singh, he was astute enough to recognise the threat of the Dogrās and thus replaced Dhiān Singh with Chet Singh Bājwa as his chief advisor.[13] A rumour was circulated to the Khālsā Army that Kharak Singh had made a pact with the British agreeing to accept their supremacy over Panjāb by way of paying tax, disbanding the Sikh army and replacing all the Sardārs with English officers.[14] They believed the rumour to be true after Dhiān Singh showed them some forged papers, so they soon confronted the king. His chief advisor Chet Singh Bājwa was killed by the Dogrās, who had also managed to manufacture a rift between Kharak Singh and his wife Māhārānī Chand Kaur, and son, Nau-Nihaal Singh. This episode highlights the extent of Dogrā influence and their power within the Lahore Darbār that they could turn the most senior Sikh ministers and generals against the man who was hand-picked by Ranjīt Singh himself.

Nau-Nihaal Singh - a glimmer of hope

Nau-Nihaal Singh took the reins in October 1839. Latif writes,

> *"His features and disposition bore a striking resemblance to those of his illustrious grandfather, and he was exceedingly popular with the army in consequence of his having chosen the profession of arms at a very tender age. He possessed an ambitious and war like spirit, which, combined with consummate forethought, a keen judgment, and a clear insight into business matter, qualified him thoroughly for the position to which he aspired".*[15]

ਪਾਤਿਸ਼ਾਹੀ ਮਹਿਮਾ – Revisiting Sikh Sovereignty

Within a year of ascending to the throne, Nau-Nihaal Singh recaptured forts such as Kamlagarh Fort in Mandi, in modern-day Himachal Pradesh.[16] He was the charismatic young leader that gave the peoples of Panjāb a new hope.

It was during this time that the British showed signs of undoing the 1809 Treaty of Lahore. They were reluctant to recognise Nau-Nihaal Singh as the de facto leader, whilst also pushing for the Lahore Darbār to allow British troops to cross Panjāb towards Kabul. Nau-Nihaal Singh is said to have allowed this, against the opinion of his Counsel of advisors. Despite this gesture of goodwill, the British maintained their position, and it was suggested Nau-Nihaal Singh became weary of this and opened talks with Dost Mohammed about a joint effort to wage war against the British.[17] However, Giānī Sohan Singh Seetal states this was another conspiracy hatched by the Dogrās to undermine the authority of Nau Nihaal Singh and make him out to be an incompetent leader like they did of his father.[18] News of this reached the British in Calcutta, who began their own preparations; however, the matter went no further.

Nau-Nihaal Singh slowly became cognizant of the Dogrās intentions and the danger of the ever-growing influence they had amassed as key ministers within the Lahore Darbār. Nau-Nihaal Singh expressed a desire to control the salt mines in the hills, over which the Dogrās held a monopoly. In response to this, the Dogrās invited Rajput Balbīr Sen to raise a revolt, but this was overcome by forces sent by Nau-Nihaal Singh, including Ventura. Balbīr Sen was imprisoned at Gobindgarh Fort, and arbitrary taxes levied by the hill rajas were all abolished. Nau-Nihaal Singh also banned "the sale of women and children, a practice common amongst the poorer sections of the hill people."[19] Panjāb, and indeed the Lahore Darbār was on a good trajectory; however, it did not last.

Nau-Nihaal Singh's death was gruesome, coming on the day of his father's funeral, who the Dogrās had poisoned[20]. As he walked back to the fort with Udham Singh Dogrā, eldest son of Gulāb Singh and nephew to Dhiān Singh, one of the upper walls of an archway gave way, instantly killing the latter and injuring the king. Nau-Nihaal Singh is said to have been instantly carried away by Dhiān Singh in a palanquin and kept inside the fort, away from anyone else. As other Sirdārs tried to enter, they were forbidden by the minister. Chand Kaur, Nau-Nihaal Singh's mother, too was prevented from seeing her son, as was his wife, Bibī Nānaki.

While writers such as Cunningham[21] and Steinbach[22] suggest the fall of the archway was contrived by Dhiān Singh Dogrā, others such as Khushwant Singh and Muhammed Latif maintained that was not the case, citing that Dhiān Singh would not have risked the life of his nephew. However, we must ask, could a part of the wall really collapse just as the king happened to be walking beneath it? It is worth considering Giānī Giān Singh's account here as well. He points to the fact that on the funeral day, the only troops on duty were those under the command of Bijay Singh, one of the key associates of Gulāb Singh Dogrā. According to the first-hand account presented by Bijay Singh, he had overheard the two Dogrā brothers hatch a plan to kill Nau-Nihaal Singh. Some of their men were dispatched to take up their position and await the arrival of Nau-Nihaal Singh. When they saw Udham Singh Dogrā was also with him, some of the men informed Gulāb Singh. According to Bijay Singh's account, his reply was that he had three children; it did not matter that one died in the course of him attaining power.[23]

Giānī Giān Singh writes Bijay Singh gave the signal, and the wall was dropped over both. For his role, Bijay Singh was promised land; however, when the Dogrās refused to keep their side of the deal, he came forward with this confession. This confession also matches the contemporary account provided by Alexander Gardner, a soldier in charge of Sikh artillery, who writes,

> "...Several of the principal sardars begged to see the Maharaja, among them the Sindhanwalias, relations of the royal family: in vain did Nao Nihal Singh's mother, in a paroxysm of rage and anxiety,

come and beat the fort gates with her own hands – admittance even to the fort there was none, still less into the Maharaja's apartment. None of the female inmates, not even his wives, were suffered to see him. The palki-bearers who had carried Nao Nihal Singh to his palace were sent to their homes; they were servants in my own camp of artillery, and were five in number. Two were afterwards privately put to death, two escaped into Hindustan, the fate of the fifth is unknown to me. One of the palki-bearers afterwards affirmed that when the prince was put into the palki, and when he was assisting to put him there, he saw that above the right ear there was a wound which bled so slightly as only to cause a blotch of blood about the size of a rupee on the pillow or cloth on which Nao Nihal Singh's head rested while in the palki. Now it is a curious fact that when the room was opened, in which his corpse was first exposed by Dhyan Singh, blood in great quantities, both in fluid and coagulated pools, was found around the head of the cloth on which the body lay. Be this as it may, when the doors were thrown open the Sindhanwalias found the young Maharaja dead, Dhyan Singh prostrate in affliction on the ground, and Fakir Nuruddin, the royal physician, lamenting that all remedies had been useless. Thus, perished Maharaja Nao Nihal Singh on the day following the death of his father."[24]

Giānī Sohan Singh Seetal also affirms this account. What these accounts do is highlight the treachery and greed of the Dogrās. As I mentioned, they had no real affiliation to the Panth or any true desire to uphold Sikh sovereignty and further the mission of the Khālsā as some of the earlier Generals and officers of Ranjīt Singh's Rāj had done. The Dogrās were too concerned with their personal and familial opportunities to fame, power, and riches.

The final bloodshed

During the subsequent claim to the throne, the British began to probe into the internal affairs of the country of Panjāb. Notwithstanding the damaging effect of internal power struggles between Maharaja Sher Singh and Māhārānī Chand Kaur and the Sandhānwāliās, the rapid decline of temporal Sikh Raj following Ranjīt Singh's death was due to a combination of British infringement and internal treachery from the Dogrā brothers. Grewal notes,

> *"The European Generals Avitabile and Ventura, who were keen to take back their earnings to Europe, and Gulab Singh [Dogra] who was eager to retain his territories, entered into small conspiracies with the British officers and diplomats".*[25]

On the surface of it, there appeared to be a split between the Dogrās, as Dhiān Singh and British agent Mr Clark propped up Maharaja Sher Singh as the rightful heir, whilst Gulāb Singh sided with Māhārānī Chand Kaur and her claim that Nau-Nihaal Singh's unborn child was the rightful heir, a position which the likes of the Sandhānwāliās supported. However, this split was just a way of ensuring whoever succeeded to the throne, one of the Dogrās remained within reach of the Darbār.[26]

By the end of 1844, Māhārānī Chand Kaur, Bibī Nānaki (who was pregnant with Nau-Nihaal's child), Maharaja Sher Singh, his son Pratāp Singh, Dhiān Singh Dogrā, Attar Singh Sandhanwāliā, Hirā Singh Dogrā, and his nephews had all been killed. Of the Dogrās, only Gulāb Singh and his one son survived. Young Duleep Singh was bestowed with the throne, and his mother Māhārānī Jind Kaur, took over the civil administration of the Lahore Darbār in 1845, as

President of a Council which included her brother Jawāhar Singh, who too was killed shortly after taking office.

Having assumed himself an independent ruler of Jammu, Gulāb Singh Dogrā began talks with both Afghan and British forces to strengthen his rule against the best interests of the Darbār in Lahore. As we know, Duleep Singh's tenure was short-lived, too, as the first Anglo-Sikh war, or rather Jang Hind Panjāb was declared later that year.

It is worth noting here, following the grotesque amount of bloodshed within the Lahore Darbār, within just six years of Ranjīt Singh's passing, in 1845 it was the Khālsā Army that had amassed the most influence over the decision making in Panjāb. After Jawāhar Singh was killed, no further Chief Minister was appointed until November 1845, when Māhārānī Jind Kaur, to show a sense of unity in the face of the the advancing British, approved the appointments of Lāl Singh and Tej Singh.[27] More on them in the next chapter.

NOTES

[1] Lieut. Colonel Steinbach, 1883, *The Punjaub; A brief account of the country of the Sikhs*, Manju Arts, Chandigarh, reprint Language Department, 2003, Punjab, p41-42

[2] Kapūr Singh, 1959, *Parasharprasna The Baisakhi of Guru Gobind Singh*, Lahore Book Shop, Ludhiana, p190-191

[3] Khushwant Singh, 1963, *A History of the Sikhs*, Vol. 1, Second Edition, 2004, Oxford University Press, p189

[4] Dr. Gurbachan Singh Nayyar, 1995, *The Campaigns of Hari Singh Nalwa*, Publication Bureau, Punjabi University, Patiala, p83

Dr. Gurbachan Singh Nayyar, 1995, *The Campaigns of Hari Singh Nalwa*, Publication Bureau, Punjabi University, Patiala, p102

[6] Giānī Giān Singh, 1891, *Tvārīkh Gurū Khālsā*, Chattar Singh Jeevan Singh, Amritsar, p331

[7] Khushwant Singh, 1963, *A History of the Sikhs*, Vol. 1, Second Edition, 2004, Oxford University Press, p277

[8] Giānī Giān Singh, 1891, *Tvārīkh Gurū Khālsā*, Chattar Singh Jeevan Singh, Amritsar, p332

[9] ਗਿਆਨੀ ਸੋਹਣ ਸਿੰਘ ਸੀਤਲ, ੧੯੪੪, ਸਿੱਖ ਰਾਜ ਕਿਵੇਂ ਗਿਆ?
Giānī Sohan Singh Seetal, 1944, Sikh Rāj Kive Giyā, Lahore Book Shop, Ludhiana, p17

[10] Gopal Singh, 1979, *History of the Sikh People*, p488

[11] ਗਿਆਨੀ ਸੋਹਣ ਸਿੰਘ ਸੀਤਲ, ਸਿੱਖ ਰਾਜ ਕਿਵੇਂ ਗਿਆ? (Giānī Sohan Singh Seetal, Sikh Rāj Kive Giyā), 1944, p25

[12] Syad Muhammad, Latif, 1891, History of the Panjab, Calcutta Central Press, Calcutta, p497

[13] ਗਿਆਨੀ ਸੋਹਣ ਸਿੰਘ ਸੀਤਲ, ੧੯੪੪, ਸਿੱਖ ਰਾਜ ਕਿਵੇਂ ਗਿਆ?
Giānī Sohan Singh Seetal, 1944, Sikh Rāj Kive Giyā, Lahore Book Shop, Ludhiana, p27

[14] Syad Muhammad, Latif, 1891, History of the Panjab, Calcutta Central Press, Calcutta, p497

[15] Syad Muhammad, Latif, 1891, History of the Panjab, Calcutta Central Press, Calcutta, p498
[16] Giānī Giān Singh, 1891, Tvārīkh Gurū Khālsā, Chattar Singh Jeevan Singh, Amritsar, p345
[17] Khushwant Singh, 1962, The Fall of the Kingdom of the Punjab, Orient Longman, reprint 2014, Penguin Books, India, p20
[18] ਗਿਆਨੀ ਸੋਹਣ ਸਿੰਘ ਸੀਤਲ, ੧੯੪੪, ਸਿੱਖ ਰਾਜ ਕਿਵੇਂ ਗਿਆ?
Giānī Sohan Singh Seetal, 1944, Sikh Rāj Kive Giyā, Lahore Book Shop, Ludhiana, p38
[19] Khushwant Singh, 1962, The Fall of the Kingdom of the Punjab, Orient Longman, reprint 2014, Penguin Books, India, p21
[20] ਗਿਆਨੀ ਸੋਹਣ ਸਿੰਘ ਸੀਤਲ, ੧੯੪੪, ਸਿੱਖ ਰਾਜ ਕਿਵੇਂ ਗਿਆ?
Giānī Sohan Singh Seetal, 1944, Sikh Rāj Kive Giyā, Lahore Book Shop, Ludhiana, p31
[21] J. D. Cunningham, 1849, History of the Sikhs, Oxford University Press, p236
[22] Lieut. Colonel Steinbach, 1883, The Punjaub; A brief account of the country of the Sikhs, Manju Arts, Chandigarh, reprint Language Department, 2003, Punjab
[23] Giānī Giān Singh, 1891, Tvārīkh Gurū Khālsā, Chattar Singh Jeevan Singh, Amritsar, p346
[24] Alexander Gardners Memoirs, 1898, p 225-226
[25] J.S. Grewal, 1994, The Sikhs of The Punjab, Cambridge University Press, p121
[26] ਗਿਆਨੀ ਸੋਹਣ ਸਿੰਘ ਸੀਤਲ, ੧੯੪੪, ਸਿੱਖ ਰਾਜ ਕਿਵੇਂ ਗਿਆ?
Giānī Sohan Singh Seetal, 1944, Sikh Rāj Kive Giyā, Lahore Book Shop, Ludhiana, p50
[27] Major G. Carmichael Smyth, 1847, A History of the Reigning Family of Lahore, with some account of The Jummoo Rajahs, The Seik Soldiers and Their Sirdars, p167

Part 3: Invasion and Occupation of Sikh territory

It is quite evident Panjāb was always on the British radar, and despite previous treaties of friendship, most notably the Treaty of Lahore, 1809, they took full advantage of the internal state of disarray at the Lahore Darbār. If the death of Ranjīt Singh did not get their attention, the bloodshed that followed certainly gave them the impetus to advance their forces. We know from the various letters exchanged between Sir William Macnaghten, Lord Auckland, and Lord Wellington, following the death of Nau-Nihaal Singh, that they had every intention of forcing an invasion on Panjāb; capturing Peshāwar was considered integral for the British, for which they had to take Lāhore.

British aggression

The plan to dismember the Lahore Darbār and take over Panjāb was perhaps the single greatest objective of the British. Cunningham notes,

> *"None of these things were communicated to the Sikh government, but they were nevertheless believed by all parties, and they were held to denote a campaign, not of defence, but of aggression."*[1]

This, coupled with Major Broadfoot's (Lieutenant Governor of Agra) actions of claiming rights of protection over territory previously agreed to be under Sikh jurisdiction, as well as his decision to cross the Sutlej, marked the first indication of the British breaking the Treaty of 1809.

> *"Again, a troop of horse had crossed the Sutlej near Feerozpoor, to proceed to Kotkupoora, a Lahore town, to relieve or strengthen the mounted police ordinarily stationed there; but the party had crossed without the previous sanction of the British agent having been obtained, agreeably to an understanding between the two governments, based on an article of the treaty of 1809, but which modified arrangement was scarcely applicable to so small a body of men proceeding for such a purpose. Major Broadfoot nevertheless required horsemen to recross; and as he considered them dilatory in their obedience, he followed them with his escort, and overtook them as they were about to ford the river. A shot was fired by the English party, and the extreme desire of the Sikh commandment to avoid doing anything which might be held to compromise his government, alone prevented a collision."*[2]

Even before Broadfoot had made such an audacious show of aggression, the signs of British encroachment were there. During the Afghan conflict, when the British set up a cantonment in Firozpur, which fell under the jurisdiction of the Lahore Darbār, assurances had been given that they would vacate within a year. On the contrary, following the conflict, the British made it a permanent cantonment, and following the death of Rani Lachman Kaur (widow of Sardar Dannā Singh, Misl Bhangīā), they merged Firozpur into their own territory.[3] Sir Charles Napier showed further aggression in the summer of 1845 as he responded to Sikh horses crossing into Sindh, who were chasing away raiders, by immediately calling up a regiment

Invasion and Occupation of Sikh Territory

of his troops. He was ready at every given opportunity to launch an attack on Panjāb.[4] Khushwant Singh notes,

> *"By the autumn of 1845, the invasion force – the largest ever assembled by the British in India – was poised on the Punjab frontier. It had been increased from 17,000 men and 66 guns in the time of Ellenborough to over 40,000 men and 94 guns".*[5]

The same writer describes how further British cantonments were set up at Ambala, Ferozepur, and in the Simla Hills. This heightened presence of troops along the frontiers with Panjāb had actually begun in 1838 when Lord Auckland had ordered the number of British soldiers positioned at Sabathoo and Ludhiana to be increased from 2500 to 7000.[6] Lord Ellenborough added more cantonments in Ambala, Kasauli, and Simla, taking the number of troops to 14,000 with 48 canons. Lord Hardinge further increased this to 32,000 troops and 68 canons, and a separate contingent of 90,000 was stationed at Maret.[7] According to Giānī Sohan Singh Seetal, the Sikh army, led by Lāl Singh and Tej Singh, had been completely convinced of the need to press forward and cross the Sutlej, based on the following four circumstances[8]:

1. British forces have amassed thousands of troops, and an attack on Lahore was imminent
2. The British were holding 18 lac rupees of Suchet Singh in the Ferozpur Bank and are refusing to return it to the Lahore Darbār
3. Lahore had a right to the estate of Suchet Singh
4. The British had prevented Sikh officers from entering the towns and cities south of Sutlej, that fell within the jurisdiction of the Lahore Darbār.

ਪਾਤਿਸ਼ਾਹੀ ਮਹਿਮਾ – Revisiting Sikh Sovereignty

Declaration of War

With this, on the 17th of November 1845, the Sikh army declared war. Notwithstanding the betrayal of Lal Singh and Tej Singh, Major G Carmichael Smyth writes,

> "Regarding the Punjaub war; I am neither of opinion, that the Seiks made an unprovoked attack, nor that we have acted towards them with great forbearance; my opinion is, that we should, as the paramount authority, long ago have adopted coercive measures with the Seiks and have assumed what kings call "a commanding attitude," but if this policy was disapproved of, no half measures should have been pursued, no middle course should have been taken; for, if the Seiks were to be considered entirely an independent state, in no way answerable to us, we should not have provoked them! - for to assert that the bridge of boats brought from Bombay, was no causa belli [act of war], but merely a defensive measure is absurd; besides, the Seiks had translations of Sir Charles Napier's speech, (as it appeared in the Delhi Gazette,) stating that we were going to war with them; and, as all European powers would have done under such circumstances, the Seiks thought is as well to be first in the field. Moreover, they were not encamped in our territory, but their own; and, although the second article of the treaty of 1809 states, "the Rajah will never maintain in the territory, which he occupies on the left bank of the Sutlej, more troops than are necessary for the internal duties", still the third article states, "in the event of a violation of any of the preceding articles,

or of a departure from the rules of friendship on part of either state, the treaty shall be consider void and null". **We have been told the Seiks violated the treaty, by crossing the river with their army; but the question is, was not the treaty null and void when they crossed? To expect a native power to make a regular declaration of war is too ridiculous; and I only ask, had we not departed from the rules of friendship first? (author's emphasis)** *The year before the war broke out, we kept the island between Ferozepore and the Punjaub, though it belonged to the Seiks, owing to the deep water being between us and the island."*[9]

Lāl Singh and Tej Singh took full advantage of the situation.

"Their desire was to be upheld as the ministers of a dependent kingdom by grateful conquerors, and they thus deprecated an attack on Feerozpoor, and assured the local British authorities of their secret and efficient good-will...the Sikh army itself understood the necessity of unity of counsel in the affairs of war, and the power of the regimental and other committees was temporarily suspended by an agreement with the executive heads of the state, which enabled these unworthy men to effect their base objects with comparative ease".[10]

Whilst Lāl Singh and Tej Singh masqueraded as leaders who had the best interests of the Lahore Darbār at heart, their battle decisions were calculated to ensure victory was handed to the British. The first indication of this came when they refused to send troops to Ferozpur, which puzzled even British writers. In 1846, M'Gregor writes,

"The Sikh troops are said to have pressed Lāl Singh to lead them against Feerozepore repeatedly, but he refused; and at length sent them to Moodkee in order to satisfy their demands, and get rid of their importunity. His excuse for not attacking that insulated post, was, that he wanted to fight the Commander-in-chief, and considered anyone else as below his notice!! Others asserted that his forbearance arose from the supposition that the cantonments had been filled with mines, since the desertion of them by the British. Whatever the real cause may have been, it was most fortunate that the Sikh army on crossing the Sutlej did not march on Feerozpore; for the least they could have done, would be to burn the barracks and officer's bungalows, and plunder the bazaars. Great consternation prevailed among the inhabitants of the city, which would have fallen an easy prey to the Sikhs, and become the scene of pillage and outrage; for which the Khālsā, and particularly the Ukhalies, have been so always celebrated. Had Runjeet Singh been ruler of the Punjab at the time of the Sikh invasion, his first act on crossing the Sutlej would have been to send the Ukhalies to burn and pillage every town and village belonging to the British or under their protection; and it is unaccountable why this mode of proceeding was neglected. We are almost tempted to believe that the Sikh leaders wished to keep their troops together, in order that the British might have a full and fair opportunity of destroying them!"[11]

Invasion and Occupation of Sikh Territory

I have included these lengthy quotes to demonstrate that even British writers, one year later, were seemingly astounded as to why such an obvious battle stratagem was not deployed by Lāl Singh.

Despite the treachery of Lāl Singh, who also purposefully withdrew his contingent of approximately 4000 troops, just as the Sikh Army was pressing the British back, the sheer ferocity with which the Sikh Army fought and maintained their hold is testament to the fighting prowess of the Khālsā.

Khālsā in battle

British commanders Gough and Hardinge were left astonished that even though the leaders had delayed or ignored prime targets of attack and eventually fled, the Sikh contingent, which numbered approximately six to seven thousand troops, continued the fight until sunset. Writers such as Giānī Sohan Singh Seetal have even noted that some of the British troops panicked and began firing amongst their own ranks and that commanders such as Colonel Malleson did not even regard the eventual victory of the British as a victory.[12]

In the battle of Ferushahar, on 21st December 1845, the Khālsā army fought with such ferocity that the British contingent "had formally decided to surrender unconditionally"[13], with the Governor General even expressing that "all state papers were to be destroyed" following their loss.[14] However, the following day, they were saved as Lāl Singh and Tej Singh refrained from sending fresh reinforcements to finish the job and guarantee victory for the Khālsā.[15] M'Gregor writes,

> *"Whatever the conduct of the political agents may have been, or by whatever means the hostile disposition of the Sikhs had been roused which induced them to cross the Sutlej, it was proved at the battle of Moodkee, that they were far superior to any*

foes the British army of India had ever encountered in the field". [16]

This was the impression within the British camp following the first war, in which the Sikh army had fought despite the damaging treachery of Lāl Singh and Tej Singh; we can only imagine the outcome had the Sikhs been able to fight the battle on an equal footing. As mentioned, some of the British generals did not regard the victory in 1845, as a victory in the true sense of the word. They had realised the Sikh army was like no other fighting force they had encountered and thus began work to bring in reinforcements in fear of an immediate response.

Stand of defiance

The final battle of the first Sikh-Anglo war, which we must remember was a war between the Sikhs of Panjab and the whole of British India, took place in Sabraon.

> *"Even upon the slaughter sustained by the Sikhs at Sobraon, and when thousands of them covered the ground, or found a watery grave in the Sutlej, those that escaped were as ready and determined to fight as if victory had crowned with success their former endeavours".* [17]

Notwithstanding further treachery from Gulāb Singh Dogrā on the eve of the battle of Sabraon on 10th February 1846, with his decision to assist the British, true Sikh warrior veterans such as Shām Singh Attārīvālā took to the battlefield in full knowledge of the situation. Shah Mohammed, in his famous Jangnama, writes, "to save the honour of their motherland, to preserve its independence and in so doing to win or die, as free men should".

There are many other accounts of Sikh valour and bravery, recorded by British officers, including the account in which M'Gregor writes, that despite having seen their fellow Sikhs fall on the battlefield and into the Satluj, those that remained fought with such courage one would think they had won the first battle.[18] Notwithstanding the fall of Ranjīt Singh and the internal capitulation orchestrated by the manipulative Dogrās, the accounts we have of Sikh battle in 1845 indicate the spirit of Sikh resistance upon which Sikh Rāj was established. Sardār Ajmer Singh writes:

"ਜਿਸ 'ਪਾਤਸ਼ਾਹੀ' (ਸੌਵਰਨਟੀ) ਲਈ ਖ਼ਾਲਸੇ ਨੇ ਪੌਣੀ ਸਦੀ ਤਕ ਸ਼ਹਾਦਤਾਂ ਦੀ ਨਿਰੰਤਰ ਝੜੀ ਲਾਈ ਰੱਖੀ ਸੀ, ਜਦ ਉਹ ਪਾਤਸ਼ਾਹੀ ਖ਼ਾਲਸਾ ਜੀ ਨੂੰ ਖ਼ਤਰੇ-ਮੂੰਹ ਆਈ ਤੇ ਖੁਸਦੀ ਜਾਪੀ ਤਾਂ ਉਸ ਅੰਦਰ ਅਜਿਹਾ ਜਜ਼ਬਾ ਤੇ ਜੋਸ਼ ਪੈਦਾ ਹੋ ਉਠਿਆ, ਕਿ ਉਸ ਨੇ ਆਪਣੀ ਜਾਨ ਨਾਲੋਂ ਵੀ ਵੱਧ ਪਿਆਰੀ ਇਸ ਅਮਾਨਤ ਦੀ ਰੱਖਿਆ ਲਈ ਜੰਗ ਦੇ ਮੈਦਾਨ ਅੰਦਰ ਆਪਣਾ ਸਾਰਾ ਲਹੂ ਵਹਾਅ ਦਿੱਤਾ ਸੀ। ਦੁਨੀਆ ਦੇ ਇਤਿਹਾਸ ਅੰਦਰ ਅਜਿਹਾ ਕਦੇ ਸ਼ਾਇਦ ਹੀ ਵਾਪਰਿਆ ਹੋਵੇਗਾ ਕਿ ਆਪਣਾ ਉਜ਼ੀਜ਼ ਆਗੂ (ਆਪਣੀ 'ਸਰਕਾਰ') ਦੇ ਸਦੀਵੀ ਵਿਛੋੜੇ ਤੋਂ ਕਿੰਨੇ ਸਾਲਾਂ ਬਾਅਦ ਅਤੇ ਆਪਣੇ ਜਰਨੈਲਾਂ ਤੇ ਵਜ਼ੀਰਾ ਦੀਆਂ ਅਣਗਿਣਤ ਕੁਚਾਲਾਂ ਤੇ ਗ਼ਦਾਰੀਆਂ ਦਰਮਿਆਨ ਲੜੀ ਗਈ ਜੰਗ ਅੰਦਰ ਕੋਈ ਫੌਜ ਏਨੇ ਸਿਦਕ ਜਲਾਲ ਨਾਲ ਲੜ ਸਕੀ ਹੋਵੇ, ਕਿ ਹਾਰ ਜਾਣ ਦੇ ਬਾਵਜੂਦ ਉਸ ਦੇ ਇਕ ਵੀ ਸਿਪਾਹੀ ਨੇ ਨਾ ਜੰਗ ਦੇ ਮੈਦਾਨ 'ਚੋਂ ਪਿੱਠ ਦਿਖਾ ਕੇ ਨੱਸਣ ਦੀ ਕੋਸ਼ਿਸ਼ ਕੀਤੀ ਅਤੇ ਨਾ ਜੇਤੂ ਦੁਸ਼ਮਣ ਦੇ ਅੱਗੇ ਆਤਮ ਸਮਰਪਣ ਕੀਤਾ। ਉਹ ਲੜੇ ਤੇ ਸ਼ਹੀਦ ਹੋ ਗਏ!"।[੧੯]

Essentially, Sardār Ajmer Singh writes when Sikh sovereignty, which the Khālsā had kept alive for three-quarters of a century, with martyrdom after martyrdom, was in danger, a renewed power awoke within the Khālsā collective. Charged with the emotion and sheer determination to uphold Sikh sovereignty at any cost, the Khālsā spilled its blood on the battlefield. Perhaps for the first time in world history, did an army fight and resist knowing that it's king had perished, ministers and generals had betrayed them and with death imminent, it continued to fight with such valour and bravery that not one Khālsā left the battlefield nor did they give up. They fought and they attained martyrdom in the name of Sikh sovereignty. The stand in the battle of Sabraon demonstrates the Khālsā were fighting for a greater cause, a higher power that was beyond the limits of any one empire. As we have discussed, the Sikhs had established various manifestations of Khālsā Rāj, building on the reign of the Gurū Sāhibān. This was the higher purpose that propelled them to resist in the way they did.

British occupation

In the Treaty of Lahore signed on 9th March 1846, the British took occupation of both the territories lying south of the Sutlej and the entire land lying between the Sutlej and Beas, as well as Kashmīr. The Sikhs were forced to "pay an indemnity of £1.5 million for war expenses",[20] and for his loyalty, the British rewarded Gulāb Singh Dogrā, who became sovereign of Kashmīr and Jammū. The British acquired a third of all Sikh territory.

In the two years since the 1846 Treaty of Lahore, the British had systematically dismantled the Sikh army, disbanded its generals and seized or destroyed its guns; "a force of 92,000 men, 31,800 cavalry and over 383 guns was now reduced to a few thousand".[21]

Despite this devasting loss, the Sikh Army, under Sher Singh Attarīwālā, fought two further victorious battles with the British in November 1848 (Ramnagar), and January 1849 (Chillīānwālā). Sher Singh had won over the support of some troops which, writes General Thackwell, had,

> *"...created much sensation. These, constituting several regiments, were raised out of the remnants of the old Khalsa army; and it is believed that the greater part of these men had been arrayed against the British flag in the battles of the Sutlege. They were stern, discontented veterans, brooding over the*

Invasion and Occupation of Sikh Territory

humbled condition of their beloved Khalsa or Commonwealth".[22]

Here we have another indication of how the Sikhs were fighting for a higher cause, one to uphold the glory and expanse that the Khālsā had amassed through its establishment of Sikh sovereignty. This demonstrates they were not necessarily fighting under the sole achievements of one man or royal house, but for the sovereignty bestowed upon them by the Gurū. In the final days of the Lahore Darbār, Panth Dhardī Gursikhs determined to fight until the very end, displayed a magnanimous final stand of defiance. Following the battle at Ramnagar, General Thackwell wrote,

> *"...the enemy had employed their heavy guns against us; for several eighteen -pound shots were discovered on the field. The perseverance and rapidity with which the Seikh gunners fired for nearly two hours, in spite of our terrific cannonade, reflected the greatest credit on them".*[23]

Many historians have recorded how the defeat in the battle of Chillīānwālā was the worst ever suffered by the British in their hundred years of waging war in South Asia.[24] Following the battle of Chillīānwālā, General Thackwell wrote,

> *"Few battles of ancient or modern times have presented such a roll of casualties – such an enormous sacrifice of life, within such a short space of time as this. None, certainly, where the results to both parties were less marked. If either party derived any advantage from this action it was the Seikhs, whose prestige was considerably raised by it".*[25]

Fall of temporal sovereignty

In all of this, the pertinent question is how a formidable fighting force such as the Khālsā eventually fell to the British in 1849. While this year marked the end of 'Sikh Empire' in Panjāb, the seeds of defeat were sown during the tenure of non-other than Ranjīt Singh himself. Sardar Ajmer Singh maintains, for all of his achievements as ruler of Panjāb, his conquests and his military foresight that saw the expansion of Sikh Rāj to the Khyber Pass, it was the decision to forgive the Hindu Hill Rājās, following their show of obedience to him, despite the decades of conflict and betrayal those Houses showed during the life of Gurū Gobind Singh, that came back to haunt the Lahore Darbār. His decision to include individuals like the Dogrās, who did not have the same love for Sikhi and the Panth as the previous officers, as close confidants within his Counsel, was perhaps his biggest failing.[26]

As we touched upon in the previous chapter, in the first two decades of his rule, Ranjīt Singh established so much due to the Panth Dhardī Gursikhs that held senior positions within both the army and government. It was upon the governance and decision making of Sikhs such as Rānī Sadā Kaur, Sardār Mit Singh Padhāniā, Sardār Attar Singh Dhārī, and Sardār Hukam Singh Attārīwālā that the Lahore Darbār was able to become the powerhouse it did under Ranjīt Singh. Following their passing, had they been replaced with individuals who shared the same love, loyalty, and allegiance to the Sikh Panth, then the disorder that followed within the Darbār after Ranjīt Singh's death would likely never have happened. However, they were replaced with the likes of the Rājpūt Dogrās, such as Dhiān Singh, Gulāb Singh, and Hīrā Singh, or Brāhmans from U.P. such as Jamādār Khushāl Singh, Rām Singh, and Tej Singh. There were others too, Kashmīrī Pandits such as Dīvān Gangā Rām and Rājā Dīnā Nāth, and Panjābi Brāhmans such as Lāl Chand, who went on to become Lāl Singh, and Panjābī Muslims such as Fakīr Azīzudīn,

Invasion and Occupation of Sikh Territory

Fakīr Nūrudīn, and Fakīr Imāmudīn.[27] And of course, there were also Europeans who held senior positions in the army, such as Ventura.

⌈By 1839, the Sikh government that was built on the accomplishments and sacrifices of Panthic personalities now rested in the hands of non-Sikhs who did not possess the same degree of allegiance to the Panth. Their own personal faith and political ambitions, shaped perhaps, by their familial goals or worldly greed, proved to supersede their loyalty to the sovereign Sikh Panth. Moreover, Kapur Singh notes the model of governance was based on "Hindu monarchy"[28], which is why Sikh polity failed to exist following the demise of Ranjīt Singh. It was his desire, as Kapur Singh puts it, to connect Sikhs to the Past, specifically the "Aitreva Brahmana of the Rig Veda...which asserted that the Law can never overpower lawlessness except through a monarch"[29].⌉

This effectively sealed the fate of Sikh Rāj under Ranjīt Singh. Those that held an unwavering amount of loyalty were largely contained within the army, perhaps the only entity of the Lahore Darbār worthy of any praise during this period. This treachery not only presented itself in the form of the Dogrās, Pūrbīās, or Pahārīs, but also from the Phoolkīān states, in particular from the Sikh chiefs of Patiālā, Jīnd, Farīdkot, and Chachrauli.[30] Furthermore, the Muslim chief of Makerkotla also sided with the British. As Sardār Kapūr Singh notes, in the act of replacing Sikh Sirdārs with the likes of the Dogrās and Pūrbīās, Ranjīt Singh not only initiated the end of his, and his own family's hold over power in Panjāb, but ultimately brought in a new era of subjugation for Panjāb. Sardār Kapūr Singh offers a fairly damning critique of Ranjīt Singh's choice of governance and polity. He writes,

> *"Within a few years after his coronation, he reduced into desuetude the supreme authority of the Sikh policy, the Gurmata, and entrusted the control of the government of his expanding territories to a cabinet of his own choice, in accordance with the*

ਪਾਤਿਸ਼ਾਹੀ ਮਹਿਮਾ – Revisiting Sikh Sovereignty

ancient Hindu monarchical tradition, but qua his own person, in whom he had gathered all the power, and authority of the state in accordance with the un-Sikh, Hindu doctrine, he never claimed independence from the Gurmata".31

It would appear this departure had roots during the Misl period. While the Sikh Sirdārs remained steadfast on the directive to establish Sikh sovereignty, sometimes this came at great personal cost. Rajinder Singh notes,

"... Superstitions began to creep in. Gurdwaras fell into the hands of the 'Udassis', who professed Sikhism, though from the outset they were a dissident group, different from the mainstream. They brought in idolatry and Hindu ritualism, from which Guru Nanak and his successors had rid their pristine faith".32

This sheds light on the extent to which Ranjīt Singh's polity was influenced by the socio-political environment of his own upbringing as a Sikh in the late 18th century. Moreover, the heads of the aforementioned Phoolkīan states readied their forces for battle with the Sikh Army of Panjāb as soon as war was announced by the British on 13th December 1846.33 A couple of years later during the second Sikh-Anglo war (1848-1849), the chiefs of Patiālā, Jīnd, and Nābhā happily presented their forces without the British asking.34

Ranjīt Singh may be fondly remembered as Sher-e Panjāb, but he was a mortal whose fatal mistake was to abandon the Guru-sanctioned mode of Sikh polity and decision-making, namely the Gurmata. With his passing, and the temporal loss of Sikh Rāj, the Sikhs entered a new political reality that they had not previously experienced. Despite the onslaught of colonial occupation, which we will consider in more depth in the next chapter, the struggle to establish Sikh sovereignty remained the number one objective.

Yearning to reestablish Rāj

As we have seen in Part One of this book, the Sikh aspiration for political rule did not start with Ranjīt Singh, and it certainly didn't end after the fall of his kingdom. While the British annexed and occupied the land of Panjāb, the immediate desire for political autonomy was entrenched deep in the souls of Panth Dhardī Gursikhs, such as Bhāī Maharaj Singh, Colonel Rashpāl Singh, Baba Rām Singh, and Prem Singh.[35] Thus, in the same year the British annexed Panjāb, the peoples of Panjāb led by the Sikhs, initiated the anti-colonial struggle.

Bhāī Maharaj Singh

Bhāī Maharaj Singh was well known and respected in Panjāb, serving the Panth under Bhāi Bīr Singh of Naurangābād. Following the martyrdom of Bhāī Bīr Singh during the attack on his encampment in 1844 led by Dhiān Singh Dogrā, Bhāī Maharaj Singh had taken over the unit at Naurangābād and subsequently shifted base to Amritsar by setting up headquarters at a place called Samdū Ka Talāb.[36] He was cognizant of the Dogrās intent, and it was from Amritsar that he began to reignite the 18th-century spirit of Sikh sovereignty, travelling from village to village and uplifting the peoples of Panjāb.

Such was the speed of movement and organization of Bhāī Maharaj Singh that he became a high priority for the British. On 9th June 1848, Assistant Resident Captain J. Abbott wrote,

> *"The dak of yesterday brought me a note from Major Napier describing the unsuccessful efforts to capture Bhai Maharaj Singh. I cannot forbear eroding that in February last I strongly urged to the officiating Resident, the importance of this man's immediate seizure".*[37]

ਪਾਤਿਸ਼ਾਹੀ ਮਹਿਮਾ – Revisiting Sikh Sovereignty

In order to maintain their hold over Panjāb, and indeed the surrounding regions, the British understood they had to stop the Khālsā. As early as 2nd June 1847, Henry Lawrence, the first British Resident at Lahore wrote,

> *"So great is their own pride of race, and of a long-unchecked career of victories that if every Sirdar and Seikh in the Punjab were to avow himself satisfied with the humbled position of his country, it would be the extreme of infatuation to believe him, or to doubt for a moment that amongst the crowd who are the loudest in our praise, there are many who cannot forgive our victory or even our forbearance and who chafe at their loss of power in exact proportion as they submit to ours".*

Bhāī Maharaj Singh, much like Bhāī Tārā Singh had done following Bandā Singh's assassination, kept the fight alive and galvanised peoples across the Jalandhar Doāb, which was a British territory. He inspired and assisted influential anti-British proponents such as Dīvān Mūl Rāj, the Governor of Multan; Sardār Chattar Singh Attārivala, the Governor of Hazārā; Bedī Bikram Singh of Una; and Rājput chiefs of the hills.[38] One of the most empowering aspects of his actions was that whilst he remained an elusive figure for the British, Bhāī Maharaj Singh simultaneously garnered support from the villagers who supported the cause. Various British officers were fired and replaced with men whom the British thought could capture him. When this failed, they tried to drive Bhāī Maharaj Singh up the Chenab into the territory of Muslim villages who did not revere him as much as others did across Panjāb. However, Bhāī Maharaj Singh was militarily astute enough to make his way around those terrains and back into friendly territory.

He soon entered Jammū, and it was during his encampment here, notes Nahar Singh[39], that Bhāī Maharaj Singh had devised a five-point plan of action:

Invasion and Occupation of Sikh Territory

1. "Plan to take Maharaja Dalip Singh away from the Lahore Fort to a place probably in the hills of Panjab, and to restart the freedom struggle in his name.
2. To organise a united front of all persons and interests who had lately suffered at the hands of the British, jagīrdārs, the ex-military men, the Rājput chiefs, and others.
3. To neutralise the British policy of using the local Muslims against the freedom fighters by forging an alliance between the rebels in Panjab, the Pathans of the North-West, and the Amīr of Kābul.
4. To approach all the important Sikh and Hindu priests and saints from Kandhār in Afghānistān to Mālwā in the cis-Sutlej for lending their whole-hearted support to the freedom struggle.
5. A programme of disrupting the administrative machinery of the new government by subversion and surprise attacks on their treasures and cantonments."

Empowered by the Pātshāhī of the Guru, it is evident from this plan, Bhāī Maharaj Singh was taking inspiration from the actions of the Sikhs in the period between Bandā Singh's departure and the rise of Ranjīt Singh. In particular, the fifth point of attacking British convoys, which had become a necessity for the Khālsā. However, soon after this plan was made, Bhāī Maharaj Singh was captured, by the aid of a British informant in Adampur. So afraid were the British of his influence that he was immediately exiled to Singapore, where he spent the remaining six years of life in solitary confinement.

British lockdown Panjāb and exile thousands of Sikhs

Following the annexation of Panjāb, it is clear the British were fearful of further Guru-inspired Sikh resistance. They felt it was imperative to quell, once and for all, the threat of any uprising led by the Sikhs. In April 1849, Lord Dalhousie, then the Governor-General, noted how the

ਪਾਤਿਸ਼ਾਹੀ ਮਹਿਮਾ – Revisiting Sikh Sovereignty

"...if we do not thus reduce to absolute subjection the people who have twice already rudely shaken our power in India, and deprive them at one of power and of existence as a nation: - if concession or compromise shall be made: - if, in short, the resolution which we adopt, shall be anything less than full assertion of absolute conquest of our enemy, and maintenance of our conquest hereafter, - we shall be considered, throughout all India, as having been worsted in the struggle. We must make the reality of our conquest felt...".[40]

In addition to removing revolutionary Sikh leaders such as Bhāī Maharaj Singh, the British exiled and imprisoned over 7000 Sikhs by sending them to foreign jails in Burma and Singapore.[41] Māhārānī Jind Kaur was separated from her son, and heir to Ranjīt Singh's kingdom, Duleep Singh. So fearful were the British of further Sikh resistance that they refused Duleep Singh to return to Panjāb on at least three occasions.

With the help of a fifty-thousand strong force of British soldiers from Bengal[42], there was a countrywide campaign to demilitarise Sikhs in Panjāb. Mark Condos also details how Notices were put up demanding the surrender of Sikh arms, in which more than 120,000 stands containing matchlocks, swords, and other weapons were taken by the British.[43] The British also threatened to impose heavy fines and even prison time for anyone who did not comply and give up their weapons; "numerous forts and other fortifications were also demolished".[44]

Whilst the British had no real interest in preserving or upholding the Sikh Dharam, they had come to understand the importance of Sikhi as a means of inspiring and motivating the Sikh fighters, which they managed to harness as a power for their own interests. It is clear from their own letters following the wars between 1845 and 1849 that the British admired Sikh fighting spirit but used that to their advantage. While the Khālsā Army was disbanded, the British began recruiting Sikhs into their army, playing on the sentiments of the Sikh's connection to their faith. They did this by allowing the Sikhs to keep their hair, wear their *dastaars* and read Gurbānī, but instead of fighting under the sovereign flags of the Khālsā, they coopted them to fight under the Union Jack. During this specific process, the Sikhs were assured that the traditions of the Khālsā, as a mere "religious" phenomenon, would be respected:

> *"The paol, or religious pledges of Sikh fraternity, should on no account be interfered with. The Sikh should be permitted to wear his beard, and the hair of his head gathered up, as enjoined by his religion. Any invasion, however slight, of these obligations would be construed into a desire to subvert his faith, lead to evil consequences, and naturally inspire general distrust and alarm. Even those, who have assumed the outward conventional characteristics of Sikhs should not be permitted after entering the British army, to drop them".*[45]

It is important to note how this marked the first moments of the Western secular confrontation for the Sikhs. That the "religious" aspects of the Khālsā would be respected, to the point that only the most ardent Khālsā, perhaps in their minds the most "religious", would be permitted and "honoured" within the British Army. It should be noted recruitment of Sikhs into British forces was not limited to the army, but the British also recruited Sikhs into the colonial police force, deploying them across Asia and Africa.

For the benefit of harnessing the power of the Khālsā, for their own colonizing and secularising mission, they reimagined the importance of the physical and outward appearance of a Sikh, especially an Amritdhāree Gursikh and placed it within the control of the British Empire, and the overarching epistemological authority and self-professed legitimacy of Western secular philosophy, which we shall consider in the next chapter.

NOTES

[1] J. D. Cunningham, 1849, *History of the Sikhs*, Oxford University Press: Oxford, p286

[2] J. D. Cunningham, 1849, *History of the Sikhs*, Oxford University Press: Oxford, p288

[3] ਗਿਆਨੀ ਸੋਹਣ ਸਿੰਘ ਸੀਤਲ, ੧੯੪੪, ਸਿੱਖ ਰਾਜ ਕਿਵੇਂ ਗਿਆ?
Giānī Sohan Singh Seetal, 1944, Sikh Rāj Kive Giyā, Lahore Book Shop, Ludhiana, p108

[4] J. D. Cunningham, 1849, *History of the Sikhs*, Oxford University Press: Oxford, p291 and; ਗਿਆਨੀ ਸੋਹਣ ਸਿੰਘ ਸੀਤਲ, ੧੯੪੪, ਸਿੱਖ ਰਾਜ ਕਿਵੇਂ ਗਿਆ?
Giānī Sohan Singh Seetal, 1944, Sikh Rāj Kive Giyā, Lahore Book Shop, Ludhiana, p109

[5] Khushwant Singh, 1963, *A History of the Sikhs*, Vol. 2, Second Edition, 2004, Oxford University Press, p42

[6] ਗਿਆਨੀ ਸੋਹਣ ਸਿੰਘ ਸੀਤਲ, ੧੯੪੪, ਸਿੱਖ ਰਾਜ ਕਿਵੇਂ ਗਿਆ?
Giānī Sohan Singh Seetal, 1944, Sikh Rāj Kive Giyā, Lahore Book Shop, Ludhiana, p108

[7] ਗਿਆਨੀ ਸੋਹਣ ਸਿੰਘ ਸੀਤਲ, ੧੯੪੪, ਸਿੱਖ ਰਾਜ ਕਿਵੇਂ ਗਿਆ?
Giānī Sohan Singh Seetal, 1944, Sikh Rāj Kive Giyā, Lahore Book Shop, Ludhiana, p108

[8] ਗਿਆਨੀ ਸੋਹਣ ਸਿੰਘ ਸੀਤਲ, ੧੯੪੪, ਸਿੱਖ ਰਾਜ ਕਿਵੇਂ ਗਿਆ?
Giānī Sohan Singh Seetal, 1944, Sikh Rāj Kive Giyā, Lahore Book Shop, Ludhiana, p112

[9] Major G. Carmichael Smyth, 1847, *A History of the Reigning Family of Lahore, with some account of The Jummoo Rajahs, The Seik Soldiers and Their Sirdars*, Introduction pXXVI

[10] Joseph Davey Cunningham, History of the Sikhs, p299

[11] W. L. M'Gregor, 1846, *The History of the Sikhs*, Vol.2, James Madden, London, p80-81

[12] ਗਿਆਨੀ ਸੋਹਣ ਸਿੰਘ ਸੀਤਲ, ੧੯੪੪, ਸਿੱਖ ਰਾਜ ਕਿਵੇਂ ਗਿਆ?
Giānī Sohan Singh Seetal, 1944, Sikh Rāj Kive Giyā, Lahore Book Shop, Ludhiana, p126

[13] Kapūr Singh, 1959, *Parasharprasna The Baisakhi of Guru Gobind Singh,* Lahore Book Shop, Ludhiana, p193

[14] Sir Robert, Cust. N., Linguistic and Oriental Essyas. VI. 48, as quoted by Kapūr Singh, 1959, *Parasharprasna The Baisakhi of Guru Gobind Singh,* Lahore Book Shop, Ludhiana, p193

[15] Kapūr Singh, 1959, *Parasharprasna The Baisakhi of Guru Gobind Singh,* Lahore Book Shop, Ludhiana, p193

[16] W. L. M'Gregor, 1846, *The History of the Sikhs,* Vol.2, James Madden, London, p94

[17] W. L. M'Gregor, 1846, *The History of the Sikhs,* Vol.2, James Madden, London, p89

[18] ਗਿਆਨੀ ਸੋਹਣ ਸਿੰਘ ਸੀਤਲ, ੧੯੪੪, ਸਿੱਖ ਰਾਜ ਕਿਵੇਂ ਗਿਆ?
Giānī Sohan Singh Seetal, 1944, Sikh Rāj Kive Giyā, Lahore Book Shop, Ludhiana, p154

[19] ਅਜਮੇਰ ਸਿੰਘ, ੨੦੦੭, ਕਿਸ ਬਿਧ ਰੁਲੀ ਪਾਤਸ਼ਾਹੀ
Ajmer Singh, 2007, Kis Bidh Ruli Paatshai, Singh Brothers, Amritsar, 3rd Edition, p40

[20] Patwant Singh and Jyoti M. Rai, 2008, *Empire of the Sikhs, The Life and Times of Maharaja Ranjit Singh*, Peter Owen Publishers, London, p249

[21] Patwant Singh, 1999, *The Sikhs*, John Murray Publishers, London, republished by Rupa Publications, 2002, Delhi, p168-169

[22] Edward Joseph Thackwell, 1851, *Narrative of the Second Seikh War,* p11-12

[23] Edward Joseph Thackwell, 1851, *Narrative of the Second Seikh War,* p97

[24] Khushwant Singh, 1963, *A History of the Sikhs,* Vol. 2, Second Edition, 2004, Oxford University Press, p79

[25] Edward Joseph Thackwell, 1851, *Narrative of the Second Seikh War,* p179

[26] ਅਜਮੇਰ ਸਿੰਘ, ੨੦੦੭, ਕਿਸ ਬਿਧ ਰੁਲੀ ਪਾਤਸ਼ਾਹੀ
Ajmer Singh, 2007, Kis Bidh Ruli Paatshai, Singh Brothers, Amritsar, 3rd Edition, p43

[27] ਅਜਮੇਰ ਸਿੰਘ, ੨੦੦੭, ਕਿਸ ਬਿਧ ਰੁਲੀ ਪਾਤਸ਼ਾਹੀ
Ajmer Singh, 2007, Kis Bidh Ruli Paatshai, Singh Brothers, Amritsar, 3rd Edition, p43

[28] Kapūr Singh, 1959, *Parasharprasna The Baisakhi of Guru Gobind Singh,* Lahore Book Shop, Ludhiana, p164

[29] As noted by Sardar Kapur Singh, Parasharprasna, p162 - Aitreya Brahmana, Rig Veda

[30] Khushwant Singh, 1963, *A History of the Sikhs,* Vol. 2, Second Edition, 2004, Oxford University Press, p53

[31] Kapūr Singh, 1959, *Parasharprasna The Baisakhi of Guru Gobind Singh,* Lahore Book Shop, Ludhiana, p188

[32] Rajinder Singh, 1988, *Five Hundred Years of Sikhism,* Amritsar Chief Khalsa Diwan, Department of History, Panjab University, Patiala, p34

[33] ਅਜਮੇਰ ਸਿੰਘ, ੨੦੦੭, ਕਿਸ ਬਿਧ ਰੁਲੀ ਪਾਤਸ਼ਾਹੀ
Ajmer Singh, 2007, Kis Bidh Ruli Paatshai, Singh Brothers, Amritsar, 3rd Edition, p45

[34] ਅਜਮੇਰ ਸਿੰਘ, ੨੦੦੭, ਕਿਸ ਬਿਧ ਰੁਲੀ ਪਾਤਸ਼ਾਹੀ
Ajmer Singh, 2007, Kis Bidh Ruli Paatshai, Singh Brothers, Amritsar, 3rd Edition, p46

[35] Tarlochan Singh Nahal, 2011, *Religion and Politics in Sikhism: The Khalsa Perspective,* Singh Brothers, Amritsar, p30

[36] Nahar Singh, 1968, *Documents Relating to Bhai Maharaj Singh,* Introduction xix

[37] Nahar Singh, 1968, *Documents Relating to Bhai Maharaj Singh,* p9

[38] Nahar Singh, 1968, *Documents Relating to Bhai Maharaj Singh,* Introduction xx

[39] Nahar Singh, 1968, *Documents Relating to Bhai Maharaj Singh,* Introduction xxvii-xxviii

[40] Dalhousie's Minute to the Secret Committee, 7 April, 1849, PP, 1849 (1075) XLI.683, *Continuation of Papers Relating to the Punjab,* no. 52, p.664, as noted by Mark Condos, 2017, *The Insecurity State Punjab and the making of Colonial Power in British India,* Cambridge University Press, p.77

[41] ਅਜਮੇਰ ਸਿੰਘ, ੨੦੦੭, ਕਿਸ ਬਿਧ ਰੁਲੀ ਪਾਤਸ਼ਾਹੀ
Ajmer Singh, 2007, Kis Bidh Ruli Paatshai, Singh Brothers, Amritsar, 3rd Edition, p52

[42] Tan Tai Yong, 2005, *The Garrison State, The military, Government and Society in Colonial Punjab, 1849-1947*, Sage Publications, p36

[43] General Report on the Administration of Punjab, 1850-51, p480, as referenced in Tan Tai Yong, 2005, *The Garrison State, The military, Government and Society in Colonial Punjab, 1849-1947*, Sage Publications, p36

[44] Mark Condos, 2017, *The Insecurity State Punjab and the making of Colonial Power in British India*, Cambridge University Press, p.78

[45] SC 38 of 23.02.1851, as referenced in Khushwant Singh, A History of the Sikhs, Second Edition, Vol. 2, p112

Western Secularism and the Colonial Encounter

What the likes of Ahmad Shah Abdali had previously failed to achieve in nine invasions, namely to nullify the threat of Sikh resistance, the British felt they had achieved following the annexation of Panjāb in 1849. Once they took occupation of Panjāb, Governor-General James Dalhousie set about working on the task that lay before him, which he wrote was,

> "...the utter destruction and frustration of the Sikh power, the subversion of its dynasty, the subjection of its people. This must be done promptly, fully and finally".[1]

One way the British did this was through brute force with the physical removal of Sikh bodies; however, another way they achieved this goal was through efforts to recondition and assimilate Sikhs on various fronts, as they had done elsewhere in the world under the project of secularisation and colonization. We will come on to the specific policies that changed the physical landscape of Panjāb, but let us first consider the roots of colonialism.

Colonialism and Western secularism v Gurmat

From a Gurmat perspective, colonialism is an extreme manifestation of *haumai,* the acceptance of one's sense of individuality, devoid of any connection to Akāl Purakh, which only serves to heighten the self-proclaimed right to own and control other bodies and lands. Dr. Gurbhagat Singh notes,

> "...colonialism or imperialism is another version of haumai whether it is of an individual or of an institution. The notion of haumai is best exemplified by the conduct of Hitler or Mussolini in our times. The political or economic imperialism of a national state in regard to the other external or internal nations/nationalities will also fall within the haumai-paradigm of the Guru Granth [Sahib].."[2]

Thus, it can be said, colonial forces occupied the land and began to introduce physical changes on the ground, but the structure of colonialism rested on the foundations of a particular epistemology, one produced by forces in the West who deemed themselves to be a superior civilization, with a self-professed right to civilise the rest of the world, which it deemed uncivilised. While the basis of this notion of superiority traces itself back to ancient Greece,

> "it was the process of colonialism [in Panjāb] that expanded a disciplining mode of knowledge-production based on the primacy of positivism and the finality of human intellect and agency. Through this myth from ancient Greece to "modern" Europe, this project continued to expand and sought to define all elements of life as it simultaneously sought to conquer the material world in its entirety."[3]

I would urge the reader to read the entire document by Samvād, referred to above. It helps to explain how, colonialism was an inevitable consequence of modernity; the logic that created modernity created colonialism, and that logic was tied to the secular. As a destructive break away from the Divine, from a Gurmat perspective, it is a manifestation of *manmat* in which the supremacy of materialism and empiricism become the new realities to worship, pursue, uphold, and propagate. During this process that originated in Europe, supremacy of logic and the ego replaced "God" as the centre of one's life, removing Dharam from the public sphere.

It is important to understand that colonization did not exist in a vacuum or on the whim of a single colonial officer, battalion, or office. It was engineered within the wider process of Western secularisation, and it was within this encounter, that the "colonial Sikh subject"[4] was framed. The emergence of "Sikhism," the "religion," arrived within this specific context too, something which subsequent Sikhs living in British occupied Panjāb internalised and carried forth into the post-1947 era of India-occupied Panjāb.

Once the framework was established, attempts were made to understand and define Sikhi within the colonial framing of "Sikhism". However, Gurū Nānak Sāhib says Gurbānī is "Dhur kī Bānī", which is manifested through their Words because they experienced the Divine; they are the Divine in that moment. Gurbānī is the pinnacle expression of the ineffable of Akāl Purakh; it is both the path and the vehicle to realizing that which Western secular writers and scholars have made an afterthought. The very first wisdom that Gurū Nānak Sāhib imparts after the Mool Mantar, in which they reveal the attributes of Akāl Purkah, is,

ਸੋਚੈ ਸੋਚਿ ਨ ਹੋਵਈ ਜੇ ਸੋਚੀ ਲਖ ਵਾਰ ॥

[Akāl Purakh] cannot be realised through mere thought, even by thinking hundreds of thousands of times.[5]

The Gurū, of course, goes on to describe how Akāl Purakh cannot be realised through silence either, nor is the spiritual hunger of Divine union satisfied through materialistic gains, but only through the acceptance and experience of Hukam, as we touched upon at the beginning of this book.

However, this was irrelevant for the coloniser and his agents, like Ernest Trumpp, whom we will consider shortly. To them,

Western secular philosophy, itself a consequence of the Protestant Reformation in Europe, was made supreme for the purposes of modernity, and it formed the basis of their approach to "defining" Sikhi. Any expression of Divine experience or revelation was to be categorised within the same restrictive parameters of Christianity that they themselves defined, based on what had preceded the Reformation in Europe.

Colonial loot

Before turning our attention to the manufacturing of "Sikhism" and considering the physical reshaping of Panjāb, let us briefly revisit how the British looted the Lahore Darbār immediately after the fall of Ranjit Singh's Rāj.

Prior to colonial occupation, Panjāb under the governance of the Darbār-e Khālsā was the strongest and most powerful country in the region. As we have seen, under Ranjīt Singh (1799 to 1839), the territory of Sikh Rāj extended to stretch from the Khyber Pass in the West, which today lies in modern-day Afghanistan, to the foothills of the Himalayas towards Tibet. My estimates place the expanse of Sikh Rāj during this period at approximately 140,000 square miles, a similar land mass as modern-day Germany, which was divided into four provinces; Lahore, Multan, Kashmir, and Peshawar.

Henry Prinsep of the Bengal Civil Service and British Agent Captain William Murray were responsible for acquiring intel on the Sikh government and the source of their political authority. According to the former, in 1834, the Sikh treasury under Ranjīt Singh was estimated to be worth £10m, raising to several million more with the lavish ornaments, jewels, shawls, elephants, horses, and the infamous Kohinoor diamond that made up the Sikh Treasury.[6]

Upon gathering intel on the economic and military might of Panjāb under Sikh Rāj, Prinsep concluded that the total annual revenue of the country under the dominion of Ranjīt Singh in 1834 was just over 25 lakh rupees (approximately £250,000). This included the customs of the whole of Panjāb, land revenue and tributes annually levied from neighbouring chiefs, and certain fees such as Mohurana, which was charged on every paper submitted for the Seal of Ranjīt Singh.[7] Intel on the military force estimated over 82000 troops on horse and foot with 376 guns.[8]

In 1847, Shahamat Ali, who was the Persian Secretary with the Mission of Lieut. Col. Sir C M Wade to Peshawar published a book on the governance of Sikh Rāj. According to his work, the total revenue derived from the country of Panjab in 1847 exceeded three Crores[9], with Multan and Kashmir bringing in almost 40 lakh each. That was an annual revenue stream of approximately £3m.

Therefore, in thirteen years, despite the death of Ranjīt Singh, the economic output of Panjāb increased 11-fold! In his assessment of the military might of the Sikh Rāj, Ali found a substantial increase in the regiments of infantry, cavalry, and artillery.

Writing two years earlier, in 1845, Lieutenant Colonel Steinbach, who served under Ranjīt Singh and his immediate successors, recorded that

> "...although much has been extracted from the royal treasury, during the constant succession of troubles, it is doubtful if any court in Europe possess such valuable jewels as the court of Lahore. Some idea of the vast property accumulated by Runjeet Singh may be formed from the circumstance of no less than thirteen hundred various kinds of bridles, massively ornamented with gold and silver, some of them even with diamonds, being found in the royal treasury."[10]

When the Lahore Khālsā Darbār of Ranjīt Singh was annexed, the British, led by Governor-General, Lord Dalhousie, had the freedom to loot the riches of Panjāb. On 2nd November 1849, Assistant Commissioner Robert Adams, who was assisting the recently appointed Head Keeper of the Sikh Treasury (Toshkhanā), Sir John

ਪਾਤਿਸ਼ਾਹੀ ਮਹਿਮਾ – Revisiting Sikh Sovereignty

Spencer Login, sent a letter to his cousin (and wife of Sir John) in which he wrote:

> *"I wish you could walk through the same Toshkhana and see its wonders! The vast quantities of gold and silver, the jewels not to be valued, so many and so rich! The Koh-i-noor, far beyond what I had imagined, and perhaps above all, the immense collection of magnificent Cashmere shawls, rooms full of them, laid out on shelves, and heaped up in bales – it is not to be described!"* [11]

In a memorandum dated 6th April 1949, Sir John Login himself had catalogued the various treasures of the Toshkhanā. Amongst them, he listed state jewels and treasures in gold, silver, and precious stones; dishes; plates; cups; cooking pots of gold; a vast store of Cashmere shawls; Ranjīt Singh's golden chair of State (which today sits in the Victoria & Albert Museum in London); arms and armoury; a plume belonging to Gurū Gobind Singh; swords that previously belonged to Mughal rulers; pavilions; and countless other relics which he stated were too numerous to note.[12] In a letter to his wife dated September 5th, 1849, Sir John Login wrote,

> *"I had the great pleasure of presenting to the Maharaja [an 11-year-old Duleep Singh], on the morning of his birthday, a lakh of rupees' worth of his own jewels from the Toshkhana which I had been empowered by Government to select and present to him. He appeared, therefore, dressed most splendidly; wearing, besides other jewels, the diamond aigrette and star I had selected. When I congratulated him on his appearance, he innocently remarked, that on his last birthday he had worn the Koh-i-noor on his arm!"* [13]

Western Secularism and the Colonial Encounter
Imposition of Colonial Logic and the reshaping of Panjāb

With their hands on Sikh treasure and riches, a primary aim of the British then became, what Dalhousie stated, "the utter destruction and frustration of the Sikh power, the subversion of its dynasty, the subjection of its people," and it was directed across many fronts. Towards the end of the last chapter, we considered how there was a countrywide operation to demilitarise Sikhs in Panjāb; however, Tan Tai Yong explains how the number of unemployed Sikhs trained and skilled in warfare was identified as a potential problem for the British, who were fearful of a rebellion. This is why there was a specific focus on recruiting from within Panjāb, which eventually led to the creation of what he has called the "Garrison State".[14] This was the process by which Panjāb was re-militarised in the image of the coloniser; to serve as the "sword arm" of the British Rāj in South Asia.

Within the campaign of co-opting aspects of Khālsāi attire and identity, which marked the first moments of the Western secular confrontation for the Sikhs, the recruitment drive initiated by the British, also had a specific campaign to convince impressionable Sikhs of Panjāb that they were superior, according to colonial logic, to the rest of British India, and for this reason, were worthy of serving in the Empire.

> "Recruiting came to be guided by a series of manuals and handbooks, which contained detailed evaluations of the military potential of various classes of recruits. Couched as ethnological and anthropological studies, these handbooks were often nothing more than observations based on colonial stereotypes and racism that imbibed an extreme form of cultural and environmental determinism."[15]

The British foreign secretary, Lord George Curzon, wrote in 1902 that the Sikhs were "the fighting race", or the "naturally hardy, independent, and robust race". In typical British manner, they

ਪਾਤਿਸ਼ਾਹੀ ਮਹਿਮਾ – Revisiting Sikh Sovereignty

championed further divisions along the lines of caste, convincing themselves that the "Jat Sikhs" in particular were of a higher social status, "by virtue of their adherence to the defining features of the Sikh religion".[16] While all Sikhs were generally portrayed as a "martial race", recruitment handbooks produced by the British spelt out who they considered suitable recruits: Sikhs from a "Jat caste" and those adhering to the Khālsā way were identified as ideal recruits, even specifying desirable districts based on their own intel.[17] Between 1858 and 1914, there was a steep increase in the number of Sikhs employed by the British Indian Army. During the First World War, the number of Sikh soldiers reached 150,000, "a quarter of all armed personnel in British India".[18]

Fifty years after the fall of Ranjit Singh's Rāj, we find Sikhs employed by the British Empire, scattered from Hong Kong and Malaya to Central Africa and Uganda, who were motivated by both pay and this new imposition of being a "martial race".

> *"One such calculation in 1898 indicated that something approaching one-tenth of the entire Sikh male population of military age, or 39,598 men of 482,500, was employed by the [British] Indian military; of these 28,146 were Jats, 2,452 Mazbis, and the remaining 9,000 were of other classes. Among Punjabi Muslims, 21,000, or some 2 percent of those eligible, were in Indian military service. On colonial service, including both volunteers from the [British] Indian Army and those recruited independently, the government counted a total of some 5,000 men. Of these 2,554 were Sikhs (scattered from Hong Kong and Malaya to Central Africa and Uganda); 1,548 were Punjabi Muslims (serving mostly in Hong Kong and East Africa); while a further 893 of other communities were employed in*

Western Secularism and the Colonial Encounter

Hong Kong, North Borneo, Ceylon, and Mauritius."[19]

Thus, it was during the colonial encounter in Panjab, that we saw the emergence of these new types of Sikh soldiers and officers within the British Empire, based on colonial categorisation along the lines of caste and social status. During this process of placing themselves in the coloniser's service to protect his interests exclusively, they ended up adopting his ideology, even concerning their own values and their own lives.

Transformation of rural to agrarian life

Perhaps on par with the devastation caused by the creation of the colonial soldier was the remapping of rural life and the transformation of land into taxable units. There was a specific ideology behind this colonial reshaping of rural to agrarian life in Panjāb. It stands on what Neeladri Bhattacharya has referred to as the notion of 'masculine paternalism'[20], a mode of governance that Henry Lawrence, John Lawrence, and James Dalhousie enforced across Panjāb. This specific ideology of colonial governance was firstly based on the idea that Panjāb's farmers needed to be ruled and governed because they were otherwise inept of doing so in an efficient manner, and secondly that it was done for the benefit of Panjāb and Panjābīs. Within the broader backdrop to colonial occupation of Panjāb, this shift was designed to accelerate the rapid development in agriculture, which of course, served the colonial aim of exploiting labour and extracting the country's resources.

Bhattacharya demonstrates that prior to annexation of Panjāb, what became the archetypal "Indian (colonial) village" was not the sole structure of rural habitation, nor was the entirety of rural life limited within those types of village settings. Instead, there were habitation settings that served to uphold a kind of "ecological balance", with different types of villages in the, *"riverine belts and fertile lands, and those in the dry belts, pastoral tracts, scrublands, or rocky hill regions; between villages with long histories and the newer implants that were bureaucratic creations; between villages with deep lineages and dense populations, and those that were agglomerations of scattered hamlets, or simply pieces of land with hadbast boundaries, often without habitation sites, cultivated fields, or inhabitants; between those that were organised around rights to land and those whose constituent social bodies were formed around rights to pastures, wells, and inundation canals."*[21]

However, colonial officers introduced the reshaping of rural life under the pretense of ideal imperial leaders, powerful for having conquered Panjāb, but also caring because they claimed to introduce policies for the betterment of rural life in Panjāb. Bhattacharya goes on to state,

"The patriarchal self-image centering on the figure of the father was forged in diverse ways, ceremonial as much as literary, as profoundly authoritarian and masculine. Within popular imperial literature this patriarchal masculinity was underlined via tales of daring, adventure and courage. In them the civil official is fearless and powerful, and... face danger with a practiced ease born of an instinct for power."[22]

Having asserted their authority upon the basis of political control and premise of superiority of intellect, colonial officers were depicted as heroes in texts books and thus began an era of rapid change in Panjāb. The colonial creation of the agrarian model, where life in Panjāb was stringently focused on cultivating the land, was imprinted upon people's minds as the totality of rural life through the systematic reorganization of villages.

Bhattacharya notes in many regions of Panjāb, the cultivated portion of land was less than fifteen per cent, with other regions at no more than forty per cent of surveyed land.[23] However, due to colonial policies geared towards maximization of fiscal return, a concerted effort was made to transform all "rural spaces into productive landscapes". By the 1890s, the proportion of cultivated land between the Satluj and Beas was up to seventy-five per cent.[24] Bhattacharya further writes how peasants were idealised as hardworking and "settled agriculture was valorised as normative and desirable". In this process, there was a refusal to accept those other spaces and habitations of Panjāb such as forests, scrublands, pastures, hilly regions, and the mountains as desirable parts of the country because the colonial aim of exploiting the labour and extracting the produce was not possible in those spaces.[25]

Bhattacharya's work is integral to understanding the radical shift brought about in Panjāb by the British through the structure of colonialism. What Bhattacharya's research demonstrates is colonisation across Panjāb was possible only through the rapid revisualisation and reconstitution of rural spaces. The physical spaces were not merely occupied but reconstructed for the purposes of exploitation of labour and revenue extraction. Panjāb was seen as a lucrative market for export, to the rest of British India, but also the world.

Land mortgages and debt

Another damning aspect of colonial rule in Panjāb was the introduction of land mortgages. During Ranjīt Singh's time, there had been favourable expansion in both agriculture and long-distance trade, with little change to the established pre-industrial 'modes of resource use'.[26] However, as we have discussed, the onset of colonial rule changed all that. Following annexation in 1849, moneylenders were established all over Panjāb, despite security and credit being at the lowest.[27]

> "The mortgage that was rare in the days of the Sikh [rule] appeared in every village, and by 1878 seven per cent of the province was pledged. In Amritsar, at much the same date (1880) there were 798 mortgages, against only 23 recorded before 1865, and in Jullundur over fourteen lakhs were raised by mortgage in the seventies (1871-81) against only Rs. 40,000 in the fifties. By 1880 the unequal fight between the peasant proprietor and the money-lender had ended in a crushing victory for the latter".[28] During the turn of the 20th century, specifically the 30-year period between 1881 and 1911, farmer indebtedness in Panjāb increased manifold, as mortgages continue to multiply at an unprecedented rate, increasing from 53,263 in 1868 to 193,890 in 1911.[29]

By 1919, a staggering 83% owners of land were caught in the grip of money lenders".[30] Farmer indebtedness rose exponentially[31], and what made matters extremely difficult for Panjāb's farmers was the colonial policy, which made it a mandatory requirement that "all farmers should pay all land taxes in cash."[32] They simply did not have the surplus money to do this and were forced to borrow money by turning to the moneylenders. One particular case highlighted by Darling shows how the spiraling debt issues in Panjāb were passed on from one generation to the next.[33]

Grain loans were even more damaging for the Panjābī farmers because where compound interest doubled for a cash loan in approximately three years, the grain loans doubled the interest in two. The sheer speed with which Panjāb was plunged into debt makes for grim reading. Within twenty years of colonial occupation, mortgages, a rarity during Ranjīt Singh's period, had become commonplace and the moneylenders powerful. By 1874 over one million acres were mortgaged, and by 1891, nearly four million. Between 1891 and 1925, whilst there was no great increase in the area under mortgage, the amount of mortgage debt increased by over 25 crores![34] In terms of the figures, Darling notes, the mortgage debt of Panjāb in 1891, including the North-West Frontier, was "7.83 crores, but assuming it was only 45 per cent of the whole, total debt in that year was around 17 crores". The corresponding figure for 1922 (excluding the Frontier Province) was 82 crores. Alarmingly, if the Frontier were excluded from the figure in 1891, the increase would be even greater. In three decades, rural debt increased by at least 50 crores and multiplied fourfold. The following table, as first depicted by Darling, shows the figures for districts that represented all parts of Panjāb:[35]

District	Mortgage Debt (in lakhs) At date specified and in 1922	
Rohtak (excluding Sonepat)	6.5 (1873-79)	83
Jullundur	32 (1886)	197
Rawalpindi	9 (1878-82)	29
Attock	7 (1878-82)	50
Jhang	11.5 (1880)	64
Muzaffargarh (excluding Leiah)	13 (1883)	80
Bhakkar and Leiah Tehsils	5 (1879)	24

The Thorburn Report on Peasant Indebtedness and Land Alienation found, colonial policymakers and legislators strong-armed lawyers and moneylenders with the introduction of the Civil Procedure Code; the setting up of the Chief Court at Lahore (1866); and the passing of the Evidence Act and Contract Act in 1872, which adversely affected the agriculturists because the legal system prolonged litigation. The report analyses how the most decisive blow that crippled the farmers came in 1874-75 with the munsiffs' courts' introduction to try debt disputes. Up until this point in Panjāb, matters pertaining to revenue had been resolved by district officers, with intimate knowledge of the farmers' problems. However, the munsiffs were largely urbanites, unaware of the dynamics of rural affairs, which resulted in often harsh and unfair decisions.[36]

Moreover, the new colonial litigation process heavily contributed to the levels of indebtedness of Panjāb's farmers. In 1889, S.S. Thorburn noted civil suits formed approximately two per cent of new debt.[37] On average, over 40% of the adult male population attended court every year, either as parties to or as witnesses in court proceedings.

At the turn of the 20th century, most cultivators in Panjāb were born in debt, lived in debt, and died in debt. In most districts, no more than a third of people were free from debt, and in some, the percentage of those free from debt was less than ten.[38] It was a cyclical travesty, which affected generations of Panjābīs, a far cry from Ranjīt Singh's land revenue extraction policies, which varied according to the needs of different types of farmers and the necessity to retain ecological balance. No such regard was given by the British, whose sole agenda of occupying Sikh homeland was to extract resources, labour, and foot soldiers, and advance colonial interests worldwide. The systematic method of economic subjugation across Panjāb was engineered through various projects.

Rail and canal developments

Between 1873 and 1903, Panjāb's rail network was extended from 400 miles to over 3000, and its irrigation canals from 2744 to 16,893.[39] According to Professor Pritam Singh, there were three main aims behind the construction of the irrigation networks and canal colonies; (i) "to increase agricultural output and therefore maximise land revenue extraction; (ii) to facilitate military recruitment by making military service an economically attractive route to land acquirement;

and (iii) to foster a loyal political base in the countryside".[40] The overriding purpose of the irrigation of canals was, of course, linked also to the agrarian reshaping of Panjāb we discussed above, which in itself served the aim of quelling Sikh resistance in the form of providing alternative work to unemployed former Sikh soldiers of the Khālsā Army. Mark Condos writes,

> "Canals and ready access to irrigation, it was believed would transform the soldier peasantry and would include them to settle down and till the land quietly – to 'turn their swords into ploughshares'... thus, the principal objectives of early British irrigation efforts in Punjab were intimately and inextricably tied up with larger military priorities of pacification."[41]

Condos' work highlights how the opening up of new irrigation systems was in reality less about Panjāb's prosperity and developing new opportunities for the overall financial and social welfare of the Sikhs, but more about nullifying the military threat of the Sikhs. The overarching aim of the British in Panjāb was to suppress the Khālsā and solidify political control. This cemented, what Condos has called the "nexus of military-agrarian interests", which became a defining aspect of colonial rule in Panjāb.[42]

It is no wonder that Patrick Wolfe stated colonialism is not a singular event; rather, it is an entire structure. It is physical and psychological, overt and discreet; it engulfs one's entire sense of being and identity. Notwithstanding the severity of persecution, this is how the colonial encounter, post-1849, differed from previous confrontations with the Mughal and Afghan regimes. Within this encounter, the British sought to claim not just the land but the bodies and the minds of peoples.

Therefore, the structure of colonialism that was enforced over Panjāb following the events of 1849 cannot be compared or measured against previous invaders that inflicted oppression upon the Sikhs

ਪਾਤਿਸ਼ਾਹੀ ਮਹਿਮਾ – Revisiting Sikh Sovereignty

and Panjāb, because the advent of British colonialism is tied to the global restructuring of the world that was initiated in the 15th century and led to what Professor Ramon Grosfuguel has called the "Four Genocides/Epistemicides of the Long 16th Century".[43]

This is important because, as we shall consider shortly, the logic that underpinned the occupation of Pānjāb, and indeed the rest of the colonised world, namely the logic of the white European male experience in Europe, was not only exercised for centuries prior to the colonial conquest of Panjāb but passed on during the transfer of power that occured in 1947 with the creation of the Indian State.

Education system uprooted

Whilst Ranjīt Singh himself was illiterate, he maintained a complex infrastructure of education across Panjāb. This should not come as a surprise considering the work done to introduce education centres during the Gurū-period, as we explored in Part One. Most of Ranjīt Singh's Court attendants were highly educated, and his own grandson, Nau-Nihaal Singh, studied advanced mathematics and astronomy under the tutorship of well-renowned scholars of the time. There were diverse centres of education for all Panjābis, including Muslims and Hindus, showcasing the freedom and opportunity Sikh Rāj provided for those seeking new skills and knowledge for improving their living standards and the society around them.

According to the Lahore District Report of 1860[44], there were 576 formal schools where some 4,225 scholars taught. In Lahore alone, in addition to conventional schools, there were special schools for technical training, languages and mathematics. There were craft schools specialising in architecture, calligraphy, miniature painting, and sketching. Almost every Panjābi woman was literate in the sense that she could read and write Gurmukhi, with 18 formal schools for girls across Lahore. The report examined how, during his last years, Ranjīt Singh collected the equivalent of approximately £1.85m, and as a percentage directed more towards education than the British did during their entire occupation. Thousands of schools belonged to Arabic, Persian, and Sanskrit centres of excellence, and students were taught to the highest standards.

In his monumental work, *History of Indigenous Education in the Panjāb Since Annexation*, first published in 1882, G.W. Leitner, a Doctor of Oriental Learning, not only sheds light on the intricacy of the indigenous education network under Sikh Rāj but also exposes the devasting effects of the colonial policies, which systematically destroyed the thriving education centres in Panjāb.[45] He outlines how any opportunities for the healthy revival and development of such schools were either neglected or perverted.

Leitner points out that before British forces annexed Panjāb, there wasn't a single village that did not take pride in devoting time and attention to education. His research showed, with the most modest of figures, that there were approximately 330,000 students in educational institutions of various denominations who were acquainted with reading and writing. Within three decades of British rule, this number plummeted to a staggering low of a little more than 190,000, dropping almost 60%.

Importantly, the substitution of Urdu for Persian, the former more a subject of study for Europeans than natives, and the latter taught in Panjāb for centuries, which exerted a natural and beneficial influence on their various vernaculars along with Arabic and Sanskrit, was perceived as a move to limit the education of the native. Urdu and indeed English soon became the mainstream avenues of language to understanding and communicating in society. Having first degraded and broken education from any mental and moral culture associated with indigenous life, the British then transformed education systems to serve the colonising means of purely worldly ambition.

The number of education centres also dropped dramatically. According to the Settlement Report of 1852[46], in the district of Hoshiarpur, there was a school to every 19:65 (adults and non-adults) of male inhabitants. Thirty years later, that figure plunged to just one

ਪਾਤਿਸ਼ਾਹੀ ਮਹਿਮਾ – Revisiting Sikh Sovereignty

Government school to every 9,028 inhabitants, or one school to every 28,187 inhabitants, including the number of ascertained indigenous schools throughout Panjāb in 1882. Leitner's work highlighted the stark contrast to the proportion of one school to every 1,783 inhabitants in the most impoverished divisions of Panjāb in 1849 when it was annexed by the British.

Indigenous masters of knowledge, such as Maulvis, Pandits, and Granthis of various disciplines, were ridiculed as any mystical or ineffable basis of education was undermined. Granthis continued to teach correct pronunciation and meaning of Gurbāni to thousands of children in Gurmukhi, but the British deemed the Sikh alphabet and the Panjābī language a threat to their mission in Panjāb. As such they were not used for elementary instruction.[47]

In the carnage of revenge that followed the military Mutiny of 1857, the British purposefully searched every house of a village and burned any book they could get their hands on, and Leitner maintains an entire tradition, far superior to what Europe had to offer, was destroyed. An extract of report No. 335, dated 6th July 1857, concludes: "That elementary, and sometimes high, oriental classical and vernacular education was more widespread in the Punjab before annexation than it is now". The report concludes that the events of 1857 "destroyed the huge endowments that kept this 'magnificent educational system intact". Leitner also records that the Lahore Khālsā Darbār had a first-rate educational system far superior to what the British offered. Women were more educated than men, and this, Leitner observes, is what made sure that with every passing year, the literacy rate increased. Once this was stopped, literacy progressively declined.

J. S. Grewal explains the auxiliary role Christian missionaries played in the spread of English education across Panjāb. Referring to the work of John C.B. Webster (1976) on Presbyterians in Panjab, Grewal writes,

> "Christian missionaries proved to be the greatest allies of the British in spreading English

education...They made the press an effective medium of communication in Punjabi, Urdu and Hindi for evangelization. In the process they denounced indigenous religious beliefs and practices, social evils and morals of the Punjabis rather openly and aggressively, partly because of their own theological assumptions and partly because they regarded the colonial rule as providential. In the popular mind they were closely allied with the rulers, and their socio-cultural programme carried a sharper edge because of this real or supposed alliance. The Punjabis reacted to the presence of the Christian missionaries also because of their spectacular success. Starting from about 4,000 in 1881, the number of Indian Christians in the Punjab rose to over 300,000 in 1921."[48]

Infiltrating Sikh spaces

The British had a specific policy to infiltrate Sikh institutions, specifically focusing on the Dhārmic groups, the result of which was evident in the emergence of large Smāgams and Akhānd Paths held for the longevity of British rule in Panjāb.[49] In a move to exert their control, the British hand-picked individuals, such as Sardār Jodh Singh, to govern Harmandir Sāhib.[50]

Various works from the likes of Lepel Griffin and Pandit Debī Prasād (author of Gulshan-e-Panjāb), were commissioned, which served as propaganda to break a Sikh's understanding of the glory of Sikh sovereignty, particularly during Darbār-e Khālsā and Ranjīt Singh. New editions of books like Sau Sākhī were published in which a story of a joint alliance of Sikh and British forces was said to have been prophesised, in which they conquered Delhi together.[51]

The long-term psychological effects of the defeat following the 2nd war with the British upon the Sikhs, were devasting. Whether through brute force or the systematic changes introduced through education and administration in Panjāb, the loss of Sikh Rāj forced many to accept the superiority of the British.

Language, Hermeneutics, and Translation

This leads us on to another devasting phenomenon that occurred during colonial rule, which wreaked havoc on Sikh minds. [Once the British gained control of political affairs, in addition to the negative changes in education across Panjāb, they were responsible for commissioning various Christian missionaries, most famously German Indologist Ernest Trumpp in 1870, who was assigned the task of translating the Gurū Granth Sāhib.]

In the Preface to his work, Trumpp begins by narrating how he asked two Granthis for assistance in his colonial endeavour. When they informed him such a task of translating the Gurū Granth Sāhib into English could not be done in the literal way that he desired, he convinced himself that though they professed to understand the Gurū Granth Sāhib, he did not believe that was the case. Trumpp explains how he sought the assistance of a couple of other Granthis, but they too refused. He wrote how the Brahmans did not come forward due to the animosity between the Sikhs and the Hindu community. Although I would assume their reasons for not coming forward were perhaps a little more nuanced, considering the ideological opposition to Brahmanism the Gurū so vehemently spoke of in their writings. By his own admission, Trumpp reveals that he eventually found three commentaries; two of which sought to explain some of the Hindu references and the other which looked at the Arabic and Persian words; thus, he began his work.[52]

Trumpp demonstrated how colonialism did not exist in a vacuum. European forces didn't just one day wake up and set sail for new lands on the premise of discovery, as is regurgitated in education today. There was a very specific motive, which was tied to the project of modernity, secularism, and the so-called

Enlightenment movement, which empowered the ego through the notion of the superiority of logic, rationale, empiricism, and materialism, to solidify power and control for European powers. In Trumpp's own words, he read Gurū Granth Sāhib based on those commentaries and returned to Europe in 1872 to begin the translation. He laments how he had to do the work twice but saw no other way if he "wished to lay down a solid foundation and give it a translation which should be of any scientific value".

In essence, Trumpp, and others trained in Western theology and philosophy, were not interested in translating Gurbānī for any genuine interest in experiencing the Shabad. For them, it was at best an intellectual exercise, and at worst, an attempt to reframe through their worldview; to assert their authority and their version of knowledge about that which they termed the "metaphysical." This is how hermeneutical interpretation allowed them to categorise Sikhī, as a religion, within their framework, thus creating "Sikhism". Trumpp writes,

> "It is for us Occidentals [Westerners] a most painful and almost stupefying task, to read only a single Rag, and I doubt if any ordinary reader will have the patience to proceed to the second Rag, after he shall have perused the first. It would therefore be a mere waste of paper to add also the minor Rags, which only repeat, in endless variations, what has been already said in the great Rags over and over again, without adding the least to our knowledge."[53]

Notwithstanding the fact Trumpp concludes the Preface by writing, "Sikhism is a waning religion, that will soon belong to history," and "English is not my mother-tongue...I was therefore often at a loss how to translate such abstruse philosophical matters clearly and correctly...", it is important to remember, as Dr. Arvind-Pal Singh Mandair has explained, this translation imposed a new intellectual framework, that of Western theology, on to Gurbānī, thus setting new ground for future discourse on Gurbānī, both within and outside Panjāb. In his chapter on "Sikhism and the Politics of Religion-Making", Dr. Arvind-Pal Singh Mandair brilliantly notes,

> "Such a transformation was enabled by the imposition of a dominant symbolic order on the indigenous cultures, followed by the appropriation of this symbolic order by the native elites...-an order exemplified by an entire discourse of colonial ethnographies, missionary literatures, and translations, implemented by a vast network of Anglo-vernacular mission schools, and maintained by a newly imposed capitalist economy – prepared the ground for a fundamental shift in the receptive psychology of the native elites in the late nineteenth and twentieth centuries."[54]

The important point Dr. Mandair goes on to make is that although Trumpp's work was met with "vociferous rejection", it built on the efforts of Malcolm and Cunningham, the former who portrayed Sikhs as Hindu reformists, and the latter who recognised there was a difference, but not to the extent that they could be separated entirely.[55] Trumpp's work, writes Dr. Mandair,

> "...helped to catalyze the theologisation of the native elite mindset, and, inadvertently, its attunement to the economy of the empire".[56]

In other words, empowered by colonial authority over Panjāb, Trumpp introduced concepts of religion, in particular Christianity, that were otherwise foreign to the Sikh, which forced the Sikh scholars to interact with them on their terms, a process in which that foreign imposition of hermeneutical interpretation was deemed superior. The process of colonial translation by Trumpp and later Macauliffe is thus regarded simultaneously as "psychoanalytical and theological exercises" by Dr. Mandair. Essentially, what the likes of Trumpp did was to re-present the otherwise mystical and ineffable experience of the Divine, as expressed in Gurbānī, which Trumpp ridiculed for lacking rationality and reason, into theological concepts that could be critiqued and questioned from the logic of coloniality. They attempted to intellectualise that which exists beyond the confines of the mind. They did this because, as Sardar Ajmer Singh explains, with the onset of Renaissance and Modernity, intellect was considered supreme. It was during this process that the conventional existence of Dharam which included, mind, body, and soul, was stripped down to just two, mind and body.[57] As we touched upon at the start of this chapter, this approach was modelled on what Martin Luther had done during the Protestant Reformation; it was the same logic applied by British Indologists after the British took control over Panjāb.

Sikhi to "Sikhism"

Dr. Mandair has termed this process "religion-making". The classification of peoples into "religions", supported the colonial project, as colonisers built on the so-called Renaissance in Europe, by not only imposing the dominance of rationale and intellect over what it deemed ineffable, but also the dominance of the white, heterosexual male, both in the form of a Christian and the secular. In the wider critique of modernity, Walter Mignolo presents what he terms "historico-structural nodes" as levels of the logic of coloniality, one of which is,

> "...a hierarchy that privileged Christians over non-Christian/non-Western was institutionalized in the globalization of the Christian (Catholic and later Protestant) Church; by the same token, coloniality of knowledge translated other ethical and spiritual

ਪਾਤਿਸ਼ਾਹੀ ਮਹਿਮਾ – Revisiting Sikh Sovereignty

practices around the world as "religions", an invention that was also accepted by "natives".[58]

From this it can be asserted that the Christian and secular coloniser both conveyed Sikhī as a "religion" within the parameters of their own logic because it served the colonial economic and political purpose in Panjāb, as well as the wider globalizing project. Darshan Singh also writes how the colonial endeavours to translate Gurū Granth Sāhib were politically motivated,

> *"Their interpretation of the Sikh faith was greatly inspired and conditioned by their own political involvement in the Sikh faith and tradition. Those aspects of the Sikh religion came to be more emphasized which could prove helpful to promote the political hold of the English on the Sikhs, those going against it were either omitted or misrepresented".*[59]

With "Sikhism" categorised as a "religion", any resistance to their control and occupation of Panjāb was violently suppressed and vilified, as we shall see in the coming chapters. Within this context it was fairly easy to define Gursikhs that resisted the coloniser as "religious zealots" or "fundamentalists", a tactic that the colonial Indian secular establishment used following its creation in 1947, and in fact, remains evident in mainstream media outlets across the Indian state today. The intention of Trumpp, and others who we shall consider in more detail shortly, was not to understand or experience Sikhī but to legitimise their own presence in Panjāb. They had to indoctrinate the notion that they were superior, as a civilised and advanced modern force. This assertion of authority is what allowed the coloniser to occupy Panjāb to solidify wealth, natural resources, and their global dominance. It was a very degrading, dehumanizing process, fueled by *haumai,* the sense of individuality, separate from Divine connection.

Sikh resistance

Despite this onslaught, as we explored in the previous chapter, there were countless Sikhs who couldn't be broken or turned from the symbiotic connection between the Sikh Dharam and Sikh Sangarsh. As mentioned earlier, Sikh resistance to colonial occupation can be traced back to the mid-19th century. The resistance offered by the likes of Bhai Maharaj Singh and the Kūkā Movement (1857) delivered effective blows to the colonial regime in Panjāb. The Kūkā Movement's opposition to British rule was quite remarkable. The rejection of government service, English education, and English law courts ultimately aggravated widespread arrest and extra-judicial killings. The British response to the Kūkās came from the Deputy Commissioner of Ludhiana when he ordered 66 Kūkās to be executed for an alleged crime. Fifty were shot by canons along the Malerkotla parade, with the other sixteen executed a couple of days later. [60]

The logic underpinning this execution's violence is present in the later acts of violence, such as the incident at Jallianwala Bagh in 1919. The colonial exertion of force, used to quell indigenous resistance movements in Panjāb and indeed the world, was to strike terror in the minds of the Sikhs. Before the turn of the 20th century, British official Sir John Lawrence once said,

> *"Our object is to make an example to terrify others. I think this object would be effectually gained by destroying from a quarter to a third of them". He went on to add, "All these should be shot or blown away from the guns, as may be most expedient. The rest I would divide into batches: some to be imprisoned for ten years, some seven some five, some three. I think that a sufficient example will then be made, and that these distinctions will do good, and not harm".* [61]

ਪਾਤਿਸ਼ਾਹੀ ਮਹਿਮਾ – Revisiting Sikh Sovereignty

Some sixty years later, this was the same rationale General Dyer provided in his testimony to the Hunter Commission, which we'll come on to shortly. The inhuman treatment did not deter the Sikhs. The desire to remove colonial forces and regain control of Panjāb was an ever-present thought in the minds of Panth Dhardī Gursikhs. While Bhāī Maharaj Singh was sent to foreign lands and kept in solitary confinement until death, and the Kūkās were literally blown apart, the flame of freedom did not die out.

[The looting of Lahore Darbār, the dismemberment of the Khālsā army and the creation of the colonial soldier, the reshaping of rural life, destruction of indigenous schools, the Renaissance and Reformation inspired distortion of Sikh writings by virtue of disseminating Christian missionaries, creation of "Sikhism" and the policies that crippled economic life in Panjāb are all examples of the systematic suppression of life in Panjāb that occurred following the fall of temporal Sikh Rāj. Under colonial occupation, such was the severity of oppression that thousands fled the country in the hope of starting a new life.]

In the next two chapters, we shall consider various Sikh movements inspired by the tradition of the Khālsā to oppose the tyranny and oppression of both the British and what became the Indian State in 1947. In doing so, we shall consider how the nature of this oppression was not so different from that which the Sikhs encountered against the Mughals, particularly under Aurangzeb's centralised model of political administration. We touched upon this briefly in Part One of the book, in the episode related to the assassination of Gurū Tegh Bahādur Sāhib. [The Mughal regime, as Sir Jadunath Sarkar chronicles, had morphed into,

> "...a political unit, with uniformity of official language, administrative machinery, coinage, and public service, and indeed a common type of civilization for the higher classes.]. The British

continued the same policy but more efficiently and over a much wider area".[62]

Let us now consider, firstly, how the Sikhs resisted British occupation at the turn of the twentieth century, and secondly, how the creation of the Indian State marked the start of a new political reality, in which Panjāb was split in half, and the governance of the region handed, despite strong opposition from the Sikhs to one centralised political entity in New Delhi.

NOTES

[1] Quoted by Neeladri Bhattacharya, 2019, *The Great Agrarian Conquest, the colonial reshaping of a rural world*, State University of New York, p27

[2] Gurbhagat Singh, 1999, *Sikhism and Postmodern Thought*, Naad Pargaas, Sri Amritsar, p20

[3] Samvad, 7th June 2020, - https://sikhsiyasat.net/samvad-releases-important-draft-for-future-course-of-sikh-struggle/ p.29

[4] Brian Axel, 2001, *The Nation's Tortured Body*, Duke University Press, Durham and London, p35

[5] Gurū Nānak Sāhib, Japjī Sāhib, First Paurī, Gurū Granth Sāhib, Ang 1

[6] Henry Prinsep, 1834, *Origin of the Sikh Power in Punjab and the Political Life of Muha-Raja Runjeet Singh*, p185

[7] Henry Prinsep, 1834, *Origin of the Sikh Power in Punjab and the Political Life of Muha-Raja Runjeet Singh*, p184

[8] Henry Prinsep, 1834, *Origin of the Sikh Power in Punjab and the Political Life of Muha-Raja Runjeet Singh*, p186

[9] Shahamat Ali, 1847, *The Sikhs and Afghans, In Connection with India and Persia, Immediately Before and After the Death of Ranjeet Singh*, London, p22

[10] Lieut. Colonel Steinbach, 1883, *The Punjaub; A brief account of the country of the Sikhs*, Manju Arts, Chandigarh, reprint Language Department, 2003, Punjab

[11] Lady Login, 1890, *Sir John Login and Duleep Singh*, W.H. Allen & Co, London, p181

[12] Lady Login, 1890, *Sir John Login and Duleep Singh*, W.H. Allen & Co, London, p 183

[13] Lady Login, 1890, *Sir John Login and Duleep Singh*, W.H. Allen & Co, London, p175

[14] Tan Tai Yong, 2005, *The Garrison State, The military, Government and Society in Colonial Punjab, 1849-1947*, Sage Publications

[15] Tan Tai Yong, 2005, *The Garrison State, The military, Government and Society in Colonial Punjab, 1849-1947*, Sage Publications, p64

[16] K. Grant et al, 2007, Beyond Sovereignty Britain, Empire and Transnationalism, c.1880-1950, Palgrave Macmillan, p159

[17] Tan Tai Yong, 2005, *The Garrison State, The military, Government and Society in Colonial Punjab, 1849-1947*, Sage Publications, p71

[18] Darshan Singh Tatla, *Sikh free and Military Migration During the Colonial Period,* The Cambridge Survey of World Migration, edited by Robin Cohen, London: Cambridge U.P. 1995, p69

[19] K. Grant et al, 2007, Beyond Sovereignty Britain, Empire and Transnationalism, c.1880-1950, Palgrave Macmillan, p158

[20] Neeladri Bhattacharya, 2019, *The Great Agrarian Conquest, the colonial reshaping of a rural world*, State University of New York, p16

[21] Neeladri Bhattacharya, 2019, *The Great Agrarian Conquest, the colonial reshaping of a rural world*, State University of New York, p105

[22] Neeladri Bhattacharya, 2019, *The Great Agrarian Conquest, the colonial reshaping of a rural world*, State University of New York, p39

[23] Neeladri Bhattacharya, 2019, *The Great Agrarian Conquest, the colonial reshaping of a rural world*, State University of New York, p67-69

[24] Neeladri Bhattacharya, 2019, *The Great Agrarian Conquest, the colonial reshaping of a rural world*, State University of New York, p68

[25] Neeladri Bhattacharya, 2019, *The Great Agrarian Conquest, the colonial reshaping of a rural world*, State University of New York, p70

[26] Madhav Gadgil and Ramachandra Guha, 1992, *The Fissured Land: An Ecological History of India*, p13

[27] Malcolm Lyall Darling, 1925, *The Punjab Peasant in Prosperity and Debt*, p202

[28] Malcolm Lyall Darling, 1925, *The Punjab Peasant in Prosperity and Debt*, p208

[29] Malcolm Lyall Darling, 1925, *The Punjab Peasant in Prosperity and Debt*, p208

[30] Babbar Akali Movement, Sikh Missionary College, Ludhiana, Publication No. 358, p5

[31] B.S. Saini, 1975 *The Social and Economic History of Punjab*, University of Michigan, Ess Ess Publications, p.342.

[32] M.S. Leigh, 1928, *Land Revenue Settlement in Punjab*, Lahore, p.1.

[33] Malcolm Lyall Darling, 1925, *The Punjab Peasant in Prosperity and Debt*, p219

[34] Malcolm Lyall Darling, 1925, *The Punjab Peasant in Prosperity and Debt*, p233

[35] Malcolm Lyall Darling, 1925, *The Punjab Peasant in Prosperity and Debt*, p234

[36] S.S. Thorburn, 1886, *Musalmans and MoneyLenders in Punjab*, William Blacwood & Sons, London, p47

[37] S.S. Thorburn, 1886, *Musalmans and MoneyLenders in Punjab*, William Blacwood & Sons, London, p.31.

[38] Malcolm Lyall Darling, 1925, *The Punjab Peasant in Prosperity and Debt*, p279

[39] The Cambridge Survey of World Migration, edited by Robin Cohen, London: Cambridge U.P. 1995, p69

[40] Pritam Singh, 2008, *Federalism, Nationalism and Development, India and the Punjab economy*, Routledge, Oxon, p113

[41] Mark Condos, 2017, *The Insecurity State Punjab and the making of Colonial Power in British India*, Cambridge University Press, p.83

[42] Mark Condos, 2017, *The Insecurity State Punjab and the making of Colonial Power in British India*, Cambridge University Press, p.86

[43] Ramon Grosfoguel, 2013 "The Structure of Knowledge in Westernized Universities: Epistemic Racism/Sexism and the Four Genocides/Epistemicides of the Long 16th Century," Human Architecture: Journal of the Sociology of Self-Knowledge: Vol.11: Iss. 1, Article 8

[44] G. W. Leitner, 1882, *History of Indigenous Education in the Panjab Since Annexation and in 1882*, Calcutta

[45] G. W. Leitner, 1882, *History of Indigenous Education in the Panjab Since Annexation and in 1882*, Calcutta, p15-17

[46] G. W. Leitner, 1882, *History of Indigenous Education in the Panjab Since Annexation and in 1882*, Calcutta, p19

[47] G. W. Leitner, 1882, *History of Indigenous Education in the Panjab Since Annexation and in 1882*, Calcutta, p29

[48] J.S. Grewal, 1994, *The Sikhs of The Punjab*, Cambridge University Press, p130

[49] ਅਜਮੇਰ ਸਿੰਘ, ੨੦੦੭, ਕਿਸ ਬਿਧ ਰੁਲੀ ਪਾਤਸ਼ਾਹੀ
Ajmer Singh, 2007, Kis Bidh Ruli Paatshai, Singh Brothers, Amritsar, 3rd Edition, p53

[50] J.S. Grewal, 1994, *The Sikhs of The Punjab*, Cambridge University Press, p136

[51] ਅਜਮੇਰ ਸਿੰਘ, ੨੦੦੭, ਕਿਸ ਬਿਧ ਰੁਲੀ ਪਾਤਸ਼ਾਹੀ
Ajmer Singh, 2007, Kis Bidh Ruli Paatshai, Singh Brothers, Amritsar, 3rd Edition, p65

[52] Dr. Ernest Trumpp, 1877, *Adi Granth, The Holy Scriptures of the Sikhs*, WM. H. Allen & Co, London, Preface, vi

[53] Dr. Ernest Trumpp, 1877, *Adi Granth, The Holy Scriptures of the Sikhs*, WM. H. Allen & Co, Preface, London, vii

[54] Arvind-Pal Singh Mandair, 2009, *Religion and Spectre of the West*, paperback edition 2016, Columbia University Press, p175

[55] Arvind-Pal Singh Mandair, 2009, *Religion and Spectre of the West*, paperback edition 2016, Columbia University Press, p179-181

[56] Arvind-Pal Singh Mandair, 2009, *Religion and Spectre of the West*, paperback edition 2016, Columbia University Press, p176

[57] Ajmer Singh, 2017, *Modernity: An Analysis,* Seminar by Samvad - https://www.youtube.com/watch?v=bpXMayRPASo

[58] Walter D. Mignolo, 2011, *The Darker Side of Western Modernity, Global Futures, Decolonial Options*, Duke University Press, Durham and London, p18

[59] Darshan Singh, 1999, *Western Perspective on the Sikh Religion*, Singh Brothers, Amrtisar, p155-156

[60] Patwant Singh, 1999, *The Sikhs*, John Murray Publishers, London, republished by Rupa Publications, 2002, Delhi, p183

[61] Sir. J. Kaye and Colonel. G. Malleson, 1890, *History of the Indian Mutiny*, p367-368

[62] Sir Jadunath Sarkar, 1950, *Fall of the Mughal Empire,* Vol. IV, M. C. Sarkar & Sons, Calcutta p338

Sikh Opposition to Colonial Occupation

At the turn of the twentieth century, Sikhs in Panjāb, notwithstanding the betrayal and treachery that led to the loss of temporal Sikh Rāj, lived under the enforced rule of colonial conquest. As we have discussed, the debilitating effects of colonial conquest and occupation caused much socio-economic hardship and grief.

> "The economic life of the people kept deteriorating particularly of the farmers of Panjab who had never pawned their land. By 1878, all of their land holdings had been mortgaged. By 1919, 83% owners of land were caught in the grip of money lenders".[1]

One of the enduring consequences of British occupation was mass displacement, which saw thousands of Panjab's Sikh populace leave their ancestral homes. In the hope of securing a more prosperous economic future for themselves and their families, and in direct response to the political and economic situation created by colonial policies that we considered in the previous chapter, thousands left for places such as Hong Kong, Singapore, Canada, and America.

This was the first encounter Sikhs from Panjāb had with the white settler-colonial states. While there was a combination of reasons for Sikhs leaving, the root cause was colonial occupation of Panjāb. As we shall see, the experience of emigrating out was the same, whether you were a decorated colonial soldier or a farmer hoping to secure a better future.

Migration to the West

While some Sikhs who served within the British Empire arrived as early as 1897[2], the first group of Sikhs, numbering forty-five in total, are believed to have travelled in 1904 to what half a century earlier had become British Columbia, Canada.[3]

Colonial settler governments, such as Canada and the US, attempted to stop this influx of Panjābī migrants with a series of legislative measures aimed at restricting their movement. Those that managed to find some refuge across the Pacific found employment in the mines, lumber mills, and the Canadian Pacific Railways laying tracks. However, their wages were significantly lower than their white counterparts, and they faced racial discrimination from both the people and the governments. Having endured the hardship of forced displacement, the Sikhs found themselves in a position of vulnerability, criminalised and exploited for their labour. Following this encounter with the West, coupled with the grim reality of political turmoil back home, a group of Sikhs started to awaken to the reality that they needed to reestablish their own sovereignty to live as free Sikhs. They started to mobilise and organise themselves, forming a movement to oppose British occupation of Panjāb that became the Ghadar Movement.

The Ghadar Movement (1913-1917)

Beginning in 1913, printing anti-colonial literature, it was evident that the sole aim of the Ghadarites was to remove the British and liberate their homeland:

> "Today, there begins in foreign lands, but in our country's language, a war against the British Raj...What is our name? Ghadar. What is our work? Ghadar...The time will soon come when rifles and blood will take the place of pen and ink."[4]

ਪਾਤਿਸ਼ਾਹੀ ਮਹਿਮਾ – Revisiting Sikh Sovereignty

Rather than recount all the accomplishments of the Ghadar Movement, in the following pages, I will focus instead on examining who they were and what inspired them.

The first and perhaps most important point to note is that when one reads the original writings of the Ghadarites, it becomes clear that the Ghadar Movement was inspired by Sikh principles of fighting oppressive systems of governance and doing so for the liberation of all peoples. This should come as no surprise, given the sternest opposition to colonial occupation of Panjāb came from the Sikhs. This is evident in the words, attire, and actions of prominent members of the Ghadar Movement. However, many Indian revisionists, especially after the creation of the Indian state in 1947, erroneously portrayed the Ghadarites as communists, secularists, and Indian nationalists[5].

Two of the leading experts on the subject matter, Rajwinder Singh Rahi, and renowned Sikh author Ajmer Singh, have corrected the narrative by providing a comprehensive history of the Ghadar Movement, using primary source material written by the Ghadarites themselves[6]. Their works are important because they illustrate how Sikh resistance at the turn of the 20th century, when exercised against the British, was later co-opted by the Indian state and re-presented in a manner that aligned it with the wider web of Indian nationalism, which we shall consider in more detail in the next chapter.

This distortion erases sovereign Sikh agency and seeks to strip away political Sikh thought and action, thus reducing Sikh action to be scrutinised within the paradigms of a "world religion" alone. So, while the actions of the Ghadarites were for decades portrayed as being inspired by non-Sikh political ideologies, from the research of the two above-mentioned writers, we have come to know how inaccurate and damaging that narrative has been.

Sikh inspiration

Ajmer Singh, in particular, has referred not only to the writings of the founding members of the Ghadar Movement but also their contemporaries, such as Bengali-Hindu revolutionary Sachindra Nath Sanyal, leader of armed resistance against the British from Bengal.[7] Sanyal speaks about the sheer number of Sikhs that returned to Panjab to fight the British. He had regular contact with prominent Ghadarite, Kartar Singh Sarabha, and was a mentor for other anti-colonialists such as Chandra Shekhar Azad and Bhagat Singh. According to Sanyal's book *Bandi Jeevan* (1930), written whilst he was in prison, seven to eight thousand Panjabis returned home during the era of the Ghadar Movement, of which 99% were Sikhs.

Sanyal recognised the distinct contribution of Sikh revolutionaries in Panjab; that their inspiration was derived from their unwavering commitment to liberate people from the clutches of oppressive regimes, which they did because that is what Gurmat and Sikh tradition demands. When the resistance of the Ghadarites is understood from this explicitly Sikh worldview, it comes as no surprise that during the struggle against colonial forces, 93 of the 121 fighters sent to the gallows were Sikh. They also made up 2147 of the 2626 sentenced to imprisonment.[8] The Sikhs gave an immense sacrifice and thus spearheaded the movement to remove the colonisers from their lands, despite only making up 1.8% of the entire population in what became British India following the annexation of Panjāb in 1849.

Primary source material

When we consider the writings of the leading Ghadarites, such as the works of Baba Sohan Singh Bhakna and Baba Vasaka Singh, and analyze their photos, we discover they were initiated Sikhs; *Nitnemī Rehitvaan Gursikhs* who adorned the Guru's insignia and sought inspiration for their revolutionary actions from Gurmats. Baba Vasaka Singh writes:

"ਕਈ ਕਹਿੰਦੇ ਹਨ ਕਿ ਮੈਂ ਕਮਿਉਨਿਸਟ ਹਾਂ ਤੇ ਰੂਸੀ ਸਾਂਝੀਵਾਲਤਾ ਮੇਰਾ ਨਿਸ਼ਾਨਾ ਹੈ। ਮੇਰਾ ਨਿਸ਼ਾਨਾ ਸ੍ਰੀ ਦਸਮੇਸ਼ ਜੀ ਦੀ ਕਰਨੀ ਹੈ ਤੇ ਮੇਰੀ ਸਾਂਝੀਵਾਲਤਾ ਗੁਰੂ ਕਿਆ ਵਾਲੀ ਸਾਂਝੀਵਾਲਤਾ ਹੈ। ੧੯੦੬-੦੭ ਈ:ਵਿੱਚ ਕਿਹੜੀ ਰੂਸੀ ਸਾਂਝੀਵਾਲਤਾ ਸੀ ਜਦੋਂ ਤੋਂ ਸਰਬੱਤ ਦਾ ਭਲਾ ਮੇਰੇ ਵਿਚਾਰ ਅਤੇ ਕਰਮਾ ਦਾ ਸ੍ਰੇਸ਼ਟ ਬਣਿਆ ਹੈ? ਮੈਂ ਜੋ ਕੁਝ ਲਿਆ ਹੈ ਇਹ ਗੁਰੂ ਘਰੋਂ ਲਿਆ ਹੈ।"

"Some call me a communist, that I share a Russian objective. My objective is to do the work of Guru Gobind Singh ji, and my commonality is with the Guru's cause. Sarbat Da Bhala has driven my thoughts and actions since 1906-07; where was the Russian connection to Sarbat Da Bhala that has been the inspiration for my thoughts and actions? Whatever [inspiration] I have, is what I have taken from the Guru's House."[9]

In fact, Baba Vasaka Singh didn't just stop there on his thoughts about how the misinformed had labelled him a communist. He went on to highlight communism can be adopted as one aspect within Sikhi, but Sikhi cannot be adopted by communism; it is much larger and distinct.

"ਕਮਿਉਨਿਜ਼ਮ ਨੇ ਗਰੀਬ ਦੁਖੀ ਦੁਨੀਆਂ ਦਾ ਬੜਾ ਭਲਾ ਕੀਤਾ ਹੈ ਪਰ ਇਸ ਵਿਚ ਅਜੇ ਤਰੁੱਟੀਆਂ ਹਨ। ਸਿੱਖੀ ਬਹੁਤ ਵੱਡੀ ਚੀਜ਼ ਹੈ। ਕਮਿਉਨਿਜ਼ਮ ਸਿੱਖੀ ਦਾ ਇਕ ਅੰਗ ਹੈ, ਇਹ ਸਿੱਖੀ ਵਿਚ ਸਮਾ ਸਕਦਾ ਹੈ ਪਰ ਸਿੱਖੀ ਇਸ ਵਿਚ ਨਹੀਂ ਸਮਾ ਸਕਦੀ। ਗੁਰੂ ਕਾ ਲੰਗਰ, ਸਾਂਝੀ ਸੇਵਾ, 'ਤੇਰਾ ਘਰ ਸੋ ਮੇਰਾ ਘਰ' ਇਸ ਦਾ ਪ੍ਰਚਾਰ ਸੈਂਕੜੇ ਸਾਲ ਗੁਰੂ ਸਾਹਿਬਾਨ ਨੇ ਕਰ ਕੇ ਸਾਂਝੀਵਾਲਤਾ ਅਤੇ ਬਰਾਬਰਤਾ ਦਾ ਰਾਹ ਦੱਸਿਆ।"

"Communism has certainly helped this poverty-grief stricken world, but it still contains some flaws. Sikhi is very expansive. Communism can be adopted as one aspect within Sikhi, but Sikhi cannot be adopted within communism. Gurū Kā Langar, common service, "your house is my house", all of these ideals were propagated for hundreds of years by the Gurū Sāhibān, which showed us the path of harmonious coexistence and equality".[10]

This demonstrates that individuals such as Baba Vasaka Singh understood very well the distinction between the Sikh principle of Sarbat Da Bhala and Communism. The former was an inextricable part of Gurmat and the Sikh movement, tied to the sacrifices of countless Sikhs that had come before the Ghadarites. It was part of their existence as Sikhs, but for others to accept this was to accept the distinction and independence of Sikh thought and polity, which did not sit well with the aim of creating and sustaining the idea of one homogenous "Indian" political identity, and of course, the Indian nationalist movement.

In addition to erasing the Sikh inspired connection to the Ghadarites, which is otherwise prevalent among their own writings, another tactic used by Indian nationalists was to downplay or even dismiss entirely the influence of those Nitnemī Rehitvaan Gursikhs and instead portray and praise individuals like Lālā Hardyāl as pivotal figures of the Ghadar Movement. However, the fact is he was only with the Ghadarites for five months before a case was registered against him in America, and he fled to Germany before moving to Sweden and then completing a doctorate in London.

Baba Sohan Singh Bhakna writes:

"ਅੰਗਰੇਜ਼ਾਂ ਦੇ ਏਜੰਟਾ ਦਾ ਇਹ ਪ੍ਰਚਾਰ ਸੀ ਕਿ ਗ਼ਦਰ ਪਾਰਟੀ ਲਾਲਾ ਹਰਦਿਆਲ ਨੇ ਖੜੀ ਕੀਤੀ ਹੈ, ਨਹੀਂ ਤਾਂ ਇਹ ਪੰਜਾਬੀਆਂ ਦਾ ਅਨਪੜ ਟੋਲਾ ਹੀ ਹੈ। ਸਕੂਲਾ ਵਿਚ ਨਵੀਆਂ ਲੱਗੀਆਂ ਕਿਤਾਬਾਂ ਵਿਚ ਅੰਗਰੇਜ਼ਾਂ ਦੇ ਪ੍ਰਚਾਰ ਦੇ ਪੱਖ ਵਿਚ ਗ਼ਦਰ ਪਾਰਟੀ ਦੀ ਜਮਹੂਰੀ ਲਾਈਨ ਨੂੰ ਇਤਿਹਾਸ ਵਿੱਚੋਂ ਨਾਬੂਦ ਕਰਨ ਖ਼ਾਤਰ ਹਕੂਮਤ ਨੇ ਵੀ ਪਾਲਸੀ ਅਖਤਿਆਰ ਕਰ ਲਈ ਹੈ। ਪਰ ਉਹ ਦਿਨ ਦੂਰ ਨਹੀਂ, ਜਿਸ ਦਿਨ ਏਹ ਸਾਰੇ ਲਿਖਾਰੀ ਲੋਕਾਂ ਸਾਹਮਣੇ ਸ਼ਰਮਿੰਦਾ ਹੋਣਗੇ ਅਤੇ ਜਾਗੀ ਹੋਈ ਕੌਮ ਅਤੇ ਦੇਸ਼ ਆਪਣੀ

ਪਾਤਿਸ਼ਾਹੀ ਮਹਿਮਾ – Revisiting Sikh Sovereignty

ਇਨਕਲਾਬੀ ਤਾਰੀਖ਼ ਨੂੰ ਸੱਚੇ ਅਰਥਾਂ ਵਿਚ ਜਨਤਾ ਦੇ ਸਾਹਮਣੇ ਲਿਆਉਣਗੇ । "

"There was propaganda by British agents that the Ghadar Party was created by Lala Hardyal, or that it was mainly an illiterate group of Panjabi people. The [Indian] government has accepted this British propaganda which has found its way into contemporary school books written by misinformed writers. But those days are not far, when these writers will be embarrassed in front of the people as the awoken Sikh Nation will preserve and present the true essence of our revolution".

Erasing the centrality of Gurmat

According to Sardār Ajmer Singh, the Ghadar Movement itself was over 95% Sikh.[11] The Ghadarites were well versed in Gurbānī and, contrary to popular belief, knowledgeable enough to understand their political environment. In the meeting that Bhagat Singh had with Bhāī Sāhib Bhāī Randhīr Singh, on 4th October 1930, we are informed about an exchange in which Bhagat Singh recognised the achievements of the Ghadarites, making specific reference to their commitment to the Khālsā traditions,

> *"It is true that my sacrifices are insignificant compared to the sacrifices of the freedom fighters of 1914-1915. But after such astounding sacrifices they did not get any publicity or praise in the papers... It is a fact that if I had maintained the Sikh appearance and if I had professed myself to be an orthodox Sikh and kept hair and beard the non-Sikh papers would not have written a word about me, just as they did not write about you and your companions."*[12]

In explaining the reasons for not keeping his Kes, despite the tradition within his own family, Bhagat Singh goes on to say,

"... I know it for certain that Hindu papers are always reluctant to write even a word in praise of Sikh patriots and freedom fighters. They do not like Sikhs being praised for anything. If I had kept hair and beard again and become a Sikh, they would have started belittling me instead of praising me. So, I hesitated to keep hair and beard again."

This provides a fascinating insight into how much of an inspiration the Ghadarites were for individuals like Bhagat Singh. It also shows how Amritdhāree Gursikhs, waged in the battle to remove colonial forces from Panjāb, were viewed by the Hindu dominant Indian papers and explains why they wrote so little about the role of Gurmat in the political actions of the Ghadarites. As mentioned, the work of Ajmer Singh has dispelled numerous misconceptions, in particular their research into the accounts of both Jathedār Kartār Singh Jhabbar and Bhāī Sāhib Bhāī Randhīr Singh, from their time in the Andaman and Hazārī Bāgh jails, which show how much Gurbānī the Ghadarites read daily.[13]

Komagata Maru, 1914

At around the same time as the mobilization of the Ghadarites, the Komāgātā Marū (1914) ship incident occurred, which highlights the racist treatment of Panjābīs by white settler colonialists. The ship (renamed by Baba Gurdit Singh to Gurū Nānak Jahāj) carrying 376 refugees[14], of which 90% were Sikhs from Panjāb, was refused entry in Vancouver. It was forced to return to the port of Calcutta.

Upon arrival, the Sikhs insisted on going to Bengal, but they were refused entry and fired upon by the British Indian authorities. Consequently, many people were injured and killed.

"Troops came running and were given the order to fire on passengers. The passengers hid in ditches, behind a hut, and in a shop. Darkness came quickly

and those who were still alive slipped away. Eighteen passengers died from the gunshots. The authorities organised a roundup of the passengers in the surrounding area, and ultimately more than 200 were arrested and jailed".[15]

This incident only served to heighten Sikh dissent towards the colonial regime, and it boosted their cause. In Canada, individuals such as Shaheed Bhāī Bagh Singh played an integral role in opposing the Canadian government's decision to reject the Komāgatā Māru passengers. Born in Panjāb, he enlisted into the army at the age of 20 but soon realised he wasn't a soldier but a slave of the British. He left for China after a short time and became a police officer. But after two and a half years, he left because of his own desires to live as a free man. He arrived in Canada and soon started a *jathebandie* with Bhāī Sundar Singh, Bhāī Balwant Singh, and Bhāī Arjan Singh, doing Gurmat Parchār with ambitions for freedom. Shaheed Bhāī Bagh Singh became one of the first Panj Pyār-e in Canada and helped establish the first Gurdwara in Vancouver.

Bhāī Sahib soon realised the existential crisis of living in foreign lands, so dedicated his life to earning as much money as possible to help the freedom movement against the British back home. He started the first Panjābī newspaper published outside of Panjāb and urged former Sikh soldiers who fought for the British to burn their medals.

As has been the case throughout history, an agent had been hired by the government of the time to spy on the activities of the Sikhs in Vancouver. On September 5th, 1914, a man called Bela, shot Bhāī Sāhib in the back whilst they were part taking in an Ardās within Gurūs Darbār. Bhāī Badan Singh was shot and killed, and others too were injured. Bhāī Sāhib was taken to hospital, but the wound was critical. His family were brought to see him, including his infant son Joginder Singh. When he arrived, Bhāī Sāhib said:

"ਇਹ ਹੁਣ ਕੌਮ ਦੀ ਦੌਲਤ ਹੈ ਮੇਰਾ ਨਹੀ ਹੈ, ਮੈਂ ਇਸ ਨੂੰ ਆਪ ਦੇ ਹਵਾਲੇ ਕਰ ਕੇ ਗੁਰੂ ਪਾਸ ਜਾ ਰਿਹਾ ਹਾਂ, ਮੇਰੀ ਇਕੋ ਚਾਹ ਸੀ ਕਿ ਮੂ ਆਜ਼ਾਦੀ ਦੇ ਮੈਦਾਨ ਜੰਗ ਵਿਚ ਸ਼ਹੀਦ ਹੁੰਦਾ। ਪਰ ਕਰਤਾਰ ਦਾ ਭਾਣਾ ਅਮਿਟ ਹੈ, ਮੇਰੀ ਇਹ ਚਾਹ ਦਿਲ ਦੇ ਵਿਚ ਹੀ ਰਹਿ ਗਈ ਅਤੇ ਮੈਂ ਹੁਣ ਵਾਹਿਗੁਰੂ ਅੱਗੇ ਅਰਦਾਸ ਕਰਦਾ ਹਾਂ ਕੇ ਅਗਲੇ ਜਨਮ ਵਿਚ ਮੇਰੀ ਇਹ ਚਾਹ ਜ਼ਰੂਰ ਪੂਰੀ ਹੋਵੇ।"[16]

"He now belongs to the [Khālsā] Nation, he is no longer mine, I hand him over to you, as I make my journey toward my Gurū. I had only one desire, to become a martyr in the battle for freedom. But the Creator's Will cannot be undone, this one desire of mine will remain in my heart, and now I offer an Ardās to Vāhegurū that this desire of mine is achieved in my next life".

Baba Bhagwan Singh Kavi was another who resisted. At the age of 25, he was forced to flee Panjāb due to his anti-colonial activities. He went to Burma, then Hong Kong, where he served as Granthī at a Gurdwārā and delivered many lectures on revolution and the struggle for freedom. Bhagwan Singh travelled to Canada under the alias Nathā Singh and delivered fiery lectures on the Ghadar Movement for freedom. He was soon on the authorities' radar but remained resolute in his opposition to colonial occupation of his homeland. Bhagwan Singh was a poet who used his art to awaken his people to the oppressive ways of the coloniser. In 1915 he travelled to San Francisco and began writing for the Ghadar paper.

"ਸਾਨੂੰ ਲੋੜ ਨਾ ਪੰਡਤਾ ਕਾਜੀਆਂ ਦੀ, ਨਹੀਂ ਸ਼ੌਕ ਹੈ ਬੇੜਾ ਡੁਬਾਵਣੇ ਦਾ। ਜਪ ਜਾਪ ਦਾ ਵਕਤ ਬਤੀਤ ਹੋਇਆ, ਵੇਲਾ ਆ ਗਿਆ ਤੇਗ ਉਠਾਵਣੇ ਦਾ।"[17]

"We do not need Pandits or Qazis, we have no desire to drown our bodies. The time for Jap and Jāp has passed, now is the time to pick up arms."

He also travelled to Japan, and in coordination with Ghadar leader Baba Sohan Singh Bhakna, supplied 200 pistols and 2,000 bullets for passengers at Yokohama port of Japan. Baba Bhagwān Singh was a Ghadarite from Amritsar who poured his heart and soul into the anticolonial movement that saw thousands of Sikhs work to remove the British. He was arrested in 1917 and imprisoned for some years. He lived through the partition of Panjāb in 1947 and died in 1962.

The Ghadarites downfall

Despite the efforts and sacrifices of the Ghadarites, the movement was eventually suppressed by the British government with the assistance of spies and police informants. Sardar Ajmer Singh explains how the precursor to this began when the Ghadarites sought to address the deficiency of resources needed to fight a war with an Empire as large as the British. The lack of arms, in particular, was a concern for the Ghadarites, and in an attempt to acquire more arms, they thought of attacking army cantonments; however, they lacked the weapons to do this successfully. In a move to overcome this, they took advice from the Bengali rebels and decided to target and loot rich households. While there was firm condemnation of this decision from individuals such as Bhāī Nidhan Singh Chunga[18], others such as Bhāī Kartar Singh Sarabha seemingly saw no other option. Perhaps they felt it was the opportune moment as the British were involved with World War I. The decision to loot rich members of the public led the Ghadarites into contact with local gang thieves, which proved to be fatal because within a short time, when some of the robberies were unsuccessful, during police interrogation, the petty thieves gave away information about the Ghadarites. When the authorities realised that the masterminds behind the lootings were the Ghadarites who had travelled back from America and planned a full rebellion, they acted swiftly. Police informants such as Kirpāl Singh were deployed to infiltrate them, and within the first few months of 1915, prominent members were arrested, and hundreds were executed by the British.

Sikh Opposition to Colonial Occupation

While the Ghadar movement was relatively short-lived, Ghadarites such as Kartar Singh Sarabha, Bhāī Bagh Singh, Baba Bhagwan Singh Kavi, and countless others, stand testament to the unwavering spirit of Sikh resistance, the inspiration for which is garnered from the perpetual struggle for remaining sovereign and opposing tyranny, as per the Gurū's command. The movement officially ended in 1948; however, the revolutionary edge prevalent during the early years had vanished. Although the movement succumbed to external influence of communists and Indian nationalists, the daring and brave actions of the early Ghadarites served as inspiration for others.

British Terror in Panjāb

While the British quelled the Ghadar Movement, the opposition to colonial occupation of Panjāb did not stop. The British unleashed a new wave of terror in Panjāb on 13th April 1919, when they fired bullets to disperse crowds that had gathered in protest of the repressive Rowlatt legislation, which was indeed part of a larger strategy to suppress those who had opposed British occupation of Panjab since 1849. The proposed Rowlatt Act sought to allow the British Indian authorities to arrest, detain, and imprison anyone, for any or no reason, without due legal process. It was being implemented with the sole aim of crushing any resistance to British occupation of the land.

There was public outrage, with riots and strikes across Amritsar. On April 13th, in keeping with Sikh tradition, several thousand people assembled in Jallianwala Bagh to express their opposition. As the crowds gathered to protest the repressive policies of British rule, the authorities responded with extreme violence. The city was brought under martial law for three months, during which time people were arbitrarily picked up, tied to frames, and publicly whipped. Other humiliating punishments, such as forcing all people to crawl when passing through the street, became the order of the day.

ਪਾਤਿਸ਼ਾਹੀ ਮਹਿਮਾ – Revisiting Sikh Sovereignty

There were major protests to the Rowlatt Bills in Amritsar and in neighbouring Lahore and Gujranwala. On 14th April 1919, a day after the Jallianwala Bagh massacre, colonial forces unleashed more bullets upon the Panjabi populace in Gujranwala. Over 100 people were killed when British RAF officers shot civilians with machine guns.[19]

Later that year, General Dyer testified that he had planned to fire in advance of arrival at Jallianwala Bagh, not just to disperse the crowds but to strike a blow of terror aimed at all of Panjab; to "reduce the morale of the rebels". He stated that he left the wounded unattended, and if possible, he would have used machine guns and armoured vehicles. In other words, if his means had been greater, the casualties would have been greater. Patwant Singh notes,

> *"Dyer was remorseless. He directed the men to fire at those trying to escape as well as aiming where the crowd was thickest. The shooting was as calm, deliberate and cruelly aimed as target practice at the butts, with every bullet made to count. It took him fifteen minutes in all to accomplish his task, for which his men fired 1650 rounds."*[20]

It is imperative to view the Amritsar massacre within the wider context of British terror in Panjab, which as we have seen, stems from the annexation of the Sikh Homeland in 1849. The bloodshed at Jallianwala Bagh directly resulted from a violent colonial policy that saw British forces exert their influence in typically oppressive fashion. The systematic occupation of Panjab fostered an environment in which the empire subjugated the people and extracted the country's natural resources.

Shaheed Udham Singh eventually travelled several thousand miles to deliver justice. He recognised General Dyer wasn't the sole perpetrator of the Jallianwala Bagh massacre, but rather he was one cog in a much larger machine steamrolling across his homeland. He assassinated Lieut. Governor Michael O'Dwyer on 13 March 1940 and wounded then Governor of Bengal, Lawrence John Lumley Dundas and Charles Cochrane-Bailie, a colonial administrator. Unlike the indiscriminate killings of the British officers, Shaheed Udham Singh's pistol was aimed solely at the perpetrators of the Amritsar massacre, and his action reaffirmed Panjāb's opposition to colonial occupation.

Emergence of Singh Sabha, Central Sikh League, Shiromanī Gurdwārā Parbandhak Committee (SGPC) and the Shirmanī Akālī Dal (SAD)

Although a deeper analysis of these institutions falls outside of the scope of this book, it is important at this juncture to briefly revisit the emergence and intended role of the Singh Sabha, Central Sikh League, SGPC, and SAD, as a direct response to colonial occupation in Panjāb. The need and emergence of these institutions arrived within a particular context, namely the need to retake control of Sikh education and institutions across Panjāb. To overcome the hurdles of both internal and external foes, the Sikh Panth evolved during the Gurū-period, however one constant feature was that Sikh sovereignty remained an integral part the Gurū's mobilisation. One pertinent question to ask therefore, is whether the above-named institutions would ever have been founded if Sikh Rāj had endured the events of the late 1840s. and Panjāb was not colonised. I would argue not; there would have been no need for them to come into existence in the way that they did.

However, as we know Panjāb was annexed by the coloniser, and Gurdwārās were occupied. Some were even demolished in part, to allow for new British buildings, like in 1911 when the British shifted their capital from Calcutta to Delhi and knocked down one of the walls of Gurdwārā Rakāb Ganj to build an official building in the vicinity of sovereign Sikh space. As seen in the previous chapter, a thriving education system had also been replaced with European systems, and the country's resources had been looted. Within this context, we come to understand the motives behind those who resisted in a different way to the Ghadarites and later the Babbar Akalīs to try and reclaim Sikh spaces. They were indeed reactionary movements initiated by the Sikhs to try and address the issues created as a result of the physical and the epistemic violence of colonialism. It is likely these movements would never have existed if it weren't for the absence of Sikh political power in Panjāb. That is something we must remember when seeking to analyze their intentions, motives, actions, and eventual shortcomings. It is far too easy to simply point toward the "what ifs" or, with the benefit of hindsight, suggest alternative decisions they could have taken.

That being said, what the SGPC, and indeed the SAD, have become today, is a far cry from what they were a hundred years ago, largely due to the subsuming nature of the political structures that came into being during the transfer of power in 1947. We will touch upon this further in the next chapter when we consider nationalism and the creation of the Indian State. Let us first briefly touch upon some of the specific incidents that led to the creation of the SGPC and SAD.

Sākā Nankānā, 1921

Shortly after the events of Jallianwala Bagh, there was the infamous Nankana Sahib incident of 1921 in which more than one hundred Sikhs achieved martyrdom opposing the occupation of the Gurdwārā by Mahant Narain Das, who was propped up by the British. It later transpired that the Mahant was supplied weapons by British Commissioner, Mr King, for the massacre at Nankana Sahib.[21] Despite just two years since Jallianwala Bagh, the British were prepared to spill more blood, to continue striking terror, if it meant they maintained their control over Sikh spaces. News of the massacre reached Sardar Kartar Singh Jhabbar, who amassed a small army of 2200 Sikhs, armed and ready for battle. Ignoring government orders, they marched towards Nankana Sahib, in true Sikh spirit. Dr. Sangat

Singh notes how the British eventually handed over the management to the Sikhs[22]; however, the infringement and violation of the Sikhs did not end there.

The Nankana Sahib incident was not an isolated attack. It was followed by various confrontations including the Chabbīān Dā Morchā (1921); Gurū Kā Bāgh Morchā (1923); and Jaito Dā Morchā (1923), to name but a few. Most of the agitations were led by the SAD to regain control of Sikh spaces. In 1925, the Sikh Gurdwaras Act was introduced, but many lives were lost during this period. Many thousands had been imprisoned by the British. One speaker, Tara Singh of Ferozepur, while debating the Gurdwara Act on 7th May 1925, said,

> "Briefly summarizing, these sacrifices (at Tarn Taran, Nanakana Sahib, Guru Ka Bagh, Bhai Pheru and Jaito) amount to 30,000 arrested, 400 killed and 2000 wounded, Rs 15 lacs of fine inflicted, including forfeiture of pensions of retired soldiers. In addition to this, a ban has been placed on civil and military recruitment of Sikhs."[23]

Sikh resistance to British occupation was relentless, which is remarkable given the loss of political power and the attacks on Sikh culture and existence that the Sikhs of Panjāb had endured for over seventy years. One wave of resistance was followed by another, and although the movements did not reach the heights of regaining Sikh sovereignty, every effort was made to uphold the tradition of safeguarding Sikh spaces, fighting oppression, and seeking liberation for all.

Babbar Akālī Lehar

Although the SGPC and SAD opted to take a new route, another revolutionary movement that began following the Nankana Sahib massacre was the Babbar Akālī Lehar. Their sole purpose was to

ਪਾਤਿਸ਼ਾਹੀ ਮਹਿਮਾ – Revisiting Sikh Sovereignty

wage war to remove oppressive forces in Panjāb. Many Ghadarites formed the basis of the Babbar Akālīs, who did not recognise or accept British law and order, and at the same time, also rejected the "Gandhian scheme of nonviolence".[24]

The newly formed SGPC had passed a resolution, which not only abstained all Sikhs from the use of force but also stated that if arrest warrants were issued, persons should give themselves up. The Babbar Akālīs chose to ignore this order of the SGPC and remained true to the Khālsā way by choosing to fight British occupation of Panjāb, with any means necessary.

As we discussed in the previous chapter, following the annexation of Panjāb in 1849, there was a countrywide campaign to demilitarise Panjāb. Over seventy years later, the British were still asserting this policy in their attempt to subdue the Babbar Akālīs. In a letter dated 19th March 1922, an order was circulated about Kirpāns,

> "The rules of wearing the kirpans already forwarded to the Chief Minister have been approved, to which is added the following rule: - Kirpans worn on the belt is contrary to the Arms Act, and they should be worn on the side being slung across the shoulder. Marching in Military formation of more than five men will be considered as an unlawful assembly".[25]

While on the one hand, the British continued to implement a policy of demilitarising the Sikhs, they continued to sanction the use of direct assaults, and in doing so, issued orders for the military personnel to "fire straight at the crowd".[26] However, there remained strong resistance from the Khālsā. Akālī Babbars such as Jathedār Kishan Singh would freely quote Gurbāṇī and passages from Sikh chronicles with the aim of uplifting and empowering the masses to break the yoke of slavery.

Sikh Opposition to Colonial Occupation

> *"Whatever we did, it was not meant to save our lives. We had reformed the enemies of the Panth and those who had deceived and harmed it. Our brothers were fighting a peaceful battle. We have fought battles as were fought by Sri Guru Hargobind Sahib and Guru Gobind Singh Ji...When our Gurus, who were true emperors and masters of the two worlds, did not care for their lives, what concern could death have for us...".*[27]

It is imperative to acknowledge, that despite the loss of Sikh Rāj, coupled with the suffocation of colonial rule, the Sikhs continued to resist. At the centre of their struggle, we find principles inspired by Gurmat and Khālsā tradition enshrined within Gurū Granth Sāhib, which propelled them to resist in the manner that they did. This was due to the sovereignty established by the Gurū Sāhibān that we discussed in Part One. The drive to resist oppressive forces, and uphold Sikh sovereignty, was still at the forefront of Sikh minds; a testament to the power of Gurbānī and the Khālsā.

An extract from the British intelligence bureau report, dated 17th October 1923, reveals,

> *"The "Babbar Sher" of Amritsar, dated the 30th September, writes that on the principle that the Jaziratul-Arab as their holy places are situated there, 'the Sikh claim the Punjab which has been held in trust for Maharaja Dulip Singh. The trust has been violated. Moreover, the land of five rivers is replete with Sikh Gurdwaras so that it itself is a vast Gurdwara. So long as the Punjab does not come under the political control of the Sikhs, neither the Sikh community can be relieved of the anxiety about its religion nor can peace be maintained in the country".*[28]

This demonstrates that some Sikhs understood Sikh homeland to be held in trust by the British for Maharaja Duleep Singh and knew there had been a violation of that agreement. Breaking trusts and treaties, was, of course, something the British thrived on, but it is also apparent from this report that they understood Sikhs wanted their homeland; they wanted Panjāb as it was the only true home they knew, as established by the Gurū Sāhibān, and the Sikhs were prepared to continue the struggle until political power was reestablished by the Khālsā.

The following extract from Mr. D. Petrie, Assistant Director of Criminal Intelligence, also confirms this position. From the work of Rajinder Singh, we come to know of how he wrote,

> *"These enthusiasts aim not merely at founding a homogeneous Sikh Community but preach the revival of a Sikh Nation which will wrest the sceptre from the hands of the British and again establish its rule in Punjab".*[29]

At the time, some Sikhs felt the SGPC and SAD were viable options; perhaps the thinking was that they might serve as a catalyst for more permanent and long-lasting change. Either way, one thing is for certain, although the Sikhs did regain control over the Gurdwārās, the emergence of the Sikh Gurdwara Act, 1925, marked a watershed moment in the governance of those Sikh spaces.

Sikh yearning for Rāj

As we shall see in the next chapter, proponents of the Indian nationalist movement also launched a nefarious campaign of lies. It is worth mentioning here, in particular, the remarks of Mohandas Gandhi, who made special reference to the Sikh desire for Rāj in the 1920s. In a letter dated 4th March 1924,[30] he asked the newly formed SGPC to guarantee five specific points concerning their movement, of which one was "full assurance of non-violence", and another, "that the

SGPC has no desire for the establishment of Sikh Raj, and as a matter of fact, the Committee is purely a religious body".

The SGPC responded by not only accepting his conditions but, in their lengthy reply dated 20th April 1924, took the unprecedented decision of unilaterally declaring, "not only the SGPC but no other Sikh body or individual entertains even in dream any idea or desire of establishing Sikh Raj".[31]

The exchange confirmed Gandhi was astutely aware of the Sikh desire for Rāj, as early as the 1920s, which is not really a surprise, given that the Sikhs were rulers of Panjāb prior to the colonial occupation, and were spearheading the campaign to remove colonial forces. We have already explored, in depth, the roots of that Rāj, which can be traced back through the Misls, Bandā Singh Bahādur and the Gurū Sāhibān, all the way back to Kartārpur Sāhib and Gurū Nānak Sāhib. However, the mindset of some SGPC leaders at the time was such that they pandered to the whims of Gandhi, and went as far as declaring no Sikh wanted Rāj, which as we have seen, simply was not true. In 1929, Gandhi declared,

> "I ask that you accept my word and the resolution of the Congress that it will not betray a single individual, much less an entire community. If it ever thinks of doing so, it will only hasten its own doom"[32]

Would-be Prime Minister Jawaharlal Nehru toyed with Sikh sentiments, pushing the rhetoric even further when he declared,

> "The brave Sikhs of Panjab are entitled to special consideration. I see nothing wrong in an area set up in the North of India wherein, the Sikhs can also experience the glow of freedom"[33],

"Sikh State"

Sardar Gurtej Singh narrates how, on 19th May, 1940, a contingent of one hundred and fifty Sikhs met at Amritsar under the leadership of Baba Gurdit Singh (of the Komāgātā Māru episode), to form a thirty-one-member body for the reestablishment of 'Gurū Khālsā Rāj'.[34] They demanded the return of the area from Jammu to Jamraud, which, as discussed earlier, they understood to have been taken by the British in trust from Daleep Singh. The SAD, seemingly convinced of the assurances from the Indian Congress, decided against this and instead proposed the 'Azad Panjab Scheme', which in essence was a show of support to non-Sikh communities that no single community would dominate the region of Panjāb.[35] However, by the mid-1940s, the talk of an 'Azad Sikh State' was being mooted as a real possibility, and the SAD became desirous of such a State, especially since the two-nation theory had been accepted following the successes of the Muslim League. Indu Banga explains,

> *"...In view of the near certainty of the creation of some sort of Pakistan after the [Muslim] League's triumph in the elections, the Akali [SAD] leadership felt obliged to declare just before the arrival of the Cabinet Mission that 'no safeguards and guarantees of constitutional nature, no weightage or protection, promised to the Sikhs by any of the majority communities can be considered adequate to protect the Sikhs and ensure their free and unhindered growth as a nationality with a distinct religious, ideological, cultural and political character'. Therefore, 'a separate autonomous Sikh State' to be carved out of the present Punjab was the 'minimum demand and political objective of the Sikh Panth as a whole'. The Sikhs are said to be claiming the right to establish themselves as the 'governing group' in the*

Sikh Opposition to Colonial Occupation

'Sikh Zone' or the 'de facto Sikh Homeland' after the exchange of population with the 'Muslim and Hindu India'."[36]

In the months that preceded the creation of the Indian State, as late as 4th July 1947, the last Viceroy of British India, Louis Mountbatten, is believed to have been convinced of the Sikh demand, which was also supported by the Governor of Panjab, Sir Evan Jenkins, and Chief of the Viceroy's staff, Lord Ismay. Mountbatten expressed his support in writing to both Jinnah and Nehru,[37] but as history records, Nehru's deceitful response convinced the SAD to throw their lot in with the Indian State, which abruptly ended that particular strive to acquire an independent Sikh state. However, as we shall see, this did not end the desire for political autonomy but marked a period of subjugation in Panjāb that surpassed the crimes of the Mughal, Afghan, and British regimes combined.

NOTES

[1] Babbar Akali Movement, Sikh Missionary College, Ludhiana, Publication No. 358, p5

[2] The Cambridge Survey of World Migration, edited by Robin Cohen, London: Cambridge U.P. 1995, p71

[3] S. Chandra Sekhar, 1986, *From India to Canada La Jolla*, Population Review Books, p17

[4] Ghadar, 1 November 1913

[5] See for example the work of Khushwant Singh, who framed the actions of the Ghadarites within a chapter entitled "Xenophobic Marxism", in which he referred to them as 'terrorists'- Khushwant Singh, *A History of the Sikhs*, Second Edition, Volume II, p168-192. Also, Harish. K. Puri, 1993, *Ghadar Movement: Ideology, Organization, Strategy*; and Sohan Singh Josh, 1970, *Baba Sohan Singh Bhakna: Life of the Founder of the Ghadar Party*

[6] See ਅਜਮੇਰ ਸਿੰਘ, ੨੦੧੩, ਗ਼ਦਰੀ ਬਾਬੇ ਕੌਣ ਸਨ? Ajmer Singh, 2013, *Ghadari Babeh Kaun San?* Singh Brothers, Amritsar and ਰਾਜਵਿੰਦਰ ਸਿੰਘ ੨੦੧੩, ਰਾਹੀ, ਗ਼ਦਰ ਲਹਿਰ ਦੀ ਅਸਲੀ ਗਾਥਾ Rajwinder Singh Rahi, 2013, *Ghadar Lehar Di Asli Gatha*

[7] Sachindra Nath Sanyal, 1931, *Bandi Jivan*

[8] Santosh Bhartiya, 2008, *Dalit and Minority Empowerment,* Rajkamal Prakashan, p356

[9] ਪ੍ਰੋ ਬਿਕਰਮ ਸਿੰਘ ਘੁੰਮਣ, ੨੦੧੬, ਗ਼ਦਰੀ ਯੋਧੇ ਸੰਤ ਬਾਬਾ ਵਿਸਾਖਾ ਸਿੰਘ, ੧੯੧

Prof. Bikram Singh Ghuman, 2016, *Ghadri Yodhe, Sant Baba Vasaka Singh*, Varis Shah Foundation, Amritsar, p191

[10] ਪ੍ਰੋ ਬਿਕਰਮ ਸਿੰਘ ਘੁੰਮਣ, ੨੦੧੬, ਗ਼ਦਰੀ ਯੋਧੇ ਸੰਤ ਬਾਬਾ ਵਿਸਾਖਾ ਸਿੰਘ, ੧੯੧

Prof. Bikram Singh Ghuman, 2016, *Ghadri Yodhe, Sant Baba Vasaka Singh*, Varis Shah Foundation, Amritsar p191

[11] ਅਜਮੇਰ ਸਿੰਘ, ੨੦੧੩, ਗ਼ਦਰੀ ਬਾਬੇ ਕੌਣ ਸਨ?

Ajmer Singh, 2013, *Ghadari Babeh Kaun San?* Singh Brothers, Amritsar p23

[12] Bhai Randhir Singh, 1972 *Autobiography*, translated by Dr. Trilochan Singh, Bhai Sahib Randhir Singh Trust, p281-288

[13] ਅਜਮੇਰ ਸਿੰਘ, ੨੦੧੩, ਗਦਰੀ ਬਾਬੇ ਕੌਣ ਸਨ?

Ajmer Singh, 2013, Ghadari Babeh Kaun San? Singh Brothers, Amritsar, p282; Appendix 6. Extracted from the Jail letters of Jathedār Kartār Singh Jhabbar (Andaman Jail) and Bhāī Sāhib Bhāī Randhīr Singh (Hazārī Bāgh), Appendix 6 is a table containing the names of 44 Ghadarites, and the Bānī they read on a daily basis, including the ones they knew off by heart, of which there were thirty(!)

[14] https://digital.lib.sfu.ca/kmpassenger-collection/komagata-maru-passenger-list

[15] Pamela Hickman and Gola Taraschi-Carr, 2014, *Righting Canada's Wrongs; The Komagata Maru*, Lorimer, p63

[16] ਜੈਤੇਗ ਸਿੰਘ ਅਨੰਤ, ੨੦੧੪, ਗਦਰੀ ਯੋਧੇ

Jaiteg Singh Anant 2014, Ghadari Yodhe, Lokgeet Parkashan, Chandigarh, p15

[17] ਜੈਤੇਗ ਸਿੰਘ ਅਨੰਤ, ੨੦੧੪, ਗਦਰੀ ਯੋਧੇ

Jaiteg Singh Anant 2014, Ghadari Yodhe, Lokgeet Parkashan, Chandigarh, p87

[18] ਅਜਮੇਰ ਸਿੰਘ, ੨੦੧੩, ਗਦਰੀ ਬਾਬੇ ਕੌਣ ਸਨ?

Ajmer Singh, 2013, Ghadari Babeh Kaun San? Singh Brothers, Amritsar, p231

[19] T. S. Nahal 2012, *Ghadar Movement: Its Origin and Impact on Jallianwala Bagh Massacre and Indian Freedom Movement*

[20] Patwant Singh, 1999, *The Sikhs*, John Murray Publishers, London, republished by Rupa Publications, 2002, Delhi, p192

[21] Babbar Akali Movement, Sikh Missionary College, Ludhiana, Publication No. 358, p9

[22] Dr Sangat Singh, 2014, *The Sikhs in History*, Singh Brothers, Amritsar, p155

[23] PLCD, 7 May 1925, p1105, as referenced in Khushwant Singh's A History of The Sikhs, Vol. 2, p213

[24] Cynthia Keppley Mahmood, 1996, Fighting for Faith and Nation, University of Pennsylvania Press, p111

[25] Dr. Ganda Singh, 1964, *Some Confidential Papers of the Akali Movement*, Chattar Singh Jiwan Singh, Amritsar, p12

[26] Dr. Ganda Singh, 1964, *Some Confidential Papers of the Akali Movement*, Chattar Singh Jiwan Singh, Amritsar, p14

[27] Babbar Akali Movement, Sikh Missionary College, Ludhiana, Publication No. 358, p4

[28] Courtesy: British Library, Oriental and India Office Collections, London – as referenced in Tarlochan Singh Nahal, 2011, *Religion and Politics in Sikhism: The Khalsa Perspective*, Singh Brothers, Amritsar p38-39

[29] Rajinder Singh, 1988, *Five Hundred Years of Sikhism*, Amritsar Chief Khalsa Diwan, Department of History, Panjab University, Patiala, p90

[30] Dr. Ganda Singh, 1964, *Some Confidential Papers of the Akali Movement*, Chattar Singh Jiwan Singh, Amritsar, p53-55

[31] Dr. Ganda Singh, 1964, *Some Confidential Papers of the Akali Movement*, Chattar Singh Jiwan Singh, Amritsar, p56-69

[32] Mohandas Gandhi, Delhi, 1929

[33] Pandit Jawaharlal Nehru, Calcutta, 6th July 1946

[34] Gurtej Singh, 1996, *Tandav of the Centaur, Sikhs and Indian Secularism, Institute of Sikh Studies*, Chandigarh, p143

[35] Gurtej Singh, 1996, *Tandav of the Centaur, Sikhs and Indian Secularism, Institute of Sikh Studies*, Chandigarh, p143

[36] Indu Banga, 1995, *"Political Perceptions And Articulation Of The Sikhs During The 1940s"*, a paper read at the ICHR sponsored seminar on Contemporary History Of The Punjab

[37] Gurtej Singh, 1996, *Tandav of the Centaur, Sikhs and Indian Secularism, Institute of Sikh Studies*, Chandigarh, p147

Part 4: Transfer of colonial Power and the Rise of Indian Nationalism

Notwithstanding the continued resistance from Sikhs, there was a new political reality on the rise in Panjāb. This new reality was, of course, Indian Nationalism. It had gathered momentum through the creation of the Indian National Congress in 1885, and while in its early phase, "demanded decentralisation of power, in order to weaken the political power of the colonial rulers,"[1] it had all the hallmarks to reassert a new era of colonial domination in Panjāb.

A series of colonial statutes aided the growth of the nationalist movement, namely The Indian Council Act, 1909 and the Government of India Act, 1919 (amended 1935). In between these two statutes, the British appointed a Statutory Commission in 1927, headed by Sir John Simon, to consider further devolution of power. However, what had initially started as a movement to decentralise power from the British, soon became a movement, under the banners of nationalism, to heavily centralise power in New Delhi.[2]

Transfer of Power, 1947

Earlier, we noted how, as a manifestation of *manmat*, the idea of the Western secular presupposes the supremacy of empiricism and rationale, which in essence become the new realities to worship, pursue, uphold, and propagate. This intellectual idolization is no different to the ritualistic idolization commonplace in organised religion, that the Gurū Sāhibān challenged and opposed. Nām is not at the centre of this worship, nor is Hukam accepted as the moral and ethical ideal. The arrival of nationalism served to exacerbate this position, and when it became clear that a new India would be created in the image of the colonising power, as an independent nation-state, a new nationalist identity was formulated. This identity is rooted in colonial logic and Enlightenment principles such rationality, modernity and industrialization, as well as democracy, it is what Partha Chatterjee has described as a "wholly a European export to the rest of the world."[3] This is an important point that cannot be underestimated. It is often overlooked when revisiting the history of the Sikhs during the twentieth century, but the ramifications of the imposition of the European nation-state were manifold and cemented the colonial-era changes that reshaped the socio-economic landscape of Panjāb. The ideological episteme of governance upon which the new India was formulated was not only rooted in Europe, but by design, an entity that continued to uphold the notion of superiority of European thought, logic, and politics.

Hindutva

While this ideological episteme was an integral part of the Indian nationalist movement, it did not merely imitate the models of European powers such as Britain and France; there was a reimagination of "national" culture, adapted to the requirements of European standards of modernity, and the economic demands of industrialisation and capitalism, but at the same time distinct for a homogeneous, unified Indian national identity.

Ever since 1947, the different political parties of the Indian State have taken up varying points on the European political spectrum that have shaped its economic and social policies, but all have participated in the politics of Hindutva. The ideology of Hindutva was formally introduced in 1923 by Vinayak Damodar Savarkar, who "stressed the need to preserve the cultural purity of the Hindu nation, and resist the incursion of alien practices."[4] Savarkar defined Hindutva as the commonality of one nation, race, and civilization that predated the Egyptians and Babylonians, different from the religion of Hinduism, marked by the development of a "sense of nationality", following the arrival of Aryans to the River Indus.[5]

While Congress became the face of Indian secular nationalism, and the BJP was, and remains, engaged in an unapologetically pro-Hindu nationalism, history shows us the demarcations are not clear cut but often overlap for the overriding objective of one homogenous "Indian" identity. This is because there is what Professor Pritam Singh has called a "Hindu bias" ingrained within the Indian constitution, which "must be read as symptomatic of the depth of institutionalised Hindu communalism in India".[6] From the naming of the Indian State as 'Bharat' to the heavy focus on centralizing power in New Delhi, his work demonstrates how the rhetoric of Hindutva, mixed with nationalism created a monstrous situation for any distinct nation in so-called India. Recognising the "Hindu bias" in the Indian constitution demonstrates how "*Hindutva* in India is widespread and deeply rooted and goes beyond what is represented by the *Hindutva* group of organisations known as the *sangh parivar.*"[7] We shall consider shortly how the Sikhs opposed this suffocating model of governance.

Indian Nationalism

> *"In its essential aspects... nationalism represents the attempt to actualise in political terms the universal urge for liberty and progress. And yet the evidence was undeniable that it could also give rise to mindless chauvinism and xenophobia and serve as a justification for organised violence and tyranny."*[8]

In his excellent theoretical work, Partha Chatterjee examines the relationship between colonialism and nationalism, highlighting how the derivative character of colonial discourse has produced both the power and problem of nationalism within the project of India. What we learn from studying the arrival of nationalism in India is reflected in many ways of how it has manifested itself in the world. Throughout the 20th century and beyond, "it has been the cause of some of the most destructive wars ever seen; it has justified the brutality of Nazism and Fascism."[9] Chatterjee goes on to say it is the "ideology of racial hatred", giving rise to some of the most "irrational revivalist movements as well as to the most oppressive political regimes in the contemporary world."

While the emphasis of Chatterjee's analysis is on the fact that nationalism is a doctrine born from the imagination of Europeans at the beginning of the 19th century, we shall see how following the advent of colonialism it was violently imposed and adapted to suit the political intent of the India project, within the context of the new global political order. This is what India has been since 1947, and Panjāb, along with other former sovereign countries of the region, has endured the onslaught of this otherwise foreign political system of governance. There would naturally be strong Sikh opposition to this ideology that sought to homogenise, what was an otherwise diverse and mutually exclusive group of peoples with their own traditions, customs, and languages.

The Sikh Position

We have discussed the origins of Sikh consciousness that seeks not only to exercise the Pātshāhī bestowed upon the Khālsā through manifestation of Rāj, but to do so in opposition to exploitative and oppressive systems and structures of control. The basis of that position, as we considered in Part One and Part Two, is grounded in Gurmat, and exemplified by the actions of the Gurū Sāhibān and the Khālsā. Thus, it should be no surprise that resistance and opposition by Sikhs to the creation of the Indian state are evident both pre-and post-1947.

In 1928, esteemed Sikh thinker, poet, and scholar Prof. Puran Singh spoke out against the imposition of one homogenous "Indian" identity when he wrote a lengthy letter to Sir John Simon, who remember, was placed in charge of Statutory Commission, within which he noted:

> *"There are Hindus, Sikhs, Moslems, Christians, Parsis and Jains in India, but very few Indians. And strange as it may sound, it is quite true that those who have removed those labels are empty bottles, without having any character of wine, of acid, or of poison. They are of no account, because, for centuries, in India the formation of character has been associated, not with the practice of broad-minded patriotism, but with certain racial prejudices and social superstitions".[10]*

The act of homogenizing all those living within what had become known as British India was for Sikh intellectuals such as Prof. Puran Singh, a move to strip away political agency from what was an otherwise diverse region of the world. In almost prophetic manner, he went on,

> *"It is, therefore, not extricable from the so-called religious bias and bigotry. Self-Government in India means Government by the very few cunning and aggressive people who, once put into possession of the authority, would twist all letters of law and constitutions to their individual wills and make them work on the communal or the so-called religious bias."[11]*

Despite strong opposition, centralised governance was favoured by proponents of both overt Hindutva and those who hid behind the façade of Indian secular nationalism because it enabled the formation of one unified Indian national identity. Sikh homeland, the once prosperous region under Ranjīt Singh, the land where sovereign flags

ਪਾਤਿਸ਼ਾਹੀ ਮਹਿਮਾ – Revisiting Sikh Sovereignty

of the Khālsā flew under Bandā Singh Bahādur, was subsumed into the neocolonial project that became the secular Indian State, with complete control in the hands of *haumai*-driven elites in New Delhi. The sheer loss of life and number of those who were permanently displaced during the creation of both the State of India and Pakistan indicates the destructive nature of the colonial encounter. The death and destruction that occurred in 1947 make for grim reading.

Role of secularism and "religion"

The emergence of the Indian state and Indian nationalism, especially so in its formative years under the Indian Congress, adopted Western secular thought. Using the work of Talal Asad, who has described how secularism gave birth to new concepts of "religion", "ethics", and "politics",[12] it can be asserted that this new categorisation, based on colonial logic, is what empowered the secular Indian state to then marginalise and criminalise Sikh dissent because "Sikhism" was deemed incompatible with their adopted structure of modernity. Here I would like to lean on how secularism, as Talal Asad puts it,

> *"...builds on a particular conception of the world ("natural" and "social") and of the problems generated by that world. In the context of early modern Europe these problems were perceived as the need to control the increasingly mobile poor in city and countryside, to govern mutually hostile Christian sects within a sovereign territory, and to regulate the commercial, military, and colonizing expansion of Europe overseas."*[13]

Thus, the notion of secular nationalism allowed the Indian state to implement a new "rational" form of control and domination over the Sikhs, and indeed other minority peoples across the subcontinent, but as I have already alluded to, and as we shall see, Hindutva and the imposition of Hindu supremacy played an integral role

317

throughout. When the Sikhs expressed and exercised their Pātshāhī, they were demonised as religious fundamentalists and extremists. The advent of Indian Nationalism and, by extension patriotism, became a new form of control for the majority Hindu population, interwoven with the totalitarianizing structure of Brahmanism.

Empowered with the ideal of *Sarbat dā bhalā*, the Sikhs could never accept this form of control and dominance. It can be said that the SAD could and did try to work within what Talal Asad has described as a "complex arrangement of legal reasoning, moral practice, and political authority"[14] of the secular, but Nām conscious Gursikhs aligned to the sovereignty of the Guru Khālsā Panth have, and will always, oppose any form of physical or mental subjugation. This forms the basis of Sikh dissent towards centralised power in India, whether founded on the "secular" or "religious". Let us examine the centralised power of the new Indian state.

Centralised Power

> "The importance given to central planning, in the Indian central state's strategy of economic development, further increased the political and economic power of the centre the interlocking and mutually reinforcing relationship between centralisation, Indian nationalism and planned development strategy became the chief driving force of Indian political economy..."[15]

In addition to the "Hindu bias", there was what Professor Pritam Singh has called a "centralist bias"[16], at the heart of the Indian nationalist movement, which pushed for a 'Union of States', purposefully rejecting the model of a 'Federation of States', as we see in the United States. While introducing the Draft Constitution in 1949, Dr. B. R. Ambedkar, who held a doctorate on American federalism, as Chairman of the Drafting Committee, declared,

ਪਾਤਿਸ਼ਾਹੀ ਮਹਿਮਾ – Revisiting Sikh Sovereignty

> *"...though India was to be a federation, the federation was not the result of an agreement by the States to join a federation, and that the federation not being the result of an agreement, **no State has the right to secede from it [author's emphasis].** The federation is a Union because it is indestructible. Though the country and the people may be divided into different States for the convenience of administration, the country is one integral whole, its people a single people living under a single imperium derived from a single source."[17]*

The iteration of this notion of centrality of power and the homogenous identity that was steamrolled through the rise of Indian nationalism, of course, was by design opposed to reinstating the temporal sovereignty of the Sikhs in Panjāb that was lost during the colonial encounter. There was no process of decolonisation but rather a substitution of one imperial power with another, with the added presence of Hindutva.

> *"Hindutva elements both before and after 1947 have been the most ardent proponents of strong centralisation and Union power. Although there were other supporters of centralisation, as pointed out above, if one were to construct a league table of support for centralisation, Hindu nationalists would come out at the top."[18]*

This is why the term neo-colonialism, or simply new colonialism, is also used to describe what India became; namely, an entity that appeared to have gained overt political independence, even though the idea of one homogenous India did not politically exist prior to 1947. The economic dependence upon colonising powers for building infrastructure and industry continued, as did the process of "civilizing".

Transfer of Colonial Power and the Rise of Indian Nationalism

The domination of the Central government was guaranteed by the constitutional framework, which, to paraphrase Prof. Puran Singh, allowed "a few cunning and aggressive people to twist all letters of law and constitutions to their individual wills". They weren't alone in this, of course, as Britain became a firm ally of the Indian State, to the extent of assisting the Indian Army during its military attack on Srī Darbār Sāhib thirty-seven years later.

Indo-Sikh confrontation

The events of 1947 ushered in a new era of subjugation for the Sikhs, as the imposition of Indian nationalism and the domination of Hindutvā reigned supreme across what became East Panjāb. The desire to build one nation crippled the diverse nations within the subcontinent. For a Sikh, the policies of successive Indian governments have surpassed the violent persecution of the Mughal and British forces that we considered in the previous chapters.

The promises of autonomy in Panjāb and the protection of Sikh rights we considered towards the end of the last chapter disappeared and were soon replaced with a tirade of statements from the elites in power of the Indian State. The Governor of India, no less, singled out the Sikh community for its "lawlessness", which "needed" to be suppressed by India,

> "the Sikhs, as a community, are a lawless people and are thus a menace to the law-abiding Hindus in the province. Hence they should be stringently suppressed."[19]

In November 1947, Mohandas Gandhi, who had already expressed his disapproval of Sikh tradition and protocols, as the "father of the nation," had the audacity to publicly insult the Sikhs, the Gurū, and the Khālsā Panth,

ਪਾਤਿਸ਼ਾਹੀ ਮਹਿਮਾ – Revisiting Sikh Sovereignty

> *"Years ago, I said at Nankana Sahib, Sikhs have given proof of their valour but the consummation of Guru Gobind Singh's ideal will be reached only when they will substitute for their kirpan, the sword of the spirit of non-violence. So long as one wants to retain one's sword, one has not attained complete fearlessness."[20]*

The new prime minister, Jawaharlal Nehru, who had previously stated he saw no problem with Sikhs enjoying the glow of freedom with greater autonomy in Panjāb, also changed his tune, declaring,

> *"I do not fancy beards or moustaches or topknots, but I have no desire to impose my canons of taste on others, though I must confess, in regard to beards, that I inwardly rejoiced when Amanullah [the then king of Afghanistan who forces devout Muslims to have off their beards], began to to deal with them in summary fashion in Kabul".[21]*

The Sikhs were completely deceived, and while no Sikh signed the Constitution, they were forced to accept the political reality of this new India. Notwithstanding the claims of just governance, Gurtej Singh notes how oppressive ideology engulfed both the Constitution and emblems of the newly established Indian State. This was indicative of the Indian State's position as a new sovereign power, capable of unlimited and unchecked violence without any moral or ethical recourse.[22] In the 1949 Constituent Assembly Debates, Bhupinder Singh Mann said,

> *"I will be failing in my duty if I do not give the reactions of my own community, the Sikhs of East Punjab, so far as this Constitution goes. Their feeling is that they cannot give unstinted support of full approval to this Constitution."[23]*

Hukam Singh, another SAD representative, said,

> "...the Sikhs feel utterly disappointed and frustrated. They feel that they have been discriminated against. Let it not be misunderstood that the Sikh community has agreed to this Constitution. I wish to record an emphatic protest here. My community cannot subscribe its assent to this historic document... In our Constitution, each article tends to sap the local autonomy and make the provinces irresponsible... The minorities and particularly the Sikhs have been ignored and completely neglected. The Provincial units have been reduced to Muncipal Boards... there is enough provision in our Constitution...to facilitate the development of administration into a fascist state."[24]

Various SAD representatives opposed the Constitution for a number of reasons; it did not take into consideration the minority groups that found themselves in this new country of India; it was heavily focused on centralizing power and had the hallmarks to descend into fascism. The Sikhs vehemently refused to sign it. It did not take long, following the creation of the Indian State, for the words of Prof. Puran Singh and the fears expressed by SAD representatives to be proven true. The "religious bias" that he had referred to, was used to vilify the Sikhs, and from the standpoint of Western secular reason, logic, and rationale, Sikhs were criminalised for any political dissent.

What began as opposition to the Constitution was followed by SAD-led Sikh mobilization against the socio-economic and political suppression imposed upon Panjāb. However, there was a marked difference in the resistance offered in a post-1947 East Panjāb, ruled by New Delhi, to the Sikh resistance that we considered in previous chapters. This, as we shall see, was because the SAD was operating as a representative Sikh political body, governed and regulated by the Indian State. It was not a wholly sovereign and autonomous entity, such as the Sikhs experienced previously. While there may have been individuals of SAD hopeful of full-autonomy, SAD as an institution was by default limited to agitate for reform or petition and protest for India to grant them "equal rights", but never to establish Khālsā Rāj. If you recall, this was one of the conditions Mohandas Gandhi had imposed upon those representing the Sikhs. Let us consider some of the socio-economic and political suppression forced upon Panjāb following the creation of the Indian State.

Stolen River Waters

Following the Indus River Treaty, the newly formed state of Pakistān had received 80% of Panjāb's river water. In 1956, of the remaining 20% in East Panjāb, which was approximately 15 MAF (million-acre feet), the non-riparian state of Rajasthan received 8 MAF, with East Panjāb receiving 7.2 MAF. Despite Sikh opposition, however limiting on the part of the SAD, the Indian State pressed ahead to systematically suppress and exploit East Panjāb, starting with the river waters.

We must ask why, or rather on what basis, an amount that constituted over half of East Panjāb's allocated share of river water was diverted to the neighbouring non-riparian state of Rajasthan. When one reads the interstate river water agreements, the main overriding reason cited for such seismic water redistribution is "national interest" and "optimum utilization of the waters."[25] "National interest", in other words, the nationalist need to increase production of produce to meet the ever-increasing demands of a capitalist society. This justification has been at the center of Panjāb's economic, social and political turmoil since 1947. It has cost life in Panjāb dearly.

After the creation of the state of Haryana in 1966, it too demanded 4.8 MAF of East Panjāb's 7.2 share. During the 1976 emergency,

Indira Gandhi issued an executive order dividing the river water – 3.5MAF to East Panjāb, 3.5 to Haryana, and 0.2 to Delhi.[26] East Panjāb's share has fluctuated since, and the Sutlej-Yumna Link (SYL) canal saga continues, but in essence, Haryana, Delhi, and Rajasthan have been stealing Panjab's water since the 1950s. A country named after the five rivers that run across its land is today reduced to a state, which has three rivers in the Sutlej, Beas, and Ravi but due to the enforced water redistribution, seventy per cent of Panjab's irrigation is dependent on underground water, which is depleting water levels at an alarming rate. Under "optimum utilization" Panjāb has been run dry to the point that environmental experts have predicted it will soon become a desert.

Furthermore, despite all the Hindu majority states in this newly created India being founded on linguistic grounds, East Panjāb was denied this right as Indian ministers desperately tried to make Hindi the official language. Having spent almost a century fighting British colonialism, the Sikhs in East Panjāb were faced with the reality of not only losing Panjāb's river waters, but also as much as 90 per cent[27] of their heritage to West Panjāb in the newly created state of Pakistān. East Panjāb was the target of further economic and social subjugation under the weight of Indian nationalism.

Panjabi Suba Movement and the SAD

Due to the reorganization of States based on linguistic grounds, the SAD launched the Panjābī Suba Movement in the 1950s; a long drawn political agitation in which the people of Panjāb fought for Panjābī to be recognised as the main language of the region.

> "Punjabi Muslims could afford to forget Punjab and live like Pakistanis. After all, they got a sovereign state to rule, offered to them on a platter. The Punjabi Hindus could afford to forget Punjab and live like Indians. What could the Sikhs do? They

ਪਾਤਿਸ਼ਾਹੀ ਮਹਿਮਾ – Revisiting Sikh Sovereignty

> *could not shrug off their language. Their very scriptures are written in it. So, the mantle of Punjab fell on the Sikhs. The Sikhs were willing to live like Punjabis, committed to Punjabi language and culture. The Punjabi Hindus were not, and they refused to acknowledge Punjabi as their mother tongue. Thus, the seeds of the problem began to bear their bitter fruit. The alienation between Hindu and Sikh began. With the erosion of Punjab, the Sikhs began to be viewed as a community rather than a people belonging to a particular province. The Sikhs began to view themselves as a nation rather than a minority".*[28]

While this was not an agitation for full sovereignty, for the Sikhs it was a fight for survival and existence as a distinct people of Panjāb. In August 1950, The Scotsman published an article covering the events in Panjāb,

> *"The Akali Dal [SAD] wants nothing less than an autonomous Punjabi-speaking State, carved out of the Punjab and a few States to the east. It is to be subjected to the Indian Union only in matters of defence, foreign affairs and communications".*[29]

We now begin to see the limitations of the SAD, that in essence, their protest and agitation could only take them to a certain point and that point was never the same destination as the Khalsā and the Panth, which was created, and functioned, independent of other political entities. The nature of the Khālsā Panth, as we examined in Part Two, is such that it cannot work within the confines of another political power. That being said, it was tens of thousands of Sikhs, under the guidance of the SAD, who protested the Indian government's anti-Sikh and anti-Panjāb position; a position which, of course, was extended to all minority communities that refused to be subsumed under the hegemony of the Indian State. The government pushed the nationalist agenda, as another report from the Scotsman read,

> "It [Indian government] says special concessions cannot be made to local minorities. The Sikhs must be Indians first and Sikhs afterwards".[30]

The policy to forcefully impose the new nationalist identity, redistribute Panjāb's natural resources at the whim of central government in New Delhi, and the decision to deny the Sikhs their language contributed to the economic, social, and ecological suffering that Panjāb endured in the post-1947 era. The imposition of Indian nationalism over the Sikhs, was of course irrational and destructive, but was nevertheless enforced by what was still in essence, law rooted in colonial logic, justified under the mandate of "nation-building".

As mentioned at the beginning of this chapter, the ideology of nationalism is a wholly European invention, whose inevitable consequence is the "annihilation of freedom".[31] This has been a defining aspect of India and the basis of the indo-Sikh confrontation since 1947. The Central government merely stepped into the shoes left by the British, both in how it wielded power and how it violently crushed dissent. Inderjit Singh Jaijee noted,

> "Every day, in every way, India was getting worse and worse for the Sikhs. They felt the chains of slavery, tighter and stronger than the Mughal, Persian, Afghan or British ones, being cast around them." [32]

In an attempt to ease the suffering, with hopes of still working within the Union of the Indian State, the SAD issued a manifesto, making their position unequivocally clear,

> "The true test of democracy, in the opinion of the Shiromani Akali Dal, is that the minorities should

ਪਾਤਿਸ਼ਾਹੀ ਮਹਿਮਾ – Revisiting Sikh Sovereignty

> *feel that they are really free and equal partners in the destiny of their country; (a) to bring home this sense of freedom to the Sikhs, it is vital that there should be a Punjabi speaking language and culture. This will not only be in fulfilment of the pre-partition Congress programme and pledges, but also in entire conformity with the universally recognised principles governing formation of provinces, (b) The Shiromani Akali Dal is in favour of formation of provinces on a linguistic and cultural basis throughout India, but it holds it is a question of life and death for the Sikhs for a new Punjab to be created immediately, (c) The Shiromani Akali Dal has reason to believe that a Punjabi speaking province may give Sikhs the needful security. It believes in a Punjabi speaking province as an autonomous unit of India"*[33]

We see here again the limitations of working within the parameters of the Indian State. On the one hand, the SAD was seeking greater autonomy, but at the same time, wanted to remain within the "unit of India". It is important to note how this position was different to that of the Khālsā Panth, which as a fully autonomous entity, has never, and will never work within the presumed sovereignty of another. Despite the SAD demanding the implementation of that which was promised prior to the creation of the Indian State, there was strong opposition to this from the Indian nationalists, in particular, the Arya Samaj and the Jan Sangh, who initiated a campaign targeting Panjābī-speaking Hindus to disown their mother tongue and instead declare it to be Hindi.

One of the key protagonists of this initiative was Lalā Jagat Narain, who at the time was the secretary of the Punjab Pradesh Congress. He mobilised Hindus to declare Hindi as their mother tongue in the 1951 census, which of course, skewed the census results. The confrontation between the SAD and the Indian government continued to escalate, to the point that in 1955, they decided to deploy police troops to attack Sikhs at Sri Darbār Sahib. The Evening Telegraph reported,

> "Police invaded the sacred Golden Temple and were showered with bricks. Police replied with tear gas bombs...[they] cordoned off the temple area and arrested the volunteers as fast as they left the temple. But for each 100 they arrested, 100 more took their places. Soon the prisons were filled with Akalis, and the resistance strategy spread to surrounding areas...independent, courageous, persistent and fearless – all describe the Sikhs. The chances are good that they will one day achieve a home of their own".[34]

The 1966 Partition of East Panjāb

Following mass protests during the Panjābī Subā Movement, Panjābī was made the official language, but this came at a huge cost. Panjābī was only recognised after the central government further divided East Panjab in 1966 with the creation of two new states: Haryānā and Himāchal.

> "It is significant to note that both Jawahar Lal Nehru and Indira Gandhi followed a set policy against the Sikhs. Both of them opposed the creation of Punjabi Suba with all the might at their command. To Prime Minister Indira Gandhi it was a matter of acute frustration that the Punjabi Suba came to be accepted in principle because of the historical necessity following the Indo-Pakistan War of 1965 This explains why both in framing the Punjab Reorganization Act of 1966 and her subsequent

policies and decisions, the Centre did everything to dwarf and crush the socio-economic growth and entity of Punjab and its people."[35]

This, in effect, was the second partition of Panjāb. Large areas of East Panjāb such as Shimlā, Kulu-Manālī, and Dharmshālā were divided and reallocated. East Panjāb was granted no rights to the Yamuna River water. As mentioned, the state of Haryana demanded 4.8 MAF of East Panjab's 7.2 share, and during the 1976 emergency Indira Gandhi issued an executive order dividing the river water – 3.5MAF to East Panjāb, 3.5 to Haryana, and 0.2 to Delhi.[36] To date, Haryana, which does not touch Ravi, Beas, and Sutlej, has a right over these rivers, but East Panjāb is denied the same right over Yamuna waters that run through Haryana. It was a harsh reality that Sikhs have endured under the governance of successive Indian governments.

This is the destructive nature of nationalism and the implementation of a centralised model of governance. Each state was viewed as a revenue stream to make the Indian State an economically and politically strong nation, for which it had to overcome its "industrial backwardness".[37] In the case of East Panjāb, such was the overarching nature of the Constitution that the centre could intervene on matters related to agriculture if it were in the "national" or "public" interest.

It had been two decades since the creation of the Indian State, and Panjāb had become a fraction of its former size. Language had been denied, river water had been stolen, and the economy of Panjāb was neglected by way of serving the wider interests of the central government in New Delhi. Professor Pritam Singh notes,

> *"The strategic politico-economic goals of the British rule in Punjab led this province to be developed on an agrarian-oriented development path. Central government policies in India after independence (especially in the 1960s) reinforced*

> *this agrarian-oriented path of development in Punjab... The Punjab economy increasingly became a food-dependent agrarian economy and the process of economic transition towards non-agricultural sectors remained neglected throughout the 1980s.*"[38]

One year before the sub-partition of East Panjāb, Sardār Kapur Singh, had echoed the voice of previous Sikhs within the SAD, that they had only agreed to the idea of India, "on the explicit understanding of being accorded a constitutional status of co-sharers in the Indian sovereignty along with the majority community."[39] However, the post-1947 experience for Sikhs was one of subjugation and suffocation as a direct result of the policies enacted by the central government.

Sikhs who had previously opposed Britain's repressive occupation of Panjāb were now resisting the unjust rule of the Indian State. Individuals such as Shaheed Darshan Singh Pheruman, who played an integral role in the Gurdwara Reform Movement and Jaito da Morcha of the 1920s, for which he was imprisoned by the British, pledged to fast upon death in protest of India's decision to remove Chandigarh, the capital, and other Panjabi speaking areas from Panjab. He attained martyrdom on the 74th day of his hunger strike in 1969. This illustrated the complete disregard for Sikhs who had fought and led the fight to remove colonial occupation of the region.

On the contrary, under the suffocating homogenous guise of Indian nationalism and patriotism, unless they were serving the new India, the Sikhs of Panjāb were criminalised.

Despite Sikh opposition and the death of prominent Sikhs who had sacrificed their all to remove colonial forces, the Indian government continued its abuse of power in East Panjāb. Due to the overarching influence of centralised power in New Delhi, the Indian State was, and remains to be entirely intolerant of dissent.

ਪਾਤਿਸ਼ਾਹੀ ਮਹਿਮਾ – Revisiting Sikh Sovereignty

The "Green Revolution"

In an earlier chapter, we looked at the colonial creation of the agrarian model, which was imprinted upon people's minds as the totality of rural life through the systematic reorganization of villages. The specific economic policies of British occupation in Panjāb that led the region towards an agrarian-orientated trajectory were reinforced by the Indian State. The "Green Revolution" was one such initiative, introduced to achieve a national goal of becoming self-sufficient in food availability. It was hailed a success by the Indian State because it fulfilled their goal of increasing agricultural production, which inevitably strengthened their position on the world stage. However, as Professor Pritam Singh has noted, the centre's policy to reduce "regional inter-state income inequalities" meant that the region of Punjab was denied other public sector investment, which adversely affected industry within Punjab.

> *"The pattern of agricultural output in Punjab shifted crucially towards two food items: wheat and rice. The Punjab economy increasingly became a food-dependent agrarian economy and the process of economic transition towards non-agricultural sectors remained neglected..."*[40]

So, while there was a rise in per capita income for the state of Punjab, this was specific to agriculture as the region was synonymised with the notion of being India's "bread basket". It was, in essence, portrayed and utilised as a large market. Other crucial industries were ignored due to the central government's actions, which went against its own constitutional provision that states industry is a state matter.

Of course, the reality for Sikhs and Panjāb was that farmers were left with astronomical debts, and the introduction of cancerous pesticides degraded the soil quality, killing off the ecosystem by disrupting levels of biodiversity across Panjāb. By 1998, estimates of farmers' suicides were placed at six thousand deaths annually across East Panjāb, indicating a "policy of economic genocide at the worst and willful criminal neglect of the farming community in Punjab at the least amounting to state economic terrorism."[41]

Inderjit Singh Jaijee notes the sharp increase in rural indebtedness, of which the interest alone amounted to eleven per cent of net income from crop production. Covering the period up to 1998, he notes how seventy per cent of farmers were in debt. Due to lack of investment in other industries, the artisans – electricians, masons, carpenters, welders, etc., were forced to find work in the oil-rich Gulf countries. As they sent money back to East Panjāb, they were caught by remittance charges from the Indian banks, which meant the vast majority of the beneficiaries were industrialists in other states, not East Panjāb.[42] Gurtej Singh writes,

> "Ever since 1947, they [the Sikhs] are in a situation in which they face an undeclared war by an imperial power under the garb of a democratic modern state. How grim the situation is, can be known from the following two facts, one that, they have already sacrificed their lives in greater number than they had done in the centuries of confrontation with the three other empires put together. Secondly, their part of the story has just begun to be told. There is no newspaper journal to which they have not introduced themselves with a piece soaked in their blood."[43]

Systematic suppression

Alcohol, drugs, and a whole array of foreign intoxicants were systematically flushed through Panjab, sabotaging entire families. Between the late 1970s and 1990s, seventy-five per cent of the state revenue was derived from excise, virtually the only tax the state was empowered to levy. Jaijee again notes,

> *"During the period between 1977-97, the sale of Punjab Medium liquor had gone up from 10 million Ml. to 37 million Ml., and of Indian made foreign liquor from 4 million Ml. to 21 million Ml.... Aside from the promotion of liquor consumption, evidence regularly surfaces that security forces are involved in transporting drugs to politically sensitive areas."*[44]

It should be noted the rate of alcohol consumption has continued to rise without intervention from any regulatory or enforcement bodies. In 2021, reports coming out of Panjāb showed the number of liquor vendors has jumped from 5,632 to 12,000 over the last decade. The excise revenue has quadrupled from Rs. 1506 crore in 2005/2006 to Rs. 5440 crores.[45]

The Anandpur Sahib Resolution (ASR)

The Anandpur Sahib Resolution (ASR) was prepared in 1973. It was a document that essentially reiterated the position held by the SAD over the decades following the creation of the Indian state, namely that East Panjāb should be given greater autonomy, specifically outlining political, economic, social, and religious demands to improve life in the region. The document was intended to serve as a blueprint for the rest of the Indian State, to receive greater rights over language, land and water; "a devolution of centralised power."[46] The Indian State's response to the agitation, however, arrived in a manner that unveiled the true face of the secular Indian State.

It is clear how the nature of economic exploitation in Panjāb during this period was grounded in the logic underpinning the colonial occupation of Panjāb between 1849 and 1947. The only difference now lay in "the effective camouflage of the written Constitution, free Press, functioning democracy, impartial judiciary,

Transfer of Colonial Power and the Rise of Indian Nationalism

elected legislature, efficient bureaucracy, active Human Rights Organizations and so on"[47], that had completely hoodwinked the masses into thinking the secular State was justified by its policies. In reality, nothing much had changed during the transfer of power and the creation of the Indian State.

It is important to recognise the evolution of the Indian state, from its colonial roots, to its neocolonial branches. For the Gursikhs, as a distinct and sovereign peoples, empowered by the Pātshāhī of Gurū Sāhib, and indeed with the worldview that centres Nām and Vismād, there was always going to be a clash. We considered in Part One how the the first battle took place in 1634, with the Battle of Amritsar, and as we shall see next, another large battle ensued 350 years later in which the Akāl Takht established by Gurū Hargobind Sāhib became the target again.

NOTES

[1] Pritam Singh, 2008, *Federalism, Nationalism and Development, India and the Punjab economy*, Routledge, Oxon, p58

[2] Pritam Singh, 2008, *Federalism, Nationalism and Development, India and the Punjab economy*, Routledge, Oxon, p56-59

[3] Partha Chatterjee, 1986, *Nationalist Thought and the Colonial World, A Derivative Discourse*, University of Minnesota Press, 2011, Sixth Edition, p7

[4] G.W. Brown, et al, 2018, *The Concise Oxford Dictionary of Politics and International Relations*, Oxford University Press, p381

[5] V.D. Savarkar, 1923, *Essentials of Hindutva*

[6] Professor Pritam Singh, 2005, *'Hindu Bias in India's Secular Constitution: probing flaws in the instruments of governance'*, Third World Quartely, 26:6, 909-926

[7] Professor Pritam Singh, 2005, *'Hindu Bias in India's Secular Constitution: probing flaws in the instruments of governance'*, Third World Quartely, 26:6, 909-926

[8] Partha Chatterjee, 1986, *Nationalist Thought and the Colonial World, A Derivative Discourse*, University of Minnesota Press, 2011, Sixth Edition, p2

[9] Partha Chatterjee, 1986, *Nationalist Thought and the Colonial World, A Derivative Discourse*, University of Minnesota Press, 2011, Sixth Edition, p2

[10] Professor Puran Singh, 28th October 1928, letter to Sir John Simon, as recorded in Gurtej Singh, 2000, *Web of Indian Secularism; Chakravyuh*

[11] Professor Puran Singh, 28th October 1928, letter to Sir John Simon, as recorded in Gurtej Singh, 2000, *Web of Indian Secularism; Chakravyuh*

[12] Talal Asad, 2003, *Formations of the Secular, Christianity, Islam, Modernity*, Stanford University Press, California, Introduction

[13] Talal Asad, 2003, *Formations of the Secular, Christianity, Islam, Modernity*, Stanford University Press, California, p192

[14] Talal Asad, 2003, *Formations of the Secular, Christianity, Islam, Modernity*, Stanford University Press, California, p255

[15] Pritam Singh, 2008, *Federalism, Nationalism and Development, India and the Punjab economy*, Routledge, Oxon, p68-69

[16] Pritam Singh, 2008, *Federalism, Nationalism and Development, India and the Punjab economy*, Routledge, Oxon, p63

[17] Constituent Assembly Debates 1949, Article 43,

[18] Professor Pritam Singh (2005), *'Hindu Bias in India's Secular Constitution: probing flaws in the instruments of governance'*, Third World Quartely, 26:6, 909-926

[19] Chandu Lāl Trivedi, Governor of East Panjab, 10th October 1947

[20] D.G. Tendulkar, Mahatma, Vol. 7, p113; quoted by Gurmit Singh, 1969, *Gandhi and the Sikhs*, Usha Institute of Religious Studies, p69

[21] Jawaharlal Nehru, 1936, *An Autobiography*, Reprint by Penguin Books, 2004, p471

[22] Gurtej Singh, 1996, *Tandav of the Centaur, Sikhs and Indian Secularism, Institute of Sikh Studies*, Chandigarh, p42

[23] Constituent Assembly Debates 1949, Article 722

[24] Constituent Assembly Debates 1949, Article 753

[25] See for example Agreement dated 31st December, 1981 - https://water.rajasthan.gov.in/content/dam/water/water-resources-department/InterstateAgreements/Ravi%20Beas%20Agreement%2031.12.1981.pdf

[26] Dr Sangat Singh, 2014, *The Sikhs in History*, Singh Brothers, Amritsar, p363

[27] Bobby Singh Bansal, 2017, *Sikh Monuments in India and Pakistan, Remnants of the Sikh Empire,* Hay House

[28] Rajinder Puri, "*What it's all about*", in *'Punjab in Indian Politics'*, edited by Amrik Singh, 1985, p55, as quoted by Ranbir Singh Sandhu, 1999, *Struggle for Justice,* Sikh Educational & Religious Foundation, Ohio, introduction xiii

[29] Rawle Knox, The Scotsman, 11th August 1950

[30] Rawle Knox, The Scotsman, Friday 11th August 1950

[31] Partha Chatterjee, Nationalist Thought and the Colonial World, A Derivative Discourse, University of Minesota Press, 1986, Sixth Edition 2011, p7

[32] Inderjit Singh Jaijee 2002, *Politics of Genocide*, Ajanta Publications, Delhi, p5

[33] The Spokesman, 29th August, 1951

[34] Evening Telegraph, 11th August 1955

[35] G.S. Dhillon, 1992, *India Commits Suicide*, Singh and Singh Publishers, Chandigarh, p190

[36] Dr Sangat Singh, 2014, *The Sikhs in History*, Singh Brothers, Amritsar, p363

[37] Pritam Singh, 2008, *Federalism, Nationalism and Development, India and the Punjab economy*, Routledge, Oxon, p127

[38] Pritam Singh, 2008, *Federalism, Nationalism and Development, India and the Punjab economy*, Routledge, Oxon, p126

[39] Sirdar Kapur Singh, 1965, "Main Resolution", General Hari Singh Nalwa Conference, Ludhiana 4th July, 1965, as cited by Gurtej Singh, 2020, *Documents on Sikh Homeland and Speeches in Parliament*, Satvic Books, Amritsar, p130

[40] Pritam Singh, 2008, *Federalism, Nationalism and Development, India and the Punjab economy*, Routledge, Oxon, p126

[41] Inderjit Singh Jaijee 2002, *Politics of Genocide*, Ajanta Publications, Delhi, p15

[42] Inderjit Singh Jaijee 2002, *Politics of Genocide*, Ajanta Publications, Delhi, p16

[43] Gurtej Singh, 1996, *Tandav of the Centaur, Sikhs and Indian Secularism, Institute of Sikh Studies*, Chandigarh, Preface, XIV (1996)

[44] Inderjit Singh Jaijee 2002, *Politics of Genocide*, Ajanta Publications, Delhi, p16

[45] https://timesofindia.indiatimes.com/india/In-Punjab-13k-govt-primary-schools-12k-liquor-vends/articleshow/51706637.cms

[46] Cynthia Keppley Mahmood, 1996, Fighting for Faith and Nation, University of Pennsylvania Press, p118

[47] Gurtej Singh, 2000, *Web of Indian Secularism; Chakravyuh*, reprint 2014, Introduction, xxiii

Dharam Yudh and the Khalistān Sangarsh

> "*Political power, according to the [Gurū Sāhibān] belongs rightly to the people, and the Order of the Khalsa was created to see that no one is allowed to usurp it. The existence of no other nobility except that of virtue and of the spirit is sanctioned by the Sikh ethos.*"[1]

In the previous three chapters, we have explored the devasting effect of the colonial encounter, both on the minds and bodies of Sikhs in Panjāb. We considered how the systemic nature of oppressive colonial ideology took on a new mutation with the arrival of the Indian State and Indian Nationalism, underpinned by both Brahmanical and Western Secular thought. Notwithstanding the resistance of the Khālsā such as Bhāī Maharaj Singh, the Ghadarites and the Babbar Akalī, following the transfer of imperial power in 1947, we considered how Sikh opposition was largely limited to working within the parameters of the modern Indian State. Despite the oppressive polity of successive Indian governments, the SAD remained committed to its ideology. By the early 1980s, it was organizing mass-scale protests and civil disobedience marches to exert pressure on the central government to implement the conditions outlined in the ASR.

The 1978 Saka and Nirankārī Sect

At around the same time, Sant Jarnail Singh ji Khalsa Bhindranwale was awakening the Sikh Panth to the realities of living as slaves in

ਪਾਤਿਸ਼ਾਹੀ ਮਹਿਮਾ – Revisiting Sikh Sovereignty

this new India. As a Sikh aligned to the sovereignty of the Khālsā Panth, he was astutely aware of the larger politics at play; that the Indian state had been waging war with the Sikhs since 1947. Despite the social, economic, and political onslaught Panjāb, and the Sikhs, endured in the decades immediately following the creation of the Indian state, the murder of thirteen Gursikhs who were opposing the government-backed Nirankari sect responsible for sacrilege and distortion of Gurmat marked a major turning point.

The Nirankari sect had announced plans to hold a large march on 13th April 1978, in which they planned to mock the Gurū Sāhibān and ridicule the creation of the Khālsā. When news of this reached Sant Jarnail Singh, he contacted the Chief Minister of Panjāb, Parkāsh Singh Bādal, with hopes of preventing the march from taking place. However, A.R. Darshi writes,

> "...partially under pressure of Morar Ji Desai, a Gujrati Brahmin, Prime Minister, and partially to please the Jan Sangh, a political party of the fundamentalist Hindus, [Bādal] allowed Nirankaris to hold their proposed gathering."[2]

A meeting was called at Manjhī Sāhib Diwān Hall in Srī Darbār Sāhib, where Sant Jarnail Singh addressed the Sikh Sangat, making it clear that while the Sikhs have no problem with others wanting to start their own religion, this was a direct challenge to the Sikh tradition and sanctity of the Khālsā, and it needed to be opposed. An agreement was reached for Sikhs to launch a counter-march, headed by Bhāī Faujā Singh. Sant Jarnail Singh wanted to join them too; however, five Sikhs, including Bhāī Faujā Singh, convened to pass an order, in the form of the Panj Pyāre, ordering Sant Jarnail Singh to stay where he was.[3]

Gursikhs from both the Damdamī Taksāl and Akhand Kīrtanī Jathā marched to oppose the Nirankaris; however, they were mowed down by bullets fired from the Nirankari sect and the police.[4] Thirteen of the Gursikhs, including Bhāī Faujā Singh, attained martyrdom.

Scottish anthropologist Joyce Pettigrew, in her interview with Dilbir Singh, a correspondent of the Tribune, noted his account of Sant Jarnail Singh's reaction,

> *"For it was a situation of terror and pessimism and that man [Sant Jarnail Singh] was physically with his own hands carrying the dead bodies and placing them in his vehicle. Afterwards, at Amritsar Medical College he and Bhai Amrik Singh personally received the bodies after the post-mortem examination. The next day the dead bodies were brought to Guru Ram Das Serai and placed there. I could not help but notice his sincerity..."*[5]

There was no justice from the state for the callous and cold-blooded murder of those Gursikhs. The perpetrators were not only acquitted of any charges but were given free reins to do as they pleased within Panjāb and against the Sikhs.

The reawakening and realignment to Sikh sovereignty

Sant Jarnail Singh took it upon himself to care for the wounded and perform the final rites of the Sikh martyrs. He called for Panthic unity, and in the stand against the injustice of the Indian state, he declared,

> *"Their justice system has failed, so now our justice system will prevail"*[6]

A Hukamnāmā was issued by the Akāl Takht in which Sikhs were informed to have no relation with the Nirankārī sect. Between 1978 and 1984, there was an unprecedented rise in Sikh consciousness, a reawakening to the reality of living under systems of governance that suppressed Divine human experience. There was a significant realignment towards Gurmat and the polity of the Khālsā, which in years immediately preceding the creation of the Indian State, had been curbed by the rise of secular thought and engulfed under the insidious framework of Indian nationalism. It was both radical and revolutionary, as Sant Jarnail Singh travelled village to village, delivering guidance to Sikhs in those troubled times. His fiery speeches reconnected Sikhs with their revolutionary roots to become Guru-oriented, empowering them to make a stand. Entire villages were awakening as he captured the hearts and souls of the Sikhs, old and young alike, inspiring them to make a stand, as per Gurū Gobind Singh Ji's instruction.

In 1980, two Singhs, Bhāī Ranjīt Singh, who went on to serve as Jathedār of Akāl Takht, and Shāheed Bhāī Kabal Singh who went on to attain martyrdom at Srī Darbār Sāhib, were dispatched to remove the head of the Nirankārī sect. Following his death, Sant Jarnail Singh publicly congratulated the Khālsā Panth for having taken matters into their own hands, as the glorious Khālsā had done previously.

> *"...they have infused a fresh breath of life into the Sikh Nation... they have shown that they could be like Sukhā Singh and Mehtāb Singh."*[7]

The Sikhs were rising, and the Indian establishment understood the ramifications of that. There was a threat to the "unity" of the Indian State, a 37-year-old political entity responsible for violently imposing itself upon Panjāb and other regions across the subcontinent. In fact, the threat, as we have seen, was always there, brimming under the surface as Sikhs had reigned over Panjāb before and were not willing to live as slaves under the oppressive nature of Indian State polity. Naturally, having ruled within Panjāb under various manifestations of Sikh Rāj for centuries, the Sikhs had wanted an independent state prior to the creation of the India State, but for the false promises of the Indian leaders, the SAD had, at the very last minute, trusted them. However, this was a decision they regretted soon after, and as we have discussed in the previous chapter, Sikh opposition to the Indian Constitution is well-documented.

Sant Jarnail Singh's mission

When examining his speeches, as they have been meticulously presented by Ranbir Singh Sandhu,[8] we find constant reference to five main directives that Sant Jarnail Singh placed before the Sikh Panth: (1) give up addictions harmful for the body; (2) read Gurbānī; (3) take Amrit and become initiated Khālsā; (4) become armed; and (5) realise the Pātshāhi of the Gurū. These were very specific objectives, aimed at tackling the problem of drugs, alcohol, and other substance abuse that systematically flushed through social life in Panjāb, as well as the obvious attacks on Sikhī, and the devasting effect that had left on Sikh psyche. Whether he was highlighting examples of slavery or police brutality, the five main directives were interwoven within his stand against the oppression of the Indian State. This was a radical alternative to that which the SAD had been propagating for over five decades. Instead of pleading for justice or organizing marches and rallies for the implementation of "civil rights", Sant Jarnail Singh focused on leading the Sikhs on a path that was in line with the tradition and way of the Khālsā.

Following decades of disillusionment and disarray under Indian governance, Sant Jarnail Singh's revolutionary approach galvanised the Sikh Panth. This rise intimidated the SAD, whose grip over Sikh affairs loosened. At this moment, they spread a rumour that Sant Jarnail Singh was an agent of the Congress[9], despite his entire mobilization being based on Khālsā tradition and polity. He instilled within Sikhs the spirit of sovereignty that had been a defining aspect of Sikhs since 1469; the undeniable spirit of Gurū's Darbār, and the spirit of the Khālsā that had initially powered 150 years of Sikhs being rebels or rulers.

ਪਾਤਿਸ਼ਾਹੀ ਮਹਿਮਾ – Revisiting Sikh Sovereignty

Sant Jarnail Singh did not overtly criticise the limited ways of the SAD, but at the same time, he pointed toward the futility of asking an oppressive regime for rights, either by way of protest or petition,

> *"If you wish to deal in matters of the Faith, [keep in mind that] if Sukha Singh and Mehtab Singh had come to Punjab to file a suit in order to catch Massa Ranghar, he would never have been caught. If Baba Deep Singh Ji had sought writs [of the courts] from here, the Haidari flag [of Afghans] would never have come down from Harmandir Sahib. If Banda Singh Bahadur had consulted with commissioners and lawyers, it is certain, Wazira would never have been captured".*[10]

While some Sikhs, under the guidance of the SAD, remained steadfast in their movement and chose instead to raise the level of civil disobedience, others, who had realised the truth contained within the words of Sant Jarnail Singh, knew that path was destined for failure. While the former planned to withhold all shipments of grain from leaving Panjāb in the hope that it would finally pave the way for a diplomatic resolution, the latter were fortifying Srī Darbār Sāhib for the attack that was considered imminent. Under the leadership of Sant Jarnail Singh, Sikhs of Panjāb were rising again.

In 1984, under the premise of a modern secular nation-state, the ideal of modernity, governed by the rule of law, the Indian government took extreme military action by deploying all three divisions of its armed forces to attack the Sikhs. Built on decades of propaganda that the Sikhs were merely a religion (framed from a Eurocentric viewpoint that we considered in the previous chapters), a bunch of criminals, uncivilised in comparison to the Western standards of life and governance that the Indian State modelled itself on. This was the fallacy which led the Indian State to declare that it had no other option but to "root out terrorists". This was the same colonial logic that had warranted extreme violence from the British, whether it was the decision to blow apart Sikh bodies by tying them to canons or unleash a reign of terror in Amritsar during the decades that preceded the transfer of power.

Battle of Amritsar and the attack on Srī Darbār Sāhib

350 years had passed since the very first Battle of Amritsar, and on June 6th, 1984, after almost a week of failed attempts to break the Sikh resistance of Sant Jarnail Singh, General Shabegh Singh, Bhāī Amrīk Singh, Baba Thārā Singh, and approximately 175 other Sikh fighters, Indirā Gāndhī, sanctioned the use of battle tanks. As many as seven according to some sources[11], to add to the platoon of military personnel from all three divisions of India's armed forces, were rolled into the Parikarmā of Srī Darbār Sāhib. The result was devasting as the tanks pumped high-explosive squash-head shells into the Akāl Takht, reducing it to rubble and annihilating any sign of life.

While the Khālsā embraced the glory of martyrdom, the extreme actions of the Indian State were exposed in front of the whole world. Joyce Pettigrew famously wrote,

> "The army went into Darbar Sahib (Golden Temple) not to eliminate a political figure or a political movement but to suppress the culture of a people, to attack their heart, to strike a blow at their spirit and self-confidence."[12]

There was of course the wider clash that we have discussed above, the clash of the secular and rational modern government, against what it painted to be the irrational group of "Sikh fundamentalists", who were then vilified and hunted. While Prime Minister Indira Gandhi publicly maintained the invasion was a last resort, former Lt. General S.K. Sinha later revealed that it was 18 months in the planning,

ਪਾਤਿਸ਼ਾਹੀ ਮਹਿਮਾ – Revisiting Sikh Sovereignty

> *"The army had begun rehearsals of a commando attack near Chakrata Cantonment in the Doon Valley, where a complete replica of the Golden Temple complex had been built".*[13]

Moreover, whilst the West only learnt of Britain's involvement[14] in the attack as recently as 2014, Sikhs on the ground in Panjāb were already aware of Britain's collusion. Writing in 1996, G.S. Dhillon noted,

> *"sources in Delhi say that two officers of the Indian secret service, Gary Saxena and R.N. Kay, of the Research and Analysis Wing [RAW], made several trips to London to seek expertise. The Indian Government then selected 600 men from different units and sent them to rehearse the assault on a life-size replica of the Golden Temple, built at a secret training camp in the Chakrata Hills, about 150 miles north of Delhi."*[15]

Although there had been a media blackout in Panjāb, news of the assault on Srī Darbār Sāhib managed to leak out to neighbouring villages, with Sikh soldiers revolted in a bid to get to Amritsar. It is interesting to note that prior to the attack, the Sikh Regimental Centre was purposefully shifted outside of Panjāb to Uttar Pradesh (by comparison, the Bihar Regimental Centre is in Bihar, and the Rajputana Rifles are based near home in Delhi). This clearly shows the intentions of the Government and their view of Sikhs. Although the Sikhs that defended Srī Darbār Sāhib kept the army at bay for over a week, had the Sikh Regiment been stationed in Panjāb, the outcome of the battle would have been very different. A.R. Darshi notes,

> *"Had the militant Sikhs been equally armed, had their numerical strength been even one-tenths of the*

Indian army, they would have pushed the army up to Delhi, or even beyond Jamuna".[16]

As we have seen, while the military attack in 1984 may have taken 18 months to plan, the indo-Sikh confrontation was over 30 years in the making. After the resistance was broken, the army had free reign. Apart from the rape and murder of pilgrims, the most distressing and inexcusable act was the torching of the Sikh Reference Library. Whilst the army maintained this was an accident, claiming the library was blown apart to create a new opening for the tanks, Tully and Jacob, in corroboration with Pettigrew's words, later rebuffed the absurdity of such claims when they noted, "any army which wants to destroy a nation destroys its culture. That is why the Indian army burnt the [Sikh Reference] library."

It was an opportunity to inflict as much damage as possible and the Indian Army took full advantage by burning the library which housed many priceless handwritten manuscripts, books and other important Sikh artifacts. During the days of the battle that raged in Amritsar, the number of lives taken by Indian security personnel is estimated to be 5000. According to various sources this number rises significantly to take account of lives lost across Panjāb to between 100,000 and 120,000.[17]

Declaration of War

The Indian government's decision to send the army in June 1984 was an act of war, the point of no return. Whether you were a Sikh living in Panjāb, Singapore, Nairobi, Canada, England, or the USA, the events of June 1984 would impact your life, changing the trajectory of your foreseeable future. Most notably, the impact on the lives of Sikhs living in Panjāb would endure the biggest change.

The events of June 1984 changed the relationship between a Sikh and the Indian State. Despite the anti-India position pre-and post-1947, the Sikhs under the SAD had persevered along diplomatic means. The communal nature of Indian polity, which was referred to by Professor Puran Singh some 56 years earlier, was exposed in both the actions of the Indian Government and the authoritative bulletins of the Indian army following the events of 1984.[18]

The supposition in 1947 that India was to be a "democratic republic", never materialised and, in fact, any such political aspirations were disregarded in 1950 when the Constitution was revealed, which is why no Sikh agreed to sign it. Sardar Gurtej Singh notes when the Constitution was written,

> *"what emerged from it was a Hindu Imperial Power claiming hegemonic control over the political affairs of minorities. It was and has remained a totally centralised set up, intolerant of dissent, both political and cultural. The exterior of a modern democratic republic was maintained for external consumption and as an effective public relations exercise".[19]*

Operation Woodrose and the Sikh Genocide

The Indian State's violent attack against Sikhs did not start in June 1984, nor did it end. On the contrary, the attack in 1984 was a precursor to the genocide that followed as the State intensified its strategy to eliminate the Khālsā. Following the attack on Srī Darbār Sāhib, an official Army circular issued in July 1984 noted,

> *"Although the majority of the terrorists have been dealt with and the bulk of the arms and ammunition recovered, yet a large number of them are still at large. They have to be subdued to achieve the final aim of restoring peace in the country. Any knowledge of Amritdharis who are dangerous people and pledge to commit murders, arson and acts of terrorism should immediately be brought to the*

notice of the authorities. These people may appear harmless from the outside but they are basically committed to terrorism. In the interest of us all, their identity and whereabouts must be disclosed".20

The monstrous military action against Sikh youth was code-named 'Operation Woodrose' because, in the eyes of the Indian government, the young Sikhs were roses "wildly" grown in the woods.[21] General Jamwal was put in charge of sealing the border, and General R.S.Dayal was to oversee the apprehension of Sikhs within Panjāb.[22] The essence of the plan was to "mop up" all Amritdhari Gursikhs, especially young males, from villages across Panjāb, and it was executed with horrific precision. Much like the years following the execution of Banda Singh, tens of thousands of Sikhs were hunted down, rounded up, detained in military camps, brutally tortured, and in many cases shot dead.

Much of the information about the sadistic nature of inhuman persecution and torture of Sikhs taken by Indian security officers come from the accounts of survivors.[23] The accounts are harrowing and continue to be a source of trauma for Sikhs around the world. To assist in the "mopping up" of Sikhs, the government compiled district wide lists on how many Amrit Sanchārs were taking place, which enabled the State to ascertain how many Amritdhari Gursikhs were coming into the Khālsā fold.[24] For three months, Sikhs were captured, tortured, and killed across Panjāb. Dr. Sangat Singh has placed the number of Sikh lives taken during the first four to six weeks of Operation Woodrose at approximately 100,000, with a further 20,000 fleeing to Pakistan.[25]

Sikh Genocide, November 1984

The Indian Prime Minister Indira Gandhi was assassinated by Shaheed Bhāī Beant Singh and Shaheed Bhāī Satwant Singh on 31st October 1984. Would-be Prime Minister Rajīv Gāndhī was among the leading Indian politicians vying for revenge following the assassination of his mother. Upon landing in Delhi later that day, he bellowed at those who had received him, "My mother has been shot dead. What are you doing here? Go and take revenge. No turban should be seen."[26]

This was followed by similar speeches from other Indian politicians, reporters, and celebrities, as the Indian capital, as well as other cities, became open hunting grounds for Sikhs. In fact, Jaijee notes how Civil and Military officers posted in the capital between 1982 to 1984 confirmed that Sikh homes had been singled out for marking by Congress officials as early as 1982.[27] The names of two-hundred and twenty-seven individuals who instigated mass scale rape, loot, and killings over the next few days were documented by the People's Union for Civil Liberties (PUCL) in a thirty-one-page booklet titled 'Who Are The Guilty'. It has been proven beyond doubt by other writers[28], how in November 1984, the Indian State mobilised to instigate the third major genocide of the Sikhs. In the years that followed, the Indian public, particularly "the middle-class Hindu had nearly complete sympathy with the killing and lynching of Sikhs."[29] "Hating Sikhs"[30], as Mahmood puts it, had become respectable. Taking inspiration from the founding fathers of the Indian State, Indian media soon manufactured the phrase "Sikh Terrorism", pushing a narrative in which the word 'terrorist' was used interchangeably as a synonym for 'Sikh.'[31]

A reign of terror, sanctioned by the full might of the Indian State and its oppressive machinery, was unleashed in the name of fighting "Sikh Terrorism". In August 1985, the Citizens For Democracy published a report on the State atrocities,

> *"...it was a terrible tale of sadistic torture, ruthless killings, fake encounters, calculated ill-treatment of women and children, and corruption and graft on a large scale."*[32]

While the government placed the death toll at 2,700, independent sources have recorded how the number of Sikhs killed between 31st October and 2nd November, 1984, surpassed 20,000.[33] Approximately 200 Gurdwaras across Delhi were attacked, some of which were razed to the ground.[34] From the Prime Minister's office to the local campaigners, the government leaders played a decisive role in murder, loot, rape, and arson.[35]

The Khalistan Sangarsh

As mentioned, the Indian Army's attack on Srī Darbār Sāhib was perceived by the Khālsā Panth as an act of war. The Prime Minister was assassinated on 31st October 1984, Lalit Makhen, a perpetrator who was named in the list compiled by the PUCL, was brought to justice by Shaheed Bhāī Harjinder Singh Jindā and Shaheed Bhāī Sukhdev Singh Sukhā on 31st July 1985, followed shortly with the assassination of Arjun Dass, another Indian politician named in the PUCL, on 5th September 1985.

Suffice to say the Khālsā response was swift and precise; a testament to the foundations Sant Jarnail Singh Bhindranwale had built through connecting Sikhs to Gurbānī and realizing the Pātshāhī bestowed upon them by Gurū Sāhib. The history of the Gurū Sāhibān, which we considered in some length at the start of this book, and the creation of the Khālsā, is what empowered the drive for Khalistan.

Sarbat Khālsā, 1986

On 26th January 1986, at the Sarbat Khālsā, a Gurmattā was passed. The Gurmattā was opened with strong reference to the decision taken by Gurū Hargobind Sāhib, following the Shaheedī of Gurū Arjan Sāhib, to raise Srī Akāl Takht Sāhib, gather horses and weapons to wage war against the oppressors.[36] The Gurmattā also referred to the historical context, both pre-and post-1947, in which Panjāb and the Sikhs were suppressed by centralised power of successive Indian governments, and listed by name those who were prime suspects for the heinous crimes against the Sikh Panth; including the names of prominent SAD and SGPC leaders for betraying the Sikh Panth. There was a strong affirmation to the Sikh principle of *Sarbat Da Bhala*, promoting the welfare of all and complete respect for other faiths and creeds. The explicit objective was to exercise arms to punish the oppressors of Delhi.

The Gurmattā announced the immediate dissolution of the SGPC, calling for Sikhs to take care of their local Gurdwāray, and the reconstruction of Srī Akāl Takht Sāhib. The formation of a Five Member Panthic Committee (FMPC), comprised of Bhāi Dhannā Singh, Bhāī Gurbachan Singh Mānochāhal, Bhāi Gurdev Singh, Bhāī Aroor Singh and Bhāī Vassan Singh, was also announced. Reference was made to the scale of the declaration. It recognised the far-reaching implications of the Indian Government's decision to attack Srī Darbār Sāhib and initiate the Sikh Genocide in November; namely, as a signal of intent to annihilate the Sikhs. Special recognition was made to various organizations like the PUCL and 'Citizens of Democracy' for highlighting the atrocities of the Sikh Genocide in November 1984. The Gurmattā ended with a resolution that stated if the Sikhs, in either Indian or Pakistani police custody, were executed, the Sikh Panth would declare them as martyrs of the Khālistān movement.

Declaration of Independence of Khālistān

The Declaration of Independence of Khālistān was made on 29th April 1986, from Srī Akāl Takht Sāhib. The Declaration announced the formation of the Khalistan Commando Force (KCF) under Manbir Singh Chaheru (alias General Hari Singh). The KCF was a major Kharku Jathebandī to wage an armed liberation movement for the establishment of Khālistān.[37] Others included the Babbar Khalsa (BK), formed in 1980, and later the Khalistan Liberation Force (KLF) and Bhindranwale Tiger Force of Khalistan (BTFK).

The Declaration explicitly states that Khālistān will function based on the principles espoused by Gurmat,

> "The Chief objective before the political and administrative structure of Khalistan will the welfare of humanity and social service, as per [Bhāī Gurdās] 'Without service, cursed are the hands and feet, and useless are other deeds" ... The policy of Khalistan will be as per the Guru's wish, Sarbat da bhala (welfare for all beings) ... The segregation of humanity based upon caste, birth, locality and colour will not be permitted, and such divisions will be abolished by the use of political power."[38]

The Declaration was a direct challenge to the centralised power structures of the Indian State that had wreaked havoc through decades of systematic suppression in Panjāb and to Sikh consciousness. The deliberate intention to abolish a political entity built on Brahmanical and colonial logic, that segregates humanity along lines of caste, birth, locality, and colour, was testament to not only the self-regulating nature of the Khālsā Panth, but also the Khālsāee will to uproot oppressive and destructive systems of power. The Declaration was the clearest and most empowering expression of collective Sikh sovereignty since 1849, reaffirming the Khālsā's mandate to establish political power based on the welfare and co-existence of all. There was constant references to the Gurū Sāhibān.

"ਵੀਰੋਂ ਇਹ ਕੋਈ ਸਾਡੀ ਚਲਾਈ ਹੋਈ ਲੜਾਈ ਨਹੀ, ਇਹ ਤਾ ਗੁਰੂ ਨਾਨਕ ਸਾਹਿਬ ਦੀ ਚਲਾਈ ਹੋਈ ਲੜਾਈ ਹੈ, ਜਿਹੜੀ ਗੁਰੂ ਸਾਹਿਬ ਨੇ ਬਾਬੁਰ ਬਾਦਸ਼ਾਹ ਨਾਲ ਲੜੀ ਸੀ"

Brothers, this is not a fight we started, this fight was initiated by Gurū Nānak, which Gurū Sāhib first fought with Emperor Bābur"[39]

ਪਾਤਿਸ਼ਾਹੀ ਮਹਿਮਾ – Revisiting Sikh Sovereignty

On 30th April 1986, one day after the Declaration for Khālistān, the Indian security forces invaded Srī Darbār Sāhib for the third time, in what became known as Operation Black Thunder I. While the government's account maintained the operation was carried out by police and paramilitary units, independent eye-witness accounts maintained five battalions of commandos were airlifted under the command of two Major Generals of the Indian Army; three battalions consisted of "black cats" and two were of the Border Security Force (BSF). Seven hundred or so commandos are said to have been involved. Any expression of Sikh sovereignty, of independent thought or action, to actualise the lofty vision of the Gurū Sāhibān was violently crushed by the totalitarian Indian State. This is how Operation Black Thunder I, much like the invasions of Srī Darbār Sāhib in 1955, 1984, and the fourth invasion that came in May 1988, code-named Operation Black Thunder II, was justified as a means of civilizing the Sikhs who were portrayed as a threat to the "peace and unity" of a thirty-nine-year-old entity.

This justification for attacking Srī Darbār Sāhib was and continues to be rooted in the secular epistemic that we considered earlier, which the Indian State has used time and time again. It is also the basis of the narrative propagated by the Indian media and its agencies that has maligned and vilified the Khālistān movement for the past forty years.[40] Any sign of dissent, or resistance to the stranglehold of dominance, the suffocating notion of a homogenised and politicised Indian identity, was instantly and violently crushed by the Indian State and its agencies on all fronts.

Despite the sustained onslaught, the *jujharoo* Khālsā remained resolute, and within four months of the Declaration, assassinated General Vaidya, Head of the Indian Army, and the person who led the attack in June 1984. Undoubtedly, Sikh *jujharoos* of the Khālistān movement took ideological inspiration from the Gurū's mandate to fight oppression and protect the weak. This is evident from their words, as recorded in jail letters and official statements to the press, and evident from the way in which they fought back for almost a decade. They also took inspiration from the military prowess of great Sikh martyrs from the 18th century, as they waged a guerilla war, clashing with Indian police and paramilitary forces across Panjāb. Writing in 1996, Mahmood noted,

> "The history of the Dal Khalsa and the Afghan wars is important for understanding what the Khalistani militancy has become today, not only because it ended up creating the only Sikh state that has ever existed, but because the organization of guerilla forces in the Dal Khalsa was a direct foreshadowing of how Khalistani militants are organised today."[41]

The Sarbat Khālsā of 1986, in similar fashion to 1748 Sarbat, passed a Gurmattā to organise the Khālsā *jujharoo* units. As we considered earlier, the mass killing of Sikhs that ensued did not deter the Khālsā from reaffirming the movement for sovereignty in 1748, and it certainly didn't deter the Khālsā in the years between 1986 and 1995. In a joint statement[42] from the KCF and KLF in August 1987, leaders of the Khālistān Sangarsh reiterated how the ideology behind the armed movement was based on the "grand ideals" of the Khālsā and the Sikh Ardās; in particular 'Rāj Karegā Khālsā' and 'Khālsā jī de bol bāle'. There was Panthic unity across the board, with similar statements issued by the Sikh Students Federation (SSF), who also asserted that the Anandpur Sāhib Resolution (ASR) was not to be confused with the armed movement to establish Khālsā Rāj because the ASR did not "clearly spell out the political aims and objectives of the Sikh Nation in the context of India's political and economic structure."[43]

The Sarbat Khālsā announced that the Sikhs were slaves within the Indian State and that the struggle to establish Khālistān was their fundamental right; a right that they were empowered to exercise with the use of arms, as mandated by the Gurū. The declaration was reminiscent of the famous words used by Rattan Singh Bhangoo to describe the mandate Gurū Gobind Singh gave to Bandā Singh Bahādur, as he declared war on the Mughal government in Delhi,

ਸਿੱਖਨ ਰੱਖ ਅਸਿੱਖ ਸੰਘਰੀਓ । ਦਾਸ ਹੋਇ ਤਾਂ ਉਸੈ ਉਬਰੀਓ ।
ਦਿਲੀਓਂ ਲਗ ਕਰ ਦੰਗਾ ਮਚਾਵੋ । ਪੰਜਾਬ ਪ੍ਰਬਤ ਸਭ ਧੁੜ ਮਿਲਾਵੋ । ੮ ।

While protecting the Guru's Sikhs, he must destroy the enemies of the Sikhs, and protect those as well who accept his sovereignty. He must create anarchic conditions from Delhi onwards, after that he must raze the whole of Punjab and Hill states to the ground.[44]

The leaders of the Khālistān movement, such as Shaheed Bhāī Labh Singh and Shaheed Bhāī Gurjant Singh Budhsinghwāle, highlighted how the Indian Constitution had suffocated the Sikhs, and they were slaves in India, declaring if the Khālsā Panth wished to execute the principles of Nām Japnā, Kirat Karnī, and Vand Ke Shaknā, then it had to capture political power.[45] Another *Jujharoo* Commander spoke how it was Gurū Nānak Sāhib who taught them how to raise their voices against injustice, that the Gurū led by example, and from the very beginning, the ideology of the Brahmin opposed their actions.[46] He went on to explain that Khālsā polity within Khālistān would seek to eliminate the inequalities of the poor and the rich by eliminating feudal or monopolistic forces. As we discussed in Part Two, this was exactly what Bandā Singh achieved. There was also the open alliance with other oppressed communities, whom the Khālsā wished to free. An appeal was made for them to support the Khālistān movement. While the Khālsā exercised the right to bear arms in the fight against oppressive forces, outlining the specific targets and the ideology that propped them up, the Indian State's reaction was wholly inhuman, and the loss of Sikh life, unprecedented.

Dharam Yudh and the Khalistān Sangarsh

Indian State Repression

A recent report published by the Khalistan Centre explains details how there were four main aspects to the oppressive strategy deployed by the State[47]:

1. "Militarising the police and overwhelming the region with an armed military presence
2. Enforced disappearances of human rights activists, journalists, and democratic Sikh political leadership
3. Incentivizing the extrajudicial murder of activists and guerrillas with impunity through an elaborate bounty system using unmarked funds
4. Crushing popular support through illegal detention, enforced disappearances, and draconian laws".

Security forces were given complete impunity, and the use of torture had the overt and explicit approval of leading politicians and law enforcers.[48] By the mid-1990s, militarised police in Panjāb exceeded over 70,000, an increase of 50,000 from 1975. This made the region the single most highly concentrated area in the subcontinent, with nearly 100 police officers per 100 square kilometers, compared to a national average of 45 officers across the country.[49]

The Indian state enacted legislation that gave authorities the same overarching powers as the Rowlatt Act during the British occupation of Panjāb. The Armed Forces Special Powers Act (AFSPA), introduced by the Indian Parliament in 1958, was enacted across Panjāb, resulting in detention, torture, rape, executions, mass cremations, and forced disappearances of hundreds of thousands of Sikhs. The National Security Act Ordinance (NSAO) was promulgated on 22 June 1984, followed by the Terrorist Affected Areas Ordinance (TAAO) on 14 July 1984, and the Terrorist and Disruptive Activities Act 1985 (TADA). All three Acts built on AFSPA, granting Indian law enforcers very wide powers of detention, including imprisonment without trial, restriction of writing, speech, and of movement in which the accused could be detained for years without a formal charge. Confessions made to police officers, usually under duress, were made admissible as evidence in a court of law. The burden of proof was placed upon the accused to prove their innocence. Exclusive courtrooms were set up to hear the cases, and the identities of "witnesses" were kept secret, a violation of international standards of right to a fair trial.

The act was later repealed only to be replaced by the Prevention of Terrorist Activities Act (POTA) 2002, which contained provisions like those found in TADA. This pattern of introducing repressive laws, designed to suppress political dissent, has been a convenient tool for oppressive and exploitative regimes across Panjāb since 1849. Indian legislature such as AFSPA, NSAO, TAAO, TADA, and POTA reinforced colonial logic, which the executive authorities insidiously used to crush Sikh resistance. The devastation of loss of life has been documented well, but Mahmood's words in particular are harrowing,

> "The disappeared have floated away as ash on Punjab's rivers or been carried skyward as smoke into Punjab's scorching heavens. The few bits of evidence we have shock and repel is... India is a place where innocent people die, where canals are clogged with bodies and crematoria sweep away nameless ashes, where human rights workers disappear or are thrown in jail. It is both a cradle and a grave."[50]

This was an inevitability that Sikh thinkers and mystics such as Prof. Puran Singh warned about in 1928. Such is the nature of the Indian State, ruled by the "few cunning and aggressive people," that it is by design programmed to violently subdue any voice of dissent; any act of resistance which either expressly, or by association, threatens to expose the fallacy of one homogenous India. Since its creation, not one year has gone by without the Indian State deploying its armed forces within its own borders.[51] Thus, whether it be in Panjāb, or elsewhere in Jammū, Kashmīr, or the north-eastern States, the fragility of the Indian project, built in the image of coloniality and modernity, and engulfed within the spectrum of Hindutva, has been exposed time and time again.

Khālsā defiance

While the Indian State violated all human rights and augmented its barbaric suppression of Sikh bodies, the Khālsā remained defiant. In 1991, the Babbar Khalsa International declared,

> *"A new era is about to begin on the land of Khalistan This new milieu will have exhaustive debates on the Khalsa culture, Khalsa vision, Khalsa rule and Khalsa society which will help us construct a beautiful model for the economic, political and social structural aspects of Khalistan... Therefore, after rejecting the Indian Constitution and boycotting the elections, we must adopt a resolution for Khalistan."*[52]

The decision to reject the Indian Constitution reaffirmed the Sikh position, as it has been since 1950. It was also backed by the KCF, KLF, BTFK, and the SSF, who referred to it as the "root of all problems".[53] Throughout the documents containing speeches and declarations from the Khārkoo Jathedbandiā, we find a constant reference to the self-regulating will of the Khālsā, of the perpetual desire to actualise Gurmat principles of Nām japnā and Sarbat Da Bhala. The constant expression is to establish governance based on ideals espoused and lived by the Gurū Sāhibān, which consider the welfare of all beings, and uproot all forms of oppression and exploitation. The spirit of Chardīkalā is found in abundance, coupled with unwavering faith in the Gurū. The words contained within the jail letters of Shaheed Bhāī Sukhdev Singh Sukha and Shaheed Bhāī Harjinder Singh Jinda stand testament to this spirit,

ਪਾਤਿਸ਼ਾਹੀ ਮਹਿਮਾ – Revisiting Sikh Sovereignty

> *"In comparison with the violence of the enemy, the violence of the Khalsa abounds in Divine qualities and spiritual blessings. The Khalsa has to give such a Divine form and beauty to its struggle that it may even burden the conscience of the enemy with the realization of its own sin. Such a moral miracle will be possible only if the concentration on the Guru of the Khalsa and rhythm of the Guru Granth Sahib remain fully connected and intact. The Guru Granth Sahib is the main source of our life-stream and spiritual power. It is also the chief spring of our inspiration to advance towards the destination of Khalistan... Our martyrdom will radiate only integration... martyrdom is a transcendence of all fears, greeds (sic), and obscene physical desires."*[54]

In previous chapters, we discussed how the Sikhs began waging an armed struggle to regain political control of Panjāb in 1849, through the actions of Bhāī Maharaj Singh, Rām Singh, and the Kūkās. At the turn of the 19th century, it was the Ghadarites who resisted colonial occupation of Panjāb, and by the 1920s, the Babbar Akālīs were agitating to re-establish Sikh sovereignty. Sikh sovereignty remained an ever-present thought in the minds of the Guru's Beloved, although as we have seen, groups and organizations emerged during the period of colonial occupation of Panjāb who submitted to the ideals of Western modernity and decided to adopt a different way to the tradition of the Khālsā.

> *"Not only do they suffer the loss of their own sense of self by rejecting their heritage, but they have not been able to formulate a new sense of "self" or a meaningful vision for the world through the project of modernity either. This is not only because the project of modernity is fundamentally premised on*

the exclusion and subordination of the non-white world, but because its corresponding secular worldview maliciously prohibits a sovereign Sikh worldview in the public (social, political, and economic) sphere."[55]

The perpetual struggle for Khālsā Rāj

Between 1984 and 1995, the Khālistān movement breathed new life into the pursuit of Khālsā Rāj initiated by the Gurū Sāhibān. The spirit and power of the Gurmukh were seen not just in the actions of *jujharoo* Khālsā, but equally evident in the defiance shown by Sikh martyrs such as Shaheed Bhāī Anokh Singh Babbar, Shaheed Bhāī Sukhdev Singh Babbar and Shaheed Bhāī Jaswant Singh Khālrā, who endured the barbaric torture of their oppressors, showing no sign of mercy or defeat. Their defiance was indicative of the Gurū's Sikhia, and a victory for the Khālistān Sangarsh. The victory is also evident in the jail letters of *jujharoos*, such as Shaheed Bhāī Harjinder Singh "Jinda" and Shaheed Bhāī Sukhdev Singh "Sukha". The letters continue to inspire Sikhs the world over. Their words are rooted in sovereign Sikh thought and action, which is Divinely inspired and drenched with love and compassion for all the sublime and beautiful values espoused by Gurū Nānak Sāhib.

Expressly condemning the Indian parliament, courts, educational institutions, and media for trying to subdue the "consciousness of the Khalsa through the subtler force of majoritarianism and material monopoly", they address the deep-rooted flaws of centralised power that give rise to the institutional framework, which seeks to suppress, exploit, and dehumanise minority communities across India. That stand of defiance, the unwavering faith in Akāl Purakh, the allegiance to Gurū Granth Sahib, the offering of their heads for the advancement of the Panth and the desire to create a just society is a testament to what the Khālsā has always strived to achieve. Their *sidak* was empowered through total submission to Hukam, which is made possible through the timeless victory of Gurū Nānak Sāhib.

> *"In the last one decade there have been very few "actual" encounters between our soldiers and your forces. But wherever those have occurred, the evidence in them of our valor and radiant heroism, we are sure, is preserved in your confidential files. A fragment of that fact once in a while slips through your newspapers as well. Our Khalsa vigor is an aspect of our spiritual heritage. In such moments of fight, spirituality radiates through the flashes of our swords."*[56]

In addition to the decades of economic suppression and forced assimilation that the Indian State imposed upon Panjāb, the years preceding, and in particular, following the attack on Srī Darbār Sāhib, saw perhaps the largest loss of Sikh life since the arrival of Gurū Nānak Sāhib.[57] While many Sikhs today continue to process the effects of intergenerational trauma, the Khālsā response to the depraved acts of violence was swift, precise, and above all, demonstrated that the enduring effects of colonialism, secularism, and nationalism begin to fade when a Sikh enters the protection of the Gurū Darbār.

The Khālsā, empowered by Nām and the eternal truth of Satgurū, existed outside the constructs of the colonial and neocolonial worlds. There was a recognition that the State-sponsored terror campaigns were underpinned by an ideology produced in a state of *haumai,* for which the Khālsā was created to uproot and destroy. The mobilization under Sant Jarnail Singh, the fortification of Srī Darbār Sāhib and the early battles for the establishment of Khālistān waged by the Khālsā are testament to this undying commitment to deliver on the Gurū's glorious mandate of acquiring political power. Revolutionary Sikh writers, intellects, speakers, singers, and fighters of the Khālistān movement reminded the ego-fueled rulers in New Delhi and their temporal allies that the power vested in the Khālsā by Gurū Gobind Singh Sāhib was as potent as ever.

While the Indian state, and its allies, continue to vilify and marginalise revolutionary Sikh thought and action, there is constant comfort and reassurance in the eternal truth that reverberates from the Gurū's Darbār. For the sake of amassing temporal power and control, the egoic minds have committed the most horrendous acts against humanity, but they only see the world through their eyes. They value the material world with no sense of fear of the unseen. Such is the state of their condition that they see not the limits of their intellect and reason. They see not the limits of empiricism and the five senses. Drunk in the malady of their own ego, they declare themselves to be invincible and unaccountable. As the Gurū reveals, righteousness has grown wings and flown away; the butchers' rule is the hallmark of temporal governance in this Age of Kaljug.

The Gurū' Sāhibān illuminated the world, and the Panth they forged served as a source of empowerment for the Shaheeds of the Khālistān Sangarsh. They were the embodiment of Gurmat, evident in their words and their sacrifices. Since 1849 we have seen, irrespective of how *haumai* has manifested, and by whichever political force, the defiant Khālsā has stood to advance Dharam Yudh, to fight the righteous war. That is the nature of the Khālsā, and there is no power capable of stopping the self-regulating Will of the Khālsā either from protecting the weak and uplifting the oppressed or from establishing Khālsā Rāj. This is the power of the Pātshāhī bestowed upon the Khālsā, and it is guaranteed by the immortal victory of Gurū Nānak Sāhib.

NOTES

[1] Gurtej Singh, 1996, *Tandav of the Centaur, Sikhs and Indian Secularism*, Institute of Sikh Studies, Chandigarh, p135-136

[2] A. R. Darshi, 1999, *The Gallant Defender*, Chattar Singh Jiwan Singh, Amritsar, p31-32

[3] Eye witness account of Iqbal Singh and Amarjit Singh as cited by Cynthia Keppley Mahmood, 1996, *Fighting for Faith and Nation*, University of Pennsylvania Press, p60

[4] Eye witness account of Iqbal Singh and Amarjit Singh as cited by Cynthia Keppley Mahmood, 1996, *Fighting for Faith and Nation*, University of Pennsylvania Press, p58

[5] Joyce Pettigrew, 1995, *The Sikhs of the Punjab, Unheard Voices of State and Guerilla Violence*, Zed Books Ltd, London and New Jersey, p33

[6] Eye witness account of Amarjit Singh as cited by Cynthia Keppley Mahmood, 1996, *Fighting for Faith and Nation*, University of Pennsylvania Press, p60

[7] Sant Jarnail Singh, early 1982, as translated by Ranbir Singh, 1999 Sandhu, *Struggle for Justice*, Educational & Religious Foundation, Ohio, p13

[8] Ranbir Singh Sandhu, 1999, *Struggle for Justice*, Sikh Educational & Religious Foundation, Ohio

[9] Eye witness account of Amarjit Singh as cited by Cynthia Keppley Mahmood, 1996, *Fighting for Faith and Nation*, University of Pennsylvania Press, p61

[10] Sant Jarnail Singh, early 1982, as translated by Ranbir Singh, 1999 Sandhu, *Struggle for Justice*, Educational & Religious Foundation, Ohio p13

[11] Dr Sangat Singh, 2014, *The Sikhs in History*, Singh Brothers, Amritsar, p380

[12] Joyce Pettigrew, 1995, *The Sikhs of the Punjab, Unheard Voices of State and Guerilla Violence*, Zed Books Ltd, London and New Jersey

[13] General S. K. Sinha (Retd.), 1984, GOC-in-C of the Western Command, Spokesman Weekly, July 16,1984

[14] http://www.sikhfeduk.com/assets/files/Sacrificing-Sikhs-Report-2017.pdf

[15] G.S. Dhillon, 1996, *Truth About Punjab,* SGPC White Paper, SGPC, Amritsar

[16] A. R. Darshi, 1999, *The Gallant Defender,* Chattar Singh Jiwan Singh, Amritsar, p136

[17] Gunisha Kaur, 2004, *Lost in History,1984 Reconstructed*, Second Edition, 2009, Sikh Spirit Foundation, p44; and Dr Sangat Singh, 2014, *The Sikhs in History*, Singh Brothers, Amritsar, p385

[18] See Baatcheet, June 1984 – as referenced by Gurtej Singh, 2000, *Web of Indian Secularism; Chakravyuh*, reprint 2014, p60; A. R. Darshi, 1999, *The Gallant Defender*, p137; and Inderjit Singh Jaijee, 2002, *Politics of Genocide*, p69-70

[19] Gurtej Singh, 2000, *Web of Indian Secularism; Chakravyuh*, Introduction, xiv

[20] As cited in Inderjit Singh Jaijee 2002, *Politics of Genocide*, p69-70; Gurtej Singh, 2000, *Web of Indian Secularism; Chakravyuh*, reprint 2014, p60; and A. R. Darshi, 1999, *The Gallant Defender*, p137

[21] A. R. Darshi, 1999, *The Gallant Defender,* Chattar Singh Jiwan Singh, Amritsar, p138

[22] Inderjit Singh Jaijee 2002, *Politics of Genocide*, Ajanta Publications, Delhi, p72

[23] Gunisha Kaur, 2009, *Lost in History, 1984 Reconstructed*, p57

[24] Inderjit Singh Jaijee 2002, *Politics of Genocide*, Ajanta Publications, Delhi, p217

[25] Dr Sangat Singh, 2014, *The Sikhs in History*, Singh Brothers, Amritsar, p386

[26] Dr Sangat Singh, 2014, *The Sikhs in History*, Singh Brothers, Amritsar, p396

[27] Inderjit Singh Jaijee 2002, *Politics of Genocide*, Ajanta Publications, Delhi, p74

[28] See G.S. Dhillon, India Commits Suicide, 1992; Inderjit Singh Jaijee (2002), Politics of Genocide; Manoj Mitta & H S Phoolka, When A Tree Shook Delhi, The 1984 Carnage and its Aftermath, 2007; and Dr Sangat Singh, 2014, The Sikhs in History, Singh Brothers, Amritsar;
[29] Cynthia Keppley Mahmood, 1996, Fighting for Faith and Nation, University of Pennsylvania Press, p141
[30] Cynthia Keppley Mahmood, 1996, Fighting for Faith and Nation, University of Pennsylvania Press, p143
[31] Khalistan Centre, 2020, 'Who Speaks for Khalistan: Narrating Sikh Liberation', Assu, Nanakshahi 552, October 2020, p20
[32] Citizens For Democracy, 1985, Report To The Nation: Oppression in Punjab, p2
[33] Inderjit Singh Jaijee 2002, Politics of Genocide, Ajanta Publications, Delhi, p382
[34] Inderjit Singh Jaijee 2002, Politics of Genocide, Ajanta Publications, Delhi, p75
[35] G.S. Dhillon, 1992, India Commits Suicide, Singh and Singh Publishers, Chandigarh, p321
[36] "Panthic Dastavej", edited by Narayan Singh Chuaura and Journalist Karamjit Singh - https://sikhsiyasat.net/wp-content/uploads/2015/12/Resolutions-of-the-Sarbat-Khalsa-1986.compressed.pdf
[37] Cynthia Keppley Mahmood, 1996, Fighting for Faith and Nation, University of Pennsylvania Press, p153
[38] 1984Tribute.com Team, The Sikh Martyrs, Volume 1, p251-256
[39] Shaheed Bhāī Jugrāj Singh Toofān, Khālistān Liberation Force
[40] Khalistan Centre's, 2020, 'Who Speaks for Khalistan: Narrating Sikh Liberation', Assu, Nanakshahi 552, October 2020
[41] Cynthia Keppley Mahmood, 1996, Fighting for Faith and Nation, University of Pennsylvania Press, p108
[42] Shaheed Bhāī Lābh Singh and Shaheed Bhāī Gurjant Singh Budhsinghwālā, 1989, "Eh Jang Sadi Jitt Nal Hi Mukkegi" Jantak Paigam (58); as cited by Birinder Pal Singh, Sikh militants' terms of discourse:

Religion, Khalistan/nation and violence, Sikh Formations, DOI: 10.1080/17448727.2017.1289679

[43] Shaheed Bhāī Lābh Singh and Shaheed Bhāī Gurjant Singh Budhsinghwālā, 1989, "Eh Jang Sadi Jitt Nal Hi Mukkegi" Jantak Paigam (58); as cited by Birinder Pal Singh, Sikh militants' terms of discourse: Religion, Khalistan/nation and violence, Sikh Formations, DOI: 10.1080/17448727.2017.1289679

[44] ਰਤਨ ਸਿੰਘ ਭੰਗੂ, ੧੮੪੧, ਸ੍ਰੀ ਗੁਰ ਪੰਥ ਪ੍ਰਕਾਸ਼
Rattan Singh Bhangoo, 1841, Sri Gur Panth Prakash, (2:35) Translation by Gurtej Singh, 2015, Vol. 1, Singh Brothers, Amritsar

[45] Shaheed Bhāī Lābh Singh and Shaheed Bhāī Gurjant Singh Budhsinghwālā, 1989, "Eh Jang Sadi Jitt Nal Hi Mukkegi" Jantak Paigam (58); as cited by Birinder Pal Singh, Sikh militants' terms of discourse: Religion, Khalistan/nation and violence, Sikh Formations, DOI: 10.1080/17448727.2017.1289679

[46] Joyce Pettigrew, 1995, The Sikhs of the Punjab, Unheard Voices of State and Guerrilla Violence, Zed Books Ltd, London and New Jersey, p154

[47] Khalistan Centre, 'Who Speaks for Khalistan: Narrating Sikh Liberation', Assu, Nanakshahi 552, October 2020, p8

[48] Gunisha Kaur, 2004, Lost in History,1984 Reconstructed, Second Edition, 2009, Sikh Spirit Foundation, p60

[49] Sikh Liberation Front, 2018, Criminalizing Sikh Dissent: Repression of Sikhs in Indian-Occupied Punjab, p6

[50] Cynthia Keppley Mahmood, Writing the Bones, p30-31 - https://www.academia.edu/7064863/Writing_the_bones

[51] Harsha Walia, 2021, Border & Rule, Global Migration, Capitalism, and the Rise of Racist Nationalism, Haymarket Books, Chicago, p176

[52] BKI (Babbar Khalsa International), 1991, "Babbar Khalsa International Wallon Sandesh." Jantak Paigam, October; as cited by Birinder Pal Singh, Sikh militants' terms of discourse: Religion, Khalistan/nation and violence, Sikh Formations, DOI: 10.1080/17448727.2017.1289679

[53] Birinder Pal Singh, *Sikh militants' terms of discourse: Religion, Khalistan/nation and violence*, Sikh Formations, DOI: 10.1080/17448727.2017.1289679, p6

[54] Shaheed Bhāī Sukhdev Singh Sukhā and Shaheed Bhāī Jarjinder Singh Jindā, 1990, Letter to the President of India

[55] Samvad, 7th June 2020, - https://sikhsiyasat.net/samvad-releases-important-draft-for-future-course-of-sikh-struggle/ p36

[56] Shaheed Bhāī Sukhdev Singh Sukhā and Shaheed Bhāī Jarjinder Singh Jindā, 1990, Letter to the President of India

[57] This assertion is based on the estimate of approximately 200,000 lives lost in the hundred years between the Gurū period and the Misls, as provided by Hari Ram Gupta, 1952, *History of the Sikhs*, Vol. 2, p255

Conclusion

In Part One of this book, we reexamined the establishment and rise of the Sikh Panth under the Gurū Sāhibān. We considered the way in which Gurū Nānak Sāhib renounced both Islamic and Brahmanical centres of social, political, and religious control in the sub-continent and instead paved a third and distinct way; the Tisar Panth. Fundamental to this revolutionary movement was the centrality of Nām consciousness and the doctrine of Sikh sovereignty, which we considered in its early formation during the Gurū-period, and the various manifestations of Sikh sovereignty throughout the 18th and 19th centuries.

Ever since Gurū Nānak Sāhib established Kartārpur Sāhib, we considered how many forces sought to establish their control over the Sikhs, and by extension, autonomous Sikh spaces. We considered how various Gurū Sāhibān were imprisoned, tortured, and executed for their revolutionary actions. Whether it was internal attacks from members of the Gurū's own family or attacks from external foes who tried to assert their limited logic and authority, the pursuit and preservation of Sikh sovereignty remained a perpetual command for Sikhs. The establishment and struggle for Sikh sovereignty were based on the distinct worldview propagated by the Gurū Sāhibān, who proactively created new paradigms of existence that offered a liberating alternative to the clutches of totalitarian and oppressive power structures. At the heart of their creation was the recognition that the Divine was manifested within every life form, no matter how large or small. Every soul upon this Earth had a Divine right to exist without fear of persecution or suppression. This mobilization has been a perpetual one since 1469, and it has propelled the Sikh Panth towards realizing its objective ever since.

ਪਾਤਿਸ਼ਾਹੀ ਮਹਿਮਾ – Revisiting Sikh Sovereignty

The rise of Sikh or Gurmukh consciousness became the source of a revolutionary transformation, which empowered the change that swept across the lands to realise the Divine power within and in every moment. Integral to this was the doctrine of Sikh sovereignty that allowed the praxis of Gurmat to exist independently. This was the overriding reason why the Gurū Sāhibān faced violent opposition from the ruling elite. It is also why the Sikhs continue to face persecution today. The Sikh way has always challenged corruption and injustice from the highest echelons of power, and it will continue to do so because the Gurū's path is fundamentally opposed to religious, social, economic, and political subjugation.

In Part Two, we considered the rise of the Khālsā, focusing on the Republic created by Bandā Singh, the Misl period, Dal Khālsā, and the rise of Ranjīt Singh. It is clear Sikhs understood that the preservation of Sikh sovereignty was needed to fully realise the Gurū's mandate and actualise Sikh ideals of Sarbat Da Bhala, the welfare of all beings, and Sānjīvāltā, the harmonious co-existence of humanity. We considered how these were not mere theories but actualised by Bandā Singh during the short-lived Republic in which he minted coins in the names of the Gurū Sāhibān, founded a capital, sovereign seal and flags which hurled across Panjāb.

Despite the horrific onslaught from the imperial regime, the Sikhs remained steadfast in their commitment to uphold Sikh sovereignty which eventually paved the way for the Misls to reign over Panjāb, and later Ranjīt Singh's Rāj. During that forty-year period it was the accomplishments of Panth Dardhi Gursikhs such as Rani Sada Kaur, Hari Singh Nalwa and Akali Phula Singh who expanded Sikh Rāj. Notwithstanding the internal disarray that ensued within the Lahore Darbār, we then looked at how Sikh Rāj in Panjāb was abruptly interrupted following the annexation of Panjāb and occupation of British forces.

In Part Three, we considered in depth some of the ramifications of the colonial encounter, both on the minds and bodies of the Sikhs of Panjāb. From the disbandment of the Khālsā Army to the specific policies which were geared towards relisting the Sikhs to serve under the British Crown, under a new identity imposed upon them by the coloniser. From the social and political reshaping of the land and restructuring of lives and traditions through the arrival of the British, to the reimagination of Sikhi through the encounter with Christianity and European secularism, the coloniser radically changed the socio-political landscape across Panjāb. Despite this onslaught, we also revisited some of the Sikh movements that resisted the colonial occupation of Panjāb, from the early rebellions of Bhāī Maharaj Singh and the Kūkās to the Ghadarites and Babbar Akālīs, and other non-military reactionary movements such as the Singh Sabha, early Shiromani Prabandhak Gurdwaran Committee, and the Shiromani Akali Dal. Whilst the latter were limited by default, we considered how they were established out of desire to regain some degree of control over Sikh matters in Panjāb.

In Part Four, having analyzed the advent of colonialism and Western secularism, we looked at the Indian nationalist movement and what it meant for both East Panjāb and sovereign Sikh political mobilization. The subsuming nature of the Indian State was such that central government in New Delhi held all the power to use and abuse Panjāb as it deemed necessary. This took its toll on Sikh and Panjābī psyche to the extent that referring to Panjāb as the "bread basket" of the Indian state perpetuated a notion of pride and allegiance to Indian patriotism and nationalism. There was a sense of responsibility, perhaps even duty, to fulfil this role – a position that is evident even today, especially within some of the rhetoric and discourse surrounding the Panjāb Farmers Protest (2020-present).

In essence following the transfer of colonial power in 1947, Panjāb, once a glorious country built on the sovereignty bestowed upon the Sikhs by Gurū Nānak Sāhib, became a market to merely serve and feed the rest of the subcontinent. We then considered how the transfer of colonial power in 1947 marked a new era of subjugation for the Sikhs who fought to keep their distinct identity and existence alive.

ਪਾਤਿਸ਼ਾਹੀ ਮਹਿਮਾ – Revisiting Sikh Sovereignty

Following the creation of the Indian State, the effects of colonization continued to haunt those who were once colonised, and the web of Indian secularism trapped the minds and bodies of Sikhs, many of whom sidelined the sovereign ways of Khālsā polity. In particular the SAD initiated a mode of resistance, or rather protest, that was new for the Sikhs. There had been no such tactic deployed by the Sikhs, or indeed the Gurū Sāhibān, up until this point which placed the political and social aspirations of the Sikhs in the hands of the oppressive power regime. Notwithstanding the sincerity of their efforts the SAD operated within a limited framework, with little to no room for sovereign Sikh action that had become a defining aspect of the Sikh movement.

It was Sikh revolutionaries such as Sant Jarnail Singh, imbued in Gurmat, who reignited the spirit of the Khālsā. The mobilization of Sikhs and the realignment to Gurmat, within a seven-year span, led to the stand of defiance in which bearing arms was but a natural Sikh progression of fighting Indian State oppression and injustice. Sant Jarnail Singh best epitomised the integrated vision of the Sikh Gurūs – Miri and Piri – that inspired men and women to acquire a Divine sense of purpose and make the ultimate sacrifices for the cause of truth and righteousness, to defend Srī Darbār Sāhib and cement the foundations for Khālistān with their blood.

The Battle of Amritsar 1984 marked a whole new chapter in the history of the Sikhs. Despite the onslaught of colonial logic and brute force that had all but subsumed Panjāb and sovereign Sikh spaces for over a century, this battle showcased to the whole world that the Khālsā was alive and ready to deliver on the perpetual Sikh mandate of waging war against oppressive regimes. No amount of praise for the 175 or so Khālsā who fought during the Battle of Amritsar 1984 is enough. They fought with such ferocity and power that it shook New Delhi to its core. The only response the Indian state had, much like the actions of 18th century Mughal rulers, was to launch a campaign to kill and remove anyone who resembled the ways of the Khālsā. Such was the threat posed by Khālistān in the 1980s and 1990s that

Bibliography

the Indian state machinery went into overdrive to violently suppress the Sikhs, paying no heed to human, let alone their own so-called civil rights. Just as Dr. Ganda Singh had described the "inexhaustible temporal resources of the then greatest Empire in the world" in relation to the way in which the Mughals captured the Khālsā following the Siege of Gurdās Nangal in 1715, the Indian state too deployed all of its own resources, and those of its allies, into capturing and executing the Sikhs who threatened to end the Indian state's oppressive forty-year existence. The effects were devasting, but the yearning for freedom, for Khālistān, lives on.

In this book, we have revisited Sikh Sovereignty, which has been a perpetual movement since Gurū Nānak Sāhib founded Kartārpur Sāhib. Sikhs have either enacted the Pātshāhī of the Gurū and established Rāj or sacrificed their lives in the pursuit of establishing a governance based on the ideals of welfare and coexistence that are enshrined within Gurmat. The significance of the Khālsā lies not only in the opposition and resistance to religious intolerance and political suppression within South Asia, but also in the stand against all structures of power that break from the Divine, irrespective of their geographical location.

The Gurū Sāhibān themselves taught that physical force, when exercised by Nām conscious souls, was a necessary and liberating tool in the pursuit of Sikh Rāj. This has been the way of the Sikh Panth since inception. During the Sikh Sangarsh of the 1980s and 1990s, the early Generals of Khālistān exposed the veil of Indian secularism and democracy, and reinstated the magnificence of the Khālsā. Whether they attained martyrdom within the glory of battle or the courage of withstanding inhuman torture, they moved within the Hukam of Akāl.

The struggle for Khālistān is the latest manifestation of sovereign Sikh mobilisation in which the Khālsā has rewritten the history books. The resistance, resilience and unwavering allegiance to the Gurū Khālsā Panth is worthy of the highest praise.

ਪਾਤਿਸ਼ਾਹੀ ਮਹਿਮਾ – Revisiting Sikh Sovereignty

BIBLIOGRAPHY

ਪੰਜਾਬੀ / ਗੁਰਮੁਖੀ

ਅਜਮੇਰ ਸਿੰਘ, ੨੦੦੭, ਕਿਸ ਬਿਧ ਰੁਲੀ ਪਾਤਸ਼ਾਹੀ
Ajmer Singh, 2007, Kis Bidh Ruli Paatshai, Singh Brothers, Amritsar, 3rd Edition

ਅਜਮੇਰ ਸਿੰਘ, ੨੦੧੩, ਗ਼ਦਰੀ ਬਾਬੇ ਕੌਣ ਸਨ?
Ajmer Singh, 2013, Ghadari Babeh Kaun San? Singh Brothers, Amritsar

ਭਗਤ ਸਿੰਘ, ੧੭੧੮, ਗੁਰ ਬਿਲਾਸ ਪਾਤਸ਼ਾਹੀ ੬
Bhagat Singh, 1718, *Gurbilās Pātshahi 6*, Edited by Dr. Gurmukh Singh, 1997, Punjabi University, Patiala

ਪ੍ਰੋ. ਬਿਕਰਮ ਸਿੰਘ ਘੁੰਮਣ, ੨੦੧੬, ਗ਼ਦਰੀ ਯੋਧੇ ਸੰਤ ਬਾਬਾ ਵਿਸਾਖਾ ਸਿੰਘ, ੧੯੧
Prof. Bikram Singh Ghuman, 2016, Ghadri Yodhe, Sant Baba Vasaka Singh, Varis Shah Foundation, Amritsar

ਗੰਡਾ ਸਿੰਘ, ੧੯੬੭, ਹੁਕਮਨਾਮੇ ਸਿੱਖ ਗੁਰੂ, ਮਾਤਾ ਸਾਹਿਬਾਂ, ਬਾਬਾ ਬੰਦਾ ਸਿੰਘ ਅਤੇ ਗੁਰੂ ਕੇ ਖਾਲਸੇ ਦੇ
Dr. Ganda Singh, 1967, *Hukamname Sikh Guru, Mata Sahiban, Baba Banda Singh and Guru Ke Khalse De*, 1967, Baldev Singh, Kapurthala, New Revised Edition, 2015

ਗਿਆਨੀ ਗਿਆਨ ਸਿੰਘ, ੧੮੭੮, ਸ੍ਰੀ ਗੁਰੂ ਪੰਥ ਪ੍ਰਕਾਸ਼
Giānī Giān Singh, 1878, *Sri Guru Panth Prakāsh*, edited Giānī Kirpāl Singh

ਗਿਆਨੀ ਗਿਆਨ ਸਿੰਘ, ੧੮੯੧, ਤਵਾਰੀਖ ਗੁਰੂ ਖਾਲਸਾ
Giānī Giān Singh, 1891, *Tvārīkh Gurū Khālsā*, Chattar Singh Jeevan Singh, Amritsar

ਪਾਤਿਸ਼ਾਹੀ ਮਹਿਮਾ – Revisiting Sikh Sovereignty

ਹਰਿੰਦਰ ਸਿੰਘ ਮਬ੍ਹੂਬ, ਸਹਿਜੇ ਰਚਿਓ ਖ਼ਾਲਸਾ
Harinder Singh Mehboob, 1988, Sahije Rachio Khalsa, Third Edition, Singh Brothers, Amritsar

ਜੈਤੇਗ ਸਿੰਘ ਅਨੰਤ, ੨੦੧੪, ਗ਼ਦਰੀ ਯੋਧੇ
Jaiteg Singh Anant 2014, Ghadari Yodhe, Lokgeet Parkashan, Chandigarh

ਭਾਈ ਕਾਨ੍ਹ ਸਿੰਘ ਨਾਭਾ, ੧੯੩੦, ਗੁਰਸ਼ਬਦ ਰਤਨਾਕਰ ਮਹਾਨ ਕੋਸ਼
Bhāī Kahn Singh Nabha, 1930, *Gurshabad Ratankar Mahan Kosh*, Publication Bureau, Punjabi University, Patiala

ਭਾਈ ਕਾਨ੍ਹ ਸਿੰਘ ਨਾਭਾ, ੧੯੩੦, ਗੁਰਸ਼ਬਦ ਰਤਨਾਕਰ ਮਹਾਨ ਕੋਸ਼
Bhāī Kahan Singh Nabha, 1930, *Gurshabad Ratnakar, Mahan Kosh,* Bāgh 1, Chattar Singh Jeevan Singh, 2004, Amritsar

ਕਵੀ ਚੂੜਾਮਣੀ ਭਾਈ ਸੰਤੋਖ ਸਿੰਘ, ੧੮੪੩, ਸ੍ਰੀ ਗੁਰਪ੍ਰਤਾਪ ਸੂਰਜ ਗ੍ਰੰਥ
Kavī Chūrāmanī Bhāī Santokh Singh, 1843, *Srī Gur Pratap Sūraj Granth*

ਕਵੀ ਚੂੜਾਮਣੀ ਭਾਈ ਸੰਤੋਖ ਸਿੰਘ, ੧੮੪੩, ਸ੍ਰੀ ਗੁਰ ਨਾਨਕ ਪ੍ਰਕਾਸ਼
Kavī Chūrāmanī Bhāī Santokh Singh, 1843, Srī Gur Nānak Prakāsh, translated by Resham Singh & Jīvanpal Singh, 2019

ਭਾਈ ਖੇਸਰ ਸਿੰਘ ਛਿਬੜ, ੧੨੬੯, ਬੰਸਾਵਲੀਨਾਮਾ ਦਸਾਂ ਪਾਤਸ਼ਾਹੀਆਂ ਕਾ
Kesar Singh Chibbar, 1769, *Bansāvalīnāmā*, Edited by Piara Singh Padam, 1997, Singh Brothers, Amritsar

ਖੁਇਰ ਸਿੰਘ, ੧੭੫੧, ਗੁਰਬਿਲਾਸ ਪਾਤਸ਼ਾਹੀ ੧੦
Koer Singh, 1751, *Gurbilās Pātshahi Dasve*, edited by Shamsher Singh Ashok, 1999, Panjabi University, Patiala,

ਭਾਈ ਨੰਦ ਲਾਲ, ੧੬੩੩-੧੭੧੩, ਗੰਜਨਾਮਾ

Bibliography

Bhāī Nand Lal, 1633-1713, *Ganjnama, Kalaam-e-Goya*, translated by Sardar Pritpal Singh Bindra, 2003, Institute of Sikh Studies, Chandigarh

ਪ੍ਰੋ. ਪਿਆਰਾ ਸਿੰਘ ਪਦਮ, ਸ੍ਰੀ ਗੁਰੂ ਗੋਬਿੰਦ ਸਿੰਘ ਜੀ ਦੇ ਦਰਬਾਰੀ ਰਤਨ
Professor Piara Singh Padam, 1974, *Sri Guru Gobind Singh Ji De Darbari Ratan*, Singh Brothers

ਰਤਨ ਸਿੰਘ ਭੰਗੂ, ਸ੍ਰੀ ਗੁਰ ਪੰਥ ਪ੍ਰਕਾਸ਼
Rattan Singh Bhangoo, *Sri Gur Panth Prakash*, Translation by Gurtej Singh, 2015, Vol. 1, Singh Brothers, Amritsar

ਰਤਨ ਸਿੰਘ ਭੰਗੂ, ੧੮੪੧, ਸ੍ਰੀ ਗੁਰ ਪੰਥ ਪ੍ਰਕਾਸ਼
Rattan Singh Bhangoo, 1841, *Sri Gur Panth Prakash*, edited by Kulwant Singh, IOSS

ਰਾਜਵਿੰਦਰ ਸਿੰਘ ੨੦੧੩, ਰਾਹੀ, ਗ਼ਦਰ ਲਹਿਰ ਦੀ ਅਸਲੀ ਗਾਥਾ
Rajwinder Singh Rahi, 2013, *Ghadar Lehar Di Asli Gatha*

ਸਤਿਬੀਰ ਸਿੰਘ, ੧੯੫੨, ਸਾਡਾ ਇਤਿਹਾਸ ਦਸ ਪਾਤਸ਼ਾਹੀਆਂ
Satbir Singh, 1957, *Sada Itihas Life Story of Ten Masters*, 7th Edition, 1991, New Book Company, Jalandhar

ਗਿਆਨੀ ਸੋਹਣ ਸਿੰਘ ਸੀਤਲ, ੧੯੫੦, ਸਿੱਖ ਰਾਜ ਕਿਵੇਂ ਬਣਿਆ?
Giānī Sohan Singh Seetal, 1950, *Sikh Rāj Kive Baniyā*, Lahore Book Shop, Ludhiana

ਗਿਆਨੀ ਸੋਹਣ ਸਿੰਘ ਸੀਤਲ, ੧੯੪੪, ਸਿੱਖ ਰਾਜ ਕਿਵੇਂ ਗਿਆ?
Giānī Sohan Singh Seetal, 1944, *Sikh Rāj Kive Giyā*, Lahore Book Shop, Ludhiana

ਸਰੂਪ ਦਾਸ ਭੱਲਾ, ੧੭੭੬, ਗੁਰੂ ਨਾਨਕ ਮਹਿਮਾ
Sārūp Das Bhalla, 1776, *Guru Nanak Mehima*, Edited by Dr. Uttam Singh Bhatia, 1971, Bhasha Vibhag, Panjab

ਪਾਤਿਸ਼ਾਹੀ ਮਹਿਮਾ – Revisiting Sikh Sovereignty

ਸਰੂਪ ਦਾਸ ਭੱਲਾ, ੧੨੨੬, ਮਹਿਮਾ ਪ੍ਰਕਾਸ਼
Sārūp Das Bhalla, 1776, *Mehmā Prakāsh*, Edited by Dr. Uttam Singh Bhatia, 1971, Bhasha Vibhag, Panjab

ਭਾਈ ਸਰੂਪ ਸਿੰਘ ਕੋਸ਼ਿਸ਼, ੧੭੯੦, ਗੁਰੂ ਕੀਆਂ ਸਾਖੀਆਂ
Bhai Swarup Singh Kaushish, 1790, *Gurū Kīān Sākhīān*, edited by Piara Singh Padam, 1986, Singh Brothers, Amritsar

ਕਵੀ ਸੈਨਾਪਤੀ, ੧੭੧੧, ਸ੍ਰੀ ਗੁਰ ਸੋਭਾ
Kavi Saināpatī, 1711, *Srī Gur Sobha*, translation by Prof. Kulwant Singh, Institute of Sikh Studies, Chandigarh

ਸੰਤ ਹਰੀ ਸਿੰਘ 'ਰੰਧਾਵੇ ਵਾਲੇ', ੨੦੧੬, ਆਦਿ ਸ੍ਰੀ ਗੁਰ ਗ੍ਰੰਥ ਸਾਹਿਬ ਜੀ ਦਾ ਸੰਪ੍ਰਦਾਈ ਸਟੀਕ, ਗੁਰਬਾਣੀ ਅਰਥ-ਭੰਡਾਰ
Sant Hari Singh Randhawa, 2016, *Aad Srī Gurū Granth Sāhib ji da Sampardai Steek, Gurbānī Arth Bhandar*, Damdami Taksal

ਭਾਈ ਵੀਰ ਸਿੰਘ, ੧੯੨੬, ਪੁਰਾਤਨ ਜਨਮਸਾਖੀ
Bhāī Vir Singh, 1926, *Purātan Janam Sākhī*
Purātan Janam Sakhi (1588), edited by Bhāī Vir Singh, 1926

English

Arvind-Pal Singh Mandair, 2013, *Sikhism A Guide for the Perplexed*, Bloomsbury

Arvind-Pal Singh Mandair, 2009, *Religion and Spectre of the West*, paperback edition 2016, Columbia University Press

A. R. Darshi, 1999, *The Gallant Defender*, Chattar Singh Jiwan Singh, Amritsar

Amandeep Singh Madra & Parmjit Singh, 2004, "Sicques, Tigers or Thieves": Eyewitness Accounts of the Sikhs (1606-1809), Palgrave Macmillan

Bibliography

Albert Memmi, 1974, *The Colonizer and the Colonized*, reprint by Profile Books, 2021, London

Babbar Akali Movement, Sikh Missionary College, Ludhiana, Publication No. 358

Brian Axel, 2001, *The Nation's Tortured Body*, Duke University Press, Durham and London

B.S. Saini, 1975 *The Social and Economic History of Punjab*, University of Michigan, Ess Ess Publications

Bobby Singh Bansal, 2017, *Sikh Monuments in India and Pakistan, Remnants of the Sikh Empire,* Hay House

Balbinder Bhogal, 2007, Text as sword Sikh religious violence taken for wonder, published in Religion and Violence in South Asia

Balbinder Bhogal, 2011, *Monopolizing violence before and after 1984*, Sikh Formations

Birinder Pal Singh, *Sikh militants' terms of discourse: Religion, Khalistan/nation and violence*, Sikh Formations, DOI: 10.1080/17448727.2017.1289679

The Cambridge Survey of World Migration, edited by Robin Cohen, London: Cambridge U.P. 1995

Clinton H. Loehlin, 1971, *The Granth of Guru Gobind Singh and the Khalsa Brotherhood*, Lucknow Publishing House

Cynthia Keppley Mahmood, 1996, Fighting for Faith and Nation, University of Pennsylvania Press

Citizens For Democracy, 1985, *Report To The Nation: Oppression in Punjab*

C. J. H. Hayes, 1926, *Essays on Nationalism*, cited in John Wolffe, 1994, *'God and Creator and Greater Britain: Religion and National Life in Britain and Ireland, 1843-1945'*, Routledge, London and New York

Darshan Singh, 1999, *Western Perspective on the Sikh Religion*, Singh Brothers, Amrtisar

Dolores Domin, 1974, *Some Aspects of British Land Policy in Panjab after 1849"*, Vol. VIII

Daniel Haines, 2013, *Building Empire, Building the Nation: Development, Legitimacy, and Hydro-Politics of Sind, 1919-1969*, Oxford University Press

Edward Joseph Thackwell, 1851, *Narrative of the Second Seikh War*

Dr. Ganda Singh, 1962, *Early European Accounts of the Sikhs*, Firma K. L. Mukhopadhyaya, Calcutta

Dr. Ganda Singh, 1935, Life of Bandā Singh Bahadur, Publication Bureau, Punjabi University, Patiala

Dr. Ganda Singh, 1964, *Some Confidential Papers of the Akali Movement*, Chattar Singh Jiwan Singh, Amritsar

Gurbhagat Singh, 1999, *Sikhism and Postmodern Thought*, Naad Pargaas, Sri Amritsar

Gurbhagat Singh, 2013, *Vismād The Sikh Alternative*, Naad Pargaas, Sri Amritsar

Bibliography

Sir Gokul Chand Narang, 1912, *Transformation of Sikhism*, Ripon Printing Press, Lahore, 3rd Edition

George Forster, 1783, *A Journey from Bengal to England*, London, p309-310

George Forster, 1793, *Travels*, edited Dr. Ganda Singh, 1962, *Early European Accounts of the Sikhs*, Firma K. L. Mukhopadhyaya, Calcutta

Major G. Carmichael Smyth, 1847, *A History of the Reigning Family of Lahore, with some account of The Jummoo Rajahs, The Seik Soldiers and Their Sirdars*

Gurtej Singh, 2000, *Web of Indian Secularism; Chakravyuh*

Gurtej Singh, 1996, *Tandav of the Centaur, Sikhs and Indian Secularism, Institute of Sikh Studies,* Chandigarh

Gurtej Singh, 2020, *Documents on Sikh Homeland and Speeches in Parliament,* Satvic Books, Amritsar

Gunisha Kaur, 2004, *Lost in History,1984 Reconstructed*, Second Edition, 2009, Sikh Spirit Foundation

Gopal Singh, 1979, *History of the Sikh People*

G.S. Dhillon, 1996, *Truth About Punjab,* SGPC White Paper, SGPC, Amritsar

G.S. Dhillon, 1992, *India Commits Suicide*, Singh and Singh Publishers, Chandigarh

G.W. Brown, et al, 2018, *The Concise Oxford Dictionary of Politics and International Relations,* Oxford University Press

G. W. Leitner, 1882, *History of Indigenous Education in the Panjab Since Annexation and in 1882*, Calcutta

Dr. Gurbachan Singh Nayyar, 1995, *The Campaigns of Hari Singh Nalwa*, Publication Bureau, Punjabi University, Patiala

Gurmit Singh, 1969, *Gandhi and the Sikhs*, Usha Institute of Religious Studies

Henry Prinsep, 1834, *Origin of the Sikh Power in Punjab and the Political Life of Muha-Raja Runjeet Singh*

H. Calvert, 2017, *The Wealth and Welfare of Punjab*, Kalpaz Publications

Harbans Singh, 1982, *Gurū Tegh Bahadur*, Sterling Publishers

Harbans Singh, 1992, The Encyclopaedia of Sikhism

Hari Ram Gupta, 1952, *History of the Sikhs*, Vol. 2, Munshiram Manoharlal, Delhi

Harsha Walia, 2021, *Border & Rule, Global Migration, Capitalism, and the Rise of Racist Nationalism*, Haymarket Books, Chicago

Inderjit Singh Jaijee 2002, *Politics of Genocide*, Ajanta Publications, Delhi

Indu Banga, 2004, *Ecology and Rights in the Punjab*, Journal of Panjab Studies, Vol. 11, Punjab University Chandigarh

Indu Banga, 1995, *"Political Perceptions And Articulation Of The Sikhs During The 1940s"*, a paper read at the ICHR sponsored seminar on Contemporary History Of The Punjab

Bibliography

Jawaharlal Nehru, 1936, *An Autobiography*, Reprint by Penguin Books, 2004

Jagjit Singh, 1981, *Percussions of History, The Sikh Revolution & in the Caravan of Revolutions*, The Nanakshahi Trust, Panjab

J. D. Cunningham, 1849, *History of the Sikhs*, Oxford University Press: Oxford

J.S. Grewal, 1994, *The Sikhs of The Punjab*, Cambridge University Press

John Malcolm, 1812, *Sketch of the Sikhs*

John Plamenatz, 1976, 'Two Types of Nationalism' in Eugene Kamenka, ed, Nationalism: The Nature and Evolution of an Idea, Edward Arnold, London

Joyce Pettigrew, 1995, *The Sikhs of the Punjab, Unheard Voices of State and Guerilla Violence*, Zed Books Ltd, London and New Jersey

Sir. J. Kaye *and Colonel. G. Malleson, 1890, History of the Indian Mutiny*

Sir Jadunath Sarkar, 1930, *A Short History of Aurangzib*, M. C. Sarkar & Sons, Calcutta

Sir Jadunath Sarkar, 1950, *Fall of the Mughal Empire,* Vol. IV, M. C. Sarkar & Sons, Calcutta

John Surman and Edward Stephenson, 1715-1719, *Madras Diary and Consultation Book*, 87 Range 239, edited by Amandeep Singh Madra & Parmjit Singh, 2004, "Sicques, Tigers or Thieves": Eyewitness Accounts of the Sikhs (1606-1809), Palgrave Macmillan

ਪਾਤਿਸ਼ਾਹੀ ਮਹਿਮਾ – Revisiting Sikh Sovereignty

Julian Huxley, 1941, *Religion without Revelation*, Watts and Co, London

Kapūr Singh, 1959, *Parasharprasna The Baisakhi of Guru Gobind Singh,* Lahore Book Shop, Ludhiana

Khalistan Centre, 2020, *'Who Speaks for Khalistan: Narrating Sikh Liberation',* Assu, Nanakshahi 552, October 2020

Dr. Kirpal Singh, 2004, *Janam Sākhī Tradition, An Analytical Study*, Singh Brothers, Amritsar

Khushwant Singh, 1963, *A History of the Sikhs*, Vol. 1, Second Edition, 2004, Oxford University Press

Khushwant Singh, 1962, *The Fall of the Kingdom of the Punjab*, Orient Longman, reprint 2014, Penguin Books, India,

K. Grant et al, 2007, Beyond Sovereignty Britain, Empire and Transnationalism, c.1880-1950, Palgrave Macmillan

Lady Login, 1890, *Sir John Login and Duleep Singh*, W.H. Allen & Co, London

Louis E Fenech, 2008, *The Darbar of the Sikh Gurus,* Oxford University Press, Delhi

Mark Condos, 2017, *The Insecurity State Punjab and the making of Colonial Power in British India*, Cambridge University Press

Mobad, 1645-46, *Dabistān-i Mazāhib, Sikhism and the Sikhs*, translated by J. S. Grewal & Irfan Habib, 2001, *Sikh History from Persian Sources,* Tulika Books, Delhi

Madhav Gadgil and Ramachandra Guha, 1992, *The Fissured Land: An Ecological History of India*

Bibliography

Malcolm Lyall Darling, 1925, *The Punjab Peasant in Prosperity and Debt*

M.S. Leigh, 1928, *Land Revenue Settlement in Punjab*, Lahore

Nahar Singh, 1968, *Documents Relating to Bhai Maharaj Singh*

Neeladri Bhattacharya, 2019, *The Great Agrarian Conquest, the colonial reshaping of a rural world*, State University of New York

Patwant Singh and Jyoti M. Rai, 2008, *Empire of the Sikhs, The Life and Times of Maharaja Ranjit Singh*, Peter Owen Publishers, London

Patwant Singh, 1999, *The Sikhs*, John Murray Publishers, London, republished by Rupa Publications, 2002, Delhi

Professor Pritam Singh, 2008, *Federalism, Nationalism and Development, India and the Punjab economy*, Routledge, Oxon

Professor Pritam Singh, 2005, *'Hindu Bias in India's Secular Constitution: probing flaws in the instruments of governance'*, Third World Quartely, 26:6, 909-926

Pamela Hickman and Gola Taraschi-Carr, 2014, *Righting Canada's Wrongs; The Komagata Maru*, Lorimer

Partha Chatterjee, 1986, *Nationalist Thought and the Colonial World, A Derivative Discourse*, University of Minnesota Press, 2011, Sixth Edition

Paul Brass, 2003, *The partition of India and retributive genocide in the Punjab, 1946-47: means, methods and purposes*, Journal of Genocide Research

ਪਾਤਿਸ਼ਾਹੀ ਮਹਿਮਾ – Revisiting Sikh Sovereignty

Pashaura Singh, 2000, *The Guru Granth Sahib, Canon, Meaning and Authority*, Oxford University Press

Professor Puran Singh, 28th October 1928, letter to Sir John Simon, as recorded in Gurtej Singh, 2000, *Web of Indian Secularism; Chakravyuh*

Professor Puran Singh, 1930, *Spirit of the Sikh*, Part 1, Publication Bureau Punjabi University, Patiala

Professor Puran Singh, 1920, *The Book of The Ten Masters*, Singh Brothers, Amritsar

Bhai Randhir Singh, 1972 *Autobiography*, translated by Dr. Trilochan Singh, Bhai Sahib Randhir Singh Trust

Rajinder Singh, 1988, *Five Hundred Years of Sikhism*, Amritsar Chief Khalsa Diwan, Department of History, Panjab University, Patiala

Ranbir Singh Sandhu, 1999, *Struggle for Justice,* Sikh Educational & Religious Foundation, Ohio

Ramon Grosfoguel, 2013 "The Structure of Knowledge in Westernized Universities: Epistemic Racism/Sexism and the Four Genocides/Epistemicides of the Long 16th Century," Human Architecture: Journal of the Sociology of Self-Knowledge: Vol.11: Iss. 1, Article 8

Dr Sukhdial Singh, 2007, *Origin and Evolution of the Khālsā Commonweatlh*, Chattar Singh Jiwan Singh, Amritsar

Dr Sangat Singh, 2014, *The Sikhs in History*, Singh Brothers, Amritsar

Sachindra Nath Sanyal, 1931, Bandi Jivan

Bibliography

Satya M. Rai, 1965, *Partition of the Punjab: A study of Its Effects on the Politics and Administartion of the Punjab (I), 1957-6*, Bombay

Santosh Bhartiya, 2008, *Dalit and Minority Empowerment*, Rajkamal Prakashan

Dr Sarbjinder Singh, 2008, *Divine Revelation*, Sikh Foundation, Delhi

S. Chandra Sekhar, 1986, From India to Canada La Jolla, Population Review Books

Samvad, 2020, - https://sikhsiyasat.net/samvad-releases-important-draft-for-future-course-of-sikh-struggle/

Shahamat Ali, 1847, *The Sikhs and Afghans, In Connection with India and Persia, Immediately Before and After the Death of Ranjeet Singh*, London

Lieut. Colonel Steinbach, 1883, *The Punjaub; A brief account of the country of the Sikhs*, Manju Arts, Chandigarh, reprint Language Department, 2003, Punjab

Syad Muhammad, Latif, 1891, History of the Panjab, Calcutta Central Press, Calcutta,

Dr. Ernest Trumpp, 1877, *Adi Granth, The Holy Scriptures of the Sikhs*, WM. H. Allen & Co, Preface, London

Tan Tai Yong, 2005, *The Garrison State, The military, Government and Society in Colonial Punjab, 1849-1947*, Sage Publications

T. S. Nahal 2012, *Ghadar Movement: Its Origin and Impact on Jallianwala Bagh Massacre and Indian Freedom Movement*

ਪਾਤਿਸ਼ਾਹੀ ਮਹਿਮਾ – Revisiting Sikh Sovereignty

S.S. Thorburn, 1886, *Musalmans and MoneyLenders in Punjab*, William Blacwood & Sons, London

Talal Asad, 2003, *Formations of the Secular, Christianity, Islam, Modernity*, Stanford University Press, California

Dr. Trilochan Singh, 1981, *Life of Gurū Har Krishan*

Trilochan Singh, 1994, *Ernest Trumpp and W.H. McLeod As Scholars of Sikh History, Religion and Culture*, International Centre of Sikh Studies, Chandigarh

Tarlochan Singh Nahal, 2011, *Religion and Politics in Sikhism: The Khalsa Perspective*, Singh Brothers, Amritsar

Teja Singh and Ganda Singh, 1950, *A Short History of the Sikhs (1469-1765)*, Volume One, Sixth Edition, Publication Bureau, Punjabi University, Patiala

Tomoko Masuzawa, 2005, *The Invention of World Religions*, University of Chicago Press, Chicago and London

Van der Veer, 1996, *Writing Violence in the Making of Hindu India: Religion, Community, and the Politics of Democracy in India*, Oxford University Press, Delhi

V.D. Savarkar, 1923, *Essentials of Hindutva*

Walter D. Mignolo, 2011, *The Darker Side of Western Modernity, Global Futures, Decolonial Options*, Duke University Press, Durham and London

W. Owen Cole and Piara Singh Sambhi, 1995, *The Sikhs and Their Religious Beliefs and Practices*, Second Edition

Bibliography

W. L. M'Gregor, 1846, *The History of the Sikhs*, Vol.2, James Madden, London

GLOSSARY OF TERMS

Akāl/Akāl Purakh   the Timeless/Immortal One

Akāl Senā – army of Sikhs raised by Guru Hargobind Sāhib

Akath – that which is indescribable

Alakh – that which cannot be uttered

Amrit – sacred nectar prepared in the iron bowl with the double-edged sword during Sikh initiation ceremony

Amrit Sanchār – Sikh initiation ceremony

Amritdhārī – initiated Sikh, one who has taken Amrit and become a Khālsā

Anand Karaj – union of two souls within the Sikh tradition

Anhad – unheard primal sound

Anhad Shabad – the unstruck melody

Ardas – Sikh supplication to Akāl/Gurū

Bandī Chhor – liberation/release from imprisonment

Baolī – an open well

Bhagat – one who is attuned, through devotional remembrance or praise, to the Divine

Bhānā – submission/acceptance to *Hukam*

Bhatt – ballad singer

Glossary of Terms

Bhujhaṅgī – a young Singh

Brahmgiān – knowledge of the Creator

Brahmgiānī – holder of knowledge of the Creator

Bungā – a dwelling place or outpost

Chandoā – royal canopy

Chardīkalā – ever rising spirit

Chaur Sahib – royal wisk

Darbār/Gurū's Darbār – the Court of Gurū

Dastaar – Sikh crown (turban)

Degh Tegh Fateh – Victory of upholding the service of food and sword

Dhādhī – traditional singers of war ballads

Dharam – righteousness

Dharamsāl – a place of dwelling like a Gurdwara

Dhur ki Bani – Word(s) inspired from the Divine source

Fakīr – holy man

Fateh – victory

Firanghi/Faranghi – foreigner, specifically in reference to the European/British coloniser

Ghallūghārā – genocide

Giān - knowledge

Gurbānī – Gurū's Word(s)

Gurgaddi – Seat of Gurū Nānak Sāhib

Gurmat – Gurū Sāhib's ideology, comprised of what they said and done

Gurmattā – decision-making assembly of the Sikhs

Gurmukh(s) - lit. those who face the Gurū, meaning those who accept and speak of the way of the Gurū

Gurū Sāhibān – respectful term for addressing all of the 10 Sikh Gurū's

Gurū/Gurū Sāhib – respectful term for addressing any of the 10 Sikh Gurū's

Halemi Rāj – political autonomy or rule of the meek, as described by Gurū Arjan Sāhib

Haumai – ego, self-centeredness, break from the Divine

Hukam – Divine Will or Order

Hukamnāmā/Hukamnāme – decree issued from Gurū's Darbār

Jagat Gurū – Gurū of the world

Janamsākhī – hagiography

Janeu – ceremonial Hindu thread

Japjī Sāhib – Sublime utterance by Gurū Nānak Sāhib, part of an Amritdhārī Sikh's daily discipline

Jathā – Sikh unit or contingent

Jathedār – head of the Sikh unit of contingent

Jot – Light

Jujharoo – Sikh fighter

Glossary of Terms

Kaljug – age of spiritual darkness

Khālsā – initiated Sikh or body of initiated Sikhs, those who have taken Amrit

Khālsā jī ke bol bāle – the writ/command of the Khālsā

Khārkoo – Sikh military fighter

Khārkoo Jathedbandī – unit of Sikh military fighters

Kirpā – Grace of the Gurū

Kirpan – Sikh sword

Kirt Karnī – honest labout

Kirtan – devotional singing of Gurbānī

Langar – communal kitchen

Mahakavi – great poet

Mahal – castle, palace or royal house

Manjhī – lit. seat, in reference to the Gurū's delegated seat of authority

Manjhīdār – holder of Manjhī

Manmat – a egoic state, where one only listens to and follows their own logic

Miri Piri – lit. the spiritual and temporal

Misl(s) – Sikh guerrilla/military unit

Mool Mantar – Subline utterance by Gurū Nānak Sāhib, the core of Sikhi

Nām – "loving and holistic meditative attunement to Vaheguru"

Nām Abiās/ Japnā – contemplative "loving and holistic meditative attunement to Vaheguru"

Nirgun – without attributes

Nishān Sāhib – Sikh flag

Pangat – lit. group or assembly

Panth – Sikh way/Nation

Panth Dhardī Gursikhs – those who have deep love for the Sikh Panth

Parchār – dissemination [of Sikh principles]

Parchārak – *one who spreads/disseminates the Gurmat*

Parikarmā – area surrounding Darbār Sāhib

Pātshāhī Mehimā – in Praise of the True Sovereign

Pauri/Pauris – specific stanza or verse from Gurbānī

Pothī/Pothīs – book

Purātan – precolonial

Qazi – magistrate or judge of Islamic court

Rāj – political autonomy or rule

Rehat – daily discipline/conduct

Rehatnāmā – order or directive issued about daily discipline/conduct

Sache Pātshāh – True Sovereign of both worlds

Sāhib – master/ruler

Sāhibzādā – lit. prince, used in reference to Gurū's sons

Sākhī - story

Glossary of Terms

Sampardai – alongside the Nirmala and Udasi traditions, this is the third major school of exposition of Gurbani.

Sangat/Gurū's Sangat – assembly of the Gurū's beloved Sikhs

Sarbat da Bhala – lit. Welfare of all, the teaching that a Sikh is to seek the welfare of every life form

Sarbat Khālsā – political decision-making assembly

Sarbloh – iron

Sargun – with attributes

Saroop – beauteous form

Satgurū – Gurū of Truth/One True Gurū

Shabad – Gurū's Word/Wisdom

Shaheed – martyr

Shaheedī – martyrdom

Siddh – an ascetic

Simran – loving remembrance of the Divine

Sukhmanī Sāhib – Sublime utterance by Gurū Arjan Sāhib

Tisar Panth – lit. the third way, attributed to Gurū Nānak's Sāhib's way, the way of the Khālsā

Toshkhanā – the Treasury

Udāssī – reference to the Gurū's travels/tours

Vaheguru – lit. Gurū is great, a name for the Almighty

Vand Ke Shaknā – to consume after first providing for others

Vismād – a state of Pure Wonder and Love of Akāl Purakh